Prevention of Delinquent Behavior

Primary Prevention of Psychopathology

George W. Albee and Justin M. Joffe, *General Editors*

Volumes in this series:

The above volumes are available from
University Press of New England
3 Lebanon Street, Hanover, New Hampshire 03755

Prevention of Delinquent Behavior

Editors

John D. Burchard
and Sara N. Burchard

Primary Prevention of Psychopathology

Vol. X

SAGE PUBLICATIONS
The Publishers of Professional Social Science
Newbury Park   Beverly Hills   London   New Delhi

For information address:

SAGE Publications, Inc.
2111 West Hillcrest Drive
Newbury Park, California 91320

SAGE Publications Inc.
275 South Beverly Drive
Beverly Hills
California 90212

SAGE Publications Ltd.
28 Banner Street
London EC1Y 8QE
England

SAGE PUBLICATIONS India Pvt. Ltd.
M-32 Market
Greater Kailash I
New Delhi 110 048 India

Printed in the United States of America

Library of Congress Cataloging-in-Publication Data

Main entry under title:

The prevention of delinquent behavior.

   (Vermont conference on the primary prevention of
psychopathology ; v. 10)
   Includes papers presented at a workshop in
Bolton Valley, Vt., in summer 1983.
   Includes index.
   1. Juvenile delinquency—United States—
Congresses.   2. Juvenile delinquency—United States—
Prevention—Congresses.   3. Criminal behavior,
Prediction of—Congresses.   4. Juvenile justice,
Administration of—United States—Congresses.
I. Burchard, John D.   II. Burchard, Sara N.
III. Series.
HV9104.P74   1986   364.3'6'0973   86-26095
ISBN 0-8039-2908-0

Contents

Introduction

This book focuses on two important concerns in the field of delinquency prevention. The first pertains to our ability to identify those children who are most at risk of becoming juvenile delinquents. The second is intervention programs designed to prevent that from happening. Those two topics were the subject of a three-day conference at Bolton, Vermont, sponsored by the Vermont Conference on the Primary Prevention of Psychopathology at the University of Vermont, the Center for Studies of Antisocial and Violent Behavior (National Institute of Mental Health) and the Office of Prevention (NIMH).

The purpose of the conference was to assemble some of the leading social scientists in each area and provide them with a forum to present and discuss their research. Experienced and qualified persons were also invited to facilitate discussion and to explore the social policy implications of the scientific data that were presented. This book contains all of the papers that were presented at the conference in addition to one that was added shortly thereafter. It is an empirically based resource book for social scientists, practitioners, and policy-makers interested in the field of delinquency prevention.

Much of the research that is reported in this book falls into the category of secondary prevention. Our reasons for emphasizing secondary prevention will be more clear following a brief discussion of recent developments in three areas of juvenile justice and delinquency prevention: (1) recent trends in the incidence and prevalence of delinquent behavior, (2) reforms in the juvenile justice system, and (3) the role of prevention.

Recent Trends in the Incidence and Prevalence of Delinquent Behavior

With respect to the incidence (number of offenses) and prevalence (proportion of juveniles who commit an offense) of delinquent behavior there is both good news and bad news. The good news is that

7

we have made significant progress in our ability to monitor delinquent behavior and the data indicate we are experiencing a decline in
its absolute frequency. The bad news is that the decline is more likely
to be a function of a change in population demographics than an
increase in the effectiveness of our prevention or rehabilitation
programs.

According to the Uniform Crime Report, there were 1,927,120
juveniles arrested in 1975, the peak year for juvenile arrests. By 1982,
that number had dropped to 1,630,226, a decline of 15%. During that
same time period the juvenile population at risk (e.g., the number of
children age 10 through the upper age of juvenile court jurisdiction)
declined by 11.7%. All else being equal the decline in juveniles at risk
should, in itself, produce a significant decline in delinquent behavior.

With respect to self-reported delinquent offenses the news is also
mixed. The National Youth Survey, which measures prevalence and
incidence of self-reported delinquent behavior on a per capita basis,
compared data on 15-, 16-, and 17-year-olds in 1976 with the same
aged juveniles in 1980. During that four year period, there was a
significant decline in the proportion of juveniles who committed one
or more delinquent offenses (prevalence) but no change in the total
number of incidents. In other words, a smaller percentage of juveniles
were involved in delinquency in 1980 as compared to 1976 but those
that were involved were committing a greater number of offenses
(Elliott, Ageton, Huizinga, Knowles, & Canter, 1983).

While it is difficult to determine whether or not there has been a
change in the per capita rate of delinquent behavior it is not difficult
to detect a significant change in the system that responds to the
juvenile offender.

Reforms in the Juvenile Justice System

A recent article entitled "The Watershed of Juvenile Justice
Reform" (Krisberg, Schwartz, Litsky, & Austin, 1985), provides ample
documentation that the pendulum has changed direction with
respect to our efforts to prevent and rehabilitate juvenile delinquents.
In short, the movement left toward a more liberal ideology and
practice has been replaced by a conservative movement to the right.

During the 1960s and most of the 1970s, the predominant opinion
was that the juvenile justice system was not working and much of the

agenda focused on deinstitutionalization, diversion, and prevention. One of the major events during this time was the formation of the President's Commission on Law Enforcement and the Administration of Justice in 1967. A primary result of the Commission was the development of programs to divert juveniles from the juvenile justice system. Although the effort was massive (it would be hard to find a major city that did not have some sort of diversion program in the mid 1970s) the outcome was largely negative. The verdict seems to be that (1) most of the clients who were served by diversion were juveniles that would have previously been lectured and released (Klein, 1979), (2) even with this less serious population the evidence regarding recidivism is equivocal, and (3) the vast majority of the programs were terminated soon after the federal resources were eliminated.

Another major event during the pendulum's swing to the left was the passage of the federal Juvenile Justice and Delinquency Prevention Act of 1974 (JJDPA). The Act called upon the federal government to (1) "develop and implement effective methods of preventing and reducing delinquency, (2) to develop and conduct . . . effective programs to divert juveniles from the traditional juvenile justice system and to provide critically needed alternatives to institutionalization, and (3) to improve the quality of juvenile justice in the United States," (U.S. Senate Committee on the Judiciary, 1975).

The JJDPA produced federal resources for prevention programs much like the President's Commission in 1967. However, there were two important differences. One was that the funding placed more emphasis on primary and secondary prevention. The second was that in order to obtain the funding the states had to make legislative and policy changes that would (1) remove status offenders from secure facilities that also contained delinquents and (2) remove delinquents from secure facilities that also contained adults.

Although the financial incentive of JJDPA was relatively small, all but five states (Nevada, North Dakota, Oklahoma, South Dakota, and Wyoming) have qualified for the program, thus producing some dramatic results. According to the Office of Juvenile Justice and Delinquency Prevention, the population of 5,000 status offenders held in public facilities in 1977 had decreased to slightly more than 2,000 in 1982, a decline of approximately 60%. During a similar time period, the population of juveniles held in contact with adults had decreased from 97,847 to 15,130, a decline of approximately 84% (Martin, 1985).

The many changes brought about by the President's Commission in 1967 and the JJDPA in 1974 raise many significant questions. Are we better able to rehabilitate delinquent offenders by separating them from adults in secure facilities? Does the removal of status offenders from the more restricted facilities for juveniles decrease the rate at which status offenders become delinquent? Are the prevention programs and the less restrictive intervention programs that were initiated by JJDPA effective in reducing either the prevalence of juvenile offenders or the incidence of delinquent behavior? Although such questions are always very difficult to answer the task has been made exceedingly more difficult by recent juvenile justice reforms in the opposite direction.

If a President's Commission and the JJDPA were the hallmark of the movement to deinstitutionalize, divert, and prevent, the "get tough" ideology of the Reagan administration has led to more recent efforts to make the juvenile justice system more restrictive and more punitive, particularly for the more serious offenders. Coinciding with such concepts as "just deserts" and "selective incapacitation" are some data that indicate that the changes are more than ideological rhetoric.

Summarizing data obtained through the children in custody survey (U.S. Census Bureau) Krisberg and his colleagues characterize the effects of the reform as follows:

> Despite a declining youth population, declining serious juvenile crime rates, and the relative high costs and limited benefits of institutional care, the number of juveniles incarcerated on a given day in detention centers and training schools is increasing. Also, juveniles are being confined in such facilities for longer periods of time. There is not solid evidence that these policies of increased juvenile incapacitation are positively affecting public safety. Incarceration policies are largely unrelated to rates of serious youth crime [Krisberg et al., 1985, pp. 36-37].

The agenda of the new reform is clear, particularly with respect to federal policy (Regnery, 1983). First and foremost is the early identification of the career offender and the suppression of his or her delinquent behavior through selective incapacitation. The second initiative involves restitution and work for probationers; the third consists of strategies and incentives to increase the private sector administration of our correctional institutions. The fourth initiative involves a concerted effort to get the federal government out of the business of delinquency prevention. The selective extinction of prevention programs was of most concern to the participants of the Bolton Conference.

The Role of Prevention

While much can be said for a "get tough" policy for the violent juvenile offender, such a policy is not likely to have much impact on the incidence of violent juvenile crime. Also needed is a "get tough" policy on prevention.

There are two important reasons why the impact of selective incapacitation will be limited, even with respect to violent crime. First, it does not address the onset of the problem. It does nothing to reduce the frequency of violent crime prior to the first arrest. Second, it applies to only a small proportion of violent juvenile offenders. On the basis of self-report data, it has been determined that only 14% of the juveniles who have committed three or more index crimes for two consecutive years have been arrested (see the chapter by Elliott, Dunford, & Huizinga in this book). Obviously to incapacitate there must at least be one arrest.

A "get tough" policy in prevention requires more preventive intervention, not less. While it is true there have been few interventions of proven value in terms of hard scientific data, it is also true that we have not done much in the area of prevention and little of what we have done has been properly evaluated.

Most of the progress that has been made in the field of prevention pertains to the identification of risk factors. While we are still uncertain as to how best to intervene in those situations, the potential is immense. For example it is not difficult to identify families where the children are extremely vulnerable with respect to delinquency, yet many of the resources that might help that family are only administered after a child has been adjudicated.

Progress in the identification of at-risk children is one of the reasons we chose to focus on secondary prevention. The other is more practical. It is clear there will be significant decline in human service resources during the next five to ten years. In addition to a national policy to remove the government from the prevention business, Congress is committed to removing more than 200 billion dollars from the federal budget over the next five years. One strategy to cope with fewer resources is to target those resources to individuals that are most at risk.

Finally, a note of caution. There are many indications that at least in terms of juvenile delinquency we are experiencing the calm before the storm. As noted above, the existing decline in delinquent behavior appears to be mostly a function of a change in population. The juvenile population will start to increase again in about five years. In addition, we are presently experiencing increases in many demographic variables that are clearly associated with the early correlates of delinquent behavior. There have been significant increases in the number of children living in poverty, the number of single parents, the number of teenage parents who are raising children by themselves, and the number of marital separations and divorces. The situation is the opposite of a delinquency prevention program that would be designed based on our knowledge of relevant research. For these reasons we believe there must be more emphasis on prevention, particularily with respect to our most vulnerable children.

The research papers making up the first five chapters of this book focus on the identification of at-risk children. They are very diversified. Chapter 1 by Emmy Werner presents a comprehensive 18-year prospective study of 698 multiracial children on the island of Kauai. This longitudinal study investigates both the factors that predispose children to delinquency and mental health problems as well as the protective factors that contribute to their resiliency under high-risk conditions.

Chapter 2 by George Spivack and Norma Cianci is part of a 15-year longitudinal study of over 600 high-risk urban youth who entered Philadelphia kindergartens in 1968. In that chapter behavior patterns are identified that emerge in the early primary grades and correlate with subsequent antisocial behavior during adolescence. The primary focus of Chapter 3 by Rolf Loeber and Thomas J. Dishion is on the development and preliminary assessment of a multiple gating technique as a more practical, cost-effective way to identify children at risk for subsequent antisocial behavior during middle childhood and early adolescence.

The process of identifying children at risk for antisocial and delinquent behavior requires some knowledge of the base rates of those behaviors. Using self-report data from the National Youth Survey, Delbert Elliott, Franklyn Dunford, and David Huizinga, in Chapter 4, provide a methodology for identifying and predicting the career offender. The final chapter in the section on identification focuses on a possible at-risk population where identification and intervention have already occurred but for different reasons. In Chapter 5, Ted Lane and Glen Davis look at the problem of child abuse and neglect and review the research literature with respect to its relationship to subsequent juvenile delinquency. An overview and critical discussion of all five chapters on early identification are provided in Chapter 6 by Carl Jesness.

The first two chapters on intervention programs focus on the family and involve efforts to improve the child-care skills of parents. In Chapter 7, David Wolfe reviews a series of studies he has conducted that involve the use of behavioral techniques to modify the behavior of abusive parents. Preliminary data are also presented from a study in progress. In Chapter 8, Robert Whaler and Jean Dumas present research that focuses on methods to modify child-directed aversive behavior of multistressed mothers by changing the stimulus control properties of the mothers' aversive experiences.

The next two chapters report intervention programs in preschool and school settings. In Chapter 9, John Berrueta-Clement, Larry Schweinhart, William Barnett, and David Weikart analyze longitudinal data from the Perry preschool project. In a comparison study involving random assignment, they examine the relationship of preschool experience on subsequent delinquent behavior. Both self-reported and officially reported delinquent and antisocial behavior are reported for the experimental and control subjects at 19 years of age. Chapter 10, by David Hawkins and Tony Lam, presents preliminary results from part of a large longitudinal delinquency prevention experiment in the public schools. Data pertaining to efforts to improve the behavior of teachers is presented and analyzed.

The final chapter in the section on intervention programs involves a paper that was not part of the Bolton Conference. As a result of the conference it was felt that it was necessary to include a review of some of the intervention procedures that focus directly on the individual regarded as being at-risk for subsequent antisocial or delinquent behavior. In Chapter 11 those procedures are reviewed critically by Larry Michelson who places a particular emphasis on techniques involving cognitive behavior modification. In Chapter 12, Harold Leitenberg provides an overview and critical discussion of the first four chapters on intervention programs.

The final chapter focuses on issues of social policy and the prevention of antisocial and delinquent behavior. In Chapter 13, Jay Lindgren looks at social policy primarily in terms of the research papers that were presented at the Bolton Conference.

The Bolton Conference and this subsequent publication are an effort to bring together and critically examine a substantial body of the most current research on identification, prevention and early intervention programs for children at risk for antisocial and delinquent behavior. Of special concern are the implications of that research for policymakers and administrators in the fields of education, social service, and juvenile corrections. The discussion chapters attempt to examine the research data from the standpoint of methodology as well as social policy.

Although this volume cannot be all-inclusive, it does provide a substantial framework and direction for both the social scientist and the policymaker. Based upon the empirical information presented, the issues framed, and conclusions drawn by the discussants, we hope that reasonable decisions relative to future directions in the prevention of antisocial and delinquent behavior can be made.

—John D. Burchard
—Sara N. Burchard

References

Elliott, D. S., Ageton, S. S., Huizinga, D., Knowles, B. A., & Canter, R. J. (1983). *The prevalence and incidence of delinquent behavior: 1976-1980*. Boulder: C/A Publications.

Klein, M. W. (1979). Deinstitutionalization and diversion of juvenile offenders: A litany of impediments. In N. Norris & M. Toury (Eds.), *Crime and justice: An annual review of research*. Chicago: University of Chicago Press.

Krisberg, B., Schwartz, I. M., Litsky, R., & Austin, J. (1985). *The watershed of juvenile justice reform*. Paper published by the Center for the Study of Youth Policy, Minneapolis, MN.

Martin, E. (1985). *Deinstitutionalization of status offenders: A national perspective*. Paper presented at the First Annual Conference for Children and Youth Council, Boise, ID.

Regnery, A. S. (1983). The juvenile justice system: A federal perspective. *The Proceedings*, National Association of Juvenile Correctional Agencies.

PART I

Early Identification of At-Risk Children

1

Vulnerability and Resiliency in Children at Risk for Delinquency: A Longitudinal Study from Birth to Young Adulthood

Emmy E. Werner

Most studies of delinquency have dealt with select samples of children and youth who have come to the attention of the criminal justice system and of correctional or mental health agencies. Few are longitudinal in nature (Feldhusen, Thurston, & Benning, 1973; Zabczyaska, 1977). Prospective studies of a whole cohort of children in an entire community, representing a wide range of socioeconomic and cultural backgrounds, are rarer still. One of these is the Kauai Longitudinal Study (1954-1986) conducted by a multidisciplinary team of pediatricians, psychologists, public health and social workers from California and Hawaii (Werner, Bierman, & French, 1971; Werner & Smith, 1977; Werner & Smith, 1982). This prospective study allows us to examine the influence of pre- and perinatal factors and the quality of the caretaking environment on the development of a multiracial cohort of 698 children from their birth in 1955 to young adulthood.

From the wealth of data available, I would like to select some that appear especially relevant to the objectives of this book: the early identification of children who are at "high risk" for engaging in delinquent behavior and the factors that prevent the occurrence of such behavior. The purpose of my report is three-fold:

(1) To examine the prognostic power of a combination of biological and psychosocial risk factors in early and middle childhood in identifying males and females with delinquency records in adolescence.
(2) To identify protective factors in the lives of children at high risk for delinquency that buffered the negative impact of constitutional vulnerability, chronic poverty, and family distress, and that prevented the occurrence of deviant behavior.
(3) To present a transactional model that stresses the bidirectionality of child-caregiver effects and the balance between risk factors and protective factors that appears to account for the difference in the development of deviant and resilient children.

I will conclude with a brief discussion of some of the implications of our findings for research and social action concerned with the identification of high-risk children and the prevention of delinquent behavior.

Methodology

The Island and the Study Population

The island of Kauai, with some 32,000 inhabitants, lies at the northwest end of the main chain of the Hawaiian islands, some 100 miles and a half-hour's flight from Honolulu. Settled between the eighth and thirteenth centuries, A.D., by voyagers from the Society Islands and Tahiti, it was an independent kingdom, until Hawaii became a territory and later the fiftieth state of the Union. The island was first visited by Europeans in 1778 when Captain Cook landed on its shores. In the nineteenth and twentieth centuries Kauai encountered successive waves of emigrants from New England, Europe, Southeast Asia, and the West Coast of the U.S. mainland. Many of the newcomers, who came to work on the sugar and pineapple plantations of the island, intermarried with the local Hawaiians.

The children in our study group are a kaleidoscope of many different ethnic groups: Japanese (33%), part and full Hawaiians (23%), Filipino (18%), ethnic mixtures other than Hawaiians (14%), Portuguese from the Azores (6%), Anglo-Caucasians (3%), Chinese (1%), Koreans (1%), and Puerto-Ricans (1%). Most of the fathers work as semi- or unskilled laborers on the sugar plantations or in the tourist industry. Most mothers did not graduate from high school, and half have only 8 years or less of formal education. Half of the families on Kauai live in chronic poverty.

The study began in 1954 with a household census followed by the assessment of the reproductive histories and the physical and emotional status of all pregnant women in the community. It continued with an evaluation of the cumulative effects of preperinatal stress and the quality of the caretaking environment on the physical, cognitive, and social development of the cohort of 698 children born in 1955, in the postpartum period, year 1, 2, 10, and 18. For two high-risk groups we now have data that extend into their 25th year of life. They are the offspring of psychotic parents (Werner & Smith, 1982) and of teenage mothers (Gonsalves, 1982).

Our assessment instruments included a variety of measures of the constitutional and behavior characteristics of the children, their families, and the larger social context in which they lived and of stressful events that occurred during the first and second decade of their lives. A detailed account of the methodology and the complete data based of the Kauai Longitudinal Study can be found in three books: *The Children of Kauai* (Werner et al., 1971), *Kauai's Children Come of Age* (Werner & Smith, 1977), and *Vulnerable, but Invincible: A Study of Resilient Children* (Werner & Smith, 1982).

**The Assessment of the Children
and of Caretaker-Child Interaction**

At birth, pediatricians evaluated the presence and severity of some 60 conditions thought to have had a possible deleterious effect on the fetus or newborn that occurred during the prenatal, labor, and delivery periods. After all conditions were scored, the pediatricians assigned to each newborn an overall perinatal stress score ranging from 0—no complications, to 3—severe perinatal complications (see Table 1).

Public health nurses conducted home visits in the postpartum period and in year 1, obtained maternal ratings of the infants' temperamental characteristics, and rated the quality of the mothers' caretaking style. They also inquired about stressful life events that had occurred since the baby was born.

In the second year of life, pediatricians and psychologists independently conducted a series of developmental examinations that assessed the physical status of the child, the presence of congenital or acquired physical defects, and sensori-motor, language, and self-help skills with the Cattell Infant Intelligence and Vineland Social Maturity Scales (Cattell, 1940; Doll, 1953). The psychologists also assessed the behavior of the toddler and parent-child interaction during the

TABLE 1.1

Summary of Scoring System for Prenatal-Perinatal Complications: Kauai Longitudinal Study

Mild (Score 1)	Moderate (Score 2)	Severe (Score 3)
mild: pre-eclampsia, essential hypertension, renal insufficiency or anemia; controlled diabetes or hypothyroidism; positive Wasserman and no treatment; acute genitourinary infection 3rd trimester; untreated pelvic tumor producing dystocia; treated asthma	marked: pre-eclampsia, essential hypertension, renal insufficiency or anemia; diabetes under poor control; decompensated cardiovascular disease requiring treatment; untreated thyroid dysfunction; confirmed rubella 1st trimester; nonobstetrical surgery: general anesthesia, abdominal incision or hypotension	eclampsia; renal or diabetic coma; treated pelvic tumor
2nd or 3rd trimester vaginal bleeding; placental infarct; marginal placenta previa; premature rupture of membranes; amnionitis; abnormal fetal heart rate: meconium stained amniotic fluid (excl. breech); confirmed polyhydramnios	vaginal bleeding with cramping; central placenta previa: partial placenta abruptio: placental or cord anomalies	complete placenta abruptio; congenital syphilis of the newborn
rapid, forceful, or prolonged unproductive labor; frank breech or persistent occipit posterior; twins; elective Cesarean section; low forceps with complications; cord prolapsed or twisted and oxygen administered to newborn	chin, face, brow, or footling presentation; emergency Cesarean section; manual or forceps rotation, mid forceps or high forceps or breech and oxygen administered under 5 minutes	transverse lie; emergency Cesarean section: manual rotation, mid forceps or high forceps or breech extraction and oxygen administered 5 minutes or more
breathing delayed 1-3 minutes; intermittent central cyanosis and oxygen administered under 1 minute; cry weak or abnormal; bradycardia	breathing delayed 3-5 minutes; gasping; intermittent central cyanosis and oxygen administered over 1 minute; cry delayed 5-15 minutes	breathing delayed over 5 minutes; no respiratory effort; persistent cyanosis and oxygen administered continuously; cry delayed over 15 minutes
birth injury excl. central nervous system; jaundice; hemmorrhagic disease mild; pneumonia, rate of respiration under 40 and oxygen administered intermittently; birth weight 1,800-2,500 gm and oxygen administered intermittently or incubator or other special care; oral antibiotic to newborn; abnormal tone or Moro reflex; irritability	major birth injury and temporary central nervous system involvement; spasms; pneumonia, rate of respiration over 40 and oxygen administered intermittently; apnea and oxygen administered intermittently or resuscitation under 5 minutes; birth weight 1,800-2,500 gm, fair suck and oxygen administered or incubator; antibiotics administered intravenously, cry absent	major birth injury and persistent central nervous system involvement; exchange transfusion; seizure; hyaline membrane disease; pneumonia; rate of respiration over 60 and oxygen administered continuously, resuscitation over 5 minutes; birth weight under 1,800 gm and oxygen administered or special feeding; meningitis; absent Moro reflex

SOURCE: Reprinted by permission of publisher from Werner, E. E. and Smith, R. S., *Vulnerable, but Invincible: A Longitudinal Study of Resilient Children and Youth.* New York: McGraw Hill, pp. 170-171.

examinations and inquired about stressful life events that had occurred since year 1.

The 10-year follow-up included (independent) assessments of the child's behavior and school achievement by teachers and parents, and the results of the 2 group tests—the Bender-Gestalt (B-G) test (Koppitz, 1964), a measure of the central nervous system (CNS) integrity, and the Primary Mental Abilities Test (PMA) (Thurstone, & Thurstone, 1954) yielding verbal, reasoning, numerical, spatial, and perceptual-motor scores. Family interviews during home visits by public health and social workers provided information on the health status of parents and children, changes in the household composition, and information on stressful life events that had occurred between the ages of 2 and 10.

The 18-year follow-up included the results of scholastic aptitude and achievement tests routinely given in the schools of the island as well as California Psychological Inventory (CPI) and Locus of Control scale scores for each youth in the cohort (Gough, 1969; Nowicki & Strickland, 1973). In addition, we conducted in-depth clinical interviews with youth who had developed serious learning disabilities or mental health problems by age 10, and with controls without problems who were matched by age, sex, ethnicity, and socioeconomic (SES) status.

At each follow-up there were special diagnostic tests for children who were considered at risk on the basis of the examinations given at birth, and at ages 2, 10, and 18 years.

The Assessment of the Home Environment

Independent assessments of the quality of the home environment were made periodically—at birth, ages 2, 10, and 18, by psychologists and graduate students in psychology, who had no knowledge of the children's status. These assessments were made on a 5-point scale ranging from 1, "very unfavorable," to 5, "very favorable." Dimensions included in these ratings were the *mother's educational level* (based on years of completed schooling, from records that also included IQ's for about half the parents); the *family socioeconomic level* at birth, age 2, and 10 (based on father's occupation, steadiness of employment, income level, and condition of housing); *family stability* from birth to age 2 (based on the information from early home visits and interviews that provided evidence of family discord, or long-term separation of the child from the mother) and ratings of the *quality of educational stimulation* and *emotional support* provided by the family at age 10 (based on interviews and observations during home visits).

Included in the interviews at the 18-year followup were a number of items that dealt with the youth's perception of the quality of the family life during adolescence. We explored their attitudes toward their parents, their feelings of security or conflict about their family, their identification with role models in the family, and stressful life events that had occurred between ages 10 and 18. We also asked for an evaluation of the help they had received from formal and informal sources of support, that is kith, kin, and community agencies. These contacts were verified in the records of the social services agencies to which we had access and that also provided an independent check on major stressful life events.

The Records of the Community Agencies

In comparison with other communities of similar size on the U.S. mainland, the island of Kauai has a great variety of community agencies and volunteer organizations that concern themselves with the needs of children and youth. They include mental health services, special educational and rehabilitation services, and, in the Police Department, a special counselor in the Juvenile Crime Prevention Unit as well as a school relations officer at one of the three high schools on the island.

We were able to monitor the records of both public and private agencies for members of the 1955 birth cohort and their families throughout the 2 decades of this study. They included records of the police and the family court, records of the schools and the department of special education, records of the family physicians, hospitals, public health and mental health agencies, and of the Department of Social Service and Housing (Divisions of Public Welfare and Vocational Rehabilitation). The Mental Health Register for the State of Hawaii in Honolulu also provided us with information on in- and out-patient treatment for the youth and their families (with confidentiality safeguarded by the use of code numbers).

Attrition Rates

Throughout the 2 decades of the study, attrition rates remained low: 96% of the 1955 birth cohort participated in the 2-year follow-up,

90% in the 10-year follow-up, and 88% in the 18-year follow-up. By comparison, the two largest follow-up studies on the U.S. mainland, the Growth and Guidance Studies of the Institute of Human Development at the University of California at Berkeley (Block, 1971) and the follow-up study of antisocial children referred to child guidance clinics in St. Louis by Robins (1966), were able to reach 75% and 82% of their original target groups.

Results

The "Casualities" of the First and Second Decade of Life

By age 10, approximately 1 out of every 3 children in this birth cohort needed some medical, educational, or mental health services, often a combination of them. Approximately 7% of the children needed medical care for moderate to severe physical handicaps (defects of the central nervous system, vision, hearing, heart anomalies, or orthopedic problems); 14% were in need of remedial education (of more than 6-months duration) in such basic skills as reading, spelling, grammar, or arithmetic; 3% were in need of placement in a class for the mentally retarded; and another 3% were in need of placement in a class for the learning disabled. (The learning disabled were children of normal intelligence, but with serious reading, attentional, or perceptual-motor problems who had also been considered "hyperactive" by their teachers and parents.) In addition, some 4% of the children were considered in need of long-term mental health care (of more than 6-months duration). Of 5 children in this group 4 were "acting out," that is, persistently aggressive, constantly bullying or quarreling, destructive, stealing, or truant from home or school.

By age 18, 10% of the cohort had mental health problems, documented in the State Mental Health Register, in the records of the Division of Mental Health or in mental hospital and community mental health centers on the island. Of the cohort, 15% (21% of the males, 11% of the females) had contacts with the police and among those 4 out of 10 had contact with the family court as well.

Among the delinquent acts (including status offenses) recorded in police and/or family court files were second- and first-degree larceny; second- and first-degree burglary; car theft; malicious injury; assault and battery; sexual misconduct; possession, sale, and abuse of hard drugs; forgery or passing of forged checks; and repeated acts of truancy, running away from home, curfew violations, and unlawful hunting (i.e., status offenses) (see Table 2). (Excluded from our statistical analyses were youths whose police record contained only a traffic citation or an occasional property trespass and who had not been referred to the family court.)

Of the youth with delinquency records in adolescence, one-third were warned and severely reprimanded; one-fifth were counseled with their parents present; 7% were placed in foster homes; 7% were placed in youth correctional facilities; 5% were placed in the Job Corps; 5% were referred to mental health clinics; 4% were placed in a state hospital; and 2% were placed on probation.

Some Salient Characteristics
of Youth with Records of Delinquent Acts

Among the youth who had a record of delinquent acts in adolescence (60% of the males, 85% of the females), 3 out of 4 lived in chronic poverty. About half of this group had been considered in need of remedial education and/or special class placement by age 10, and about 1 out of 5 had been considered in need of mental health services by this age. The combined rates of educational and mental health problems for these youth by age 10 was twice as high as that for the cohort as a whole.

There were nearly twice as many males (N = 67) as females (N = 35) among the youth with records of delinquent acts. Among middle class males in this group, there was a significantly higher proportion ($p < .01$) who had been diagnosed by pediatricians *at birth* as having "chronic conditions possibly leading to minimal brain dysfunctions" than among lower-class males or among females with a record of delinquent acts.

The females, in turn, had more multiple problems in the second decade of life than the males and more repeated contacts with the police during adolescence. By age 18, more than half of the females, but only 1 out of 6 among the males with a record of delinquent acts, had serious mental health problems necessitating in- or out-patient treatment. Half of all the teenage pregnancies were among the females with delinquency records, although they constituted only 11% of the women in this birth cohort.

There were significant differences in exposure to stressful life events between youth *with* delinquency records and same sex peers *without* delinquency records and/or mental health problems (Chi-

TABLE 1.2
The Proportion of Delinquents Engaging in Delinquent Acts
as Recorded in Police and/or Family Court Files
(1955 Birth Cohort, Kauai)

	Male Delinquents[1] (N = 67) %	Female Delinquents[2] (N = 35) %
Traffic citation	31.3	45.7
Car accident: malicious injury	9.0	2.9
Car theft	6.0	2.9
Trespassing	9.0	2.9
Larceny, second degree	32.8	31.4
Larceny, first degree	6.0	5.7
Burglary, second degree	17.9	8.6
Burglary, first degree	13.4	5.7
Running away from home	11.9	54.3
Truant from school	4.5	2.9
Curfew violations	7.5	0
Assault and battery	14.9	17.1
Sexual misconduct	0	5.7
Drug abuse	0	14.3
Unlawful possession of drugs	0	2.4
Forgery and passing of forged checks	4.5	0

1. Total Males: 320; 2. Total females: 313.

square tests, $p < .05$). Among both sexes, a higher proportion of those with delinquency records were exposed to stressful life events that disrupted their family unit (see Tables 3 and 4). A higher proportion of males with police and/or court contact were exposed to such stressful life events in childhood (see column 1, Table 3), while a higher proportion of females with police and/or court contact were exposed to such stressful life events in adolescence (see column 1, Table 4). Females with delinquency records also had a higher proportion of family members with learning and/or behavior problems than did males with delinquency records.

Predictors of Delinquency for the Females in the 1955 Cohort on Kauai

Predictions of delinquency in adolescence from data obtained in the first decade of life were generally better for the girls than for the boys. However, predictions increased for *both* sexes from modest correlations based on the data available by age 2, to substantial

TABLE 1.3

Stressful Life Events Which Differentiated Significantly Between
Males With Delinquency Records and Males Without Delinquency
Records and/or Mental Health Problems
(1955 Birth Cohort, Kauai)

Stressful Life Events	Males With Delinquency Records (N = 67) %	Males Without Delinquency Records (N = 206) %
In Infancy		
Mother pregnant or birth of younger sibling before M was 2 years old	38.3	15.0
In Childhood		
Older sibling left household	38.3	15.0
Serious discord between parents	14.9	4.4
Maternal mental health problems	8.5	1.0
Father lost job	8.5	.5
Father permanently absent	8.5	3.4
Male changed schools in lower grades	8.5	1.0
Brother handicapped, with serious learning or behavior problems or in trouble with law	4.3	1.0
Mother remarried, stepfather moves in house	4.3	.5
In Adolescence		
Problems in relationship with father	23.4	6.8
Maternal mental health problems	17.0	1.0
Problems in relationship with mother	12.8	2.9

multiple correlations, based on 10-year data or on a combination of variables from *both* the 2- and 10-year follow-up.

The most powerful predictor among the 2-year data for the girls was a Cattell IQ score below 80, with a correlation coefficient of $r = .38$. Equally powerful a predictor was the presence of a congenital defect ($r = .37$). The multiple correlation coefficient (measuring the relationship between a combination of all the variables available and the outcome variable) rose to an $R = .44$ for the girls, with most of the added predictive power contributed by a low level of maternal education (8 grades or less of formal schooling), the presence of a moderate to severe degree of perinatal stress, birth weight below 2500 gm, as well as distressing feeding or sleeping habits or temper tantrums noted by the mother in year 1 and by the psychologists during the 2-year follow-up examination.

TABLE 1.4

Stressful Life Events Which Differentiated Significantly
Between Females With Delinquency Records and Females Without
Delinquency Records and/or Mental Health Problems
(1955 Birth Cohort, Kauai)

Stressful Life Events	Females With Delinquency Records (N = 35) %	Females Without Delinquency Records (N = 233) %
In Infancy		
Mother pregnant or birth of younger sibling before F was 2 years old	58.6	18.5
Serious marital discord	6.9	.5
Maternal mental health problems	3.4	0
In Childhood		
Maternal mental health problems	13.8	.9
Sister handicapped or serious learning or behavior problems	17.2	1.7
Brother handicapped or serious learning or behavior problems	13.8	.9
Female changed schools	3.4	1.3
Female was placed in foster home	3.4	0
Death of brother	3.4	.9
In Adolescence		
Problems in family relationship	69.0	9.8
Teenage pregnancy	41.4	2.0
Problems in relationship with mother	48.3	3.9
Problems in relationship with father	51.7	2.0
Teenage marriage	24.1	1.0
Father absent permanently (deserted, divorced)	17.2	3.9
Mother absent permanently (divorced)	17.2	2.0
Maternal mental health problems	17.2	1.0
Severe marital discord between parents	20.7	2.0
Problems with peers	13.8	3.9
Mother absent temporarily	13.8	2.9
Father absent temporarily	17.2	1.0
Sibling left home	10.3	0
Teenage marital stress	17.2	0

The single most powerful predictor of delinquency in girls at age
10 was a need for long-term mental health services (of more than
6-months duration), with a correlation of $r = .30$. When we added the
other diagnostic data obtained at age 10, we obtained a multiple

correlation of R = .74. A (low) socioeconomic status rating, a (low) PMA IQ (more than 1 standard deviation below the mean), and a recognized need for remedial education at age 10, added most of the predictive power to the multiple correlation for the girls. The addition of the data available from the 2-year exam to the 10-year data, raised the multiple correlation for the girls from R = .74 to R = .81.

Predictors of Delinquency for the Males in the 1955 Cohort on Kauai

The single most powerful predictor among the 2-year data for the boys was a low rating of family stability (r = .19). When we combined all of our data available by age 2, the multiple correlation rose to a modest R = .32. A low level of maternal education and a low standard of living at birth, the presence of a congenital defect, and a high activity level rating by the mother when the infant was 1 year old, as well as below average self-help skills reflected in a low Vineland Social Quotient (SQ) at age 2, contributed most of the added predictive power for the boys.

The two most powerful predictors of delinquency in boys at age 10 was a low PMA IQ (r = .24) and a need for remedial education (r = .24). The addition of other diagnostic data obtained during the 10-year follow-up raised the multiple correlation to an R = .46 for the boys, with most of the added predictive power contributed by a low socioeconomic status, a low level of maternal education, and the presence of a moderate to severe physical handicap (necessitating medical care) at age 10. The addition of the data available by age 2 to the data from the 10-year follow-up raised the multiple correlation for the boys from a modest R = .46 to a substantial R = .79.

Key Predictors of Delinquent Behavior

A combination of about a dozen variables occurred most frequently as the best predictors of deviant outcomes in the 1955 birth cohort. Among the *medical* variables were the presence of moderate to severe degrees of perinatal stress, a congenital defect, or an acquired physical handicap by age 10. Among the *sociological* variables were a low standard of living at birth and also at ages 2 and 10, a low rating of family stability by age 2, and a low level of maternal education. Among the *behavioral* variables were maternal ratings of activity level of the infant (very high or very low at age 1), a Cattell IQ below 80 at age 2, a PMA IQ below 90 at age 10, and a recognized need for placement in a learning-disability class or long-term mental health care by age 10.

The presence of 4 or more of these key predictors in the records of the children in this cohort by age 2 appeared to be a realistic dividing line between most youth who had delinquency records (72%) and most children in the cohort who did not develop any serious learning or behavior problems or had no trouble with the law (73%). We are aware that even our largest correlations between predictor variables and outcomes, though statistically significant, do not permit accurate predictions in each individual case. As Robins (1966) has pointed out in her follow-up study of deviant children, if resources are ample and intervention imposes no distress on children who may not need help, those concerned with the prevention of delinquent behavior may choose to lower the number of predictors required, thus including not only *all* children at high risk for delinquency, but also a number of children who would not develop any deviant behavior. If resources are scarce, we might explore an additional avenue: the identification of protective factors in the lives of children at high risk for delinquency that buffer the negative impact of constitutional vulner-abilities, poverty, and family distress, and prevent the occurrence of deviant behavior.

Protective Factors in the Lives of Children at Risk for Delinquency

In our cohort of 698 children, about half lived in chronic poverty. Among those in poverty were 72 children (42 females, 30 males) who had each encountered 4 or more risk factors before age 2 that were key predictors of delinquency (*including* poverty, exposure to perinatal stress, a mother with 8 grades or less of education, and family distress). But none of these high-risk children developed any serious learning or behavioral difficulties during childhood or adolescence, none had any contacts with the police or family court, and none had received remedial education or mental health services. Yet they "worked well, played well, loved well and expected well" when we interviewed them at age 18.

We contrasted these resilient children with peers of the same age and sex in the cohort who also had encountered 4 or more risk factors in early childhood (including poverty) and who had committed delinquent acts by adolescence. A number of constitutional variables, household-structure variables, and personality characteristics differentiated the two high-risk groups from each other. Most of these characteristics were shared by both sexes, but some were sex specific.

Presented here is a brief summary of the (statistically) significant differences between the resilient and delinquent-prone high-risk groups. The interested reader is referred to the book *Vulnerable, but Invincible* (Werner & Smith, 1982) for a detailed account of the data (especially in Chapters 6 through 10, and the appendix).

Protective factors within the children. A significantly higher proportion among the resilient than among the delinquent high-risk children were firstborn. Although rates of perinatal stress, congenital defects, and physical handicaps were above the norm for the cohort, the high-risk resilient children had fewer serious illnesses during early and middle childhood and recuperated more quickly from them than did their high-risk peers with delinquency records in adolescence.

The mothers of the resilient children perceived them as "very active," "affectionate," "cuddly," "good-natured," and "easy to deal with" when they were infants. The psychologists noted their pronounced autonomy and positive social orientation when they were toddlers. Developmental exams in the second year of life indicated appropriate physical, sensori-motor, and language development as well as advanced self-help skills. In middle childhood, these children possessed adequate problem-solving and reading skills, and their perceptual-motor development was age appropriate. Parents and self-reports indicated activities and interests that were not narrowly sex typed.

Characteristics that differentiated between high-risk resilient youth and youth with a delinquency record in adolescence were better verbal skills, a more internal locus of control, a higher self-esteem, and higher scores on the CPI scales of responsibility, socialization, achievement, and femininity for *both* sexes, reflecting a more nurturant and responsible attitude toward life than that of the delinquents. Resilient girls differed from girls with a delinquency record on a number of additional CPI dimensions such as dominance, sociability, achievement via independence, intellectual efficiency, and a sense of well-being.

Protective factors in the caregiving environment. Key factors in the caregiving environment that appeared to contribute to the stress resistance of resilient children in the midst of poverty were the age of the opposite-sex parent (younger mothers for resilient males; older fathers for resilient females); the number of children in the family (four or less); the spacing between the index child and the next-born sibling (more than 2 years); the availability of alternate caretakers within the household (father, grandparents, older siblings); the amount of attention given to the child in infancy by the primary caretaker; the availability of a sibling as a caretaker or confidant in childhood; the work load of the mother; discipline and rule enforcement in the household in adolescence; and the presence of an informal multigenerational network of kin and friends including neighbors, teachers, and ministers who were supportive and available for counsel in times of crises or major life transitions.

For the resilient girls, early mother-daughter relationships had been consistently positive, and there were other females present in the household as support and models for them. Permanent absence of the father and long-term employment by the mother outside of the household seemed to push them into the direction of greater autonomy and competence that included care for younger siblings. Resilient boys were more often first-born sons and grew up in households that were less physically crowded. There were fewer children, but some adult male model was present in their family who provided rules and structure for their lives.

Factors that increased vulnerability in children at risk for delinquency. Structure and strong social bonds were absent in the lives of most high-risk children who had a delinquency record in adolescence. The lack of emotional support was most devastating to children with a constitutional tendency toward withdrawal and passivity, with low activity levels and irregular feeding or sleeping habits.

In comparison with the resilient children, delinquent-prone children of both sexes were more often later-born children in large families whose mothers were often pregnant again and gave birth to another sibling before the index child was 2 years old. As infants their mothers rated them as less socially responsive than their siblings, considered them more difficult to handle, and were also more distressed by their temper and eating and sleeping habits. To psychologists, they appeared less autonomous and more dependent during the development examinations at age 2.

During childhood delinquent-prone children moved and changed schools more often. They also lost more close friends or siblings through departure and death. They were exposed to more parental illness, including mental illness (which affected a higher proportion of girls), and to family discord and permanent father absence (which affected a higher proportion of boys). There were fewer alternate caregivers in the household for these children, even though their mothers worked (but more sporadically than mothers of resilient children). Caretakers who were strangers appeared to affect the boys more negatively than the girls. More parental marriages among these families ended in divorce or separation of one parent from the family. This appeared to affect the boys more negatively in childhood, the girls more negatively in adolescence.

By age 18, a higher proportion of delinquent than resilient youth had an external locus of control orientation and a very low estimate of themselves. They felt that events happened to them as a result of luck, fate, or other factors beyond their control. Professional assistance sought and obtained by community agencies during adolescence was generally considered of "little help" to them.

Crucial for these youth was not the experience of failure per se, but loss of control over reinforcement, a perceived lack of synchrony between their actions and feedback from the environment. On the contrary, the experience of the resilient children in coping with and mastering stressful life events through their own actions appeared to build immunity against such "learned helplessness" and produced an attitude of "hopefulness" instead (Seligman, 1975).

Key Discriminators

We now present a set of predictors that maximally differentiated between children who lived in poverty and committed delinquent acts and their resilient peers of the same age and sex who shared similar risk factors (including chronic poverty) but had no contact with the police and/or courts during the first 2 decades of life and did not develop any learning and/or behavior problems. A total of 36 variables (characteristics of the child and of the caretaking environment) at age 10 and a total of 42 variables at age 18 were entered as predictors in forward stepwise discriminant analyses. One variable was either added to or removed from the equation until optimum discriminant functions were achieved. The variable added was the one that, when partialled on the previously entered variables, had the highest multiple correlations with the groups. The effectiveness of the discriminant functions was tested by reclassifying the boys and girls into delinquent and resilient groups and computing the rates of correct classification. The variables that contributed to optimum discriminant functions at ages 10 and ages 18 are listed in Tables 5 and 6.

Discriminant Function Analyses
Using Predictors at Age 10

By age 10, 20 of the 36 predictor variables entered in the stepwise analysis separated the high-risk resilient girls from the high-risk girls who committed delinquent acts in adolescence (see Table 5, column 1). The 20 variable discriminant function correctly classified 88% of the resilient girls and 91% of the girls with delinquency records (misclassifying 4 resilient and 2 delinquent girls). The separation between the 2 groups was highly significant ($p < .0001$). The canonical correlation for the 20 variable function was .92.

By age 10, 14 of the 36 predictor variables entered in the stepwise discriminant analysis separated the high-risk resilient males from the high-risk males who committed delinquent acts in adolescence (see Table 5, column 2). The 14 variable discriminant function correctly classified 82% of the high-risk resilient boys and 88% of the boys with delinquency records (misclassifying 4 resilient and 5 delinquent boys). The separation between the 2 groups was highly significant ($p < .001$). The canonical correlation for the 14 variable function was .73.

Discriminant Function Analyses
Using Predictors at Age 18

By age 18, 14 of the 42 variables entered in the stepwise discriminant function analysis differentiated significantly between high-risk resilient females and high-risk females who committed delinquent acts in adolescence (see Table 6, column 1). The 14 variable function correctly classified 92% of the resilient females and 91% of the females with delinquency records (misclassifying 3 resilient and 2 delinquent females). The separation between the 2 groups was highly significant ($p < .0001$). The canonical correlation for the 14 variable function was .95.

By age 18, 22 of the 42 variables entered in the stepwise discriminant function analysis differented significantly between high-risk resilient males and high-risk males who committed delinquent acts in adolescence (see Table 6, column 2). The 22 variable function correctly classified 95% of the resilient males and 95% of the males

TABLE 1.5
Significant Discriminators Between Resilient Youth
and Youth With Delinquency Records — All of Whom Live
in Chronic Poverty — Using Predictors at Age 10
(1955 Birth Cohort, Kauai)

Variables Entered in Stepwise Discriminant Function Analysis	Standardized Discriminant for Females	Function Coefficients for Males
In Infancy		
Evidence of low mental functioning in parents	−1.34	
Evidence of maternal mental illness (birth-2 years)	−1.25	
Evidence of maternal mental illness (2-10 years)	−.57	
Birth order	−1.24	−.99
Prolonged separation of infant from mother (year 1)	−.37	
Prolonged disruption of family life (year 1)	−1.22	
Infant perceived as "good-natured, easy to deal with" (year 1)		+.40
In Second Year		
Physical status of child (20 months)		+.25
Autonomy (20 months)		+.85
Information processing skills (20 months)	+.67	
Parent-child interaction (20 months)	+1.84	+.83
Conflict between parents (birth-2 years)	−.65	−.51
Father absent since birth	+.89	
Serious or repeated illness of child (birth-2 years)	−.62	
Cumulative number of stressful life events (birth-2 years)		−.44
In Childhood		
Serious or repeated illness of child (2-10 years)	−1.55	−.63
Parental illness (2-10 years)	−.56	
Father dead or permanently absent (2-10 years)	−1.29	
Father temporarily absent (2-10 years)	−1.65	−.53
Death of sibling (2-10 years)		−.94
Departure of sibling from household (2-10 years)	−.54	−.67
Number of children in household by age 10	−.37	−.25
Number of adults in household by age 10		−.49
Emotional support provided in household (2-10 years)	+.44	
Cumulative N of stressful life events (2-10 years)	−2.62	
Bender Gestalt error score at age 10	−1.11	−.50

TABLE 1.6
Significant Discriminators Between Resilient Youth and
Youth With Delinquency Records—All of Whom Live in
Chronic Poverty—Using Predictors at Age 18
(1955 Birth Cohort, Kauai)

Variables Entered in Stepwise Discriminant Function Analysis	Standardized Discriminant for Females	Function Coefficients for Males
In Infancy		
Evidence of low mental functioning in parents	−1.16	
Age of opposite sex parent at birth of child		−.47
Birth order		−.78
Attention given to infant (year 1)	+.40	
Prolonged separation of infant from mother (year 1)	−.97	−1.43
Distressing habits of infant (year 1)		−.38
Infant perceived as "cuddly, affectionate" (year 1)		+.66
Infant perceived as "good-natured, easy to deal with" (year 1)	+.29	
Mother's way of coping with infant (ratio ±) (year 1)		+.74
In Second Year		
Physical status of child (20 months)		+.43
Social orientation (20 months)	+.51	
Autonomy (20 months)		+.46
Self-help skills (20 months)		+.51
Parent/child interaction (ratio ±) (20 months)	+1.79	+.31
Serious or repeated illness of child (birth-2 years)		−1.39
Prolonged disruption of family life (year 1)		−.34
Conflict between parents (birth-2 yhears)		−.65
Cumulative number of stressful life events (birth-1 year)	−1.17	
In Childhood		
Father absent permanently (2-10 years)		−1.04
Chronic family discord (2-10 years)	−.97	−.52
Mother worked long-term (2-10 years)		−.66
Repeated or chronic parental illnesses (2-10 years)		−.72
Death of a sibling (2-10 years)		−.55
Departure of sibling from household (2-10 years)	+.52	
Number of children in household by age 10	−1.32	
Number of additional adults in household (besides parents) (by year 10)	+1.10	
Emotional support in home (2-10 years)		+.80
Bender-Gestalt error score (10 years)		−.52

TABLE 1.6 Continued

Variables Entered in Stepwise Discriminant Function Analysis	Standardized Discriminant for Females	Function Coefficients for Males
In Adolescence		
Quality of family relationships (10-18 years)	+1.02	+1.45
Quality of relationships with mother (10-18 years)	+3.54	
Cumulative number of stressful life events (10-18 years)	−3.44	−2.79

with delinquent records in adolescence (misclassifying 1 resilient and 2 delinquent males). The separation between the 2 groups was highly significant ($p < .0001$). The canonical correlation for the 14 variable function was .87.

An examination of Tables 5 and 6 shows that among significant discriminators in infancy between high-risk children who committed delinquent acts by adolescence and those who did not were the age of the mother, birth-order of the child, the mother's perception of the infant's temperamental characteristics, and the health of the infant. The other discriminating variables in infancy were characteristics of the caregiving environment critical for attachment and the establishment of a secure bond between the infant and the primary caretaker, that is, the amount of attention given to the infant and the quality of the early caretaker/child relationship.

Among significant discriminators in the second year of life between high-risk children who committed delinquent acts by adolescence and those who did not were the physical status of the toddler, his autonomy and social orientation, and the quality of parent/child relationships observed during the developmental examinations.

During childhood most of the significant discriminators between high-risk resilient children and those who committed delinquent acts by adolescence dealt with the composition and coherence of the household: the number of children and adults in the family, the presence or absence of the father, the departure or death of siblings, the employment of the mother, the presence or absence of chronic family discord, and the cumulative number of stressful life events experienced. Characteristics that differentiated the high-risk children who later became delinquent from those who did not were CNS integrity and good health. Additional discriminators among the girls were parental IQ and mental health status of the parents, especially the mother.

By age 18, the youth's own perception of the quality of the family relationship during adolescence as well as the cumulative number of stressful life events experienced since age 10 were additional significant discriminators between high-risk males and females who had delinquency records and high-risk youth without any problems in adolescence. For females the quality of their relationship with their mothers was an added significant discriminator.

A Transactional Model of Development

The results of the Kauai Longitudinal Study appear to lend some empirical support to a transactional model of human development that takes into account the bidirectionality of child-caregiver effects. In the words of Sameroff (1983, p. 12), "The development of a child appears to be multiply determined by what the child brings to the situation, what s/he elicits from the situation, what the environment can offer and what it does offer."

In Figure 1 we show some of the interrelations between major risk factors at birth, and some of the most common stressful life events that *increased vulnerability* in this birth cohort as well as protective factors within the child and the caregiving environment that *increased stress resistance*. The contribution of risk factors, stressful life events, and protective factors appear to differ with the sex of the child and with the stages of the life cycle.

Constitutional factors (such as health and temperament) appeared to pull their greatest weight in infancy and early childhood (to age 2), while ecological factors (household structure and composition) and cognitive skills gained in importance in childhood (to age 10). Inter- and intrapersonal factors (locus of control, self-esteem) were of greatest importance in adolescence judging from the weight assigned to these variables in the discriminant analyses. Stressful life events appeared to make boys more vulnerable in early and middle childhood and girls more vulnerable in adolescence.

To the extent that the boys and girls in this study were able to elicit predominantly positive responses from their environment, they were found to be stress-resistent, even if they had a physical handicap or lived in chronic poverty or in a home with a psychotic parent. To the extent that the children elicited negative responses from their environment, they were found to be vulnerable, even if they were reared in more affluent homes.

Optimal adaptive development appears to be characterized by a balance between the power of the person and the power of his or her

Major Risk Factors (at birth)
Chronic poverty
Mother with little education
Moderate-severe perinatal complications
Developmental delays or irregularities
Genetic abnormalities
Parental psychopathology

VULNERABILITY

Major Sources of Stress ————————→ *Major Sources of Support*

In Childhood and Adolescence	*Protective Factors Within the Child*	*Caregiving Environment*
Prolonged separation from primary caretaker during first year of life	Birth order (first) CNS integrity	Four or fewer children spaced more than two years apart
Birth of younger sib within two years after child's	High activity level	Much attention paid to infant during first year
Serious or repeated childhood illnesses	Good-natured; affectionate disposition	Positive parent-child relationship in early childhood
Parental illness	Responsive to people	Additional caretakers besides mother
Paternal mental illness		
Sib with handicap or learning or behavior problem	Free of distressing habits	Care by siblings and grandparents
Chronic family discord	Positive social orientation	Mother has some steady employment outside of household
Father absent		
Loss of job or sporadic employment of parent(s)	Autonomy	Availability of kin and neighbors for emotional support
Change of residence	Advanced self-help skills	
Change of schools	Age-appropriate sensorimotor and perceptual skills	Structure and rules in household
Divorce of parents		
Remarriage and entry of step-parent into household		Shared values—a sense of coherence
Departure or death of older sib or close friend	Adequate communication skills	Close peer friends
Foster home placement (for F: teenage pregnancy)	Ability to focus attention and control impulses	Availability of counsel by teachers and/or ministers
	Special interests and hobbies	Access to special services (health, education, social services)
	Positive self-concept	
	Internal Locus of Control	
	Desire to improve self	

RANGE OF PROBABLE DEVELOPMENTAL OUTCOMES
Adaptive   Maladaptive

Fewer	Risk Factors Stressful events	}	:	{ More	Risk Factors Stressful events
More	Protective factors in child in caregiving environment	}	:	{ Fewer	Protective factors in child in caregiving environment

SOURCE: Reprinted by permission of publisher from Werner, E. E. and Smith, R. S., **Vulnerable, but Invincible: A Longitudinal Study of Resilient Children and Youth.** New York: McGraw Hill, 1982, pp. 134-135.

Figure 1.1 Model of Interrelation Between Risk, Stress, Sources of Support and Coping (Based on Data from the Kauai Longitudinal Study)

social and physical environment (Wertheim, 1978). Intervention aimed at the prevention of delinquent and deviant behavior in children may thus be conceived as an attempt to restore this balance, either by *decreasing* a child's exposure to biological risk or stressful life events or by *increasing* the number of protective factors (competencies, sources of support) that she or he can draw upon.

Discussion

The results of our longitudinal study need replication in other sociocultural contexts. We draw encouragement, however, from the fact that some of the risk factors and the protective factors that we noted in this predominantly Asian and Polynesian population living on a small rural island, have also been reported by other investigators on the U.S. mainland and in Europe. The background characteristics of the delinquent youth on Kauai in the mid-1970s were strikingly similar to those reported by Robins (1966) in her follow-up study of black and Caucasian children who had been referred to child guidance clinics in metropolitan St. Louis for antisocial behavior in the 1920s and 1930s. The preponderance of educational problems in the early grades in the backgrounds of future delinquents have been repeatedly noted in more recent longitudinal studies of the development of delinquency in the United States (Feldhusen et al., 1973; Venezia, 1971), in Great Britain (Rutter, 1979), and in Poland (Zabczyaska, 1977). A number of protective factors in children's responses to stress and disadvantage, such as a good-natured temperament (Rutter, 1979; Thomas & Chess, 1977), close personal bonds with at least one member of the family, and a high self-esteem (Rutter, 1979), and the positive effects of a smaller family size and the presence of alternate caretakers such as grandparents (Kellam et al., 1977; Robins, 1966; Robbins, West, & Herjanic, 1975), have been noted in high-risk black and Caucasian children in the United States and in England as well.

The Identification of Children at High Risk for Delinquent Behavior

Information on these variables can be fairly routinely obtained from available school records in the early grades as well as from the records of well-baby clinics and the federally mandated early and periodic screening, diagnostic, and treatment program (EPSDT) for children who are recipients of Aid to Families with Dependent Children (AFDC). Some states such as California now have mandated such early screening for all children below the age of 6. We have seen on Kauai that the inclusion of a temperament rating scale for parents and/or teachers and of a checklist of stressful life events could enhance this identification process. But a developmental screening program is only useful if it plugs into practical intervention programs and if there is a periodic follow-up to determine the efficacy of the intervention.

The Kauai Longitudinal Study began before the matter of identification of high-risk children became a concern of the federal and state governments. Our findings, however, have some relevance to this concern. Our cohort was periodically assessed (at birth, in early childhood, and in the early grades). Letters with suggestions for follow-up, when indicated, went to the parents, and with parental consent, diagnostic information was made available to the educational, health, and mental health agencies in the community. These agencies were relatively well-staffed for the size of the island's population (32,000), were easily accessible to everyone regardless of ethnic or socioeconomic status, and had a tradition of mutual cooperation. Yet in what one might call an optimal setting for intervention if we contrast the small island of Kauai with many big "inner cities" on the U.S. mainland, only a minority of high-risk children (one-third) received some form of professional help, and less than half of those who did improved (Werner & Smith, 1977). On Kauai, in the mid-1970s, at the height of the community mental health and crisis intervention movements, some 70% of the youth with delinquency records received *no help* whatsoever from any agency—a proportion identical with that reported by Robins (1966) half a century earlier for the antisocial children who came to the attention of child-guidance clinics in the late 1920s. This aspect of our findings makes one pause for some serious reflection about the extent and efficacy of intervention in the lives of high-risk children, most of whom live in poverty.

Social Class and Vulnerability

Although most of the children who became delinquent were poor, it needs to be kept in mind that *poverty alone* was not a sufficient condition for the development of antisocial behavior. A low standard of living increased the likelihood of exposure of the child to *both* biological and psychological risk factors. But it was the joint impact of constitutional vulnerabilities and early family instability that led to serious and repeated delinquencies in *both* middle-class as well as lower-class children on Kauai. Our findings again complement those of Robins (1966) who followed antisocial Caucasian and black children in St. Louis into middle age. She noted "that childhood behavior and family patterns rather than class position lead to the hopelessness and alienation found largely in the bottom stratum is argued by the fact that antisocial children reared in middle class homes develop into much the same kind of impulsive and imprudent adults that lower class antisocial children do" (p. 304).

Regardless of social-class standing, children with "difficult temperaments" who interacted with distressed caretakers in disorganized, unstable families had a greater chance of developing delinquent behavior than children who were perceived as rewarding by their caretakers and who grew up in supportive homes.

Sources of Support

We were impressed by the pervasive effects of the quality of the mother-child interaction in infancy and early childhood that were documented as early as year 1 by home visitors and that were verified independently by the psychologists during the developmental examinations in the second year. They were also noted by the classroom teachers at age 10, and commented on by the youth in the age 18 interview.

The role of the father appeared more crucial in middle childhood and adolescence, especially for the children with learning disabilities and for the pregnant teenagers, half of whom had delinquency records in adolescence. The father's understanding and support, or lack of it, appeared to play a crucial role in the positive or negative resolution of the developmental problems of his offspring. Parental attitudes differentiated significantly between high-risk children whose behavior improved in adolescence and those whose behavior did not. Exposure to different types of intervention by community agencies for the minority who obtained such help in adolescence did not differentiate between those who improved and those who did not.

We had not anticipated the considerable influence of alternate care-givers such as grandparents, siblings, aunts, and uncles, parents of boy or girl friends, on the children and youth in this cohort. The emotional support of such elders or peer friends was a major protective factor in the midst of poverty, parental psychopathology, and serious disruptions of the family unit.

Among the people of Kauai, an informal network of kin and neighbors and the counsel and advice of a favorite teacher or clergyman were more often sought and more highly valued than the services of the mental health professionals, whether they were counselors, probation officers, psychologists, psychiatrists, or social workers.

Competence and Locus of Control

Equally pervasive appeared to be the positive effects of competence in reading and writing "standard" English among the children of Kauai. Competence in these skills was a major ameliorative factor among the resilient youth who coped well in spite of poverty or family distress. Lack of these skills led to cumulative problems in school and were prevalent among youth with a delinquency record.

The degree to which the youth had faith in the effectiveness of their own actions was positively related to the way they utilized their self-help skills and intellectual resources. An external locus of control, that is pronounced lack of faith in the effectiveness of one's own action, was especially notable among the delinquent youth; an internal locus of control was a significant correlate of resiliency even in high-risk conditions.

Implications

What then are some of the implications of our findings?

Future research in the study of vulnerability and stress resistance needs to consider the consequences of changing demographic trends such as later age of marriage and childbirth, smaller families, and single parenthood as well as changing sex role expectations that may alter substantially the nature of the caregiving environment and the stress resistance of contemporary children and youth in the modern, industrialized world.

We need to know more about the role of alternate caregivers, whether they are siblings, grandmothers, kith, or kin, as sources of support in times of stress. Cross-cultural studies and studies of child abuse have made us aware that a mother's emotional stability and

42   Emmy E. Werner

warmth toward her children is greater when there are more adults around to help and when she has fewer of her own children to handle (Werner, 1984).

Outside of the family unit, there is need to explore other informal sources of support. Among the most frequently encountered in our study were peer friends, teachers, ministers, and neighbors.

A strengthening of already existing informal support systems should focus especially on those children and families in a community that appear most vulnerable because they—temporarily or permanently—lack some of the essential social bonds that appear to buffer stress. Among them are working mothers of young children, with no dependable alternatives for child care; single, divorced, or teenaged parents with no other adult in the household; hospitalized children in need of special care who are separated from their families for extended periods of time; children of psychotic parents (and the well spouse in such a marriage).

The central component of effective coping with the multiplicity of inevitable life stresses appears to be a sense of *coherence* (Antonovsky, 1979)—a feeling of confidence that one's internal and external environment is predictable, that life has meaning and that things will work out as well as can be reasonably expected.

Young children maintain a relatively small number of relationships that give them feedback and shape their sense of coherence. But in the course of this longitudinal study we learned from the resilient youth ((Werner & Smith, 1982) that even under adverse circumstances constructive change *is* possible when older children or adolescents develop new competencies and meet people who give them positive reinforcement and a reason for commitment and caring.

References

Antonovsky, A. (1979). *Health, stress and coping: New perspectives on mental and physical well-being.* San Francisco: Jossey-Bass.
Block, J. (1971). *Lives through time.* Berkeley: Bancroft.
Cattell, P. (1940). *The measurement of intelligence of infants.* New York: Psychological Corporation.
Doll, E. A. (1953). *Measurement of social competence.* Minneapolis: Educational Testing Bureau.
Feldhusen, J. F., Thurston, J. R., & Benning, J. J. (1973). A longitudinal study of delinquency and other aspects of children's behavior. *International Journal of Criminology and Penology, 1,* 341-351.

Gonsalves, A. M. (1982). *Follow-up of teenage mothers at age 25: A longitudinal study on the island of Kauai.* Master's thesis, University of California, Davis.

Gough, H. (1969). *California Psychological Inventory Manual* (rev. ed.) Palo Alto: Consulting Psychologists Press.

Kellam, S. G., Ensminger, M., & Turner, D. J. (1977). Family structure and the mental health of children. *Archives of General Psychiatry, 34,* 1012-1022.

Koppitz, E. (1964). *The Bender-Gestalt test for young children.* New York: Grune and Stratton.

Nowicki, S., & Strickland, B. (1973). A locus of control scale for children. *Journal of Consulting and Clinical Psychology, 40,* 148-154.

Robins, L. N. (1966). *Deviant children grown up.* Baltimore: Williams & Wilkins.

Robins, L. N., West, P. A., & Herjanic, B. L. (1975). Arrests and delinquencies in two generations: A study of black urban families and their children. *Journal of Child Psychology and Psychiatry, 16,* 125-140.

Rutter, M. (1979). Protective factors in children's responses to stress and disadvantage. In M. W. Kent & J. E. Rolf (Eds.), *Primary prevention of psychopathology, Vol. III. Social competence in children* (pp. 49-74). Hanover, NH: University Press of New England.

Sameroff, A. J. (1983). Resilient children and how they grew. *Contemporary Psychology 28,* 12.

Seligman, M. E. (1975). *Helplessness.* San Fancisco: W. H. Freeman.

Thomas, A., & Chess, S. (1977). *Temperament and development.* New York: Brunner/Mazel.

Thurstone, L., and Thurstone, T. G. (1954). *SRA primary mental abilities: Trainer's manual.* Chicago: Science Research Associates.

Venezia, P. S. (1971). Delinquency prediction: A critique and a suggestion. *Journal of Research in Crime and Delinquency, 8* 108-117.

Werner, E. E. (1984). *Kith, kin and hired hands: A cross-cultural perspective on alternate caregivers.* Baltimore: University Park Press.

Werner, E. E., Bierman, J. M., & French, F. E. (1971). *The children of Kauai: A longitudinal study from the prenatal period to age ten.* Honolulu: University of Hawaii Press.

Werner, E. E., & Smith, R. S. (1977). *Kauai's children come of age.* Honolulu: University of Hawaii Press.

Werner, E. E., & Smith, R. S. (1982). *Vulnerable, but invincible: A longitudinal study of resilient children and youth.* New York: McGraw Hill.

Wertheim, E. S. (1978). Development genesis of human vulnerability: Conceptual re-evaluation. In E. J. Anthony, C. Koupernik, & C. Chiland (Eds.), *The child in his family: Vulnerable children, Vol. IV* (pp. 17-36). New York: John Wiley.

Zabczyaska, E. (1977). A longitudinal study of the development of juvenile delinquency. *Polish Psychological Bulletin, 8,* 239-245.

2

High-Risk Early Behavior Pattern and Later Delinquency

George Spivack
Norma Cianci

The present chapter reports on findings from a larger parent 15-year longitudinal study, the major purpose of the latter being to identify high-risk early signs that a youngster, already a member of a broader high-risk urban group, is further at risk for delinquency and its related academic and emotional problems during his or her life time. The parent study cohort of 660 children was selected at random from center city Philadelphia kindergartens in the fall of 1968, and a broad range of information on them has been collected since then, including data on delinquency in the community and school, academic performance, special class placement, retention in grade, emotional well-being, teenage alcohol and drug use, specific indices of behavioral adjustment to the school environment throughout the years, attitudes toward family, school, and the law in adolescence, and work history and adjustment during adolescence and young adulthood.

The purpose of the present chapter is to address the question of whether behavior patterns emerging in school during kindergarten and the primary school years indicate the ability of the child to adapt to the school environment and whether these patterns discriminate

Authors' Note: This contribution was prepared under grant number 76-JN-99-0024 from the National Institute for Juvenile Justice and Delinquency Prevention, Office of Juvenile Justice and Delinquency Prevention, Law Enforcement Assistance Administration, U.S. Department of Justice. Points of view or opinions in this document are those of the authors and do not necessarily represent the official position or policies of the U.S. Department of Justice.

children who may be at risk for subsequent delinquency and misconduct in both school and community. What is meant by *ability to adapt* is the child's ability to control and regulate his or her own behavior and thinking, ability to attend and work independently, and ability to comprehend and become involved in the learning process.

Implicit in this question is the assumption that early inability to adapt or cope with life tasks and interpersonal demands (e.g., at school) is prognostic of later-life failure in a variety of areas. Discovery of early signs of poor coping that have both predictive and explanatory power would substantially aid those concerned with initiating preventive efforts, as well as those interested in a variety of developmental and clinical issues.

Background

Prediction of Adjustment and School Success from Early Adjustment Levels in School

Two studies have attempted to relate behavioral adjustment in nursery school to subsequent adaptive functioning. Westman, Rice, and Bermann (1967) had clinicians make a variety of ratings using 130 nursery school to subsequent adaptive functioning. Westman, Rich, relations with teacher and peers, and signs of "immaturity" or "eccentricity." Although no one index related to later measures of adjustment, a combined index did relate significantly. They concluded that the nursery school "is a strategic outpost of mental health screening and intervention" (p. 731). In a similar study, Chamberlain and Nader (1971) made overall adjustment ratings of 40 nursery school children based on perusal of teacher records. Although too few cases were involved for detailed statistical analysis, these ratings significantly related to adjustment through the elementary school years. Neither study could specify what specific behaviors had predictive significance.

T'seng and Sonstegard (1971) had professionals observe the classroom behavior of kindergarten children, and make ratings on 17 behavioral attributes. They discovered a variety of attributes significantly related to subsequent academic achievement up to the 10th grade. More recently, Perry, Guidebaldi, and Kehle (1979) found teacher ratings of disruptiveness/conformity in kindergarten to predict third grade achievement, and that teacher ratings of peer acceptance, school interest, and academic activity were as strong predictors of achievement as early academic achievement and IQ.

Baker and Holzworth (1961) did a retrospective study of 71 children hospitalized during adolescence. They found that 66% had exhibited school problems in the first 2 grades. Glavin (1972) has provided evidence of the persistence of less severe behavioral problems. Children "nominated" as poorly adjusted in primary grades tended to be so classified 3 years later.

Perhaps the most extensive longitudinal study of maladjustment in the school setting has been carried out by Cowen, Zax, and their coworkers (Cowen, Pederson, Babigian, Izzo, & Trost, 1973; Cowen, Zax, Izzo, & Trost, 1966; Zax, Cowen, & Rappaport, 1968). As part of a larger school intervention study, a group of children were "red tagged" in first grade as at risk, employing a wide variety of measures. These youngsters, when in third and then seventh grades, were found to be doing less well academically and exhibiting signs of emotional disturbance. It was discovered, 11 to 13 years later, that significantly more had come into contact with mental health agencies. The authors have repeatedly emphasized the need to streamline and simplify their early identification process, and the need to identify the specific early signs that indicate high risk. Zax et al. (1968) make the point of how necessary it is to develop early information that leads to preventive action.

Kellam, Ensminger, and Simon (1980) have reported on the predictive significance of teacher-rated behavioral signs in the first grade for subsequent life adjustment among urban children from poor families. They report that for both sexes first graders rated as more aggressive were more likely 10 years later to self-report drug use, and for males more aggressiveness, law-breaking, and absence of feelings of well-being.

**Prediction of Delinquency
from Prior Nondelinquent Events**

Most well-known in this area is the work of the Gluecks, and attempts to validate the *Glueck Social Prediction Table (SPT)* (Glueck & Glueck, 1950), which employs mostly parental child-rearing and parent-child "home" variables. All but one of these studies have been retrospective, often involving a reanalysis of previous data (e.g., Glueck, 1962, 1963). The exception to this is the study by the New York City Youth Board (1956) that applied the table in a delinquency-prone neighborhood to youngsters age 6, with a follow-up 8 years later. Some predictive power was revealed, although difficulty employing the table was noted. Glueck (1966) has suggested it may be possible to predict delinquency at age 2 or 3 by supplementing the SPT with added measures of restlessness, resistance to authority, and destructiveness, noting, however, that it might be difficult to obtain such information reliably.

Hampton (1969) developed a *Minnesota Multiphasic Personality Inventory (MMPI)* type measure with which a mother could supply answers about her 10- to 12-year-old child's behavior as well as parental behaviors: *The Personality Inventory for Children (PIC)*. Significant predictive power 6 to 8 years later was revealed, even though Hathaway and Monachesi (1973) previously had not found predictive success employing the standard MMPI scales and some newly devised scales. Gibson and West (1970) studied boys when they were 8 and 9, following them up 5 to 6 years later. They discovered that socioeconomic status and intelligence related to subsequent delinquent behavior independently.

Few studies have attempted to predict delinquency from specific prior classroom behavior even though studies have suggested teachers may be very good predictors of delinquency in children (see Venezia, 1971). Farrington and West (1971) found that teacher-judged behavior at ages 8 and 9 related to delinquency at age 14 and 15. "In the present study, the best available measure of misconduct at an early age was provided by classroom teacher's responses to a questionnaire seeking their observations on the behavior of the boys in their class" (p. 344). Feldhusen and Benning (1972) employed a battery of procedures when youngsters were in grades 3, 6, and 9, to predict delinquency and level of adjustment 5 years later. They concluded that teacher judgments of children were the best predictor variables.

Perhaps the most extensive study relating early (first grade) school performance and adjustment to later (adolescent) delinquent behavior is that of Kellam et al. (1980) noted earlier. From teacher ratings, children were classified as aggressive, shy-aggressive, or shy, and 10 years later interviewed about their delinquent behaviors (e.g., thefts, assaultiveness, and vandalism). Among males only, those classified as aggressive or shy-aggressive later self-reported more delinquent behavior than males classified in the first grade as shy or well-adjusted.

The Kellam et al. finding indicating early childhood aggressiveness is a high-risk sign for later delinquent behaviors is consistent with findings of others. Roff (1961) studied the relationship between childhood symptoms in a clinic cohort to later adaptation in the armed services. Cases described by teachers as excessively aggressive, dominating, blaming of others, and prone to tantrums were significantly more likely in service years to go AWOL and exhibit rule violations and bad conduct than clinic cases manifesting other symptoms. Robins (1966) has reported similar findings: Clinic children of both sexes manifesting "antisocial" behaviors were more likely than other clinic cases to manifest "sociopathic" behaviors later in life, as well as hysterical and alcoholism problems. Robins and Wish (1977) have also reported that this relationship between childhood antisocial behavior and adult diagnosis is especially strong among black males. Two longitudinal studies in England (Douglas, Ross, Hammond, & Milligan, 1966; Mulligan, Douglas, Hammond, & Tizard, 1963) have also reported that preadolescent antisocial and aggressive behaviors are evidenced in the histories of boys who later become delinquent. Kramer and Loney (1978) discovered this relationship between preadolescent aggressiveness and adolescent delinquency in a sample of boys manifesting hyperactivity during preadolescence. They discovered that adolescent delinquent behavior was related to preadolescent aggressiveness but not to degree of hyperactivity.

Finally, two other studies are worthy of note, for although the results do not pertain directly to delinquency or misconduct, they suggest a relationship between aggressiveness in young children and indices of poor inner control that are of direct relevance to the current study. In the first, Rubin and Krus (1974) examined the relationship between teacher-rated, poor self-control and acting out in the first grade, to fourth grade similar behavior as well as measures of behavior and attitude problems and need for special services. The results indicated consistency in poor self-control behaviors over the 3-year period, and a significant relationship between poor control in first grade and subsequent problems as well as need for special services. First grade teacher ratings of anxious or neurotic behaviors did not have predictive power, consistent with other data indicating little prognostic significance of early childhood signs of introversion (e.g., Michael, 1957) or withdrawal (Morris, Soroker, & Burruss, 1954).

The second study (Ledingham, 1981) examined the relationship between aggressive behaviors and ratings of the specific classroom behaviors employed in the present study. These data indicated that aggressive children tended to manifest classroom disturbance, impatience, disrespect-defiance, external blaming, and irrelevant responsiveness behaviors previously identified as reflecting poor self-regulating capacity among children (see Spivack, Cianci, Quercetti, & Bogaslav, 1980). This relationship between aggressiveness and other behaviors helps to specify the meaning of aggressiveness in children by suggesting the processes underlying aggressiveness that may bode ill for chances of effective adjustment in later years.

Delinquency Theory and Early Ability to Cope as a Sign of High Risk

In the main, delinquency theory has not been directed toward identification of potential high-risk signs as reflected in the child's inability to cope and to the specific forms this inability may take. Early longitudinal studies (e.g., Ferguson, 1952; West, 1969; West & Farrington, 1973, 1977; Wolfgang, Figlio, & Sellin, 1972) have specified the association of delinquency with low socioeconomic level, race, unstable parents, poor academic achievement, lower than expected IQ, and school dropout. From the mid-1950s through the mid-1960s, subculture theories dominated the scene, but these sociological approaches implicating cultural processes of conformity, value reflection, and cultural strain or frustration, viewed delinquency as a solution to a problem with no implication of association with inability to cope or insufficiency in social competency. The same is true of subsequent theories of labeling, social control, and social deviance (see McCartney, 1974).

At the other end of the spectrum is the research and theorizing of Mednick and his colleagues (e.g., Mednick, 1979; Mednick & Christiansen, 1977). Mednick provides evidence in support of the notion that delinquent behavior reflects a deficiency in capacity to inhibit, such deficiency supposedly blocking the developing child's ability to use the experience of punishment in a fashion that would (through learning) inhibit antisocial behavior. Mednick traces this deficiency to a slow autonomic nervous system recovery rate that is an inherited quality. Although somewhat narrow in its potential explanatory power, Mednick's notions do have direct and broader implications for the child's developing capacity to cope, although these are not noted.

More recently, Hawkins and Weiss (1984) have attempted to integrate control theory (e.g., Hirschi, 1967) and a social-learning approach into a broad social-development model of relevance to delinquency prevention. The model proposes a sequence of variables/circumstances that begin with the child's attachment to parents, subsequent commitment and attachment to school and the moral order (including the law), subsequent (or accompanying) exposure to peers, ending finally at the behavioral level. The more a child becomes positively attached to parents, the more likely he or she is said to become committed and attached to school and societal order. The more this occurs, the less likely the child will become involved with delinquent peers and acts. The model provides a very practical guide for certain preventive efforts, and has implicit in it the capacity of the child to deal or cope with his or her environment, given all the elements required to "bond" the child to conventional society. The implication is that the child will "learn" conventional behavior, but left untouched are issues that determine how well (or not well) attachments take place, or the ability of the child to do what he or she must do to be acceptable.

Elliott and Voss (1974) have proposed a relationship between schooling and delinquency that attempts to integrate some elements of coping ability and quality with beliefs and exposure to delinquency. Failure to achieve valued goals (e.g., academic success), if it leads to external blaming, may cause a sense of normlessness that, when accompanied by exposure to delinquent influences, will lead to delinquent acts. Academic subject failure, then, and a coping style that includes the blaming of others or circumstances, would constitute early high-risk events when they occur in combination, especially if followed by insufficient inner standards and exposure to others who are delinquent. More recent data of Elliott, Huizinga, and Ageton (1982) indicate bonding to delinquent peers as a "necessary cause," with weak bonds to conventional groups, other peers and activities serving as prior and only indirect causative factors.

Farnworth (1982) has provided further evidence of relevance to the issue of the relationship between early school experience, academic success, early behavioral adjustment, and later attitudes toward school and self-reported delinquent behavior. Reporting on the High/Scope longitudinal project, Farnworth notes that early school failure and IQ were not found to be related to self-reported delinquency in the teenage years. These findings are inconsistent with social-bonding theory, which holds that low levels of ability increase chances of delinquency through intermediate school failure and negative attitudes. On the other hand, Farnworth reports that teacher ratings of conduct and personality in kindergarten and first grade related to 3 out of the 4 delinquency measures employed. It is these behavioral elements that are said to affect mediating school success and attitudes that accompany delinquent behaviors. Teachers ratings of antisocial behavior in kindergarten and first grade were found to relate directly to self-reported conning, lying, and stealing behavior 10 years later.

These data suggest that it may not be the experience of failure per se but how the child behaves and copes with failure or stress in early life that may define early high risk for delinquency, and perhaps its related problems. The present report presents some evidence of relevance to this question.

Methodology

Overview of Data Collection Through Time

The subset of data to be reported is from a longitudinal program of data collection begun with a random sample of 660 inner-city children, half boys and half girls, who entered kindergarten in the fall of 1968 and who are still being followed. The initial data collection period covered 1968-1972, during which time, among other data, the currently reported measures for coping and adjustment to the early school experience were obtained. The second data collection period began in 1975, during which time then-current data were obtained, as well as data covering the intervening years, 1972-1975. The currently reported data on lifelong officially reported delinquency, school delinquency, and conduct disturbance in the classroom were gathered during this second period. This pattern of data collection was dictated by the funds available from different sources over the total period of years.

Initial Selection of Subjects and Tracking from 1968-1972

Initial data collection including numerous administrative clearances in the schools began in October of 1968 in 29 schools from four inner-city school districts. This area was and still is characterized by all of the usual signs of poverty and underprivilege found in large urban centers. Children were selected randomly with the following constraints: there would be half boys and half girls, half would be in morning and half in afternoon kindergarten classes, and half of each of these would have had preschool (Head Start) experience. It was also planned that no teacher would have more than 12 children to rate.

Having met the above criteria, all 56 kindergarten teachers from the 29 schools agreed to participate. Meeting in small groups, teachers were told that this was a longitudinal study of children for the purpose of studying classroom behavior patterns and how these would relate to subsequent learning and adjustment. They were told that the long-range goal was to identify high-risk behaviors, perhaps as early as in kindergarten, which call for preventive measures in the classroom. All teachers saw these purposes as reasonable and seemed eager to participate. A brief 30-minute training period in how to use the Devereux Elementary School Behavior Rating Scale (DESB) (see Spivack & Swift, 1967) followed. After all questions were answered, each teacher was given his or her list of students to rate and asked to return completed ratings to the principal's office within 2 weeks.

In May of 1969 (7 months later), each teacher was again contacted for a second rating of each youngster. By this time 127 youngsters (19% of the original sample) were no longer in the same kindergarten and could not be rated. Each of the remaining 533 children was rated after a brief "refresher" training meeting with the teachers.

Early in the fall of 1969 (beginning first grade) an intensive tracking of "lost" cases began. The children, originally in 29 schools, were now dispersed among over 60 schools, and in the classrooms of over 100 first grade teachers. Despite this tracking effort, and in part due to parochial school transfers (N = 35), there was continued attrition down to a sample of 443 children. Some teachers were unwilling to participate, and this contributed to loss of ratings. At this point 428 children were rated in 52 schools. This sample constituted 65% of the original sample rated at the beginning of kindergarten, 19 months earlier.

The same process was repeated 1 year later (spring of 1971) to locate as many children in the sample as possible, obtain classroom behavior ratings, and collect all other available school record information.

During the fall of 1971, when the sample was entering third grade, a complete tracking search was made for all children initially involved in the study. This search was abetted by a new computer system operated by the Division of Research of the Philadelphia Schools. With the assistance of the computer, and meetings with district superintendents, principals, and teachers, 611 (93%) of the original sample were successfully tracked. Ratings were obtained from 216 teachers in 91 schools located throughout the city.

Process of Data Collection from 1975 On

The first and rather substantial task in 1975 was to locate as many of the original 660 youngsters as possible through existing records. The search began with the computerized Pupil Directories of the Philadelphia Public Schools, the location of each child requiring numerous telephone calls and cross-checks into school files. This procedure had to be followed each year, with each year bringing added tracking difficulties due to mobility of families and unreliable school records and student attendance. In 1975, for example, data on only 500 of the original 1968 sample of 660 were obtained.

Having identified where children were currently enrolled each year, we held meetings with principals of each school to describe the nature and purpose of the study, and to demonstrate (through letters) the approval by the District Superintendents, teacher's union, and Department of Research and Evaluation. The interviews with principals were crucial in obtaining the variety of academic, attendance, deportment, special class placement, retention in grade, and counselor information desired, beyond the data on school delinquency and teacher ratings of classroom conduct disturbance presently being reported.

A similar clearance procedure was initiated beginning in 1975 with the Philadelphia Police Department in order to obtain police contact information. Following approval to conduct the project from the Police Commissioner, we established a system to obtain detailed descriptions of all police contact episodes on every member of the cohort throughout their life histories. This required cooperation from, and close working relationships with, staff of the Juvenile Aid Division, and especially staff of the Records Division. Each year up to 1980 this search was updated. This process, as did the search of school records, required the creation of a system of confidentiality, such that all names were removed from data, and data were submitted to the research team by I.D. number.

Data

The subset of data presently reported consists of classroom behavior ratings obtained between 1968 and 1972, measures of official police contact between the ages of 6 and 17, measures of school offenses between the ages of 13 and 15, and measures of conduct disturbance manifest in the classroom between the ages of 14 and 15. These criterion measures of delinquency loaded on a single factor for both sexes, when factor analyses were performed on 29 measures of delinquency, emotional and behavioral problems, academic failure, attitudes, and alcohol and drug use during adolescence.

Classroom behavior ratings. Classroom behavior ratings were obtained from teachers employing the DESB rating scale (Spivack & Swift, 1966, 1967; Swift & Spivack, 1973). Ratings were made at the beginning and the end of kindergarten and first grade, and the end of second and third grades. The 47-item, 11-factor scale measures how well the child adapts to the variety of task and social demands made upon the child in the usual, structured classroom. Validity and reliability data are reported in the manual and elsewhere (Spivack & Swift, 1967, 1973). The 11 factors measure:

(1) *Classroom Disturbance*: extent to which child teases and torments classmates, interferes with others' work, is quickly drawn into noisemaking, and must be reprimanded or controlled.

(2) *Impatience:* extent to which child starts work too quickly, is sloppy in his or her work, is unwilling to go back over work, and rushes through his or her work.

(3) *Disrespect-Defiance:* extent to which child speaks disrespectfully to teacher, resists doing what is asked of him or her, belittles the work being done, and breaks classroom rules.

(4) *External Blame:* extent to which child says teacher does not help him or her, never calls on him or her, blames external circumstances when things do not go well for him or her, and is quick to say the work assigned is too hard.

(5) *Achievement Anxiety:* extent to which child gets upset about test scores, worries about knowing the "right" answers, is overtly anxious when tests are given, and is sensitive to criticism or correction.

(6) *External Reliance:* extent to which child looks to others for direction, relies on the teacher for direction, requires precise directions, and has difficulty making his or her own decisions.

(7) *Comprehension:* extent to which child gets the point of what is going on in class, seems able to apply what he or she has learned, and knows material when called upon to recite.

(8) *Inattentive-Withdrawn:* extent to which child loses his or her attention, seems to be oblivious to what transpires in the classroom, and seems difficult to reach or preoccupied.

(9) *Irrelevant-Responsiveness:* extent to which child tells exaggerated stories, gives irrelevant answers, interrupts when teacher is talking, and makes irrelevant comments during classroom discussion.

(10) *Creative Initiative:* extent to which child brings things to class that relate to current topics, talks about things in an interesting fashion, initiates classroom discussion, and introduces personal experiences into class discussion.

(11) *Need for Closeness to Teacher:* extent to which child seeks out the teacher before or after class, offers to do things for the teacher, is friendly toward the teacher, and likes to be physically close to the teacher.

Official police contact data. Working cooperatively with the police records personnel, detailed descriptions of every recorded crime were obtained up to the age of 17. Each offense was scored for seriousness using the Sellin-Wolfgang scoring method (Sellin & Wolfgang, 1978) and these scores totaled for each subject. Reported below are 2 scores for each subject: total number of police contacts and total seriousness score for all crimes allegedly committed. While these 2 scores correlated .64 in males, the correlation was only .39 in females. Very few females had more than 1 police contact, making the distribution too narrow for correlational purposes. For this reason, the total seriousness score was needed as a second measure.

Total school offense scores. The raw data from which this score emerged were the in-school forms used in Philadelphia junior and senior high schools by teachers and administrators to record formally the description of any student offense warranting disciplinary action. These "pink slips" were gathered from each school yearly by the research staff and a coding system devised and standardized to assign "total seriousness" scores for each student each year (see Spivack, Cianci, Quercetti, & Bogaslav, 1980). The system categorized offenses as being against persons, property, or institutional rules, further classifying the first 2 categories into minor or major offenses. A student's score each year was the total of minor and institutional violations, plus 2 times the number of major offenses. Assignment to categories of offense and ratings of seriousness were quite reliable.

Classroom conduct disturbance. This measure reflects the extent to which classroom behavior is characterized by (1) over-emotionality and quickness to anger or upset, (2) uncooperativeness, disobedience, or disruptiveness, and (3) assaultiveness and quarrelsomeness. Scores were derived from annual teacher ratings. Factor analysis of these, and ratings of other behaviors, indicated these 3 items defined a single factor that was labeled "conduct disturbance." The original pool of items was derived from scales previously developed by the senior author (Spivack & Spotts, 1967; Swift & Spivack, 1969.) Specific items were selected for the present purpose because they loaded on factors of relevance to the study (e.g., "inability to delay"). Teachers employed a 5-point frequency ratings scale in rating each item. Reliability of ratings was suggested by significant correlations between ratings done in different classrooms (English and Math), and over a 1-year period. Ratings from English classes are employed in the current report.

Results

Early Behavior and Later Delinquency and Misconduct

In order to examine relationships between early behavioral signs of problems with coping in the classroom and later indices of delinquency and misconduct, a series of regression analyses were conducted relating the specific 11 behavioral factors from the *Devereux Elementary School Behavior Rating Scale (DESB)* and criteria of delinquency over the subsequent preadolescent and adolescent years. The latter criteria included total number of official police contacts in the life history, the police contact seriousness scores, the total school offense scores, and the conduct disturbance scores.

Early behavior and life history of police contacts. Table 1 and Table 2 present correlational and regression findings for both sexes for each DESB factor in kindergarten, first grade, second grade, and third grade in relationship to total number of police contacts and seriousness scores of these offenses. Table entries include first order correlations, *R* values, and significant beta values when *R* values are significant. Interpretation of these (and subsequent) tables derives

7

TABLE 2.1

Multiple Regression Analyses Describing the Relationships
Between K-3 Classroom Behavior and Total Number of
Police Contacts for Males[1]
(significant correlations are presented)

DESB Factors	Kindergarten (N = 27)	Grade 1 (N = 212)	Grade 2 (N = 237)	Grade 3 (N = 247)
(1) Classroom disturbance	.19**	.17**	.27**b	.22**
(2) Impatience	.20**b	.16*	.18**	
(3) Disrespect defiance	.20**B	.17**	.25**	.25**B
(4) External blame			.21**	.15*
(5) Ach. anxiety				
(6) External reliance			.16**	
(7) Comprehension		−.13*	−.17**b	
(8) Inattentive withdrawn			.19**	
(9) Irrelevant responsiveness	.13*		.21**	
(10) Creative initiative		−.14*		
(11) Needs closeness		−.13*		
Multiple R	.27*		.31**	.33**

1. The infrequent occurrence of more than one police contact among females made number of contacts an insensitive measure for females, and so only total seriousness of crimes for females is presented in Table 2.
B = beta < .05; b = beta < .05-10.
* = p < .05; ** = p < .01.

from exploration of the significant *R* values, examining which individual factors have significant correlations when the *R* value is significant, and finally which significant correlations also have accompanying significant betas. A significant *R* value indicates that the total of 11 factors significantly predict the criterion (e.g., number of police contacts). Exploring the significant correlations suggests which of the factors are making the contribution to this prediction. A significant beta indicates which factors are especially important, in that they are uniquely contributing to predictive significance above and beyond what the other factors are contributing. Repeated significance of certain factors from analysis to analysis reveals the most likely behaviors of predictive significance that may define an early high-risk behavior pattern.

Examining the findings for males first, Table 1 indicates that, as early as kindergarten, a grouping of DESB factors (1, 2, 3) significantly define a high-risk behavior grouping for subsequent number of official contacts over about a 10-year period. A similar pattern

TABLE 2.2

Multiple Regression Analyses Describing the Relationships Between K-3 Classroom Behavior and Total Seriousness of Police Contact Crimes, for Both Sexes

	Males				Females			
DESB Factors	Kindergarten (N = 270)	Grade 1 (N = 212)	Grade 2 (N = 237)	Grade 3 (N = 247)	Kindergarten (N = 275)	Grade 1 (N = 212)	Grade 2 (N = 231)	Grade 3 (N = 256)
(1) Classroom disturbance	.13*	.16*	.24**		.15*	.23**	.13*	.21**
(2) Impatience		.14*	.17**		.16**	.15*	.23**	.19**
(3) Disrespect defiance	.18**	.15*	.20**	.26**	.13*	.17*		.17**
(4) External blame				.17**		.18**		
(5) Anchievement anxiety					.14*			
(6) External reliance			.15*			.16*		.16*
(7) Comprehension			-.19**	-.13*			-.17**	-.14*
(8) Inattentive withdrawn			.22**					.15*
(9) Irrrelevant responsiveness			.16*	.16*	.13*		.22**	.17**
(10) Creative initiative		-.14*						
(11) Needs closeness								
Multiple R			.31**	.32**		.32*	.32**	.28*

* = p < .05; ** = p < .05.

58

emerges in grades 2 and 3. The relevance of these factors is confirmed by Table 2 findings relating these factors to total seriousness of police recorded offense. In some instances factors 4, 7, and 9 also enter the picture. In the main, the grouping of significant factors suggests a young child who exhibits a variety of cognitive and behavioral signs of socially annoying and intrusive behaviors, impatience, and poor cognitive control.

These findings do not emerge among females when the criterion of number of police contacts is employed. This was to be expected, since the number of police contacts in the female group was generally low and thus the distribution of dependent variable scores quite restricted. In contrast, when total seriousness of police contacts was considered (Table 2) a similar combination of factors emerges as defining a high-risk grouping (1, 2, 3, and 9) at times accompanied by factors 6 and 7 for both sexes. At this stage of data analysis, it would appear that official delinquency in the community over a span of years is preceded with significant frequency by an early classroom behavior pattern characterized by impatience or inability to wait, a disturbing and socially annoying social pattern, and defiant negativeness. These may be accompanied by a cognitive responsiveness typified by lack of reflectiveness and social relevance, as well as poor comprehension. It is also of interest to note behaviors *not* of significance, or so rarely so as to suggest at best a very weak involvement in an early high-risk pattern for subsequent delinquent behavior in the community. Such behaviors include inattentiveness (factor 8), creative involvement in school work (factor 10), and quality of relationship to the teacher (factor 11). These behaviors do bear directly upon the quality of purely academic performance in school at the time they occur (see Spivack & Swift, 1966).

Early behavior and school offenses. Table 3 summarizes the findings for both sexes of all regression analyses relating DESB factor scores at kindergarten and grades 1-3 to total school (pink slip) offense scores when students were 13, 14, and 15 years of age, and for total scores when these scores were combined for adjacent years (13-14, 14-15). The latter two combined years measures were included as likely representing more reliable scores since they covered behavioral reports over 2-year periods. The resulting decreased Ns, however, also decreased chances for statistical significance. The table entries are the total significant correlations and betas (in parentheses) for each year separately, adjacent years combined, and the totals for each. The total

TABLE 2.3

Summary Table of Multiple Regression Analyses, for Both Sexes, Providing Total Number of Significant Correlations and Betas (in parentheses), and Multiple Rs, When Behaviors in Kindergarten and Grades 1-3 Were Related to Total School Offense Scores at Age 13, 14, and 15, and to Combined Scores at Ages 13-14 and 14-15[1]

| | Age | | | | | | | | Combined Ages Scores | | | | |
| | 13 | | 14 | | 15 | | Σ 13-15 | | 13-14 | | 14-15 | | |
DESB Factors	M	F	M	F	M	F	M	F	M	F	M	F	rs/Rs^2
(1) Classroom disturbance	2 (1)	1	3 (2)	2	4 (2)	2 (1)	9 (5)	5 (1)	4 (1)	2	4 (3)	2	.16 – .36
(2) Impatience	1 (1)	2 (2)	3 (2)	2 (2)	2	2 (1)	6 (3)	6 (5)	3	2 (2)	3	2 (2)	.18 – .39
(3) Disrespect defiance	1	3 (2)	4 (1)	2 (1)	1	2	6 (1)	7 (3)	4 (1)	2 (1)	4	2 (1)	.16 – .32
(4) External blame	3	2	2	1 (1)	0	2	5	5 (1)	4 (1)	1 (1)	2	1 (1)	.13 – .30
(5) Achievement anxiety	0	0	0	1	1	0	1	1	0	0	0	0	.14 – .19
(6) External reliance	0	2	2	1	2	1	4	4	0	2	2	1	.14 – .25
(7) Comprehension	1	0 (1)	3	1	2	0	6	1 (1)	1 (1)	1	2	1	.15 – .20
(8) Inattentive withdrawn	1 (1)	1	3 (2)	2	1	1 (1)	5 (3)	4 (1)	2 (1)	3 (1)	3 (2)	1	.14 – .37
(9) Irrelevant responsiveness	1	1	3	1 (1)	2 (1)	2 (1)	6 (1)	4 (2)	3	1	3 (1)	2	.13 – .32
(10) Creative initiative	0	1 (1)	0	0	0	0	0	1 (1)	0	1 (1)	0	0	.18 – .18
(11) Needs closeness	0	1	0	0	1	0	1	1	0	0	0	1 (1)	.14 – .17
Multiple R	2	2	3	2	2	3	7	7	2	3	3	2	.31 – .45

1. Ns in these analyses varied between 137 and 205. All significant correlations were positive, except for factors 7, 10, and 11.
2. Range of significant rs and Rs.

number of significant Rs are at the bottom of the table. The maximum number of significant findings in each separate age cell is 4, there having been regressions involving kindergarten and the first 3 school grades.

The table indicates consistency across sex, indicating 2 or 3 significant Rs for each sex on each occasion. Factors 1, 2, and 3 are most often significant in terms of correlations and betas, followed by factors 9, 4, and 8. Factor 7 was often significant for males, but seldom among females. The grouping of factors 1, 2, 3, 4, and 9 is similar to that emerging when police contact in males was the criterion, with the addition of factor 8. This latter factor of inattentive/withdrawn behaviors may reflect the fact that a poorly "self-regulated" child may not be attending to what is going on in the classroom because she or he generally is unreflective in style and thus prone to action without attending or first listening to others.

Early behavior and classroom conduct disturbance. These analyses related early classroom behaviors to misconduct in the classroom during the adolescent years (i.e., ages 14 and 15). The misconduct measure includes behaviors such as quickness to anger or emotional upset, uncooperativeness and disobedience, and assaultiveness and quarrelsomeness. In contrast to the school offense measure, which reflects a variety of behaviors leading to disciplinary action, the conduct disturbance measure focuses specifically upon poor emotional control and manifest negativeness.

Examination of Table 4 reveals a pattern quite similar to that which emerged in analyses of school offenses. Factors 1, 2, and 3 dominate, followed by 9, 4, and 8. These data, in combination with police contact data, for males, indicate that the behavioral factors most consistently predictive of later criteria are 1, 2, 3, and 9, with factor 4 next, followed by factors 7 and 8. While such summary analysis risks the loss of subtleties in interpretation, given the variability of findings from year to year and between measures, the consistency of the pattern of significant relationships between certain behavior ratings and criterion measures across years makes for confidence in their predictive importance. Within this high-risk cohort, children of both sexes between the ages of 5 and 8 who exhibit poor control or regulation of their cognitive and behavioral patterns are especially at risk.

TABLE 2.4

Summary of Table of Multiple Regression Analyses, for Both Sexes, Providing Total Number of Significant Correlations and Betas (in parenthesis) and Multiple Rs, When Behavior in Kindergarten and Grades 1-3 Were Related to Classroom Conduct Disturbance Scores at Ages 14, 15, and Combined Scores of Ages 14-15[1]

DESB Factors	Age 13		14		Combined Ages Scores		rs/Rs²[2]
	M	F	M	F	M	F	
(1) Classroom disturbance	4 (2)	3 (1)	3	3 (1)	4 (1)	3 (1)	.21 – .43
(2) Impatience	2	4 (1)	2	3 (1)	1	3 (1)	.16 – .38
(3) Disrespect defiance	4	4	3	2	3 (1)	4	.16 – .44
(4) External blame	3 (2)	2	0	1	2	2	.18 – .35
(5) Achievement anxiety	1	1	0	0	0	0	.14 – .18
(6) External reliance	0	0	2	0	0	0	.17 – .18
(7) Comprehension	2 (1)	1	0	0	0	0	.17 – .27
(8) Inattentive withdrawn	2	2	1	2 (1)	1	0	.16 – .25
(9) Irrelevant responsiveness	3	2	3	2 (1)	2	3	.15 – .34
(10) Creative initiative	1	0	0	0	0	0	.18 – .18
(11) Needs closeness	0	1	1	0	1 (1)	1 (1)	.14 – .19
Multiple R	2	3	0	3	2	2	.38 – .59

1. Ns in these analyses varied between 79 and 178: Cell maximum is 4 because 4 analyses were done: K-3.
2. Range of significant rs and Rs.

Total High-Risk Behavioral Aberrance
and Later Delinquency and Misconduct

As a further check upon the regression findings, a high-risk total aberrance score was devised, consisting of the total number of at-risk factors in a child's early behavior profile that exceeded the normal (+1 SD) range of the DESB rating scale standardization sample (see Spivack & Swift, 1967). Factors 1, 2, 3, and 9 were selected as best defining high risk, and thus scores could vary from 0 (none aberrant) to 4 (all high-risk factor scores exceeding the normal range). Analyses of variance were performed, with high-risk total aberrance score the independent variable for DESB ratings in kindergarten and in grade 3, the 2 points in time when Ns were largest.

Table 5 provides the results of these analyses. With rare exception, the findings support the notion that elevated scores on these selected factors *as a group* quite early in the school history of such youngsters define risk for subsequent delinquent and/or serious misconduct in the community and schoolroom. The more of these behavior factors that are aberrant at any point in time, the greater the chances of subsequent delinquency, misconduct, and poorly emotionally controlled behavior. Examination of the mean criterion scores indicated that the relationships between total aberrance scores and criterion scores were linear in all cases. Invariably, there was more delinquency or misconduct when aberrance scores were 3 or 4 than when they were 0 or 1. As would be expected, the most frequent significant Newman-Keuls tests emerged because of the differences between extreme cells (e.g., 4 or 3 versus 0 or 1).

Chronicity of the High-Risk Pattern
and Later Delinquency and Misconduct

When we had identified the individual factors that define high risk, demonstrated their relevance to a variety of objective delinquent criteria, and shown that the more of such behavior at any one time (kindergarten or grade 3) the greater the chance for subsequent delinquency, it was decided to assess whether chronicity of such early behavior was a further "bad sign."

To examine this issue, we defined four groups of children. The chronic high-risk group was defined as those who exhibited 3 or 4 high scores on high-risk factors at *both* kindergarten and grade 3. The next most chronic group consisted of those who exhibited fewer than

TABLE 2.5

Analyses of Variance Describing the Relationships Between Total Number of High-Risk Aberrant Behavior Factor Scores in Kindergarten and Grade 3, and Subsequent Criterion Scores of Delinquency and Conduct Disturbance, for Each Sex

Dependent Variables	Males Between/Within F Ratio				Females Between/Within F Ratio			
Number of Police Contacts	K	(N = 331)	4/326	2.99*	K	(N = 328)	4/323	.80
	3	(N = 331)	4/326	2.58*	3	(N = 328)	4/323	.65
Seriousness of Police Contact Crimes	K	(N = 270)	4/265	2.10	K	(N = 275)	4/270	2.19
	3	(N = 247)	4/242	2.69*	3	(N = 256)	4/251	7.86**
Seriousness of School Offenses								
Age 13	K	(N = 167)	4/162	1.77	K	(N = 181)	4/176	6.28**
Age 14	K	(N = 193)	4/188	3.18*	K	(N = 205)	4/200	2.94**
Age 15	K	(N = 172)	4/167	1.32	K	(N = 180)	4/175	1.31
Ages 13-14	K	(N = 151)	4/146	1.85	K	(N = 170)	4/165	4.80**
Ages 14-15	K	(N = 156)	4/151	2.39*	K	(N = 169)	4/164	2.53*
Age 13	3	(N = 163)	4/158	1.72	3	(N = 188)	4/183	4.97**
Age 14	3	(N = 198)	4/193	3.45**	3	(N = 215)	4/210	4.47**
Age 15	3	(N = 170)	4/165	2.78*	3	(N = 188)	4/183	.93
Ages 13-14	3	(N = 150)	4/145	3.01*	3	(N = 175)	4/170	5.48**
Ages 14-15	3	(N = 159)	4/154	3.71**	3	(N = 178)	4/173	4.61**
Classroom Conduct Disturbance								
Age 14	K	(N = 165)	4/160	2.35	K	(N = 178)	4/173	2.79*
Age 15	K	(N = 134)	4/129	2.76*	K	(N = 126)	4/121	3.27**
Ages 14-15	K	(N = 105)	4/100	2.61*	K	(N = 101)	4/96	3.30**
Age 14	3	(N = 166)	4/161	4.06**	3	(N = 178)	4/173	5.02**
Age 15	3	(N = 133)	4/128	2.19	3	(N = 127)	4/122	4.19**
Ages 14-15	3	(N = 108)	4/103	2.10	3	(N = 101)	4/96	5.55**

*p = .01; **p = .05.

3 elevated factor scores in kindergarten, but exhibited 3 or more by the time they reached grade 3. The next group consisted of those who exhibited 3 or more elevated factor scores in kindergarten, but fewer than 3 by third grade. The lowest group consisted of those who exhibited fewer than 3 elevated high-risk factors scores both in kindergarten and third grade. Analyses of variance compared these four groups on the basis of the 4 subsequent criterion measures of delinquency and misconduct.

Table 6 indicates that chronicity of the high-risk behavior pattern is more likely to characterize the early behavior pattern of both males and females with subsequent delinquency in the community and in school. As with the findings regarding total aberrance scores, the relationships between early chronicity and subsequent criterion variables were all linear. The most frequent significant Newman-Keuls test indicated significance between chronic aberrance and no aberrance, or aberrance only in kindergarten or grade 3. As noted earlier, number of police contacts as a criterion measure for females is less sensitive than the total seriousness score because of the very narrow range of scores (i.e., few females with more than one contact). The absence of significant findings for males for the conduct disturbance measure is not easily explained, since data in Table 5 indicate significance when aberrance at kindergarten and grade 3 are considered separately. It would appear that, in this instance, high risk as measured by total aberrance pattern at either point in time warrants concern in males, and that high-risk pattern at both points in time adds nothing significant predictively to such a fact.

Discussion

As noted earlier, there is currently ample evidence that, at least among males, early signs of excessive aggressiveness and/or antisocial behavior are high-risk signs for later antisocial and delinquent behavior. A recent review of much of the literature by Loeber (1982) suggests that early onset and high density of antisocial behavior during preadolescence predicts such behavior in later years. Robins, Murphy, Woodroff, and King (1971) have reported that this relationship is particularly striking among blacks.

The present findings add to the current body of data by the following: (1) studying behavior patterns that typify children prior to

TABLE 2.6
Analyses of Variance Describing the Relationships Between
Chronicity of High-Risk Aberrant Behaviors in Kindergarten
and Grade 3, and Subsequent Criterion Scores of Delinquency
and Conduct Disturbance, for Each Sex

Dependent Variables	Males Between/Within F Ratio		Females Between/Within F Ratio	
Number of Police Contacts	3/200	5.81**	3/216	1.71
Seriousness of Police Contact Crimes	3/200	5.82**	3/214	4.45**
Seriousness of School Offenses				
Age 13	3/133	2.03	3/163	4.00**
Age 14	3/157	2.83*	3/183	5.40**
Age 15	3/136	3.54*	3/160	2.74*
Ages 13-14	3/120	1.60	3/154	5.39**
Ages 14-15	3/125	2.49*	3/153	6.50**
Classroom Conduct Disturbance				
Age 14	3/134	1.86	3/149	4.50**
Age 15	3/108	1.02	3/106	5.45**
Ages 14-15	3/86	1.36	3/84	5.39**

*$p = < .05$; **$p = < .05$.

the emergence of those behaviors that society labels "antisocial" or
"criminal," (2) identifying these behaviors through the use of reliable
measurement devices that may be employed in normal school
settings, (3) demonstrating the existence of the same high-risk pattern
in both sexes, and (4) defining a high-risk pattern that discriminates
among youth who are at risk for delinquent and disturbed behaviors
due to their socioeconomic circumstances. Finally, the pattern
emerges prior to significant academic experiences (e.g., in kindergarten).

The core elements in this early high-risk pattern deserve scrutiny
for what they may tell us about such vulnerable children. They
exhibit: (1) the tendency in the classroom to become involved in
poking and annoying social behavior, as well as excessive talking and
noisemaking, (2) impatience, reflected in the tendency to rush into
things before listening or judging what is best to do, and apparent
need to move ahead constantly without looking back or reflecting
upon the past, (3) negative and defiant behavior with the teacher, and
(4) self-centered verbal responsiveness characterized by interruption
of others, irrelevance of what is said in the context of ongoing
conversation, and blurting out personal thoughts with insufficient

prior self-examination. Examination of these behaviors reveals that they reflect problems in the interpersonal sphere (which often elicit adult attempts to enforce external controls), as well as problems in the cognitive sphere. In their extremes, *such youngsters are overly involved socially, and unwilling or unable to modulate their own motor and cognitive behaviors so as to accommodate to others around them.* They appear unable to contain tension and their own desires. What comes into their minds they say, and where there is "action" they are drawn to it like a moth to light. If they do appreciate the perspective of others (and they may very well not), they do not manifest evidence of willingness to take the needs of others into account.

Given this syndrome of elements, it is easy to see how such a child might easily come into early conflict with adult authority, especially in settings that demand self-restraint and accommodation to numerous social and task demands, such as in the classroom. Although such behaviors may not have their origins in hostile intent, it is easy to imagine such children quickly becoming involved in negative peer interchanges and angry adult reactions, all of which would quickly snowball, with increasing age, into the kinds of behavior we label as antisocial.

The fact that this high-risk pattern emerges in both sexes prior to experience with formal academic training does not necessarily preclude academic failure as playing a part in an early causative pattern. Current analyses are underway examining the role of early academic failure in the emergence of this behavior pattern. Rather, it suggests the possibility that there may be a variety of social and task demands made upon the growing child, including those that occur in the classroom, that bring out this reaction or coping pattern in some young children. Further, what may be unique is not the stressful circumstances alone or even this response pattern to these circumstances, but these in interaction with how adults and others react to this high-risk behavior.

Such an interactive conception is consistent with the work of Chess and her colleagues (Chess 1966, 1967; Chess, Thomas, Rutter, & Birch, 1963). In this longitudinal work they suggest that one must consider the interaction of the child's basic temperament and the particular quality of stresses with which he or she is confronted in trying to determine whether the child will manifest a behavioral disturbance. Of three temperament groups of children identifiable quite early in life (Chess, 1966), one seems quite relevant to the present data. This child exhibits early signs (i.e., during early months of life) of irregularity, nonadaptability to change, predominantly negative responses to new stimuli, predominantly negative mood, and intense emotional reaction. Of special interest is the fact that for such a "difficult child," the most stressful circumstances are generally those that demand socialization, and alteration in spontaneous responses and patterns in order to conform with family, school, or peer group. Disturbance occurs when such adult demands are made in an inconsistent, impatient, or punitive manner (Chess, 1967). When these children manifest disturbance, the latter involve "active symptoms," such as tantrums, aggressive behavior, and habit disturbances (Chess et al., 1963).

One notes some similarity between elements of the "difficult child," temperamentally speaking, and the early behavioral pattern of the high-risk child in the current longitudinal study. It suggests the possibility that the high-risk signs reflect the failure of a temperamentally "difficult child" to adapt to the early demands in school for socialization (e.g., in kindergarten) and/or the subsequent demands in primary grades, demands to sit still in class, pay attention to the teacher, accommodate inner desires and wishes to those of others, and conform in the variety of ways that are not consistent with the child's temperament, yet are requirements of most early learning environments.

Chess (1966) suggests that such children require unusual firmness, patience, consistency, and tolerance on the part of adults when they are under stress in order to avoid subsequent problems with them. Very similar advice has been offered to teachers in the handling of children who demonstrate the high-risk classroom behavior pattern (see Swift & Spivack, 1975). Bates (1980), in his discussion of the concept of difficult temperament, extends the dynamics of what occurs between mother and child by proposing that it may be the mother's perception of the meaning of the difficult behavior that makes the difference. If such behavior is perceived in a negative light, mothers react adversely with negative feelings and rejection (Milliones, 1978) and such negative rejection has been shown to lead to serious acting out and aggressive problems (Lorion, Cowen, Kraus, & Milling, 1977). There is no reason to doubt that the same dynamics may continue to operate in the classroom from kindergarten on, initial signs of the high-risk pattern reflecting an early pattern of stress-temperamental reaction-negative adult perception and reaction-high-risk coping behavior-negative adult reaction, and so on, that soon is transformed into the more blatant antisocial and delinquent behaviors. It would certainly be likely that youngsters caught up early in such negative interactions with their social environments would not evolve positive bonds to family or school or the social "order." Such a child is unable to do what must be done to "learn" conventional behavior because he or she cannot contain tension, reflect, and modulate action to make the needed accommodations, and these deficiences become compounded with negative affect.

The data also suggest that if this childhood pattern is not caught early and is allowed to snowball during the primary grades, matters get worse. These findings are consistent with a study of Hancock (1982) employing the author's database. Hancock found that among the males with at least 1 police contact, those exhibiting a chronic high-risk pattern in primary grades, when compared with controls (a) were significantly more often in later years to become chronically delinquent (more than 4 police contacts), (b) had significantly more frequent delinquency contacts within the schools in eighth and tenth grades, (c) were significantly more often placed in special classes, and (d) had significantly more absences in eighth and tenth grades (though *not* significantly poorer teacher marks in English or standardized test scores).

Two possible lines of new research would seem worthwhile. One line is to further articulate the nature of the cognitive and behavioral characteristics of such children and to trace their precursors during early developmental years. Uncovering such precursors would not only add to our understanding of vulnerability, but might suggest specific preventive interventions appropriate to very early developmental years. One avenue of such research might examine the issue of "match" between parental child rearing styles and child temperament, hypothesizing that the high-risk pattern will emerge with greatest frequency when children with a "difficult" temperament have parents who perceive such behavior in a negative light (e.g., as reflecting negatively upon them as people, or causing them anxiety and annoyance), and thus respond to the child impatiently, punitively, and without understanding of the child's needs and feelings. A parallel process may also be operating in such a match, one in which the child with such a temperament is quick to model his or her behavior after parents with similar temperaments or behavior patterns.

70   Spivack and Cianci

The possibility of such an interactive mode is supported by the work of Bronson (1966a, 1966b). Analysis of the Berkeley Guidance Study longitudinal data indicated a placid-controlled/reactive-explosive behavioral dimension or "central orientation" that remained a relatively stable quality between the ages of 5 and 16. At one end of this dimension are such behaviors as overreactivity to stimulation, poor control, and generally nonconforming or rebellious behaviors. Correlates of this dimension included the tendency to complain, quarrelsomeness, tantrums, and restlessness. Such behaviors seem quite similar to the qualities of "difficult temperament" as well as the present high-risk pattern. Of relevance to the present point, however, is that Bronson (1966a), in relating this dimension to early family relationships, discovered that reactive-explosive behaviors through-out childhood were related *in both sexes* to hostility and indifference exhibited in the father-mother relationship, as well as erratic and poor maternal discipline with the child, qualities noted by Chess (1966) as creating a snowballing negative effect when combined with an infant's "difficult temperament." This was further coupled with hostility in the relationship between each parent and child. Eron (1980) has pointed out that the more a child is punished for aggression at home, the more aggressive the child is at school, adding that punishment may very well provide a model for the child.

It will also be recalled that one element of the high-risk pattern is the tendency of such a child to become overly involved socially in annoying behavior and to stir up and interfere with the work of others. It could very well be that such children naturally gravitate to active engagement with others, and through this get reinforcement for such a behavioral style. In a similar sense such children might be attracted to aggressive or exciting content on T.V., or to delinquent peers, if exposed to either, because the activities presented by both are a match for the personality and cognitive styles that develop out of early developmental interactions.

A second line is to research means of intervention that might ameliorate this behavioral pattern and thus decrease the development of an antisocial pattern. One possible form of intervention has already demonstrated effectiveness in decreasing certain elements of the high-risk pattern by enhancing the child's interpersonal cognitive problem-solving skills (see Spivack & Shure, 1982). Such training enhances the child's interpersonal cognitive sensitivities and general reflectiveness about how to deal with problems in terms of options and consequences, and seems to increase the ability or willingness of the child to contain tension as well as think through a problem situation. A second form of prevention might be to specify the best styles of response to such high-risk children that adults (e.g., parents, teachers) might adopt so as to avoid or interrupt the child-adult negative cycle, and to teach these to child rearers and caregivers. Significant elements in such training would be to establish a productive adult perception of high-risk behaviors and what they mean, and a child-rearing style that is firm (but not hostile), consistent (but not rigid), and oriented toward enhancing those social cognitive skills that function as mediators of self-regulated functioning.

References

Baker, J. W., & Holzworth, A. (1961). Social histories of successful and unsuccessful children. *Child Development, 32*, 135-149.

Bates, J. E. (1980). The concept of difficult temperament. *Merrill-Palmer Quarterly, 26*, 300-318.

Bronson, W. C. (1966a). Central orientations: A study of behavior organization from childhood to adolescence. *Child Development, 37*(a), 125-156.

Bronson, W. C. (1966b). Early antecedents of emotional expressiveness and reactivity control. *Child Development, 37*(b), 793-810.

Chamberlain, R. W., & Nader, P. R. (1971). Relationship between nursery school behavior patterns and later school functioning. *American Journal of Orthopsychiatry, 41*, 597-601.

Chess, S. (1966). Individuality in children, its importance to the pediatrician. *Journal of Pediatrics, 69*, 676-684.

Chess, S. (1967). The role of temperament in the child's development. *Acta Paedopsychiatrica, 34*, 91-103.

Chess, S., Thomas, A., Rutter, M., & Birch, H. G. (1963). Interaction of temperament and environment in the production of behavioral disturbances in children. *American Journal of Psychiatry, 120*, 142-147.

Cowen, E. L., Pederson, A., Babigian, H., Izzo, L. D., & Trost, M. A. (1973). Long-term follow-up of early detected vulnerable children. *Journal of Consulting and Clinical Psychology, 41*, 438-446.

Cowen, E. L., Zax, M., Izzo, L. D., & Trost, M. A. (1966). Prevention of emotional disorders in the school setting. *Journal of Consulting Psychology, 30*, 381-387.

Douglas, J.W.B., Ross, J. M., Hammond, W. A., & Milligan, D. G. (1966). Delinquency and social class. *British Journal of Criminology, 6*, 224-302.

Elliot, D. S., Huizinga, D., & Ageton, S. S. (1982). *Explaining delinquency and drug use* (National Youth Survey Project Report No. 21). Boulder, CO: Behavioral Research Institute.

72   Spivack and Cianci

Elliot, D. S., & Voss, H. (1974). *Delinquency and drop-out.* Lexington, MA: D. C. Heath.

Eron, L. D. (1980). Prescription for reduction of aggression. *American Psychologist, 35,* 244-252.

Farnworth, M. (1982). *Schooling and delinquency: The influence of preschool and school achievement on self-reported delinquency at age 15.* Paper presented at a symposium at the American Educational Research Association, New York.

Farrington, D. P., & West, D. J. (1971). A comparison between early delinquents and young aggressives. *British Journal of Criminology, 11,* 341-358.

Feldhusen, J. F., & Benning, J. J. (1972). Prediction of delinquency, adjustment, and academic achievement over a five-year period. *Journal of Educational Research, 65,* 375-381.

Ferguson, T. (1952). *The young delinquent in his social setting.* London: University Press.

Gibson, H. B., & West, D. J. (1970). Social and intellectual handicaps as precursors of early delinquency. *British Journal of Criminology, 10,* 21-32.

Glavin, J. P. (1972). Persistence of behavior disorders in children. *Exceptional Children, 38,* 367-376.

Glueck, E. T. (1962). Toward improving the identification of delinquents. *Journal of Criminal Law, Criminology and Police Science, 53,* 164-170.

Glueck, E. T. (1963). Toward improving the identification of delinquents. *Journal of Criminal Law, Criminology and Police Science, 54,* 178-180.

Glueck, E. T. (1966). Identification of potential delinquents at 2-3 years of age. *International Journal of Social Psychiatry, 12,* 5-16.

Glueck, S., & Glueck, E. T. (1950). *Unraveling juvenile delinquency.* Cambridge, MA: Harvard University Press.

Hampton, A. C. (1969). *Longitudinal study of personality of children who become delinquent; using the Personality Inventory for Children (PIC).* Unpublished doctoral dissertation, University of Minnesota.

Hancock, B. J. (1982). *Early chronic high risk behaviors of adolescent urban delinquent males.* Unpublished master's thesis, Hahnemann University College of Medicine.

Hathaway, S. R., & Monachesi, E. D.(1973). *Adolescent personality and behavior: MMPI patterns of normal, delinquent, dropout, and other outcomes.* Minneapolis: University of Minnesota Press.

Hawkins, J. D., & Weiss, J. G. (1984). The social development model: An integrated approach to deliquency prevention. *Journal of Primary Prevention.*

Hirschi, T. (1967). *Causes of delinquency.* Berkeley: University of California Press.

Kellam, S. G., Ensminger, M. E., & Simon, M. B. (1980). Mental health in first grade and teenage drug, alcohol, and cigarette use. *Drug and Alcohol Dependency, 5,* 273-304.

Kramer, J., & Loney, J. (1978, August 31). *Predicting adolescent antisocial behavior among hyperactive boys.* Paper presented at American Psychological Association, Toronto, Canada.

Ledingham, J. E. (1981). Developmental patterns of aggressive and withdrawn behavior in childhood: A possible method for identifying pre-schizophrenics. *Journal of Abnormal Child Psychology, 9,* 1-22.

Loeber, R. (1982). The stability of antisocial and delinquent child behavior: A review. *Child Development, 53,* 1431-1446.

Lorion, R. P., Cowen, E. L., Kraus, R. M., & Milling, L. S. (1977). Family background characteristics and school adjustment problems. *Journal of Community Psychology, 5,* 142-148.

McCartney, J. L. (1974). A review of recent research in deliquency and durance. *Journal of Operational Psychiatry, 5,* 52-68.

Mednick, S. A. (1979). Biosocial factors and primary prevention of antisocial behavior. In S. A. Mednick & S. G. Shohan (Eds.), *New paths in criminology* (pp. 45-54). Lexington, MA: Lexington Press.

Mednick, S. A., & Christiansen, K. O. (1977). *Biosocial bases of criminal behavior.* New York: Gardner.

Michael, C. M. (1957). Relative incidence of criminal behavior in long term follow-up studies of shy children. *Dallas Medical Journal, 43,* 22-26.

Milliones, J. (1978). Relationship between perceived child temperament and maternal behavior. *Child Development, 49,* 1255-1257.

Morris, D. P., Soroker, E., & Burruss, G. (1954). Follow-up studies shy withdrawn children I: Evaluation of later adjustment. *American Journal of Orthopsychiatry, 24,* 743-754.

Mulligan, G., Douglas, J.W.B., Hammond, W. A., & Tizard, J. (1963). Delinquency and the symptoms of maladjustment: The findings of a longitudinal study. *Proceeding of the Royal Society of Medicine, 56,* 1083-1986.

Perry, J. D., Guidebaldi, J., & Kehle, T. J. (1979). Kindergarten competencies as predictors of third grade classroom behavior and achievement. *Journal of Educational Psychology, 71,* 443-450.

Robbins, L. N. (1966). *Deviant children grows up: A sociological and psychiatric study of sociopathic personality.* Baltimore: Williams and Wilkins.

Robins, L. N. & Wish, E. (1977). Childhood deviance as a developmental process: A study of 223 urban Black men from birth to 18. *Social Forces, 56,* 448-473.

Robins, L. N., Murphy, G. E., Woodroff, R., & King, L. J. (1971). Adult psychiatric status of Black school boys. *Archives of General Psychiatry, 24,* 338-345.

Roff, M. (1961). Childhood interaction and adult conduct. *Journal of Abnormal Social Psychology, 63,* 333-337.

Rubin, R. A., & Krus, P. H. (1984, April 18). *Predictive validity of a school behavior rating scale.* Paper presented at the American Educational Research Association, Chicago.

Sellin, T., & Wolfgang, M. (1978). *The measurement of delinquency.* Montclair, NJ: Patterson Smith.

Spivack, G., Cianci, N., Quercetti, L., & Bogaslav, B. (1980). *High risk early school signs for delinquency, emotional problems, and school failure among urban males and females* (Report to NIJJDP, LEAA, Grant (#76-JN-990024).

Spivack, G., Haimes, P. H., & Spotts, J. (1967). *The Devereux adolescent behavior rating scale: Manual.* Devon, PA: Devereux Foundation.

Spivack, G., & Shure, M. B. (1982). The cognition of social adjustment: Interpersonal cognitive problem solving thinking. In B. B. Lahey & A. E. Kazdin (Eds.), *Advances in child psychology* (pp. 323-372). New York: Plenum.

Spivack, G., & Spotts, J. (1967). Adolescent symptomatology. *American Journal of Mental Deficiency, 71,* 74-75.

Spivack, G., & Swift, M. (1966). The Devereux elementary school behavior rating scale: A study of the nature and organization of achievement related disturbed classroom behavior. *Journal of Special Education, 1,* 71-91.

Spivack, G., & Swift, M. (1967). *Devereux elementary school behavior rating scale manual.* Devon, PA: Devereux Foundation.

Spivack, G., & Swift, M. (1973). The classroom behavior of children: A critical review of teacher administered scales. *Journal of Special Education, 7,* 55-91.

Swift, M., & Spivack, G. (1969). Achievement related classroom behaviors of secondary school normal and disturbed patients. *Exceptional Children, 35,* 677-684.

Swift, M., & Spivack, G. (1975). *Alternative teaching strategies: Helping behaviorally troubled children achieve.* Champaign, IL: Research Press.

T'seng, M. S., & Sonstegard, M. A. (1971). Identifying preschool children with learning problems. *Proceedings of the Annual Convention of the American Psychological Association, 6,* 563-564.

Venezia, P. S. (1971). Delinquency prediction: A critique and suggestion. *Journal of Research in Crime and Delinquency, 8,* 108-117.

West, D. J. (1969). *Present conduct and future delinquency.* London: Heinemann.

West, D. J., & Farrington, D. P. (1973). *Who becomes delinquent?* London: Heinemann.

West, D. J., & Farrington, D. P. (1977). *The delinquent way of life.* London: Heinemann.

Westman, J. C., Rich, D. L., & Bermann, E. (1967). Relationship between nursery school behavior and later school adjustment. *American Journal of Orthopsychiatry, 37,* 725-731.

Wolfgang, M. E., Figlio, R. M., & Sellin, T. (1972). *Delinquency in a birth cohort.* Chicago: University of Chicago Press.

Zax, M., Cowen, E. L., & Rappaport, J. (1968). Follow-up study of children identified early as emotionally disturbed. *Journal of Consulting and Clinical Psychology, 32,* 369-374.

3

Antisocial and Delinquent Youths: Methods for Their Early Identification

Rolf Loeber
Thomas J. Dishion

Anyone watching children in kindergarten or elementary school may marvel at the variety of behaviors displayed in such settings. Some play cooperatively with others, others appear more daring or perhaps even physically aggressive. On the other hand, some may seem more withdrawn or do sneaky things such as teasing others behind their backs, or stealing or grabbing things belonging to others. The onlooker may speculate whether these early behaviors are somehow connected with the kinds of adults these children will eventually become; specifically it raises the following questions: Which of these children will continue to be aggressive later in life? Which of them will continue to steal, or eventually be identified as chronic delinquents by the courts? Ruminating about the likelihood of these futures may lead us to wish for ways to prevent such outcomes from taking place.

To prevent these outcomes we need to be able to identify children who are most at risk. One of the main reasons for improving methods

Authors' Note: The authors are greatly indebted for the advice and encouragement they received from Dr. G. R. Patterson in conducting this research. Drs. J. B. Reid and M. Stouthamer-Loeber, also of the Oregon Social Learning Center, Eugene, Oregon, provided most helpful comments on earlier drafts of this chapter. The research was completed with financial support from grants MH 32857 and MH 37940 from the Center of Studies in Crime and Delinquency, National Institute of Mental Health.

for identifying children at risk for chronic antisocial or delinquent behavior is to improve prevention programs. Screening of youths saves time in juvenile courts, juvenile service agencies, and child health clinics by allowing staff to spend more of their efforts on those cases that are at highest risk, rather than on children that ultimately would, even without their help, not enter a career of crime. Further, it is difficult to judge the effectiveness of prevention programs in the absence of screening methods as the not at-risk youths will show a favorable outcome regardless of what prevention efforts are employed.

Successful prevention has two fundamental requirements: first, the prevention procedures must effectively alleviate the conditions largely responsible for the outcome of concern, and second, it must be possible to identify cost-effectively those persons most in need of preventive intervention. This last requirement is of special importance when screening for a low base rate phenomenon such as chronic delinquency.

The prevention of delinquency can be cast as a three-stage process: first, the identification of the relevant precursors to delinquency; the development of practical measures and screening procedures based on these early precursors or risk factors to identify children at risk for delinquency; the implementation of a prevention strategy for changing the risk factors and reducing the child's chances of engaging in criminal behavior.

In this chapter first we will briefly review a considerable body of evidence implicating specific precursors that have been found to be the most predictive of adolescent delinquency and recidivism. Second, we will discuss patterns of early antisocial behavior that are prognostic of chronic forms of delinquency. In the third section, we will demonstrate a preliminary screening device, called multiple gating, that is not only effective in identifying multiple offending youths, but is also less costly than traditional screening techniques. An appendix contains information on the presetting of cutting scores so that eventually correct identifications are optimized, and particular types of errors—false positive or false negative errors—are adjusted for in advance rather than occurring as an unpleasant surprise years later.

As the emphasis is on early behavioral precursors of antisocial and delinquent behaviors, we need to define these terms. We use the definition of *antisocial behavior* developed by Simcha-Fagan, Langner, Gersten, and Eisenberg (1975), which refers to the "recurrent violation of socially prescribed patterns of behavior" (p. 7). In that sense, it includes physical or verbal abuse of a person, damage to or theft of property, or victimless clandestine juvenile behaviors such as truancy or alcohol or drug use. *Delinquent acts* are those antisocial acts that are illegal and bring a youth in contact with the police. *Recidivism* refers to 2 contacts with the police involving one or more illegal acts. *Multiple offending* refers to 3 to 4 contacts and *chronic delinquency* refers to 5 or more police contacts. The contacts all involve alleged offenses rather than adjudicated offenses.

The Best Known Predictors of Delinquency

One of the best longitudinal investigations in delinquency is the Cambridge Study in Delinquent Development (West & Farrington, 1973, 1977). Farrington (1980, p. 4) summarized the results as follows:

> The major findings were that juvenile delinquents tended to come from large, poor families and to have criminal parents and siblings. They also tended to have parents who were in conflict with each other, who had cruel, passive or neglecting attitudes, and harsh or erratic discipline. While many aspects of family environment were related to delinquency, schools did not seem to be important.

Many of these variables are also mentioned in other studies (e.g., Craig & Glick, 1963; Robins, West, & Herjanic, 1975; McCord, 1979). The question relevant here is to what extent do early precursors predict later delinquency? In other words, which variables are the *best* predictors?

Since a sufficient review of the literature on predictors of juvenile delinquency showing the relative efficiency of various predictors does not appear to exist, we prepared a review of relevant studies in the United States and abroad (Loeber & Dishion, 1983a). Most of these were prospective longitudinal studies, although some were retrospective ones. Samples in these studies varied from normal children to children seen in child health clinics. The time between the measurement of predictor and outcome was from 1 to 10 years. The predictor criterion was most often arrest, but high self-reported delinquency was also an outcome measure included in the review.

Table 1 summarizes the results of the prediction studies in terms of median value of the Percent Relative Improvement Over Chance (RIOC) (ranges are indicated wherever variance among studies was large). This index, unlike most other prediction indices, is less affected by the relation between incidence of delinquency in a sample (called *base rate*) and the number of youths selected as at risk (called *selection ratio*). This makes it possible to compare the predictive efficiency of a variety of studies using different predictor variables that vary in respect to the selection ratios adopted and the base rate of delinquency in the sample. The formula to compute the relative improvement over chance (RIOC) is,

$$RIOC = \frac{\text{percentage total correct minus percentage random correct}}{\text{percentage maximum correct minus percentage random correct}}$$

The following is an example of how the RIOC is calculated. Table 2 shows a 2 × 2 prediction table based on the work by Feldhusen et al. (1973). They had teachers rate the aggression of 1,550 elementary and high school students. The police records of these students were checked 8 to 9 years later. As shown in Table 2, 273 of the students had been rated as agressive and had incurred at least 1 police contact (this group is called the *Valid Positives*). Table 2 also shows that 766 students were rated low or nonaggressive, and did not incur a police contact (this group is called *Valid Negatives*). The Valid Positive and Valid Negative subjects together constitute the percentage total correct, which equals (273 + 766)/1550 × 100 = 67.0%. The values of the Valid Positives and the Valid Negatives are influenced by the marginal values in the table. These marginal values alone will produce by chance a certain proportion of Valid Positives and Valid Negatives. The percentage random correct value can be computed in the following way: the random correct value for the Valid Positive cell in Table 2 is (489/1550) × (568/1550) × 100, or 11.6%. The similar value for the Valid Negatives is 43.4%. Thus, by chance, the correct predictions of the Valid Positives and Valid Negatives could have been 55.0%. There is one more complicating factor, that is, each 2 by 2 prediction table has a maximum ceiling on accuracy, which is a function of the match between the selection ratio and base rate. This is explained in more detail in Appendix 1. In the present example, the percentage maximum correct in Table 2 is 94.9%. Using the above formula, the RIOC for the data in Table 2 amounts to .30.

In the Loeber and Dishion (1983a) review of predictors of delinquency, the best predictors were composite measures of parental

TABLE 3.1
Rank Order of Predictors of Delinquency and Recidivism
in Terms of Median Relative Improvement Over Chance

Predictor	Median Relative Improvement Over Chance	
For Delinquency		
(1) Composite measures of parental family management techniques	.50	(.31−.82)
(2) Child problem behavior and aggressiveness	.32	(.15−.78)
(3) Stealing, lying, or truancy	.26	(.22−.58)
(4) Criminality or antisocial behavior of family members	.24	(.08−1.0)
(5) Poor educational achievement	.23	(.11−.46)
(6) Single measures of parental family management techniques	.23	(.13−.23)
(7) Separation from parents	.20	(.07−.80)
(8) Socioeconomic status	.18	(.10−.31)
For Recidivism		
(1) Stealing, lying, or truancy	.46	(.31−.60)
(2) Child problem behavior	.38	(.26−.56)
(3) Criminality or antisocial behavior of family members	.36	(.26−.45)
(4) Prior delinquency	.36	(.30−.60)
(5) Socioeconomic status	.14	(.12−.49)

SOURCE: Loeber and Dishion, 1983a.

TABLE 3.2
The Prediction of Police Contacts by Means of Teacher
Ratings of Aggression in Elementary and High School Boys

	Police Record	No Police Record	
High Aggressive	273 Valid Positives	295 False Positives	568
Low or Nonaggressive	216 False Negatives	766 Valid Negatives	982
	489	1061	1550

SOURCE: Feldhusen et al. (1973).

family management techniques (supervision and discipline) and family functioning, which produced a median RIOC of .50 (range .31 to .81). The importance of the family also appears from studies on criminality or antisocial behavior of family members. These factors led to a median RIOC of .24 in the prediction of delinquency and .36 for recidivism.

Another group of reasonably good predictors was based on child behavior. The child's early troublesomeness, problem behavior, and specifically aggressiveness, led to a median RIOC of .32 for the prediction of delinquency and .38 for recidivism. Stealing, lying, or truancy produced a RIOC of .26 for delinquency in general and .46 for recidivism. The importance of the child's own behavior is also apparent from studies on prior delinquent records or high self-reported delinquency as a predictor of recidivism (median RIOC of .36). The relative predictive importance of poor academic performance led to a median RIOC of .23 for delinquency, although its predictive power for recidivism remains unknown. In comparison, the parents' socioeconomic status or the fact that the child had been separated from the parents was only slightly predictive of delinquency (see Table 1).

This review has a number of limitations. First, it is quite possible that the ranking of predictors shown in Table 1 would have been different if the studies had been based on only self-reported delinquency. Second, the review suggests that combinations of the most powerful predictors, such as child-rearing practices and early antisocial child behavior, may have promise in producing better predictive results compared to using such predictors individually. Although a portion of the studies referred to recidivism as an outcome, the prediction of chronic offending was usually not the goal of most studies.

Early Indicators of Chronic Offending

The early identification of later chronic offenders is a particularly challenging task. For one, this is a rather small group of individuals with a base rate of about 5% among males (see, e.g., Shannon, 1980; Wolfgang, Figlio, & Sellin, 1972). Second, the early identification is particularly important because this group is responsible for about 40%-50% of all offenses in study cohorts (Shannon, 1980; Wolfgang et al., 1972). The question, then, is which indicators are known to predict chronic offending? Formulated differently, is it possible to identify a group of children who persist in delinquency rather than desist over time?

In a review of longitudinal studies on antisocial and delinquent behavior, Loeber (1982) emphasized the following patterns, which are indicative of such continuity: (a) the *density* hypothesis—the more frequent the antisocial behavior is, the more stable it tends to be; (b) the *multiple setting* hypothesis—if the antisocial behavior is noted by adults in more than one setting, it tends to be more stable over time than when it is only noted in one setting; (c) the *variety* hypothesis—the more varied the types of antisocial behavior a child displays, the more likely it is that these behaviors will persist over time; (d) the *early onset* hypothesis—the earlier the antisocial pattern becomes evident, the more likely it will become stable. The evidence for these hypotheses is substantial but not final by any account. Nevertheless, the available evidence can be of great use in the designing of screening devices.

A screening device for chronic offenders should thus identify extreme cases in terms of frequency, variety, seriousness, age of onset, and the number of settings in which the behavior tends to occur. A word of caution is in order here: although the four hypothesized patterns are indicative of chronic forms of official delinquency, they may not necessarily be sufficient to identify chronic patterns of self-reported crime.

The Use of a Multiple Gating Technique

A major criterion for the use of screening devices is their cost. The most expensive strategy is to use a number of assessment devices on *all* youths in a clinic or court setting, or as part of a larger survey to identify high-risk individuals. This procedure is often costly due to the relatively low base rate of delinquency. For example, 25% to 35% of all youths by the age of 18 have at least 1 police contact (Polk, Frease, & Richmond, 1974; Wolfgang et al., 1972). That means that, out of every 3 or 4 randomly sampled youths between the ages of 6 and 10, only one would become delinquent. This in turn implies that, in order to identify 100 youths at risk, about 300 youths need to be assessed, of whom 200 are not directly relevant to the formulation of the risk group.

Another strategy is to set up a stepwise screening method (here called *multiple gating*). One would first use the least expensive screening procedure on all subjects, and later only the more expensive devices on the high-risk groups. The multiple gating procedure systematically narrows down a high-risk group in a cost-effective manner. Before giving an example of such a multiple gating procedure, we need to emphasize one more cost-saving measure.

It is important to know whether a screening instrument can be used by less specialized community agents or whether it requires the use by highly trained professionals. Ideally, a screening device becomes most useful when it can be used by a wide variety of community agents. We see early identification as not solely the task of highly trained, and therefore expensive, professionals. In line with Bell and Pearl (1982), we see improvements in early identification as possible through the participation of community agents such as teachers and parents. Although a number of studies have shown that teachers and parents can successfully use certain procedures to identify future delinquents or recidivists (see Loeber & Dishion, 1983a), there are, to our knowledge, no screening devices that can readily be used by these community agents.

The multiple gating procedure that we designed used community agents' reports in a stepwise and economic fashion to identify youths at risk for delinquency. At the first gate, we used teacher ratings to identify those youths who scored high on antisocial behavior problems. Instead of screening this whole group again with another device, only the high-risk group was reassessed. This time, five daily telephone interviews with the parents were used to assess the child's antisocial behavior in the prior 24-hour period. These two gates led to the identification of children who were seen as conduct problems by teachers and parents. This strategy thus emphasized the capturing of extreme behaviors spoken of in terms of density, setting, and variety. The third gate consisted of more expensive assessment of the mother's child-rearing methods, particularly the degree to which she mon- itored or supervised the activities, whereabouts, and companionship of her son, and the degree of disobedience with which she was faced. Details of these assessment procedures have been reported in Loeber, Dishion, & Patterson (1984).

The sample on which the multiple gating was practiced was 58 seventh grade and 44 tenth grade boys from high schools in a medium-size West Coast town. As the subjects and their parents were asked to cooperate in a more intensive assessment, the sample cannot be considered representative. For that reason, the following results are only thought of as exploratory rather than confirmatory.

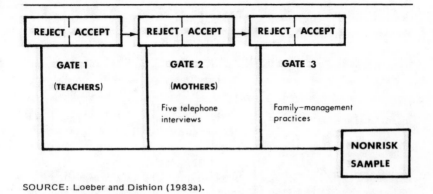

SOURCE: Loeber and Dishion (1983a).

Figure 3.1   Outline of the Multiple Gating Procedure to Identify Youths at Risk for Delinquency

The boys' court records were first assessed in 1980 and again 3 years later. For that reason, the following results, shown in Table 3, are both concurrent and prospective, as a number of youths were already delinquent at time 1. The screening procedure correctly identified 13 (or 56.5%) of the 23 delinquents. The results were virtually equivalent for boys of the seventh and of the tenth grade. Expressed in terms of the Relative Improvement Over Chance of .47, the results are encouraging, but the screening device still would have to be improved before it can be used on other populations.

A first post hoc analysis focused on ways to further optimize the multiple gating procedure by examining the behavioral profile of boys in the False Negative group. These youngsters behaved not in a clearly antisocial manner, at least as evident from the telephone interviews with the mothers and from the teacher ratings. However, the post hoc analyses showed that the youngsters sought out troublesome friends more often than nondelinquent youths. Specifically, the mothers' reports demonstrated that of all the boys in the study who sometimes or often associated with youths who got into trouble, 42% and 47% fell in the False Negative and Valid Positive categories, respectively, compared to only 10.5% in the remaining categories. A similar picture was evident from the peer nominations indicating which boys in the False Negative and Valid Positive groups were seen by their peers as more attracted to a tough peer group compared to boys in the False Positive and Valid Negative groups; $F(3,97) = 3.11$; $p = .03$. These results suggest that the inclusion

TABLE 3.3
The Results of the Multiple Gating Procedures
to Identify Delinquent Boys
(multiple offenders indicated in parentheses)

	At Least One Police Contact	Nondelinquent	
Identified as at Risk	13 (8) Valid Positives	10 False Positives	23
Identified as Nonrisk	9 (2) False Negatives	70 Valid Negatives	79
	22	80	102

of peer association in the gating procedure will further improve its effectiveness in identifying youths at risk for delinquency.

A second set of post hoc analyses showed that the reasons for arrest for the Valid Positive groups tended to be for more serious offenses than was the case for the False Negative group. Of the boys in the Valid Positive category, 77% were arrested for index crimes (mainly theft and burglary), compared to 44% of the boys in the False Negative group. The latter group was more involved in nonindex crimes such as law violation, endangering others, reckless burning, criminal mischief, and so on. These post hoc results suggest that the multiple gating procedure tended to identify those boys who committed more serious crimes.

A last analysis focused on the number of the multiple offenders correctly identified with the multiple gating procedure. As shown in Table 3, the procedure correctly identified a majority of the multiple offenders. Using the same selection ratio as for the identification of delinquents, the multiple gating identified 8, or 80%, of the 10 multiple offenders. Thus, it missed 2 multiple offenders and incorrectly identified 15 youths as multiple offenders (the False Positive category), 5 of whom had already been arrested once by the police. The RIOC index amounted to .74, which places the results among the highest reported in the literature (Loeber & Dishion, 1983a).

Although these results are promising, they are certainly not the final word in this area. First, as we were unable to reassess the youths for their self-reported delinquency at the time of follow-up, it remains unclear whether youths with high degrees of self-reported law-breaking were later correctly identified. (For the early identification of high self-reported delinquents, see the chapter by Elliott et al. in this volume.) Second, there is an obvious need to replicate our findings on other populations of youths in other areas before the procedure is more widely used. Third, it may well be the case that different screening procedures are necessary to capture different degrees and types of lawbreaking. Fourth, it should be noted that the current 3-year follow-up of the subjects needs to be extended so that the long-term effectiveness of the multiple gating technique will become apparent.

Finally, we need to consider the cost effectiveness of the multiple gating procedure compared to using a single-stage screening procedure. In terms of staff salary, the multiple gating for 102 subjects has cost $1,850. This compares with a cost of $4,455 for a single-stage assessment on all subjects. The total saving by using the multiple gating procedure amounted to 58%. To this can be added the time saved in having to contact increasingly fewer families at each gate. Thus, multiple gating procedures are expected to save considerable amounts of time and money in clinical settings, juvenile justice departments, and in large-scale screening programs, compared to conventional screening techniques.

Conclusions

The screening of youngsters for delinquency or chronic careers of crime has still to come of age. We see the improved identification of risk factors, the multiple gating procedure, and the careful setting of cutting scores (see Appendix 1) as only initial steps toward this goal. Throughout this chapter we have indicated where improvements in these areas are necessary. In addition, truly primary preventive work with high-risk youngsters to steer them away from delinquency is a field where there is a great need for advances in intervention techniques (Billis, 1981; Farrington, 1980; Office of Juvenile Justice and Delinquency Prevention, 1977, 1980; Wright & Dixon, 1977). One of the advantages of the multiple gating procedure is that it identifies youngsters who are *currently* engaged in antisocial behaviors; preventive efforts can then be aimed directly at alleviating the present problems. In sum, we see progress possible on all three fronts: the identification of risk factors, the identification of high-risk youths, and the prevention of conditions that make these youths vulnerable to long-term careers in crime.

APPENDIX 1

Optimal Prediction Strategies

In our review of longitudinal studies on antisocal child behavior and delinquency, we found that many investigators used less than optimal screening procedures, which unnecessarily produced many false positive or false negative errors (Loeber & Dishion, 1983b). In itself less than optimal screening procedures are quite understandable. Most investigators probably were aware that when both the base rate and the selection ratio are 50%, predictions become most accurate and lead to the fewest errors (Meehl & Rosen, 1955). However, these conditions frequently do not exist. First, the base rates of delinquency years ahead are not easy to guess, and second, such base rates rarely reach the 50% level.

It is not generally recognized that even when base rates are lower than 50%, optimal predictions still occur when the base rate matches the selection ratio (Loeber & Dishion, 1983b). Thus, for example, when the anticipated rate of delinquency is estimated to be 30% at age 18 (on the basis of existing studies), then a screening device used, say, at age 12 can be best preset at a selection ratio of 30%.

In addition, it may be important to favor particular types of errors. For example, if one screens for juvenile court, one wants to minimize the inclusion of nonrisk or innocent cases (i.e., reducing the percentage False Positives). In contrast, when screening for preventive intervention, one does not want to miss high-risk cases, and for that reason, one wants to minimize False Negative errors. Rather than leaving one open to unexpected outcomes, Figure 2 (and the more precise tables in Loeber & Dishion, 1983b) may help one to determine in advance the type and amount of error that eventually will occur.

Before explaining this, we need to clarify the concept of *maximum percentage errors*. A 2 × 2 identification table has a maximum percentage possible correct identifications depending on how well the selection ratio matches the base rate. Table 4A shows that when both the base rate and the selection ratio are 50%, it is theoretically possible to correctly identify 100% of the cases. By comparison, as shown in Table 4B, when the base rate is 20 percentage points lower than the selection ratio, it is simply impossible to identify correctly all cases, for at least 20% False Positive errors must occur. The total maximum correct identification in that instance will be 80%.

Figure 2 is a quick guide toward maximum ceilings in identification, together with an indication of the type and amount of errors that one expects.

TABLE 3.4
Examples of Correct Identification in Identification Tables

(A) Base Rate Matches Selection Ratio

50 Valid Positives	0 False Positives	50 Base Rate	
0 False Negatives	50 Valid Negatives	50	Maximum Correctly Identified 100%
50 Selection Ratio	50	100	

(B) Base Rate Deviates 20 Percentage Points from Selection Ratio

30 Valid Positives	20 False Positives	50 Base Rate	
0 False Negatives	50 Valid Negatives	50	Maximum Correctly Identified 80%
30 Selection Ratio	70	100	

For example, if the base rate is 20 percentage points *higher* than the selection ratio, the maximum percentage error we can anticipate is the reverse of the example in Table 4B (i.e., a minimum of zero percentage False Positive errors and a minimum of 20% False Negative errors, and as a result a maximum 80% correct identifications). For a more precise procedure of determining in advance the type of errors in identification studies, the reader is referred to Loeber and Dishion (1983b).

References

Bell, R. Q., & Pearl, D. (1982). Psychosocial change in risk groups: Implications for early identification. *Journal of Prevention in Human Services, 1*(4), 45-59.
Billis, D. (1981). At risk of prevention. Journal of Social Policy, 10, 367-380.
Craig, M. M. & Glick, S. J. (1963). Ten years' experience with the Gluck social prediction table. *Crime and Delinquency, 9*, 249-261.

88

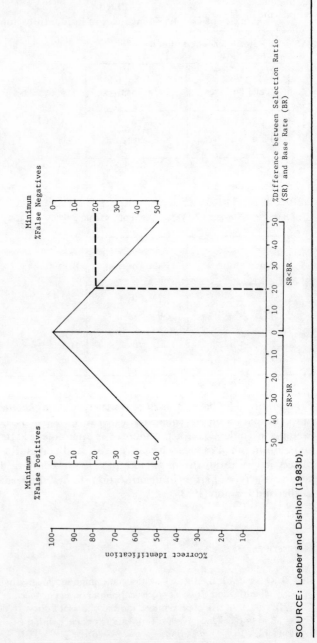

SOURCE: Loeber and Dishion (1983b).

Figure 3.2 The Relationship Between Bae Rates, Selection Rate, and False Positive and False Negative Errors

Farrington, D. P. (1980). *Prevention of juvenile delinquency: An introduction.* Paper presented at the 14th Criminological Research Conference, Strasbourg, October, 1980.

Feldhusen, J. F., Thurston, J. R., & Benning, J. J. (1973). A longitudinal study of delinquency and other aspects of children's behavior. *International Journal of Criminology and Penology, 1,* 341-351.

Gottfredson, S. D., & Gottfredson, D. M. (1980). Screening for risk: A comparison of methods. *Criminal Justice and Behavior, 7,* 315-331.

Loeber, R. (1982). The stability of antisocial and delinquent child behavior: A review. *Child Development, 53,* 1431-1446.

Loeber, R., & Dishion, T. J. (1983a). Early predictors of male delinquency: A review. *Psychological Bulletin, 94,* 68-99.

Loeber, R., & Dishion, T. J. (1983b). *Strategies for identifying at-risk youths.* Unpublished manuscript, Oregon Social Learning Center, Eugene.

Loeber, R., Dishion, T. J., & Patterson, G. R. (1984). Multiple gating: A multistage assessment procedure for identifying youths at risk for delinquency. *Journal of Research on Crime and Delinquency, 21,* 7-32.

MacNaughton-Smith, P. (1965). *Some statistical and other numerical techniques for classifying individuals.* London: HMSO.

McCord, J. (1979). Some child-rearing antecedents of criminal behaviour in adult men. *Journal of Personality and Social Psychology, 9,* 1477-1486.

Meehl, P. E., & Rosen, A. (1955). Antecedent probability and the efficiency of psychometric signs, patterns, or cutting scores. *Psychological Bulletin, 52,* 194-216.

Office of Juvenile Justice and Delinquency Prevention. (1977). *Preventing Delinquency. Vol. 1.* Washington, DC: Department of Justice.

Office of Juvenile Justice and Delinquency Prevention. (1980). *Prevention of delinquency through alternative education.* Washington, DC: Department of Justice.

Polk, K., Frease, D., & Richmond, F. L. (1974). Social class, school experience, and delinquency. *Criminology, 12,* 84-96.

Robins, L. N., West, P. A., & Herjanic, B. L. (1975). Arrests and delinquency in two generations: a study of black urban families and their children. *Journal of Child Psychology and Psychiatry, 16,* 125-140.

Shannon, L. W. (1980, November). *Assessing the relationship of juvenile careers to adult criminal careers.* Paper presented at the annual meeting of the American Society for Criminology, San Francisco.

Simcha-Fagan, O., Langner, T. S., Gersten, J. C., & Eisenberg, J. G. (1975). *Violent and antisocial behavior: A longitudinal study of urban youth.* Unpublished manuscript, Columbia University, New York.

West, D. J., & Farrington, D. P. (1973). *Who becomes delinquent?* London: Heinemann.

West, D. J., & Farrington, D. P. (1977). *The delinquent way of life.* London: Heinemann.

Wolfgang, M. E., Figlio, R. M., & Sellin, T. (1972). *Delinquency in a birth cohort.* Chicago: University of Chicago Press.

Wright, W. E., & Dixon, M. C. (1977). Community prevention and treatment of juvenile delinquency: A review of evaluation studies. *Journal of Research in Crime and Delinquency, 14,* 35-69.

4

The Identification and Prediction of Career Offenders Utilizing Self-Reported and Official Data

Delbert S. Elliott
Franklyn W. Dunford
David Huizinga

Criminologists have long been interested in studying the processes by which sustained patterns of criminal behavior develop and are maintained. The identification of social and psychological conditions and developmental processes that differentiate between the one-time or occasional offender and the chronic or career offender has obvious implications for our understanding of the causes of criminal behavior, for criminal justice policy and practices, and for treatment objectives and strategies.

Early studies of criminal careers typically involved case histories, observational studies, autobiographies, and biographies of individual career offenders (Einstadter, 1966; Jackson, 1969; MacKenzie, 1955; Martin, 1952; Reynolds, 1953; Shaw, 1930; Shaw & Moore, 1951; Sutherland, 1937; Thrasher, 1927; Whyte 1943). These studies provided rich descriptive data, not only about the evolution of criminal activity over time, but also about social and psychological develop-

Authors' Note: This study was supported by grants from the Center for Studies of Crime and Delinquency, NIMH, U.S. Department of Health and Human Services (MH 27552), the National Institute of Justice, U.S. Department of Justice (82-IJ-CX-0011), and the National Institute for Juvenile Justice and Delinquency Prevention, U.S. Department of Justice (78-JN-AX-0003). Points of view or opinions expressed in this article are those of the authors and do not necessarily represent the official position or policies of the Department of Health and Human Services or the Department of Justice.

mental processes, situational factors, and the social environments that contributed to the formation and maintenance of a criminal career. The conceptualization of a criminal career as a sustained, evolving pattern of criminal activity, generated and supported by particular developmental processes, unique attitudes, values, and social definitions, and a network of criminal associates, was derived largely from this body of research. However, the significance of these studies was limited to descriptive findings and the generation of a number of hypotheses about criminal career patterns and process. Findings could rarely be compared across studies and there was no basis for estimating the prevalence of career offenders in the offender population, or the extent to which the career patterns and processes identified could be generalized to all career offenders.

More recent studies of criminal careers have focused upon large, representative samples, examining officially recorded arrest histories and the arrest process in an effort to understand the criminal behavior patterns and processes underlying the observed arrests (Blumstein & Cohen, 1979; Blumstein, Cohen & Hsieh, 1982; Blumstein & Moitra, 1980; Bursik, 1980; Farrington, 1981; Hamparian, Schuster, Dinitz, & Conrad, 1978; Polk, 1978; Shannon, 1981; West & Farrington, 1977; Wolfgang, Figlio, and Sellin, 1972).[1] These studies are quite sophisticated methodologically and have generated an impressive body of findings relative to such issues as the prevalence of career offenders in the general population and the offender population; demographic correlates of criminal careers; offense patterns (e.g., increasing seriousness or specialization in offense patterns); crime rates and career lengths.

Although few have challenged the validity or utility of this official arrest-history approach to identifying career offenders and to studying the underlying criminal behavior patterns and career development processes, there are both conceptual and empirical grounds for viewing the findings from these studies with some caution. Relatively little attention is given in this body of research to the conceptualization of a "criminal career." In most instances, the identification of career offenders is based upon some rather arbitrary minimum number of justice system contacts, arrests, or convictions. While most would agree that the frequency of offending is one defining characteristic of a criminal career, historically this concept involved a number of other dimensions such as the duration of one's criminal activity, commitment to crime as a lifestyle or basic coping mechanism, the demonstration of proficiency and skill in the commission of crime, a criminal identity, membership in a criminal subculture, a low risk of apprehension, and personal attitudes, perceptions, and values that are tolerant or supportive of criminal behavior (Becker, 1970; Cohen, 1966; Gibbons, 1977; Inciardi, 1975; Lemert, 1951; Schur, 1971; Sutherland, 1937). Although criminologists disagree over the precise set of characteristics that define a criminal career, none of the recent arrest-history studies have attempted to validate their classification of offenders relative to any of these potential dimensions of a career.[2] Further, many even lack face validity on the frequency dimension. Is a record of 5 offenses over a 10- to 15-year period (i.e., 1 offense every 2 to 3 years) sufficient evidence for classifying an individual as a career or a chronic offender; is a record of 5 arrests over a 3-month period with no prior and no subsequent arrests sufficient evidence for identifying a career offender?

The second critical issue concerns the representativeness of arrest records as a measure of criminal behavior. The use of arrest data to establish the social, psychological, or demographic characteristics of career offenders and to describe the patterning or sequencing of criminal activity over the course of careers assumes that arrestees are a representative sample of all offenders and that arrest offenses are a representative sample of each individual's criminal behavior. This implies that arrest offenses constitute an unbiased subset of all criminal acts, known and unknown to the police. A substantial body of research challenges this assumption. The fact that offense specific clearance rates vary substantially (Webster, 1977, 1980) indicates that some offenses known to the police are much more likely to appear in arrest records than are others.[3] Research also indicates that, given a police contact, the probability of arrest is related not only to the seriousness of the offense and the number of prior justice system contacts, but also to such factors as local departmental policies, the age, race, sex, and socioeconomic class of the suspected offender, the demeanor of the suspected offender, and the presence or absence of a complainant (Black, 1970, 1971; Black & Reiss, 1970; Cameron, 1964; Cohen & Kluegal, 1978; Green, 1970; Hindelang, 1974; Monahan, 1970; Piliavin & Briar, 1964; Pollak, 1950; The President's Commission, 1967; Reasons & Kuykendall, 1972; Skolnick, 1966; Terry, 1967; Weiner & Willie, 1971). Although it must be acknowledged that the evidence of an arrest bias relative to the attributes of offenders is mixed, there is sufficient evidence in the available research at least to question the assumption that arrest offenses are representative of crimes known to police or that arrested offenders are representative of suspected offenders. Further, self-reported victimization and offender surveys suggest that crimes reported to the police may not be representative of all crimes committed (Elliott & Voss, 1974; Gibbons, 1977; Gold, 1966; Gold & Reimer, 1975; Gould, 1969, 1981; Haney & Gold, 1973; Hindelang, 1973, 1978; Hirschi, 1969; Murphy, Shirley, & Witmer, 1946; Nye & Short, 1957; Schneider, 1975; Skogan, 1976; Short & Nye, 1958; Sutherland & Cressey, 1974; Williams & Gold, 1972). In sum, police arrest data reflect official reactions to some portion of observed or known criminal acts, and there is little evidence to support the claim that arrests provide an unbiased estimate of offenses, offenders, or patterns of offending. This problem is acknowledged by Wolfgang et al. (1972) when they note that police behavior may be as important a determinant of arrest rates as is criminal behavior (p. 207).

An alternative approach to studying criminal careers involves the use of self-reported offender data in prospective longitudinal studies tracing the onset and evolution of criminal careers through offenders' own reports of their involvement in criminal activity. This approach has a number of advantages. Self-reports of criminal acts provide a more direct measure of criminal behavior that is free from distortions associated with police surveillance, victim reporting, police discretion, differential enforcement policies, and other factors known to influence the official record-generating process. Self-resports also come closer to providing a compete enumeration of each individual's criminal acts. Prior self-report studies suggest that between 1% and 5% of reported offenses are known to the police (Elliott & Voss, 1974; Williams & Gold, 1972). The increased volume of self-reported crimes facilitates the analysis of individual crime trends and patterns. It also affords a more meaningful offender classification in which the differences between occasional offenders and chronic, repetitive offenders are more substantial. And finally, the collection of offender reports of crime typically involves confidential personal interviews in which measures of a variety of other career-related variables can be obtained. Self-report studies thus have greater potential for developing multidimensional classifications of offenders and validating these classifications with respect to the conceptualization of a criminal career. In a sense, self-reported approaches to the study of criminal careers provide the type of data used in the early biographical and observational studies of criminal careers, but with large representative samples that permit generalizations to the entire population of offenders.[4]

The objectives of this report are twofold. First, to describe the development and validation of a career offender classification with longitudinal self-reported data on criminal activity obtained from a representative national youth panel. Second, to describe the results of a predictive study that attempted to identify which offenders would subsequently become career offenders. Although this is not the first study of criminal careers using self-reported offense data (see Chaiken & Chaiken, 1982; Greenwood, 1982; Petersilia, Greenwood, & Lavin, 1978); it is the first study involving a large probability sample of the general population and a prospective design, tracing the criminal activity of persons primarily through their own self-reports of criminal behavior each year. Estimates of the number of career offenders in the population, the description of their offense patterns, and an examination of the variables that differentiate between those offenders who subsequently become career offenders and those whose involvement is temporary or occasional, requires this type of sample and research design.

Description of the Study

The National Youth Survey (NYS) employed a probability sample of households in the continental United States based upon a self-weighting, multistage, cluster sampling design. The sample was drawn in late 1976 and contained approximately 2,360 eligible youth aged 11-17 at the time of the initial interview. Of these, 1,725 (73%) agreed to participate in the study, signed informed consents, and completed interviews in the initial (1977) survey. An age, sex, and race comparison between nonparticipating eligible youth and participating youth indicates that the loss rate from any particular age, sex, or racial group appears to be proportional to that group's representation in the population. Further, with respect to these characteristics, participating youth appear to be representative of the total 11-through 17-year-old youth population in the United States as established by the U.S. Census Bureau (Elliott, Ageton, Huizinga, Knowles, & Canter, 1983).

Respondent loss over the five surveys was relatively small. The cumulative loss over the total period was 13.4%. The sample N for the fifth (1981) survey was thus 1,494. A comparison of participants and nonparticipants at waves 2 through 5 revealed some selective loss by ethnicity, class, and place of residence (urban/suburban/rural) at waves 2 and 3; a selective loss by sex at wave 4; and by age at wave 5. There did not appear to be any selective loss relative to self-reported levels of delinquency on any wave.

Although the comparison of participants and nonparticipants at each wave after the first revealed some small but significant differences, a comparison of those participating at each wave with the initial sample at wave 1 revealed no significant differences by age, sex, race, class, place of residence, or level of delinquency. The selective loss was thus very small and did not influence the underlying distribution of these variables (as establised on the first survey) in any substantial way. We thus conclude that representativeness of the sample with respect to these variables has not been affected in any serious way by the loss over the five surveys. For a more detailed description and documentation of the sample see Elliott et al. (1983).

The Measure of Delinquent Behavior

The primary measure of delinquency employed in the National Youth Survey was a self-reported measure. While there is general agreement that self-reported delinquency (SRD) measures have greater conceptual validity as measures of delinquent behavior than do measures based upon official law enforcement records, prior SRD measures have been subject to serious criticism (Elliott & Ageton, 1980; Farrington, 1973; Hindelang et al., 1975, 1979, 1981; Nettler, 1974; Reiss, 1975). A new SRD measure was developed for the National Youth Survey, designed specifically to address the major criticisms of prior self-report measures. These criticisms included the unrepresentativeness of offense items (i.e., a narrow range of offenses, overrepresentation of trivial and underrepresentation of serious and violent offenses), imprecise or restricted frequency response sets (e.g., "never," "sometimes," and "often," or "none," "once or twice," and "three or more times"), item overlap leading to multiple counting of single offenses, and excessive recall periods (e.g., "over the past 3 years," "ever," "in your lifetime").

The self-report measure developed for the NYS included 47 items that were selected to be representative of the full range of official acts for which juveniles could be arrested. The set included all but one of the Uniform Crime Report's (UCR) Part I offenses (homicide was excluded); 60% of UCR Part II offenses, and a wide range of UCR "other" offenses. An attempt was made to construct items with more precise descriptions of behavior so as to reduce or eliminate the potential of item overlap and double counting. The measures employed a two-part response set: a raw frequency count and a categorical response set that provides for better discrimination at the high end of the frequency continuum. Compared with other self-reported crime measures, this measure involves a moderate recall period (1 year), and permits a direct comparison to other self-report and official measures that are reported by calendar year (see Elliott et al., 1983, for more details).

The items of the self-report measure were combined into a set of scales, each involving a relatively tight, homogeneous grouping of offenses with respect to the nature and the degree of seriousness of the acts committed. The set included eight offense-specific scales (felony assault, minor assault, robbery, felony theft, minor theft, damaged property, hard drug use, and illegal services). Two summary scales were also constructed; a global general delinquency scale, which includes 22 different offenses (excluding all age dependent or "status" offenses); and an index offense scale comprised of 9 offense items that reflect UCR Part I offenses (excluding homicide, arson, and petty larceny). The items and scales are illustrated in Table 1.

The Conceptualization of Career Offenders

We propose a conceptual definition of career offenders that includes several behavioral dimensions identified in the earlier conceptual work on career criminals and separates elements in the definition of a career from variables more properly viewed as hypotheses about the conditions and processes that lead one to become a career offender. In the earlier conceptual discussions found in the literature, the two most critical behavioral dimensions involved in the identification of criminal career offenders appear to be the frequency at which these individuals commit offenses and the persistence of their offending over time. As an initial definition of

TABLE 4.1
Self-Reported Delinquency Scales

Offense-Specific	*Summary*
Felony Assault	Index Offenses
(1) Aggravated assault	(1) Aggravated assault
(2) Sexual assault	(2) Sexual assault
(3) Gang fights	(3) Gang fights
Minor Assault	(4) Stole motor vehicle
(1) Hit teacher	(5) Stole something greater than $50
(2) Hit parent	(6) Broke into building/vehicle
(3) Hit students	(7) Strong-armed students
Robbery	(8) Strong-armed teachers
(1) Strong-armed students	(9) Strong-armed others
(2) Strong-armed teachers	General Delinquency
(3) Strong-armed others	(1) Stole motor vehicle
Felony Theft	(2) Stole something greater than $50
(1) Stole motor vehicle	(3) Bought stolen goods
(2) Stole something greater than $50	(4) Carried hidden weapon
(3) Broke into building/vehicle	(5) Stole something less than $5
(4) Bought stolen goods	(6) Aggravated assault
Minor Theft	(7) Prostitution
(1) Stole something less than $5	(8) Gang fights
(2) Stole something $5-$50	(9) Sold marijuana
(3) Joyriding	(10) Hit teacher
Damaged Property	(11) Hit parent
(1) Damaged family property	(12) Hit students
(2) Damaged school property	(13) Disorderly conduct
(3) Damaged other property	(14) Sold hard drugs
Hard Drug Use	(15) Joyriding
(1) Hallucinogens	(16) Sexual assault
(2) Amphetamines	(17) Strong-armed students
(3) Barbiturates	(18) Strong-armed teachers
(4) Heroin	(19) Strong-armed others
(5) Cocaine	(20) Stole something $5-$50
Illegal Service	(21) Broke into building/vehicle
(1) Prostitution	(22) Panhandled
(2) Sold marijuana	
(3) Sold hard drugs	

career offenders we thus propose that persons committing delinquent or criminal acts at a high frequency over a prolonged period of time be classified as career offenders.

Although the inclusion of only two behavioral dimensions in the identification of career offenders is probably overly simplistic, it is a

98   Elliott et al.

more complex definition than that employed by most researchers attempting to select or identify career offenders. The earlier cited work of Wolfgang et al. (1972), Hamparian et al. (1978), Shannon (1981), and others relying upon official record data, involved a single dimension—frequency. In these studies, there were no minimum periods during which youth were required to maintain some specified rate of offending in order to be classified as a chronic, habitual, or career offender. The requirement for some minimum annual offense rate sustained over some minimum number of years is clearly a more stringent requirement than used in most career offender research.

It should be noted that seriousness, age of first offense, special-ization in offending, police/court disposition, and other dimensions of criminal behavior and processing associated with career offenders in the literature are not included in this definition. In our judgment these variables all involve hypotheses about conditions or processes that lead one into a career or facilitate the maintenance of a career and are not properly viewed as defining variables. Neither are crim-inogenic environments; personal attitudes, beliefs, or values that encourage or tolerate criminal behavior; labeling responses of police, parents, teachers, and others; or association with other delinquents or adult criminals properly included as definitional characteristics of a criminal career. Limiting the definition to the frequency and persistence of illegal behavior allows for these variables, which have been tied to criminal careers theoretically, to be used in the validation of the career offender classifications or in tests of empirical claims about the causes and consequences of criminal careers.

Our objective is to identify career offenders among youth in the NYS sample on the basis of high frequency and persistence in self-reported offending, to validate this classification with official arrest data and a set of demographic, personal attitude, perceived environ-ment, and delinquent peer association measures, and to examine the feasibility of predicting which offenders will subsequently become career offenders.

Identifying Career Offenders

The first step in the identification of career offenders involved the development of a frequency of offending classification for each year based upon NYS cross-sectional data. We refer to this annual classification as *patterned offender* classification. Four patterned offender types were identified in terms of the *frequency* of all reported offenses and the *frequency* of serious reported offenses (i.e., UCR Part I offenses included in the index offense scale):

Patterned Offender Classification

(1)	Nonoffenders	Youth reporting 0 to 3 self-reported delinquent offenses and no Index offenses.
(2)	Exploratory Offenders	Youth reporting 4 to 11 self-reported offenses and no more than 1 Index offense.
(3)	Nonserious Patterned Offenders	Youth reporting 12 or more total offenses and no more than 2 Index offenses.
(4)	Serious Patterned Offenders	Youth reporting 3 or more Index offenses.

Using this classification scheme, youth in the NYS were placed in one of these four patterned offender types for each of the 5 years of the study based on the frequency of total and serious offenses reported. Given that a clear majority of all youth report an occasional nonserious delinquent act, and that the range of offenses included in our measure of self-reported delinquency is quite broad, the status of *nonoffender* was defined to include youth who have committed as many as 3 offenses (i.e., general delinquency scale scores of 0-3) as long as none of the offenses was serious enough to be classified as an index offense. In this way essentially nondelinquent youth would not be forced into an offender status. *Exploratory offenders* included youth engaging in illegal behavior at a rate averaging less than 1 offense per month (i.e., 4 through 11 self-reported offenses per year) with no more than 1 index offense over the same period. This definition allowed for more than incidental involvement in delinquent activity with at least 1 serious offense, but clearly represented a nonpatterned offending profile in terms of sustained annual involvement. The definition for *patterned nonserious offenders* intended to capture youth who were steadily engaged in illegal behavior across any given year (12 or more self-reported illegal acts per year), while limiting the seriousness of their activity to no more than 2 index offenses. The goal was to identify youth who were patterned violators in the sense that illegal activities were a regular part of their lives (averaging at least 1 offense per month), but who had no sustained involvement in serious delinquency (3 or more index offenses). This was done under the assumption that involvement with index offenses beyond 1 or 2 offenses per year was indicative of more than a simple experimentation with serious crime. A self-reported commission of 3 or more offenses of the burglary, felony assault, or felony theft variety was deemed grave enough to warrant placing a respondent in the *serious patterned offender* category irrespective of the total number of offenses admitted to for the year in question.

The attempt to incorporate the frequency of both total and serious offenses into the classification resulted in one potential problem. It is possible for a youth to be classified as a serious patterned offender (Type 4) having reported fewer than 12 total offenses (i.e., reporting only 3 index offenses). This aspect of the classification was troublesome, but was adopted, nevertheless, for the following reasons. First, all of the alternative definitions explored resulted in either too many offender types or some inequity that was worse than the one existing here. Second, the vast majority of the youth identified as serious patterned offenders reported committing delinquent acts at a rate far exceeding 12 offenses per year (e.g., in 1976, only 19% reported fewer than 12 offenses; 3% fewer than 6; and the mean number of offenses reported by those in this classification was 118). Finally, inasmuch as the development of the patterned offender classification was only preliminary to identifying career offenders (i.e., those with a sustained involvement in delinquent behavior), the probability of a youth reporting fewer than 12 total offenses being classified as a serious patterned offender in consecutive years was estimated to be low.

The second step in developing a career offender classification involved adding a duration dimension to the patterned offender classification (which was based upon a frequency dimension of offending). Unfortunately, the SRD measure involved annual data, limiting the period of time that could be required to establish a career offender status to multiples of annual units of time, that is, to 2, 3, 4, or 5 consecutive years. Given the assumption that a sustained involvement should reflect more than a single reporting period, the minimum career duration was thus 2 consecutive years. This period seemed appropriate conceptually and also generated a reasonable number of career offenders. *Career offenders* were thus defined as all youth classified as patterned offenders (nonserious or serious) for 2 or more consecutive years.

The career offender classification incorporating both frequency and duration dimensions included the following four types:

<u>Career Offender Classification</u>

Serious Career Offenders	Persons classified as Serious Patterned Offenders for 2 or more consecutive years.
Nonserious Career Offenders	Youth classified as Patterned Offenders (Serious or Nonserious) for 2 or more consecutive years, excluding those who were serious Patterned Offenders for 2 or more consecutive years.
Noncareer Offenders	Any combination of annual offender types, excluding those involving Patterned Offender types for 2 or more consecutive years and those involving 5 years as Nonoffender types.
Nonoffenders	Youth classified as Nonoffenders all 5 years.

All youth in the NYS who participated in all five surveys (N = 1,439) were classified into one of these offender classes. *Nonoffenders* are youth who reported no more than 3 nonserious offenses and no index offenses in any year; *noncareer offenders* have a sporadic pattern of offending over the years, but did not sustain a minimum of 12 total or 3 index offenses per year for any 2 consecutive years; *nonserious career offenders* have a sustained offending pattern of 12 or more offenses for at least 2 consecutive years, but with no sustained involvement in index offenses; and serious career offenders have a sustained involvement of 3 or more index offenses for 2 or more years.

The number and proportion of youth classified as career offenders is indicated in Table 2 by the length of their sustained patterned involvement in delinquency over the 1976-1980 period. During this 5-year period, over 18% of youth in the national sample were classified

TABLE 4.2
Distribution of Career Offender Types by Career Length

Career Length	Nonserious Career Offenders		Serious Career Offenders		Total Career Offenders	
Years	N	%	N	%	N	%
2	109	58	43	54	152	57
3	46	24	16	20	62	23
4	17	9	13	16	30	11
5	16	9	8	10	24	9
Total N	188	100	80	100	268	100
Percentage of population		13.1		5.6		18.6

as career offenders with nearly ·6% classified as serious career offenders. The vast majority of career offenders (70%) were classified as nonserious career offenders and a majority (57%) had a sustained, continuous involvement in patterned offending that appears to have lasted for only 2 years. During this same period, which represents only part of the adolescent years for NYS youth, approximately 8% of all career offenders were serious career offenders for 4 or more years.

Validating Career Offender Types

The first approach to validating the career offender classification involved a construct validation examining the relationship between career offender types and a set of variables that have been linked conceptually or theoretically to career offenders. The early descriptive studies of criminal careers suggested that career criminals were characterized by personal beliefs and attitudes that were supportive or at least tolerant of their involvement in crime; that their interpersonal networks included other criminals and persons who encouraged or were tolerant of their criminal activity; and that they perceived of themselves as criminals.

A number of scales reflecting these variables were available from the NYS. Each of these scales is described briefly in Table 3. Support for the construct validity of the career offender classification requires that career offender types differ significantly on these measures with career offenders exhibiting more prodelinquent attitudes, less commitment to prosocial norms, lower probabilities of parental sanc-

TABLE 4.3
Description of Validation Scales

Scale Name	Items	Reliability* (Alpha)	Homogeneity* (HR)	Description
(1) Attitudes toward deviance	9	.84–.85	.39–.42	A set of items asking the respondent how wrong it is to engage in 9 specific deviant/criminal acts.
(2) Family normlessness	4	.64–.74	.31–.42	A measure of the belief that it is necessary to violate conventional norms in the family, school, and peer contexts, in order to realize valued goals in these contexts.
(3) School normlessness	5	.60–.75	.23–.38	
(4) Peer normlessness	4	.60–.73	.28–.41	
(5) Perceived family sanctions	9	.84–.86	.37–.42	A measure of the perceived disapproval of parents if the respondent committed a set of deviant/criminal acts.
(6) Negative labeling by family	12	.81–.88	.27–.39	Perceived negative labeling by parents.
(7) Negative labeling by school	12	.84–.89	.32–.41	Perceived negative labeling by teachers.
(8) Exposure to delinquent peers	10	.81–.83	.34–.38	A measure of how many of the respondent's friends have engaged in 10 deviant criminal acts.

*Alpha refers to Cronbach's (1951) Alpha, an internal consistency measure of reliability and HR refers to Scott's (1968) Homogeneity Ratio, a measure of the weighted average inter-item correlation. The range of coefficients across all five years of the National Youth Study is indicated.

103

tioning of deviant/criminal behavior, and more exposure to delinquent friends as compared to nonoffenders and noncareer offenders. The results of this comparison are presented in Table 4 utilizing 1977 data, the first year for which the full offender classification can be established.

There are significant differences between career offender types on each of the validation measures. In every case the differences are substantial and in the expected direction. Moreover, mean scores increase monotonically with the progression from nonoffenders to serious career offenders. The expected differences between career offenders and nonoffenders/noncareer offenders with regard to attitudes toward crime, perceived sanctions for crime, perceived negative labeling by others, and exposure to delinquent friends are in fact observed, lending credibility to the career offender classification.

A second validity test involved an examination of differences between career offender types with respect to demographic variables and the actual frequency and range of self-reported delinquency involvement (see Table 4). There were significant relationships between the career offender classification and the sex, age, and rural/suburban/urban characteristics of offenders with career offenders being disproportionately older urban males. The relationship between social class (Hollingshead Index of Social Position, Hollingshead & Redlich, 1958) and the career offender classification was not significant. Further, there was no relationship between the race of youth and their career offender status.

The observation that self-reported career offenders are disproportionately older, urban, and male, is consistent with conventional stereotypes of career offenders that are based primarily upon official data and case histories. Given the current controversy over the relationship between officially recorded crime and social class (Braithwaite, 1981; Clelland & Carter, 1980; Hindelang et al., 1978, 1979, 1981; Tittle & Villemez, 1977; Tittle, Villemez, & Smith, 1978), it is unclear what the expected social class, career offender relationship should be. However, the finding that there is no relationship between race and career offender status is clearly contrary to expectation. Virtually all of the official career studies have found blacks to be overrepresented among career offenders (Hamparian et al., 1978; Shannon, 1981; Wolfgang et al., 1972). Those identified as self-reported career offenders do appear to differ from officially defined career offenders on this characteristic, but given our concern

TABLE 4.4

Comparisons of Career Offender Types (1976 and 1977) on Validation Scales,
Self-Reported Delinquency Scales, and Demographic Variables – 1977

Predictor Scales	N^f	Total 1,389 $\bar{x}$	Nonoffender 688 $\bar{x}$	Noncareer 562 $\bar{x}$	Nonserious Career 104 $\bar{x}$	Serious Career 35 $\bar{x}$	Anova Sig.
Validation Scales: mean score							
Normlessness—family			7.95	9.06	10.34	10.57	*
Normlessness—peers			7.85	8.81	9.69	10.86	*
Normlessness—school			10.12	11.52	13.19	14.00	*
Negative labeling—family			23.38	25.69	28.68	31.86	*
Negative labeling—school			23.30	25.93	28.98	31.12	*
Perceived sanctions—parents			41.67	40.80	40.08	38.20	*
Attitudes toward deviance			32.21	29.94	26.94	24.66	*
Exposure to delinquent peers			14.48	18.30	23.77	27.05	*
Self-Report Delinquency: mean annual frequency							
Illicit drug use[a]			5.11	5.23	5.90	6.74	*
Felony assault			.00	1.12	1.07	6.89	*
Minor assault			.28	4.13	10.06	22.23	*
Robbery			.00	.32	.30	2.20	*
Felony theft			.01	.33	3.96	12.74	*
Minor theft			.06	1.03	8.60	9.69	*
Damaged property			.79	2.70	7.95	10.52	+
Illegal services			.02	.56	11.34	27.14	*
Index offenses			.00	1.58	3.76	13.80	*
General delinquency (C)			.56	14.79	63.16	139.31	*

TABLE 4.4 Continued

Predictor Scales	N^f	Total 1,389	Nonoffender 688	Noncareer 562	Nonserious Career 104	Serious Career 35	Anova Sig.
Demographic Variables: mean score							
Sex[b]		1.60	1.39	1.30	1.14		*
Race[c]		1.31	1.26	1.30	1.31		NS
Social class[d]		43.48	43.24	41.51	47.27		NS
Urban-suburban-rural[e]		2.12	2.02	1.84	1.89		*
Age		14.67	14.85	15.24	15.17		+

NS = p > .05.

a. Category scores rather than raw frequency scores.

b. Males coded 1; females 2.

c. Whites coded 1; blacks 2.

d. Hollingshead Index of Social Position, range 11 to 77 with higher scores reflecting lower class positions.

e. Urban coded 1; suburban 2; rural 3.

f. Fifty subjects were missing data on one or more of these measures and were not included in this analysis.

*p < .0001.

+p < .05.

over systematic biases in official record data, it is not clear whether this finding has significance for the validity of the self-reported career offender classification.

The use of self-reported delinquency scales as validation measures requires explanation. By definition there will be differences in the frequency of offending between career offender types on these scales. If we were to find that the magnitude of differences between types on the self-reported delinquency measures were limited to the levels specified by their definitions, we would have no basis upon which to claim that the typology is validated by such measures. If, however, the differences between the delinquency types are found to surpass the minimal levels specified by their definitions, we would have additional reason to believe that the typology is making meaningful distinctions and that the types therein reflected represent substantially different behavior patterns. In part, we are interested in noting if the volume of delinquency reported by career offenders accounts for the majority of all reported delinquency, a finding frequently reported in official arrest studies. We are also interested in noting the rates of nonindex offending for serious career offenders, since the minimum level of total offenses involved in this classification is only 3 offenses per year.

The relationship between the frequency of particular types of self-reported offenses and the career offender classification is quite dramatic (see Table 4). Differences between types clearly exceed those built into the classification. Serious career offenders not only report a higher rate of offending on index offenses than do nonserious career offenders, but they also report higher offense rates on *every type* of offense, although this was not required by definition. Those committing serious offenses are also committing nonserious offenses at a very high frequency. The ordering of career offender types clearly reflects an increasing frequency of total offenses as well as serious offenses.

The SRD data in Table 4 also indicate that career offenders account for a substantial proportion of all self-reported offenses. Although career offenders constitute 10% of the sample in 1977, they account for 57% of all reported offenses (General Delinquency), 50% of all reported index offenses, and 36% of all serious violent offenses (i.e., felony assaults and robberies) reported in 1977. The proportion of youth classified as serious career offenders is quite small in 1976-1977 (2.5%), but this highly delinquent group of offenders accounts for approximately 1 of every 4 violent, index, and total offenses reported in 1977. Although nonserious career offenders contribute approximately 3 times their proportionate share of offenses, serious career offenders contribute over 10 times their proportionate share to the total volume of reported offenses. These findings are fairly consistent with those in official arrest studies if the shorter time span involved is taken into account. The levels of self-reported offenses reported by serious career offenders are also similar to those reported for a sample of adjudicated youth on probation (Krisberg & Austin, 1983), and to those reported by a sample of prisoners (Chaiken & Chaiken, 1982).

A final validation test involves an analysis of the number of arrests by career offender type. To the extent the career offender classification reflects valid distinctions in the frequency of total and serious offending and the probability of arrest is even crudely related to the frequency and seriousness of offending, there should be a relationship between the career offender classification and arrest. The percentage of youth with 1 or more arrests and the mean number of arrests for youth in each career offender classification are presented in Table 5.[5] Arrest data are presently available for 1976-1978 only.

Career offender types are clearly differentiated by arrest, with the percentage and mean frequency of arrest increasing systematically from very low rates for nonoffenders to relatively high rates for serious career offenders. With each advance in offender classification, the percentage arrested more than doubles, that is, the percentage of noncareer offenders arrested is approximately twice that for non-offenders; the percentage of nonserious career offenders arrested is twice that for noncareer offenders and the percentage of serious career offenders arrested is over twice that for nonserious career offenders. This escalating probability of arrest by career offender status is even more pronounced when examining the frequency of arrest. The arrest rate for serious career offenders is over 6 times that for nonserious career offenders. There is clear support in these data for the validity of the career offender classification.

Overall, the validation tests offer good support for the validity of the self-reported career offender classification. Those identified as career offenders were clearly differentiated from nonoffenders and noncareer offenders on the basis of their prodelinquent attitudes, negative labeling by others, perceived sanctions for delinquency, and exposure to delinquent friends, providing evidence of the construct validity of the classification. Demographically, self-reported career

TABLE 4.5
Number of Arrests 1976-1978 by Career Offender Type

Number of Arrests 1976-1978	Nonoffenders	Noncareer	Nonserious Career	Serious Career
Number of offenders*	470	542	172	70
Percentage arrested	1.9	4.8	10.5	24.3
Chi-Square		$X^2 = 44.87$ df = 2 p ≤ .001		
Mean number of arrests	.026	.066	.169	1.086
ANOVA		F = 36.887	p ≤ .0001	

*The N for this analysis is 1,254, the number of subjects participating in all 5 survey waves who consented to police record searches and had record searches completed (see note 5).

offenders appear to have the same general characteristics as do offi-cially identified career offenders, that is, they tend to be dispropor-tionately older, urban males. The finding from arrest studies that only a small proportion of youth become career offenders but that they account for a sizable proportion of all delinquent behavior in the population was also confirmed with this self-reported career offender classification. Finally, self-reported career offenders, particularly serious career offenders, had substantially higher arrest rates than did nonoffenders and noncareer offenders. These data thus provided evi-dence for the predictive validity of the self-reported classification.

Comparing Official and Self-Reported Classifications

We argued earlier that self-reported measures had greater con-ceptual validity than official records as indicators of criminal behavior and that the use of SRD measures might well lead to a different classification of individuals and a different set of findings relative to criminal careers than have been observed in arrest studies. Table 6 compares the results of an official arrest classification (defining career offenders as persons with 5 or more arrests) with those from the self-reported career offender classification for the 1976-1978 period.

All of those classified as career offenders on the basis of arrest data were also classified as career offenders on the basis of the self-report classification. However, very few of those classified as career offenders on the self-reported classification are identified as career offenders on the basis of arrest data. Only 2% of those reporting frequent and

TABLE 4.6
Comparison of Official and Self-Reported Career
Offender Classification Schemes: 1976-1978

	Self-Reported Career Offender Classification			
Official Arrest Classification	Nonoffenders	Offenders	Career Offenders (Nonserious and Serious)	Total
Nonoffenders: 0 Arrests				
N	461	516	207	1184
Row percentage	49	44	17	100
Column percentage	98	95	86	94
Noncareer Offenders:	9			
1-4 Arrests				
N	9	26	29	64
Row percentage	14	41	45	100
Column percentage	2	5	12	5
Career Offenders: More than 5 Arrests				
N	0	0	6	6
Row percentage			100	100
Column percentage	100	100	2	1
Total				
N	470	542	242	1254
Row percentage	38	43	19	100
Column percentage	100	100	100	100

serious offenses over a sustained period of time (2 or 3 years) have 5 or more arrests; in fact, only 14% of those classified as self-reported career offenders had *any* arrests during this period. The vast majority of self-reported career offenders are unknown to the police.

The data in Table 6 also indicate that half of those who were arrested were classified as nonoffenders or noncareer offenders on the self-reported classification. It would appear that a record of 1 or 2 arrests is insufficient to make judgment about the frequency or seriousness of the individual's true offending pattern, and it is not until one has 5 or more arrests that a clear determination of a sustained, high-frequency offending pattern can be made.

Two observations seem warranted. First, the identification of career offenders on the basis of 5 arrests means that all but a tiny fraction of youth engaging in frequent and serious offending will be overlooked. Second, to define career offenders on the basis of 5 arrests and then to describe the character of career offending patterns and test career development hypotheses with this very restricted sample of career offenders seems very risky. Although it is beyond the scope of this chapter to address the broader question of the representativeness of arrest data, our analysis of the relationship between self-reported offense and arrest distributions in the NYS sample indicated that: (1) youth who are male, lower-class, suburban, older, doing poorly in school, and from single-parent or step-parent homes are over-represented in the arrest distribution as compared to the self-reported offense distribution; (2) serious offenses are overrepresented in the arrest as compared to the self-reported distribution; (3) the relationship between arrest and self-reported frequency of offending involves a threshold effect in which the probability of individuals having an arrest record is very low until their rate of self-reported offending exceeds 100 offenses per year (Dunford & Elliot, 1983); and (4) the probability of an arrest given an offense decreases as the level of self-reported offending increases, that is, high-frequency self-reported offenders have a lower risk of arrest per offense than do low-frequency offenders. In the light of these findings, care should be exercised in generalizing the findings of arrest studies to the general population of offenders.

Predicting Career Offenders

Two separate predictive analyses were conducted, both utilizing the self-reported career offender classification. The first involved an attempt to predict which youth classified as nonoffenders and noncareer offenders in 1976 would subsequently become career offenders over the next 4 years (i.e., 1977 to 1980). The second involved an attempt to predict, at the point of a youth's first arrest, whether she or he was currently or would subsequently become a career offender. The first prediction is more difficult than the second, since it involves a "true" prediction in which the predictors (1976 measures) are all temporally prior to the observed outcome and the time interval between the prediction and observed outcome is in some instances relatively long (4 years). The second predictive analysis is more "practical" reflecting the type of decision facing a police officer at the point of a youth's first arrest. This prediction is not always a "true" prediction in the sense that the predictor measures used are NYS interview measures obtained during the *same year* as the arrest. Further, the outcome being predicted is a current *or* future career offender status. The predictors are thus typically more proximate to the outcome and in some cases are obtained after the subject has already entered a career offender status.

The predictor measures in both analyses include the set of social psychological scales described earlier as validation measures plus a set of three involvement scales (involvement with family, peers, and school academic activities—3 items each) that reflect the relative amount of time spent in each of these social contexts or activities, a peer involvement/exposure to delinquent peers index in which the peer involvement scale is weighted by the prosocial or deviant orientation of the peer group, measures of family and school strain (5-item scales) that reflect the perceived discrepancy between aspirations/goals and present achievement in these two contexts, educational and occupational aspirations, school and work status, GPA, a family crises measure, and basic demographic variables. This set of predictors was developed to test a theoretical model of delinquency and a number have been demonstrated to be relatively good predictors of future delinquent behavior and drug use (for a description of the entire set of measures, and the psychometric properties of the scales, see Elliott et al., 1982). The results of the first prediction analysis, a stepwise discriminant analysis, are presented in Table 7.

The discriminant function was primarily the result of the following 6 variables (ordered by their standardized function coefficients): sex, peer involvement/exposure to delinquent peers index, perceived family sanctions, age, occupational aspirations, and negative labeling by the school. The overall accuracy of the prediction (70%) is low relative to the simple prediction that no youth would be career offenders (with a 90% accuracy). Further, it involves a high proportion of false positives. Although over 70% of eventual career offenders were correctly predicted to be career offenders, only 22% of those predicted to become career offenders actually did so. This analysis suggests it is difficult to make long range predictions about which youth will become career offenders, even when using measures that are known to differentiate between career offenders and non-career/nonoffenders.

The second predictive analysis involved the same set of predictors, with the addition of a measure of the seriousness of the arrest offense.

TABLE 4.7
Prediction of Which Nonoffenders and Noncareer Offenders
in 1976 Would Subsequently Become Career Offenders,
1976 Predictor Measures and 1977-1980 Career
Classification Outcomes

Observed Outcome		Predicted to Be Career Offender No	Yes	Total
No	(N)	756	324	1080
Row	%	70.0	30.0	100.0
Column	%	95.5	78.5	89.6
Yes	(N)	36	89	125
Row	%	28.8	71.2	100.0
Column	%	4.5	21.5	10.4
Total	(N)	792	413	1205
Row	%	65.7	34.3	100.0
Column	%	100.0	100.0	100.0

*128 subjects were excluded from this analysis since they were classified as career offenders in 1976. An additional 106 subjects were excluded as a result of missing data on 1 or more of the predictor measures.

The arrest seriousness scale was based upon the following classification of the most serious arrest offense: status offense = 1; misdemeanor = 2; nonindex felony = 3; index felony = 4. The results of this analysis are presented in Table 8.

In this predictive test, 81% of subjects (i.e., youth with a first arrest between 1976 and 1980) were correctly classified with respect to their current or future career offender status. The proportion of false positives is relatively low, with 84% of those predicted to be career offenders actually being or becoming career offenders. The proportion of observed career offenders correctly identified was also substantial (84%).

The discriminant function involved 6 variables (ordered by their standardized function coefficients): peer involvement/exposure to delinquent peers index, negative labeling by family, school involvement, family strain, seriousness of arrest offense, and family involvement. High levels of involvement with delinquent peers and labeling by the family were the major factors discriminating between career offenders and noncareer offenders at the point of first arrest. Seriousness of the arrest offense did contribute to the prediction of a career offending status although it was a relatively weak predictor. None of the standard demographic variables contributed to the

TABLE 4.8
Prediction At First Arrest of Current
or Future Career Offender Status

| | | Predicted to Be Career Offender | | |
Observed Outcome		No	Yes	Total
No	(N)	28	8	36
Row	%	77.8	22.2	100.0
Column	%	77.8	16.0	41.9
Yes	(N)	8	42	50
Row	%	16.0	84.0	100.0
Column	%	22.2	84.0	58.1
Total	(N)	36	50	86
Row	%	41.9	58.1	100.0
Column	%	100.0	100.0	100.0

prediction.[6] Using only those variables typically known to the police at the time of arrest as predictors (e.g., age, race, class, place of residence, school and work status, GPA, and offense seriousness), the accuracy of classification was only 55%. Since one could achieve an accuracy of 58% by predicting that all persons arrested are career offenders, there is no predictive efficiency (improvement in accuracy over this base rate) with this latter set of predictors. The social psychological scales, on the other hand, do provide a good level of predictive efficiency with a 40% increase in accuracy over this base rate.

Discussion

We have proposed the use of longitudinal self-reported crime data as an alternative to arrest data in the study of criminal careers. The career offender classification, based upon self-reported data from a representative national youth panel, appears to provide a meaningful and valid classification of offenders. When compared to an official classification, several important differences emerge. First, the proportion of the adolescent population identified as career offenders is substantially greater using a self-reported classification. Second, most self-reported career offenders are unknown to the police, that is, have never been arrested. Third, the actual volume of total and serious crime as revealed by self-reported career offenders is very great, greater than many would have guessed. Fourth, career offenders with a pattern of serious offending (i.e., serious career offenders) are also committing nonserious offenses at a very high rate. This last observation may account for the failure to find evidence for increasing seriousness during the career when using arrest data (Shannon, 1981; Wolfgang et al., 1972), although this hypothesis is confirmed when using self-reported data (Dunford et al., 1983). The number of "hidden" career offenders also raises questions about the impact of a selective incapacitation policy. The current popularity of this policy is due in part to the findings from earlier arrest studies that a small portion of offenders accounts for a majority of all crime. However, the removal of those youth with 5 or more arrests would have little effect on the overall delinquency rate in the adolescent population if 86% of the career offenders were unknown to the police.

In at least two respects, self-reported offenders are similar to officially identified offenders. First, they are disproportionately older, urban, and male. Second, they account for a majority of all self-reported offenses in the population.

The predictive analysis indicates that it is difficult to predict which youth in the population will subsequently become career offenders, even when using measures that are known to discriminate (post hoc) between nonoffenders, noncareer offenders, and career offenders. The problem is one of over predicting, that is, a high false positive rate. A majority (71%) of future career offenders were predicted to be career offenders, but 78% of those predicted to become career offenders did not, at least during the next 4 years.

The attempt to identify which youth were or would become career offenders at the point of their first arrest was more successful. While the increase in the overall accuracy of the prediction was not dramatic (from 70% to 81%), the utility, cost, and predictive efficiency of this prediction was substantially better. Of those who were or would become career offenders, 84% were correctly identified (utility) and only 16% of those identified as current or future career offenders were incorrectly identified in the prediction (cost). The predictive efficiency was 40%. The fact that seriousness of the arrest offense was a relatively weak predictor and that none of the offender's attributes contributed to this prediction was surprising, since these are often the basis for postarrest processing decisions. In any case, it does appear possible to render a reasonably accurate judgment about the likelihood that a first-time arrestee is or will become a career offender. Although there may be some practical problems associated with obtaining valid measures of the predictor variables (e.g., information on the kind of friends a subject has and how much time he spends with them, perceived negative labeling by parents, and level of involvement in school related activities) for use in processing decisions, this type of information is often available to clinicians and others involved in delinquency treatment programs.

Notes

1. These studies all rely primarily upon official arrest data. Other recent approaches to the study of criminal careers involve (1) a clinical perspective and small clinical and/or institutional samples (e.g., Ganzer & Sarason, 1973); and (2) studies with a focus on physiological or biological determinants of criminal careers (e.g., Christiansen, 1974; Hutchings & Mednick, 1975; Mednick, Volavka, Gabrielli, & Itil, 1981). While these latter studies clearly have a different orientation from the studies cited, they all use arrest or court data to identify career offenders and to describe criminal behavior patterns. The criticisms of official arrest studies are thus applicable to these studies as well.

2. Several researchers utilizing arrest histories (e.g., Wolfgang et al., 1972) are careful to avoid using the term "career offender," using the term "chronic offender" instead. This particular conceptual problem is less relevant to these studies, although the other criticisms remain relevant.

3. If this source of error were systematic, it would be possible to adjust arrest rates to correct for it. Unfortunately, relatively little is known about this potential source of bias. While the UCR reports both the volume of crimes known to the police and arrests by offense each year, the offender characteristics associated with uncleared offenses are not known, precluding an analysis of how these variables are related to the clearance by arrest process.

4. The most frequently cited disadvantage of self-reported crime data is that they lack validity as a measure of crime (Nettler, 1974; Reiss, 1975; West, 1973). Two things may be said in response to this criticism: (1) official arrest data are also subject to this criticism (Gibbons, 1977; Gould, 1971; The President's Commission, 1967; Schneider, 1975; Sherman & Glick, 1982; Sutherland & Cressey, 1974; Ward, 1970; Wolfgang, 1963); and the available evidence suggests that the validity of self-report data is reasonably good compared to most social science measures (Elliott et al., 1983; Hindelang et al., 1981).

5. Police record search consents were obtained and searches completed for 86% of the original sample. Among subjects participating in all 5 waves, record searches were completed for 87% (N = 1254). We noted earlier that sample loss from wave to wave was not related to wave 1 self-reported delinquency and did not affect the original sample distributions on age, sex, race, or class. However, we have not yet examined the

possibility of some selective bias in refusals to consent to the police record search among subjects participating in all 5 waves. While the possibility of some selective bias cannot be ruled out, it seems unlikely that it could have any serious impact on the findings discussed here, given the relatively small loss rate (13%).

6. Sex was not included as a variable in this analysis as there were very few females with an arrest. In a predictive test of current or future serious career offender status, the measure of the seriousness of the arrest offense did not contribute to the discriminant function, although GPA, place of residence, and school status (in or out of school) did. The peer involvement/exposure to delinquent peers index was again the strongest discriminating variable and the overall accuracy of the classficiation was 93% with only 3% false positives.

References

Becker, H. S. (1970). Sociological Work. Chicago: Aldine.

Black, D. J. (1970). Production of crime rates. American Sociological Review, 35, 733-748.

Black, D. J. (1971). The social organization at arrest. Standord Law Review, 23, 1087-1111.

Black, D. J., & Reiss, A. J., Jr. (1970). Police control of juveniles. American Sociological Review, 35, 63-77.

Blumstein, A., & Cohen, J. (1979). Estimation of individual crime rates from arrest records. Journal of Criminal Law and Criminology, 70, 561-585.

Blumstein, A., Cohen, J., & Hsieh, P. (1982). The duration of adult criminal careers. Pittsburgh: School of Urban and Public Affairs, Carnegie-Mellon University.

Blumstein, A., & Moitra, S. (1980). The identification of "career criminals" from "chronic offenders" in a cohort. Law and Policy Quarterly, 2, 321-334.

Braithwaite, J. (1981). The myth of social class and criminality reconsidered. American Sociological Review, 46, 36-57.

Bursik, R. J., Jr. (1980). The dynamics of specialization in juvenile offenses. Social Forces, 58, 851-864.

Cameron, M. O. (1964). The booster and the snitch. London: Free Press.

Chaiken, J., & Chaiken, M. (1982). Varieties of criminal behavior. Santa Monica, CA: Rand Corporation.

Christiansen, K. O. (1974). Seriousness of criminality and concordance among Danish twins. In R. Hood (Ed.), Crime, criminology and public policy. New York: Free Press.

Clelland D., & Carter, T. J. (1980). The new myth of class and crime. Criminology, 18, 319-336.

Cohen, A. K. (1966). Deviance and control. Englewood Cliffs, NJ: Prentice-Hall.

Cohen, L. E., & Kluegel, J. R. (1978). Determinants of juvenile court dispositions: Ascriptive and achieved factors in two metropolitan courts. American Sociological Review, 43, 162-176.

Cronbach, L. J. (1951). Alpha and the internal structure of tests. Psychometrika, 16, 297-334.

Dunford, F. W., & Elliott, D. S. (in press). Identifying career offenders with self-reported data. *Journal of Research in Crime and Delinquency.*

Dunford, F. W., Elliott, D. S., & Huizinga, D. (1983). *Assessing the seriousness hypothesis with self-reported data: A study of chronic offenders.* Boulder, CO: Behavioral Research Institute.

Einstadter, W. J. (1966). *Armed robbery: A career study in perspective.* Ann Arbor: University Microfilms, Inc.

Elliott, D. S., & Ageton, S. A. (1980). Reconciling race and class differences in self-reported and official estimates of delinquency. *American Sociological Review, 45,* 95-110.

Elliott, D. S., Ageton, S. S., Huizinga, D., Knowles, B.A., & Canter, R. J. (1983). *The prevalence and incidence of delinquent behavior: 1976-1980* (The National Youth Survey Report No. 26). Boulder, CO: Behavioral Research Institue.

Elliott, D. S., Huizinga, D., & Ageton, S. S. (1982). *Explaining delinquency and drug use* (The National Youth Survey Report No. 21). Boulder, CO: Behavioral Research Institute.

Elliott, D. S., & Voss, H. L. (1974). *Delinquency and dropout.* Lexington, MA: Lexington Books.

Farrington, D. P. (1973). Self-reports of deviant behavior: Predictive and stable? *Journal of Criminal Law and Criminology, 64,* 99-110.

Farrington, D. P. (1981). *Delinquency from 10 to 25.* A paper presented at the Society for Life, History Research, Monterey, CA.

Ganzer, V. J., & Sarason, T. G. (1973) Variables associated with recidivism among juvenile delinquents. *Journal of Consulting and Clinical Psychology, 40,* 1-5.

Gibbons, D. C. (1977). *Society, crime and criminal careers (3rd ed.).* Englewood Cliffs, NJ: Prentice-Hall.

Gold, M. (1966). Undetected delinquent behavior. *Journal of Research in Crime and Delinquency 3,* 27-46.

Gold, M., & Reimer, D. J. (1975). Changing patterns of delinquent behavior among Americans 13 to 16 years old: 1972. *Crime and Delinquency Literature, 7,* 483-517.

Gould, L. C. (1969). Who defined delinquency? A comparison of self-reported and officially reported indices of delinquency for three racial groups. *Social Problems, 16,* 325-336.

Gould, L. C. (1981). Discrepancies between self-reported and official measures of delinquency. *American Sociological Review, 46,* 367-368.

Green, E. (1970). Race, social status, and criminal arrest. *American Sociological Review 35,* 476-490.

Greenwood, P. W. (1982). The violent offender in the criminal justice system. In M. E. Wolgang & N. Weiner (Eds.), *Criminal violence.* Beverly Hills, CA: Sage.

Hamparian, D. M., Schuster, R., Dinitz, S., & Conrad, J. P. (1978). *The violent few.* Lexington, MA: Lexington Books.

Haney, W., & Gold, M. (1973). The juvenile delinquent nobody knows. *Psychology Today, September,* 49-55.

Hindelang, M. J. (1978). Race and involvement in common law crimes. *American Sociological Review, 43,* 93-109.

Hindelang, M. J. (1973). Causes of delinquency: A partial replication and extension. *Social Problems, 20,* 471-487.

Hindelang, M. J. (1974). Decisions of shoplifting victims to invoke the criminal justice process. *Social Problems, 21*, 580-593.

Hindelang, M. J., Gottfredson, M. R., & Garofalo, J. (1978). *Victims of personal crime: An empirical foundation for theory of personal victimization.* Cambridge, MA: Ballinger.

Hindelang, M. J., Hirschi, T., & Weis, J. G. (1975). *Self-reported delinquency: Methods and substance.* Proposal submitted to the National Institue of Mental Health, Department of Health, Education, and Welfare, MH27778.

Hindelang, M. J., Hirschi, T., & Weis, J. G. (1979) Correlates of delinquency: The illusion of discrepancy between self-report and official measures. *American Sociological Review, 44*, 995-1014.

Hindelang, M. J., Hirschi, T., & Weis, J. G. (1981). *Measuring delinquency.* Beverly Hills, CA: Sage.

Hirschi, T. (1969). *Causes of delinquency.* Berkeley: University of California Press.

Hollingshead, A. B. & Redlich, F. C. (1958). *Social Class and Mental Illness.* New York: Wiley.

Hutchings, B., & Mednick, S. A. (1975). Registered criminality in the adoptive and biological parents of registered male criminal adoptees. In R. R. Fieve, D. Rosenthal, & H. Brill (Eds.), *Genetic research in psychiatry.* Baltimore: Johns Hopkins University Press.

Inciardi, J. A. (1975). *Careers in crime.* Chicago: Rand McNally.

Jackson, B. (1969). *A thief's primer.* New York: MacMillan.

Krisberg, B., & Austin, J. (1983). *The impact of juvenile court interventions on delinquent careers: An interim report.* San Francisco: National Council on Crime and Delinquency.

Lemert, E. M. (1951). *Social pathology.* New York: McGraw-Hill.

Martin, J. B. (1952). *My life in crime.* New York: Harper & Row.

MacKenzie, D. (1955). *Occupation: Thief.* Indianapolis: Bobbs-Merrill.

Mednick, S. A., Volavka, J., Gabrielli, W. F., Jr., & Itil, T. M. (1981). EEG as a predictor of antisocial behavior. *Criminology, 19*, 219-229.

Monahan, T. (1970). Police dispositions of juvenile offenders in Philadelphia: 1955-1966. *Phylon, 31*, 134.

Murphy, F. J., Shirley, M. M., & Witmer, H. M. (1946). The incidence of hidden delinquency. *American Journal of Orthopsychiatry, 16*, 686-696.

Nettler, G. (1974). *Explaining crime.* New York: McGraw-Hill.

Nye, F. P. & Short, J. F. (1957). Scaling delinquent behavior. *American Sociological Review, 22*, 326-331.

Petersilia, J., Greenwood, P. W., & Lavin, M. (1978). *Criminal careers of habitual felons.* Washington, DC: Government Printing Office.

Peterson, M., Braiker, H., & Polich, S. (1980). *Doing crime: A survey of California inmates.* Santa Monica, CA: Rand Institute.

Piliavin, I., & Briar, S. (1964). Police encounters with juveniles. *American Journal of Sociology, 70*, 206-214.

Polk, K. (1978). *Teenage delinquency in small town America* (Research Report 5, National Institute of Mental Health). Washington, DC: Government Printing Office.

Pollak, O. (1950). *The criminality of women.* Philadelphia: University of Pennsylvania Press.

120   Elliott et al.

President's Commission on Law Enforcement and Administration of Justice. (1967). *The Challenge of Crime in a Free Society.* Washington, DC: Government Printing Office.

Reasons, C. E., & Kuykendall, J. L. (eds.) (1972). *Race, crime and justice.* Pacific Palisades, CA: Goodyear.

Reiss, A. J., Jr. (1975). Inappropriate theories and inadequate methods as policy plagues: Self-reported delinquency and the law. In N. J. Demarath, III, et al. (Eds.), *Social policy and sociology.* (pp. 211-222). New York: Academic Press.

Reynolds, Q. (1953). *I, Willie Sutton.* New York: Farrar, Straus & Giroux.

Schneider, A. L. (1975). *Crime and victimization in Portland: Analysis of trends: 1971-1974.* Eugene: Oregon Research Institute.

Schur, E. M. (1971). *Labeling deviant behavior.* New York: Harper

Scott, W. A. (1968). Attitude measurement. In G. Lindzey & E. Aronson (Eds.), *The handbook of social psychology vol. II* (pp. 204-273). London: Addison-Wesley.

Shannon, L. (1981). *Assessing the relationship of adult criminal careers to juvenile delinquency: A study of three birth cohorts.* Final Report to the National Institute of Juvenile Justice and Delinquency Prevention, LEAA.

Shaw, C. (1930). *The jack roller.* Chicago: University of Chicago Press.

Shaw, C., & Moore, M. E. (1951) *The natural history of a delinquent career.* Philadelphia: A. Saifer.

Sherman, L. W., & Glick, B. D. (1982). *The regulation of arrest rates.* Paper presented at the American Sociological Association, San Francisco, CA.

Short, J. F. & Nye, F. I. (1958) Extent of unrecorded juvenile delinquency: Tentative conclusions. *Journal of Criminal Law and Criminology, 49,* 296-302.

Skogan, W. G. (1976, February). Citizen reporting of crime: Some national panel data. *Criminology, 13,* 535-549.

Skolnick, J. H. (1966). *Justice without trial.* New York: John Wiley.

Sutherland, E. H. (1937). *The professional thief.* Chicago: University of Chicago Press.

Sutherland, E. H., & Cressey, D. R. (1974). *Criminology* (9th ed.). Phildelphia: J. B. Lippincott.

Terry, R. M. (1967). Discrimination in the handling of juvenile offenders by social control agencies. *Journal of Research in Crime and Delinquency, 4,* 218-230.

Thrasher, F. M. (1927). *The gang.* Chicago: University of Chicago Press.

Tittle, C. R., & Villemez, W. J. (1977). Social class and criminality. *Social Forces, 56,* 474-502.

Tittle, C. R., Villemez, W. J., & Smith, D. A. (1978). The myth of social class and criminality: An empirical assessment of the empirical evidence. *Amerian Sociological Review, 43,* 643-656.

Webster, W. H. (1977). *Crime in the United States: 1976.* Washington, DC: Department of Justice.

Webster, W. H. (1980). *Crime in the United States: 1979.* Washington, DC: Department of Justice.

Weiner, N. L. & Willie, C. V. (1971). Decisions by juvenile officers. *American Journal of Sociology, 77,* 199-210.

West, D. J. (1973). *Who becomes delinquent?* London: Heinemann.

West, D. J., & Farrington, D. P. (1977). *The delinquent way of life.* New York: Crane Russak.

Whyte, W. F. (1943) *Street corner society.* Chicago: University of Chicago Press.
Williams, J. R., & Gold, M. (1972). From delinquent behavior to official delinquency. *Social Problems, 20,* 209-229.
Wolfgang, M. E., Figlio, M., & Sellin, T. (1972). *Delinquency in a birth cohort.* Chicago: University of Chicago Press.
Wolfgang, M. E. (1963, April). Uniform crime reports: A critical appraisal. *University of Pennsylvania Law Review, III,* 708-738.

5

Child Maltreatment and Juvenile Delinquency Does a Relationship Exist?

Theodore W. Lane
Glen E. Davis

There is a belief common among professionals involved in child and youth services delivery that a disproportional number of abused and neglected children subsequently come in contact with juvenile justice agencies because of antisocial or delinquent behavior. Discussions with helping professionals often reveal that certain multiproblem families come to the attention of social service agencies that, over a period of years, grapple with a host of problems usually including some form of child abuse or neglect as well as juvenile offenses at a later point in time. Many social scientists have suggested a link between parental lack of affection, excessive punishment, rejection, neglect, or abuse and conduct disorders or delinquency in children (Andrew, 1981; Button, 1973; Feshbach, 1973; Goode, 1971; Glueck & Glueck, 1968). From the standpoint of delinquency prevention, such an association would be noteworthy.

Child abuse and neglect have long been considered by researchers to result in many enduring physical, emotional, and social disturbances in their victims. Child abuse and neglect have been associated with delayed physical development, failure to thrive, and neurological damage (e.g., Smith & Hanson, 1974), poor impulse control (e.g., Gil, 1970), difficulties in school adjustment (e.g., Roberts & Lynch, 1979), disturbances in social sensitivity and perspective-taking abilities (e.g., Barahal, Waterman, & Martin, 1981), and institutionalization and death (e.g., Elmer & Gregg, 1967). While the evidence is equivocal (Elmer, 1977), many studies indicate sustained deficits many years after the initial reports of abuse (Friedman & Morse, 1974; Martin, Beezley, Conway, & Kempe, 1974; Morse, Sahler, & Friedman, 1970). Few empirical investigations have been conducted to assess whether an association between childhood maltreatment and subsequent delinquency exists, and if so, to what extent the association holds true.

Our purpose in this chapter is to review the empirical research that is currently available that explores and specifies the relationship between child abuse and neglect and subsequent delinquency. The methods and results of these studies are critically evaluated and suggestions for future empirical investigations are presented. The implications of this body of research for prevention efforts and intervention programs are also discussed.

Physical Punishment and Aggression

A number of studies have been conducted that examine the parallel between physical punishment and subsequent aggression (Eron, Walder, & Lefkowitz, 1971; Lefkowitz, Eron, Walder, & Huessman, 1972; McCord, & Howard, 1961; Welsh, 1976). While physical punishment does not equal child abuse, such research suggests a trend that might be expected when examining the link between more severe abuse and child behavior problems. These studies suggest that a relationship exists between the level of physically punitive discipline and threats and the amount of aggressive behavior exhibited by young boys as well as both male and female adolescents as measured by behaviorial observations and peer report. In addition, rejection by one or both parents resulted in higher levels of aggression for children of both sexes. However, neither the level of physical punishment nor parental rejection was significantly predictive of aggressive behavior evident during a 10-year follow up (Lefkowitz et al., 1977). Although such studies do not directly assess the negative ramifications of child abuse or neglect, they do suggest that exposure to excessive physical punishment or rejection is closely connected with aggressive behavior.

Maltreatment and Aggression

Several studies have looked at the behavioral disturbances resulting from child abuse and neglect. Although the relationship between abuse or neglect and delinquent behavior is not specifically examined, these studies assess the relationship between child maltreatment and subsequent aggressive behavior. One such research effort is the study by Reidy (1977; Reidy, Anderegg, Tracy, & Cotler, 1980).

Reidy and associates compared 20 abused children with 16 nonabused but neglected children referred from the Illinois Department of Children and Family Service and 22 normal controls, with groups matched on age, race, sex, and parental income. Aggressiveness was measured by (1) responses to a set of Thematic Apperception Test (TAT) cards, (2) the rate of occurrence of aggressive behavior in a free play situation, and (3) behavior problem checklists completed by the children's classroom teachers. Interrater reliability was assessed for the scoring of TAT responses and incidence of aggressive behavior in the free play situation, and was reported as exceeding .89 in both cases.

Abused subjects reported significantly more aggressive themes in response to the TAT cards than either the nonabused neglected children or the control children in this study. In addition, abused children exhibited significantly more aggressive behavior in the free play situation than either the neglect or control groups. On the behavior problem checklist, both the abused and nonabused neglected groups were judged as significantly more aggressive by classroom teachers than were controls. There was no significant difference between the abused and nonabused neglected groups on this latter measure.

One potential confound is that both the abused and nonabused neglected groups scored significantly lower on measures of intelligence as assessed by the Peabody Picture Vocabulary Test (Reidy et al., 1980). It is possible that teachers' perceptions of aggressive behavior as reflected in checklist ratings were influenced by the children's level of intellectual functioning, which was shown to be higher for the control subjects.

The Reidy (1977; Reidy et al., 1980) study indicating a relationship between child maltreatment and aggressive behavior, is but one of a number of studies that demonstrate that child abuse or neglect frequently results in increased aggression and disruption of social relationships (e.g., George & Main, 1979; Kent, 1980; Timberlake, 1981; Martin & Beezley, 1977; see Maurer, 1974, or Maden & Wrench, 1977, for reviews). While the link between abuse or neglect and aggressive behavior seems clear, no direct link is forged between child maltreatment and subsequent delinquent behavior. The following studies were designed to assess directly such an association.

Maltreatment and Delinquency

Bolton, Reich, and Gutierres (1977) reviewed 5,392 cases that were referred to the Arizona State Department of Economic Security as a result of child abuse and identified 774 (14.4%) of these in the juvenile court records as perpetrators of juvenile crimes or status offenders. The authors compared the types of crimes committed by these subjects to the types of crimes committed by a random sample of 900 juvenile offenders. In addition, sibling cohorts for each of these two groups were included in the study. Offenses were classified by Bolton et al. as "escape crimes" (e.g., truancy, run away), or "aggressive crimes" (e.g., assault, armed robbery), and the relative frequency of offenses in the "escape" and "aggressive" categories across the four groups was examined. Their results indicate that youths with histories of abuse had exhibited more "escape crimes" and fewer "aggressive crimes" than the other three groups.

This study is of merit in that it is one of the few that compares delinquents that have a history of being abused with a random sample of delinquents as well as two sibling cohorts. However, no comparisons were conducted between the groups on such demographic variables as age, sex, socioeconomic status, and so on. Without such analyses, the significance of how these groups were similar or differed from one another is ambiguous. For example, the delinquents with a history of abuse may have been significantly younger than the randomly selected delinquent group, and thus a greater proportion of "escape" crimes (which include only status offenses) would not be surprising.

Retrospective

Sack and Mason (1980) and Mouzakitis (1981) examined the relationship between child abuse and juvenile delinquency by retrospectively studying reports of child-rearing practices among delinquent populations. Sack and Mason obtained self-reports of childhood abuse from 112 convicted male felons following their release from penal institutions and compared these with prison histories and police records. A randomly selected control group of 376 noninstitutionalized male adults also completed the self-report measure. Reports of spanking or verbal abuse were not included in this analysis.

The results of this study indicate that childhood abuse was significantly more prevalent among the sample of noninstitutionalized adults, even when the comparisons were controlled for the effects of age, education, and income. Over one-fourth of the felons reported severe abuse as children, compared with 2.7% of the control subjects. A nonsignificant trend ($p < .06$) was noted that suggested a relationship between abuse and conviction for a sex crime as an adult. Felons who have been abused as children were approximately eight times as likely to have committed sex crimes as adults relative to nonabused institutionalized adults.

This study is one of few that, although relying on retrospective self-report, compared an adult criminal sample to a non-institutionalized control group. Although subjects were not matched on various demographic factors, the effects of age, income, and education were factored out of the analyses, which remained significant. This study provides evidence that physical abuse during childhood may be a factor in later criminal activity as an adult, especially in relation to sex crimes. This general finding has been substantiated by other investigators. For example, Tanay (1969) reviewed the clinical records of 53 homicide offenders to evaluate their child-rearing history, and found that 67% of the sample had suffered severe corporal punishment during their childhood. A study that examines the link between abuse and neglect and subsequent delinquency during adolescence (in contrast to adulthood) is examined next.

Mouzakitis (1981) reports the results of a retrospective study conducted at the Arkansas Girls Training School during 1977. The author obtained responses to a self-report questionnaire from 60 adolescent women at the Training School who had been adjudicated as delinquent (45% of the sample) or had appeared in court as the result of committing 1 or more status offenses (55% of the sample). Respondents were between the ages of 12 and 17, with a mean age of 14.8 years. The questionnaire was designed to assess respondents' perceptions of their home environment and perceptions of discipline techniques used in the home. Results are reported as frequencies and no control group was included in the study.

Regarding discipline at home, 86% of the respondents recalled being physically punished. Only 20% of the entire sample reported no physical effects such as bruises, scars, or bleeding as a result of being punished. One-fourth of the participants claimed they were punished physically since infancy, and 33% stated they were punished at least once a day. Of those who were physically punished, 44.8% responded to their parents' abusive behavior by running away or taking to the streets. Also of interest is that 53% of the respondents reported being forced to engage in sexual intercourse against their will.

Although these results are dramatic, it must be kept in mind that there are several methodological difficulties that make the interpretation of these data ambiguous. First, all information included in this study was obtained through recollection and self-report, and the validity of such information was not assessed. Since no control group was included, the results cannot be compared to frequency data from other samples.

Prospective

Pfouts, Schopler, and Henley (1981) examined the relationship between child abuse and juvenile delinquency by prospectively documenting reports of delinquent behavior that were exhibited by a group of child abuse victims. These authors investigated the emotional and physical development of 141 children from 73 families in which reports of domestic abuse had been substantiated at some time between 1971 and 1977 by protective service workers in the Orange County Department of Social Services in North Carolina. Cases of neglect and sexual abuse were not included in the sample. The 73 families involved in the study included 35 families in which child abuse alone was substantiated, 16 families in which wife abuse alone was substantiated, and 22 families in which both child abuse and wife abuse were documented. Data for the study were collected by interviewing the social worker or supervisor associated with each case, focusing on parent-child interaction patterns, children's behavior, and descriptions of family members. Information was not provided on the length of time between initial agency contact and social worker report of delinquent behavior, and it is unclear whether social worker reports included information on children and families that was apparent just at the time of the interview or at any time since the initial contact with the agency.

According to social worker reports, 40.0% of the children were truant, 29.9% engaged in stealing, 30.2% had assaulted someone, 24.1% had engaged in vandalism, and 17.9% had appeared in juvenile court. These findings take on added significance when the ages of the children at the time of the study are considered: 73.8% of the children were 12 years of age or younger, while nearly half of the sample were under 9 years of age. Of the sample, 32% were preschool or kindergarten age. Of the children enrolled in school, 72% were functioning below average or failing.

As indications of neglect or abuse increased (none, weak, strong), as judged by the investigators on the basis of caseworker interviews and protective service records, so did the degree of deviancy of the child. A series of multiple regressions were conducted to determine which factors accounted for the most variability in the degree of children's deviancy (normal, mild, or severe). Two factors, child's role in family violence (bystander of wife abuse, bystander of sibling abuse, or victim of child abuse) and family climate (parent-child relationship marked by ambivalence or parent-child relationship marked by rejection; no category was listed that could include normal parent-child relationships) accounted for 32.9% of the variance of the degree of deviancy. This indicates that children who were abused by their parents and who had parent-child relationships marked by rejection were most at risk for severe deviancy. Of the 87 children abused solely by father, father substitute, or mother, the variables of family climate, paternal versus maternal abuser, and indications of abuse (none, weak, or strong) accounted for 38.2% of the variance in the degree of deviancy data. Children who were rejected by their parents, abused by their mothers, and had the strongest indications of abuse exhibited the greatest degree of deviancy overall in this analysis.

This study suffers from several of the methodological flaws described previously. Data are reported in terms of frequencies and no comparisons with any control group are attempted. Thus data from this group cannot be contrasted to the results of other groups. The methods for measuring many of the variables and the reliability of such ratings are not reported. It is not stated whether reports of delinquent behavior and/or poor academic performance were evident before as well as following reports of domestic abuse. In addition, all data were obtained through interviews with social workers and supervisors. Although such a method may produce richer information on subjects, the data may be systematically biased in that social workers' perceptions of a link between childhood violence and subsequent delinquency may influence the data reported. There is no mention of attempts to verify the interview information. While the results of the factor analyses provide information on which variables place a child most at risk for subsequent deviancy, they should be considered with these difficulties kept in mind.

Retrospective and Prospective

One final study provides information on the relationship between child abuse and neglect and subsequent juvenile delinquency by combining retrospective and prospective methods of investigation. The New York State Assembly Select Committee on Child Abuse received a grant from the New York State Division of Criminal Justice Services to perform a longitudinal study evaluating the association between child maltreatment (i.e., child abuse and neglect) and subsequent social deviance (i.e., delinquency and status offenses). The major findings are reported by Alfaro (1981), with subsequent analyses reported by Carr and associates (Carr, 1977, 1978; Carr, Gelles, & Hargraves, 1978).

The study utilized 2 different samples of children and their families. The first study sample (1950 sample) included all children and their siblings reported for suspected maltreatment in the early 1950s within eight counties in New York State (Broome, St. Lawrence, Suffolk, Westchester, Erie, Kings, Monroe, and New York counties). The children were identified from the records of public or private child protective agencies and the Children's Court. The sample includes siblings of the identified maltreated child, who may or may not have also been identified formally as maltreated. The final 1950 sample included 5,136 children from 1,423 families. Of the 5,136 children in the 1950 sample, 4,465 (87%) had official reports of suspected child abuse or neglect and/or juvenile misconduct during the sample year (Alfaro, 1981). These children were then traced through the county-based records of the Family Court forward and backward in time for other agency contacts including both juvenile offenses and child maltreatment. The sample was followed forward for 20 years which allowed the youngest child in the sample to have become 18-years-old before the last year that agency records were examined (Carr et al., 1978). The majority of the contacts included in the study (across both samples) were between 1950 and 1972; however, some go back as far as 1930 (Alfaro, 1981).

Each official contact was coded as to the referral reason(s) that describe the experiences that led to a child's being reported as abused or neglected, or the behavior that the child had engaged in leading to the report of its being in need of supervision or delinquent. Thus, the data in this study are based on the type of child maltreatment and/or juvenile offense, rather than on the legal label applied to a child (Alfaro, 1981). Out the 11,314 contacts in the 1950 sample, approximately 85% involved reports of suspected child maltreatment. Of these, 8% were for child abuse and 92% were for neglect. Out of the total child maltreatment contacts in the study, 79% were subsequently substantiated. Approximately 15% of the contacts in the 1950 sample involved court contacts for some type of juvenile offense (Alfaro, 1981).

The second sample (1970 sample) consisted of 1,963 children from 1,851 families reported to the Family Court or Probation Intake Service as delinquent or in need of supervision in the same eight New York Counties in 1971 or 1972. In this sample, the histories of the children were subsequently traced backward for prior involvement with official agencies for maltreatment. Although the same data collection procedure was utilized, siblings of the identified children were not included in the 1970 study sample.

Total contacts for the 1970 sample included 2,688 with the Family Court, 2,379 with the Court's Probation Intake Service, and 688 with public or private child protective agencies (Alfaro, 1981). Approximately 83% of these contacts involved juvenile offenses. The distribution of referral reasons in the 1970 sample for juvenile contacts was compared to the distribution of the referral reasons for all juvenile cases in New York State between July, 1971, and July, 1972. The lack of clear differences between the two suggests that the 1970 sample was representative of the state as a whole in this regard.

The findings of the study have been reported in Alfaro (1981) and Carr (1977, 1978; Carr et al., 1978). Given the voluminous number of findings reported, only a selected number will be reviewed here. Findings include the following:

(1) Of the families in the 1950 sample with at least one substantiated child maltreatment contact, 42% (range = 25% to 64% across counties) had 1

or more children who had juvenile court contacts. This percentage increases to 49% (range = 38% to 64%) when the three counties with incomplete records are excluded from the analysis (Alfaro, 1981).

(2) In the 1950 sample, 1.3% of the children with a first agency contact for physical abuse and 14.9% of the children with a first agency contact for neglect had at least one later court contact for a juvenile offense. Among the children in the 1970 sample, 2.4% had been reported earlier in time at their first agency contact as physically abused and 13.5% as neglected (Carr et al., 1978).

(3) In Monroe County, the juvenile offense rate each year between 1957 and 1967 for the 1950 sample averaged 9.6% (i.e., number of sample children between 10 to 16 years of age with a juvenile offense contact during a given year divided by the total number of sample children between 10 to 16 years of age during the same year). In contrast, the average annual juvenile offense rate for all children in Monroe County between 10 to 16 years of age was 1.47% (Alfaro, 1981).

Carr et al. (1978) evaluated the relationship between family composition, child maltreatment, and juvenile delinquency (delinquency or status offenses) utilizing both the 1950 and 1970 study samples. Given the limited number of abused delinquents in the study samples (i.e., children who were physically abused at first agency contact and later had an agency contact for a juvenile offense), only the findings reported regarding neglected delinquents will be reviewed here. The findings reported by Carr et al. include the following:

(1) Neglected delinquents (i.e., children who were maltreated, but not physically abused, at first agency contact and later had some type of juvenile delinquency contact) were more prevalent when the mother alone was present, but only in the 1970 sample. Of the children living in such households, 25% were neglected delinquents, versus 13% of the children living in households with both parents present.

(2) An association was found between family size and neglected delinquents. In both samples, larger percentages of neglected delinquents were found as family size increased. For example, in the 1950 sample 21.1% of the children in families with 8 or more children were neglected delinquents versus 8.4% of the children in families with only 1 child.

(3) An association was found in both samples between being a neglected delinquent and the combination of being in a large household with only the mother present. For example, 45.8% of the children in a family of at least 8 children with only the mother present were neglected

delinquents in the 1970 sample, versus 5.8% from female-headed families with only 1 child.

(4) A relationship was found between being born out of wedlock and becoming a neglected delinquent (22.6% versus 12.1%), but only in the 1970 sample.

(5) When parental presence and wedlock status at the time of the child's birth were combined, an association was found between being a neglected delinquent and the combination of being born out of wedlock and having only the mother present in the household, but only for the older 1970 sample.

(6) The presence of a paramour in the household was associated with being a neglected delinquent in both samples. In the 1950 sample, for example, 27.2% of the children living in such households were neglected delinquents, versus 15.0% of the children not living in such a household.

(7) No relationship was found between the presence of a relative in the household and being a neglected delinquent.

Each of the above findings were subsequently analyzed as a function of sex, race (black versus white), and substantiation of child maltreatment (founded versus unfounded). Whereas the above mentioned findings generally held true for both sexes and races, the relationship of family background to maltreatment and juvenile contacts was greatly diminished or nonexistent in those cases where the maltreatment was not substantiated.

In summary, the major findings reported by Alfaro (1981) and Carr (1977, 1978; Carr et al., 1978) are as follows:

(1) Approximately 50% of families with at least 1 reported maltreated child subsequently have at least 1 child who comes in contact with the court for a juvenile offense.

(2) Approximately 15% of neglected children subsequently commit a juvenile offense (status or delinquent). Only 1% to 2% of physically abused children subsequently commit a juvenile offense.

(3) The probability of becoming a neglected delinquent increases as a function of having only the mother present in the home, having a relatively large family, being born out of wedlock, and having a paramour present in the home.

A number of problems should be noted concerning the methodology of the study that influence the interpretation of the results, most of which have been discussed by Alfaro (1981). In three of the eight counties studied, a substantial number of records were missing due to their destruction and/or change in record-keeping policies. Additionally, most of the Probation Intake Service Agencies routinely destroyed their records within one year that particularly influenced the data base of the 1950 sample. The population of some counties changed a substantial amount during the course of the study. Suffolk County, for example, increased in population by 116.5% between 1950 and 1960, and an additional 49.3% between 1960 and 1970 (Alfaro, 1981). Migration also was substantial in some counties. In Broome County, for instance, the nonwhite population almost tripled between 1950 and 1970, but the total population decreased during the same time period (Alfaro, 1981). The data collection procedure was county based, and therefore there was no way to account for children and families who moved in or out of the county they were initially identified in. The data were based on official records, so not all children who were maltreated or delinquent were represented. At least 1% of the 1950 sample had died by the time the data were collected, and an unknown number of children were institutionalized or had their last names changed (e.g., due to adoption). In addition to these problems, no control group was included in the design of the study. Therefore, it is impossible to evaluate how the findings reported above would compare to other samples of children.

Summary and Implications

A number of studies reviewed in this chapter were undertaken to assess whether an association exists between child abuse or neglect and subsequent juvenile delinquency. In terms of child abuse, percentages of abused children who later committed juvenile offenses ranged from approximately 1 to 25 across studies, while approximately 15% of neglected children later committed juvenile offenses. Unfortunately, these studies contain numerous methodological problems that make the interpretation of these data ambiguous. The major issues in this regard include the following:

(1) The sample of maltreated children examined in these studies were not representative of the general population of maltreated children. The only study that approached using a representative sample is the study reported by Alfaro (1981) and Carr (1977, 1978; Carr et al., 1978). In this case, however, only eight New York Counties were included, and due

to loss of records and migration the data base was substantially reduced.

(2) Appropriate control groups were not included in the design of these studies. While the finding that approximately 15% of neglected children subsequently engage in delinquent behavior may appear dramatic, there is no way to fully interpret the significance of this finding without comparable figures from children who have not been neglected matched across relevant variables.

(3) The age of the children at the time of initial or subsequent maltreatment contact, in addition to age at the time of juvenile offense contact, was not specified or controlled for in the majority of studies reviewed. The impact of child maltreatment, for example, in all probability varies as a function of age in general, and as a function of the age of the child at the time the maltreatment initially occurs.

(4) Prospective studies that are carried out while the sample is going through childhood and adolescence (in contrast to reviewing records after the fact) would allow more flexibility in terms of the variables examined. Thus, for example, it would be possible to include self-reports of delinquency in addition to official records.

In the absence of control groups, however, longitudinal research studies on crime and delinquency can be utilized to shed some light on the significance of these data. These studies have recently been reviewed by Farrington (1979). Some of the relevant data presented in his review are summarized below:

(1) The British National Survey of Health and Development found that 18% of males and 2.5% of females were convicted or officially cautioned before their 21st birthdays (Douglas, Ross, Hammond, & Mulligan, 1966; Wadsworth, 1979).

(2) In a representative sample of children born in Newcastle in 1947, 22% of males and 3.7% of females had been convicted by their 17th birthdays (Miller, Court, Knox, & Brandon, 1974).

(3) The Cambridge study found that 20% of males were found guilty in court for more serious offenses by their 17th birthdays (West & Farrington, 1973, 1977).

(4) In Philadelphia, 35% of a cohort of males were arrested before their 18th birthdays (Wolfgang, 1973).

The above prevalence rates are similar to or greater than the percentages of abused and neglected delinquents reported in the studies reviewed in this chapter, particularly for males. This suggests that there is no unique association between child abuse or neglect and juvenile delinquency. While it could be argued that a well-designed and controlled prospective longitudinal study may find such an association, the fact that no study to date has found an association between child abuse or neglect and delinquent behavior that varies significantly from the above prevalence rates argues against such a contention.

Another focus of the research literature to date involved an examination of family characteristics in terms of their association with child maltreatment and juvenile misconduct. Mouzakitis (1981), for example, reported that 73% of the study sample came from female-headed households, and 50% of the families were on public assistance. Carr et al. (1978) report associations between being a neglected offender and a number of family variables including family size, parental presence in the home, wedlock status at the time of the child's birth, and the presence of a paramour in the home. Additionally, Pfouts et al. (1981) present findings indicating an association between family interaction and extent of social deviance among maltreated children. It seems clear, based on these studies, that the probability of being a maltreated offender varies as a function of different family characteristics. However, similar family characteristics also increase the probability that children who are not abused or neglected will become juvenile offenders (e.g., West & Farrington, 1973).

If reliable differences can be demonstrated between families with maltreated offenders and families with no maltreated offenders, these differences can be useful in suggesting prevention and/or intervention strategies following a matching-to-sample methodology. Unfortunately, the research designs utilized in these studies limit the kinds of family variables that could be examined. Differences, for example, have been found between the interaction patterns (measured via behavioral observation systems) of families including an abused or neglected child and families not including an abused or neglect child (e.g., Burgess & Conger, 1978), as well as between families with versus families without a delinquent child (e.g., Alexander, 1973).

In summary, the following suggestions appear warranted based on this review:

(1) Child abuse and neglect are associated with a variety of negative outcomes other than subsequent delinquency, including death. It is crucial, therefore, to put forth efforts to prevent their occurrence in the first place. Effective treatments need to be identified that will reduce

the probability of these negative outcomes occurring, both prior to and following the emergence of child abuse and/or neglect.

(2) There is an indication that intervention with *families* of abused or neglected children may serve to prevent the siblings of the maltreated child from becoming abused, neglected, or committing a juvenile offense, in addition to preventing the reoccurrence of maltreatment toward the target child and preventing the target child from committing a juvenile offense. These results, however, need to be empirically demonstrated.

References

Alexander, J. F. (1973). Defensive and supportive communications in normal and deviant families. *Journal of Consulting and Clinical Psychology, 40*, 223-231.

Alfaro, J. D. (1981). Report on the relationship between child abuse and neglect and later socially deviant behavior. In R. J. Hunner & Y. E. Walker (Eds.), *Exploring the relationship between child abuse and delinquency*. Montclair, NJ: Allanheld, Osmun.

Andrew, J. M. (1981). Delinquency: Correlating variables. *Journal of Clinical Child Psychology, 10*, 136-140.

Barahal, R. M., Waterman, J., & Martin, N. P. (1981). The social cognitive development of abused children. *Journal of Consulting and Clinical Psychology, 49*, 508-516.

Bolton, F. G., Reich, J. W., & Gutierres, S. E. (1977). Delinquency patterns in maltreated children and siblings. *Victimology, 2*, 349-359.

Burgess, R. L., & Conger, R. D. (1978). Family interaction in abusive, neglectful, and normal families. *Child Development, 49*, 1163-1173.

Button, A. (1973). Some antecedents of felonious and delinquent behavior. *Journal of Clinical Child Psychology, 2*, 35-37.

Carr, A. (1977). *Some preliminary findings on the association between child maltreatment and juvenile misconduct in eight New York counties*. A report to the Administration for Children, Youth, and Families: National Center on Child Abuse and Neglect.

Carr, A. (1978). *Refinements on the relationship between being reported as a maltreated child and later being reported as a juvenile offender*. Prepared as part of a final report submitted to: National Center on Child Abuse and Neglect.

Carr, A., Gelles, R. J., & Hargraves, E. F. (1978, April). *Family composition and its relation to child maltreatment and juvenile delinquency*. Paper presented at the Third Annual Conference on Child Abuse and Neglect.

Douglass, J.W.B., Ross, J., Hammond, W., & Mulligan, D. (1966). Delinquency and social class. *British Journal of Criminology, 6*, 294-302.

Elmer, E. (1977). A follow-up study of traumatized children. *Pediatrics, 59*, 273-279.

Elmer, E., & Gregg, G. S. (1967). Developmental characteristics of abused children. *Pediatrics, 40*, 596-602.

Emery, R. E. (1982). Interparental conflict and the children of discord and divorce. *Psychological Bulletin, 92*, 310-330.

Eron, L. D., Walder, L. O., & Lefkowitz, M. M. (1971). *Learning of aggression in children*. Boston: Little, Brown & Co.

Farrington, D. F. (1979). Longitudinal research on crime and delinquency. In N. Morris & M. Torey (Eds.), *Crime and justice: An annual review of research*. Chicago: University of Chicago Press.

Fesbach, N. D. (1973). The effects of violence in childhood. *Journal of Clinical Child Psychology, 2*, 28-31.

Friedman, S. B., & Morse, C. W. (1974). Child abuse: A five year follow-up of early case findings in the emergency department. *Pediatrics, 54*, 404-410.

George, C., & Main, M. (1979). Social interactions of young abused children: Approach, avoidance, and aggression. *Child Development, 50*, 306-318.

Gil, D. G. (1970). *Violence against children*. Cambridge: Harvard University Press.

Glueck, S., & Glueck, E. (1968). *Delinquents and nondelinquents in perspective*. Cambridge: Harvard University Press.

Goode, W. J. (1971). Force and violence in the family. *Journal of Marriage and the Family, 33*, 624-636.

Green, A. N. (1978). Psychopathology of abused children. *Journal of the American Academy of Child Psychiatry, 17*, 92-103.

Kent, J. T. (1980). A follow-up study of abused children. In G. J. Williams & J. Money (Eds.), *Traumatic abuse and neglect of children at home*. Baltimore: Johns Hopkins University Press.

Lefkowitz, M. M., Eron, L. D., Walder, L. O., & Huessman, L. R. (1977). *Growing up to be violent: A longitudinal study of the development of aggression*. New York: Pergamon.

Maden, M. F., & Wrench, D. F. (1977). Significant findings in child abuse research. *Victimology, 2*, 196-224.

Martin, H. P., & Beezley, P. (1977). Behavioral observations of abused children. *Developmental Medicine and Child Neurology, 19*, 373-387.

Martin, H. P., Beezley, P., Conway, E. F., & Kempe, C. H. (1974). The development of abused children. *Advances in Pediatrics, 21*, 25-73.

Maurer, A. (1974). Corporal punishment. *American Psychologist, 29*, 614-626.

McCord, W., McCord, J., & Howard, A. (1961). Familial correlates of aggression in nondelinquent male children. *Journal of Abnormal and Social Psychology, 62*, 79-93.

Miller, F. J. W., Court, S., Knox, E., & Brandon, S. (1974). *The school years in Newcastle upon Tyne*. London: Oxford University Press.

Morse, C. W., Sahler, O. J. Z., & Friedman, S. B. (1979). A three-year follow-up study of abused and neglected children. *American Journal of Diseases of Children, 120*, 439-446.

Mouzakitis, C. M. (1981). An inquiry into the problem of child abuse and juvenile delinquency. In R. J. Hunner & Y. E. Walker (Eds.), *Exploring the relationship between child abuse and delinquency*. Montclair, NJ: Allanheld, Osmun.

Pfouts, J. H., Schopler, J. H., & Henley, H. C. (1981). Deviant behavior of child victims and bystanders in violent families. In R. J. Hunner & Y. E. Walker (Eds.), *Exploring the relationship between child abuse and delinquency*. Montclair, NJ: Allanheld, Osmun.

Reidy, T. J. (1977). The aggressive characteristics of abused and neglected children. *Journal of Clinical Psychology, 33*, 1140-1145.

Reidy, T. J., Anderegg, T. R., Tracy, R. J., & Cotler, S. (1980). Abused and neglected children: The cognitive, social, and behavioral correlates. In G. T. Williams & J. Money (Eds.), *Traumatic abuse and neglect of children at home.* Baltimore: Johns Hopkins University Press.

Roberts, J., & Lynch, M. (1979). A follow-up study of abused children and their siblings: How their teachers saw them. In A. W. Franklin (Ed.), *International congress on child abuse and neglect abstracts.* London: Pergamon.

Sack, W. B., & Mason, R. (1980). Child abuse and conviction of sexual crimes. *Law and Human Behavior, 4,* 211-215.

Smith, S. M., & Hanson, R. (1974). 134 battered children: A medical and psychological study. *British Medical Journal, 3,* 666-670.

Tanay, E. (1969). Psychiatric study of homicide. *American Journal of Psychiatry, 125,* 1252-1258.

Timberlake, E. M. (1981). Child abuse and externalized aggression: Preventing a delinquent life style. In R. J. Hunner & Y. E. Walker (Eds.), *Exploring the relationship between child abuse and delinquency.* Montclair, NJ: Allanheld, Osmun.

Wadsworth, M.E.J. (1979). *Roots of delinquency: Infancy, adolescence and crime.* London: Martin Robertson.

Welsh, R. S. (1976). Severe parental punishment and delinquency: A developmental theory. *Journal of Clinical Child Psychology, 5,* 17-21.

West, D. J., & Farrington, D. P. (1973). *Who becomes delinquent?* London: Heinemann.

West, D. J., & Farrington, D. P. (1977). *The delinquent way of life.* London: Heinemann.

Wick, S. C. (1981). Child abuse as causation of juvenile delinquency in Central Texas. In R. J. Hunner & Y. E. Walker (Eds.), *Exploring the relationship between child abuse and delinquency.* Montclair, NJ: Allanheld, Osmun.

Wolfgang, M. (1973). Crime in a birth cohort. *Proceedings of the American Philosophical Society, 117,* 404-411.

PART II

Discussion
Early Identification of At-Risk Children

6

Early Identification of Delinquent-Prone Children An Overview

Carl F. Jesness

Just prior to the first session of this conference, on which this book is based, a very wealthy oilman approached two of the participants with a proposition. He told them that his adopted son had recently been involved in several different antisocial acts and he wanted to do something about it. "I am very worried about it—so much so that I will pay one of you experts $100,000 a year for the next three years if you prevent his becoming a criminal. If you fail, however, you pay me back the $300,000." Both of our participants wanted to ask a lot of questions, but the man said he was late to catch a plane and had time for only one question. Both of our experts (surprisingly) asked the same question—"How old is your son?"—but when he told them the boy was 8, they (equally surprisingly) gave different answers, one saying no to the challenge while the other said yes.

My question to you is whether the conferee who said no to the proposition had done his research in early identification and prediction, or in the area of early prevention and intervention. My guess is, of course, that the pessimist was here to present data about prediction. The pessimist knew that the extent and diversity of antisocial acts, and the first age of involvement in such acts, were predictive of chronicity. The more optimistic prevention researcher believed that the oilman was offering just what was needed—an opportunity to intervene early in the youth's career with plenty of time and resources to do so. I hope the optimist is right, but the data we have heard at this conference are not encouraging; we can attach rough probabilities to our predictions, but not to our odds for success

140

in our prevention efforts. The question of just how accurate these predictions are at present, and how best to improve upon them, is the main focus of my overview. In the first part of this chapter I briefly review each of the studies presented here. In the final section I make some general observations and take the liberty of adding some conjectures (some of which may sound like editorials).

Review of Presented Papers

Antisocial Behavior and Later Delinquency

As is true of several of the other participants at this conference, Loeber and Dishion have been able to give us only a sample of the extensive research activities of the Oregon Social Learning Center, which has been engaged in sustained research on juvenile delinquency over a period of more than 10 years. In their contribution the authors present a very brief overview of delinquency prediction studies, describe antisocial behavior patterns that are related to chronic delinquency, and introduce some new techniques for evaluating the predictive efficiency of data from different predictive studies. Their primary purpose, however, is to describe the technique called "Multiple Gating" that they believe may be more cost-effective than traditional screening methods.

In their condensed review of the literature the authors compared available studies meeting certain criteria based on their index of prediction efficiency. In that summary they come up with a few surprises. For one, the fact that parental management techniques are shown to be more efficient than measures that are much more directly related to the phenomenon being predicted may in part be related to the authors' rather generous inclusion of data from some studies that have been faulted for methodological looseness. Loeber and Dishion mention this fact, but do not give us much help in sorting out the good studies from the bad. As with all meta-analyses there are problems involved in lumping together these various studies, as can be seen by the large range of scores obtained on their index of efficiency from various studies using similar variables.

Their gauge of predictive power, called the Relative Improvement Over Chance (RIOC), although not possessed of the kind of verisimilitude or face validity that would allow us to greet its use with immediate recognition or appreciation, has considerable merit in seemingly taking account in one figure of all the complexities involved in juggling the costs and benefits from various combinations of true-positives, false-positives, true-negatives, false-negatives, base rates, and so forth. However, errors in one direction are often much more important than errors in another, and, regardless of the purpose of the prediction, one really needs all the information to evaluate properly predictive effectiveness. In their as yet unpublished extensive review of early predictors, the authors do present more complete information (Loeber & Dishion, in press). (Incidentally, it would have helped the reader to understand the derivation of the index if the formula had been applied to the data presented in the tables.)

It is difficult to evaluate the effectiveness of the multiple gating procedure as presented in their brief paper. It would have been helpful, for example, to know a little more about the youths in the sample. Aside from the fact that cooperative parents were involved, just who were these 102 boys? It appears that many were already into minor 601-type delinquency—all showed serious behavioral problems. In other words, they were a highly selected group that the authors additionally indicate was not a representative sample. Even as an exploratory study, however, the results are encouraging. Focusing some attention on the extent of association with delinquent peers, as the authors suggest, would appear to be a useful addition to the screening method, although just how one would go about getting such information might pose a problem.

Loeber has elsewhere presented a detailed description and research data that provides support for his elegant set of hypotheses related to the continuity and stability of antisocial behavior (Loeber, 1982). This review, which I would highly recommend for all to read, indicates that the frequency and density of antisocial acts, the age of onset, and the variety of environments in which the antisocial acts occur are all singly and collectively predictive of chronicity. A multiple gating technique would surely identify youths with a high potential for continued delinquency.

Nevertheless, the exclusive attention on variables that get at overt antisocial behaviors may not enable the identification of a fairly large number of conforming or withdrawn youths who later become delinquent. The researchers at the Oregon Social Learning Center have elsewhere described different types of youths who engage in somewhat different types of antisocial acts. I think they have come up with a very useful distinction between youths who engage in covert antisocial acts (such as lying, stealing, and conning) and those who engage in more obvious overt acts (such as aggression and fighting) (Loeber, 1982). This acknowledgment of the presence of individual differences among delinquents suggests that to further improve their screening procedures, some additional measures of the youths' self-perceptions, attitudes, and beliefs may need to be included.

Early School Behavior and Delinquency

The paper by Spivack and Cianci, which used data from a longitudinal study of a cohort of 660 kindergarten children first evaluated in 1968, focused on the extent to which behavior patterns seen in kindergarten and primary school were predictive of later delinquency. The authors in their review of the literature point to the consistency with which early indications of aggressive behavior and school failure were found to be predictive of later antisocial problems. They hypothesize that it may not be school failure per se but the child's response to this failure that may be predictive of later delinquency.

The basic results are presented in several tables showing correlations between the teacher's ratings on the Devereux Elementary School Behavior Rating Scale (DESB) and later offenses. Although the correlations are fairly low, with approximatly 10% of the variance accounted for, the data clearly establish a statistically reliable relationship. Minor classroom antisocial misbehavior (including annoying and interfering with others, poor work habits, and so forth) observed even as early as kindergarten are related to later delinquency. As one would expect, the relationships with later school disciplinary problems are somewhat higher, and point to continuity in classroom misbehavior from kindergarten through high school. Even more similar in content to the predictor variables (i.e., the DESB) were the teachers' ratings of classroom conduct. Here the correlations appear slightly more consistent, generally being around .30.

The paper concludes with several analyses of variance using a simple scheme relating the number of instances in which the child's behavior exceeded the normal range (by some unstated degree) on the most predictive factors of the DESB to the three criteria. In most analyses, statistically significant relationships were shown. The authors conclude from these findings that the more of these behaviors that are shown in the early school years the greater is the chance for later delinquency. However, it is my impression that only tests of linearity would allow one to draw such a conclusion. To me, the data presented only suggested that (a) for males there was a statistically significant relationship between number of offenses and ratings made in kindergarten, and (b) for both sexes a relationship was shown between the seriousness of later delinquency and ratings made in Grade 3.

Overall, although the results are impressive, I found some problem relating the data presented to the rather emphatic conclusions drawn in the report. First, there is the usual danger of finding spurious significant values when large numbers of tests are run. This study involved separate analyses of males, females, 4 grade levels, 11 predictor scales, and 4 outcome criteria measured at 3 or 4 different points. The several predictor variables are highly intercorrelated as is evident from the small increases between the bivariate and multi-variate correlations. Would a factor analysis of these variables have helped simplify the results? Possibly not. Information is often lost through this process. In fact, I would have liked to learn about the specific behavior items that were the most predictive. Here even simple t-tests of means would have given me a better appreciation of the data.

But these are relatively minor matters. The main findings of the study appear to stand. As was concluded by the Gluecks more than thirty years ago, the classroom has once again shown itself to be the first testing ground of the child's capacity for socialization in a structured environment (Glueck & Glueck, 1950). Annoying social behavior, impatience, and self-centeredness as revealed as early as kindergarten are modestly predictive of later disciplinary and school conduct problems, and to a slightly lesser degree of later delinquency. But as I will point out elsewhere in this chapter, overtly aggressive antisocial behavior is only one part of the phenomenon to be explained. Delinquents are not all the same. Aggression is not equivalent to or totally predictive of delinquency.

The finding that conduct problems appearing in kindergarten prior to the child's exposure to formal academic work are predictive of later behavior problems is interesting and important. Of course, one could argue with the assumption that no pressures related to learning are experienced—some children do in fact have difficulty keeping up with the class even in kindergarten where a goodly number learn to read by the end of the year. But I think most kindergarten teachers would agree that conspicuous individual differences in behavior are evident among these children very shortly after they enter school. Just what teachers with 30 children in their classes can be expected to do to effectively intervene in an individualized way with the variety of undersocialized, aggressive, and fearful children they encounter is another matter. I am sure that there are some very bad mismatches between child and teacher personalities that aggravate already existing behavioral problems. What we as researchers need to do is to obtain sufficient unequivocal data that will convince the public (and ourselves) that greater resources should be provided for schools to ensure that the school experience itself does not exacerbate these early adjustment problems, and that enough flexibility is provided to enable a better fit of classroom, teacher, and child.

Child Abuse and Delinquency

The purpose of the paper presented by Lane and Davis was to review the research that explores the commonly held belief that child abuse and neglect are precursors of delinquent behavior. Although 28 studies are listed, the review relies most heavily on the data of Alfaro (1981) and Carr (1977, 1978) from two (1950 and 1970) New York State samples.

In the large (1950) sample, which included 5,136 children from 1,423 families, most of the 11,314 agency contacts were for neglect (92%); only 8% were for child abuse. (Consequently, let us keep in mind that the results reported refer primarily to child neglect.) The main findings were that 42% of the families had one or more children with juvenile justice contacts. Also, 25% of the males and 17% of the female children with at least one substantiated maltreatment contact were found to have at least one subsequent juvenile contact. Carr, the second author who looked at the same data, reported that 18.8% of the maltreated children had at least one official contact. (We are not told the reason for the discrepancy.) Analyses of the data from the retrospective 1970 study showed that of the juveniles reported as delinquent or "ungovernable," 21% of the boys and 29% of the girls had been reported as abused or neglected children (Alfaro, 1981). Separate delinquency rates for the neglected and child abuse cases are not presented.

Lane and Davis conclude that while a relationship appears to exist between child maltreatment and juvenile delinquency, they are cautious about interpreting these findings; they believe that most studies in this area have contained serious methodological problems.

I couldn't agree more. In reading the review by Lane and Davis as well as some of the original papers, it appears that firm conclusions about the strength of the relationship between child maltreatment and later delinquency await further study; the available data suggest that the connection is a weak one. As a matter of fact, these data leave open the question of whether the delinquency rates of abused children exceeds that of the general population.

A number of available studies indicate that the base rate for delinquency among males ranges from 17% to 35% depending on the geographical area and the criteria used to define juvenile delinquency. The grandfather of them all was, of course, the Philadelphia Cohort Study (Wolfgang, Figlio, & Sellin, 1972) in which 35% of the male sample were found to have had at least one police contact by age 18. In one of our California Youth Authority studies, 23% of the males and 13% of females in a 1959 birth cohort had at least one official juvenile arrest recorded (Wedge & Jesness, 1981). In a second, more recent study, 25% of males and 13% of females in one of the less affluent school districts in the Sacramento area had one or more probation referrals (Jesness, 1983). West found that by age 18, 25% of his sample of youth in a working class district in London had a conviction for a delinquent offense (West, 1982).

These data suggest that delinquency rates among abused or neglected children so far as we know are not much different from those we would expect in a broader, more representative sample. Frankly, I am surprised by these data. Even taking into account the many problems in the data pointed out by the authors (which would indicate that the data err on the low side), I would have expected the rates to be much higher within selected samples of abused-neglected children than for youth in general.

How can we reconcile the seeming contradictions between these data and those of the Gluecks, which show, for example, a high relationship between delinquency and parental rejection and lack of supervision? Probably a partial explanation lies in the poor data. More important, perhaps, is the questionable assumption that often seems to be made to the effect that rejection and abuse/neglect are equivalent. These variables need to be disentangled. Abuse and neglect are not equivalent to rejection. One might expect that the combination of rejection in addition to abuse/neglect would be the most highly predictive of later delinquency, but that remains to be seen.

One often overlooked aspect of the problem is contributions of the child to the situation that precipitates the abuse. In a recent study of the circumstances related to child maltreatment it was concluded that the instigation or stimulus to the abusive behavior was the incorrigible, negative, aggressive, or irritating behavior on the part of the child occurring in interaction with a parent lacking in coping skills (Herrenkahl, Herrenkahl, & Egolf, 1983). In neglect cases this was not the case—here the problem appeared to be exclusively related to the inadequate skills and lack of motivation of the parent.

I point this out because in reading the literature on child abuse, the conclusions are generally presented in such a manner that one tends to ignore the fact that there were two or more actors involved in the events. To what extent is the child to blame? Why are some children in a family abused, while others are not? How early in life does the child as an individual personality become in part responsible for the events that occur? From the data reported by Werner, it appears that these individual differences are evident and relevant very early in the child's life.

The Kauai Study

In a very unusual study of a type that will appear only rarely in the literature, Emmy Werner and her collaborators have performed the remarkable task of following a cohort of 698 children from birth to adulthood. In the paper presented at this conference she has confined her remarks to an analysis of the power of early risk factors in predicting later delinquency and to a summary of data helpful in understanding why some children apparently at high risk for delinquency defy the odds by not becoming involved in delinquency. The data enable us to examine the effects of problems occurring at the time of birth and during very early developmental history. Although it is not clear just how many variables were involved, it is clear that no effort was spared to tap all areas that could conceivably be related to later psychopathology.

What does this study tell us about the relationship between biological, psychological, and environmental events and later delinquency? First of all, of the 102 who became delinquent (67 male and 35 female), 75% lived in what is described as "chronic poverty," By age 10, 50% were not making expected progress in school, and 20% had been considered as showing mental health problems. More of the females than males had been rated as having mental health problems (about 50%) and/or as experiencing more stressful life events.

At age 2, the strongest correlates of later delinquency for females were IQ ($r = -.38$) and the presence of a congenital defect ($r = .37$). (These two were apparently highly intercorrelated since the multiple correlation that included these two and other variables was only .44.) For males, the highest 2nd year correlate was a rating of low family stability ($r = .19$). At age 10, IQ ($r = .24$) and school progress ($r = .24$) were the best predictors. The author indicates that using all variables available at age 10, very high multiple correlations were found with later delinquency. Because the number of variables involved are not given, it is difficult to judge the dependability of these results. Similarly, in concluding that if four or more of 13 "key" predictors are present (and most of these variables were recorded by age 2) a high proportion of the delinquents (73%) and nondelinquents (72%) could be identified. Here again we are somewhat at a loss as to how to evaluate these data without more information about the total number of variables involved.

A final section of the paper is aimed at learning more about the "false positives," that is, the 72 children who showed 4 or more of these risk factors before age 2 but did not develop serious "coping problems" (which I assume means involvement with delinquency). The results indicated that these "resilient" children were characterized by a number of personality, environmental, and constitutional variables that distinguished them from the vulnerables. (I assume these were statistically significant differences, but that it is not clear, nor are we sure about the number of variables involved in the analysis.) The resilient were healthier, were more often perceived as active, affectionate, independent, better adjusted infants who learned more quickly, were more positive about themselves, came from smaller families, and had supportive adults in their environments.

In a final data analysis, a large number of variables (36 at age 10, and 42 at age 18) were entered in discriminant function analyses run separately for males and females. That the discriminant correctly classified most of the 33 resilient and 22 delinquent females comes as no surprise, nor are we surprised that a similar high degree of separation was shown between the 22 resilient and 42 delinquent males. We are not surprised because when dealing with a large number of independent variables in the context of a relatively small sample, the problem of shrinkage and the possibility of profiting from chance variations in the correlations can lead to highly over-optimistic results. Perhaps the use of factor analysis could have brought more order to this mass of data. As it is, we must view the study as exploratory, and as offering many hypotheses that should be tested in other contexts.

Werner, too, has data that might further be explored to test, for example, the relationships between abuse and neglect separately and later delinquency both separately and in combination.

I do not want to detract unnecessarily from the important contribution made by this study by nit-picking about the statistical analyses. But it is a fact that the rich findings of the study may be discounted by those who would do so. One should not ignore the findings, however, for they suggest important avenues for early intervention in the lives of potential delinquents.

The most discouraging finding of the study was that only a minority of the vulnerable children received professional help (only 30% of those with delinquent records). Although the author was dissatisfied that less than half of those who did receive help improved, I would interpret this finding quite differently; I think the fact that half were helped is the good news.

Predicting Career Offenders from Self-Reported Data

The objective of the Elliott, Dunford, and Huizinga study were to describe the development and validation of a career offender classification, and to predict which minor offenders would become career offenders. The sample consisted of a national cross section of 1,725 youths from 11 to 17 years of age who were followed for 4 years beginning in 1976. The authors' primary measure of delinquency was a 47-item self-report measure. Their predictor variables were attitude scales developed to reflect an integrated theoretical model that included dimensions of control, social learning, labeling, and differential association theories. Clearly, a tremendous amount of effort went into the overall study of which we here only glimpsed a small part.

The authors justify the use of self-report rather than recorded offenses as the basis for identifying career offenders primarily on the basis that arrests do not constitute an unbiased representation of crimes committed. Consequently, they classified the youths into one of four groups on the basis of their self-report delinquency—serious career offenders, nonserious career offenders, noncareer offenders, and nonoffenders. The target for their predictions were those in the most serious offender category.

Two types of predictions were reported. The first involved predictions from the entire sample; the second involved predictions of career offenders from the subset of youth who had at least one arrest. The results of the first attempt were not very successful. Career offenders (as defined by self-reports) could not accurately be predicted from the entire sample using the particular psychological/sociological measures. The variables entered in the stepwise discriminant analysis identified 55% of the career offenders, but at a high cost of false-positives. Only 16% of those predicted to become career offenders actually were eventually shown to be career offenders; in other words there were 84% false-positives. According to other data relating self-reported to official data, only a handful (14%) of these 16% showed an official arrest record. It is apparent from these data that a very large proportion of the less serious offenders in the sample (35.4%) held attitudes and beliefs that were similar to those expressed by the serious offenders. However, once the sample was restricted to those who had an arrest, these same attitudinal variables did discriminate quite successfully between the transient and chronic offenders, with 75% correctly classified.

The more successful predictions of recidivism with those having one arrest were related to (a) the fact that the base rate was closer to the 50% "ideal" that is desirable for maximum predictive accuracy, (b) the inclusion of current as well as future SRD reports, and (c) the use of multiple regression or discriminant function procedures with a large number of predictors and a relatively small sample.

Nevertheless, the point is made—early identification is enormously simplified if one starts with a sample of youth who manifest overt behavior indicative of delinquency proneness. The authors discuss at some length the comparative validity of self-reported versus official data as a gauge of delinquent activity, and appear to be convinced that self-reports provide a superior measure of delinquent behavior. But much remains to be understood about the large discrepancies that appear in the literature between the two indices. In our own, yet to be completed study, we have found a very low correlation of .14 between self-reported delinquency and probation referrals (Jesness, 1983). In regressions predicting SRD and separate predictions of probation referrals, very different predictor variables emerged. For probation referrals the best predictors were almost exclusively behavioral/background rather than attitudinal variables (i.e., school dropout, disciplinary referrals, prior record, self-reported truancy, age at first referral, and self-rated obtrusive behavior). These showed a multiple correlation with number of probation referrals of .40 on cross validation. Only one of these same variables (self-reported truancy) entered the SRD solution; psychological/attitudinal variables accounted for most of the variance in self-reported delinquency (multiple correlation of .78 on cross validation).

Although this somewhat unexpected outcome can be attributed in part to shared method variance between the predictors and SRD outcome criterion, we continue to wonder just what is going on here. Much remains to be learned about these discrepancies. Hindelang, Hirschi, and Weis (1979) believe the discrepancy between self-report and official measures of delinquency is an "illusion" related primarily to the inclusion of many trivial antisocial behaviors as items in SRD scales. It would be of interest to learn about the relationship in Elliott's data between official data and SRD scales that included only the more serious offenses. However, we believe that there is more going on than that. The self-report data described in the series of Rand reports would indicate that the more intensive offenders must regularly work overtime in order to accumulate the enormous number of offenses they report. Although we find these extremely high rates of criminal activity hard to believe, it is nevertheless well established that a relatively small number of juvenile and adult offenders commit a highly disproportionate number of crimes. Seemingly very costly efforts at early intervention could easily be justified on a cost-benefit basis if one could identify these intensive offenders. The data presented by Elliott et al. in this report are encouraging in this regard, as are data presented by others at this conference. It would appear that if anyone could clearly demonstrate effective intervention programs with these offenders they might have very few problems getting funds to support their prevention efforts.

Conclusions and Implications

What are some of the conclusions and implications that can be drawn from the several studies presented here as well as other current research studies on the early identification of delinquent youth? I will approach the task of trying to tie some of the results together by briefly discussing (a) methodological problems, (b) the nature of serious and chronic delinquency, (c) individual differences among delinquents, and (d) labeling theory and the problem of false-positives.

Methodology

Specific problems in the design and analyses used in some of the studies have been referred to previously. In general, the main problems were related to the slippery, somewhat unpredictable nature of low correlations, especially when those low correlations are combined in multiple regression or discriminant analysis. Longitudinal studies are very expensive, both in terms of money and the personal commitment of time made to them, and it is understandable and even laudable that some of the researchers, myself included, are tempted to include as many measures of potentially important variables as they can. But doing so leaves them with the problem of how to deal with this mass of data.

Factor analysis can help, but even so, caution must be exercised in avoiding certain pitfalls. For one, correction for shrinkage becomes increasingly essential as the number of variables increases relative to the number of subjects in the sample. To pick an extreme example, if we have 50 variables, an N of 100 subjects and an R^2 of .60, $\hat{R}$ (the shrunken R^2, which provides a less biased estimate) reduces to .20. In addition, selection of variables from a pool of variables tends to capitalize on chance fluctuations in the relationships. Marked decreases in multiple correlations on cross validation can be expected where large numbers of independent variables and rather low bivariate correlations with the dependent variable are involved. In these instances it is imperative that some type of cross-validation procedure be used, perhaps of the type suggested by McNemar wherein variables selected from a regression run on one half the sample are used with the second half of the sample to derive a final set of regression weights (McNemar, 1969).

A second approach to the problem is to design the data collection around a theory. The danger here is, of course, that a too narrowly defined theory may take one down the wrong road. Without intending to imply that the authors were on a wrong track I wished, for example, in reading the Elliott et al. study, that other data that were irrelevant to their theory had been collected during this major effort such as, for example, data on school achievement. I would have been equally curious to see the behaviorally oriented researchers supplement their data with a few attitudinal variables related to other psychological/sociological points of view. Although theory can stimulate research and clarify important issues, it is possible that we have been somewhat premature in even using the word theory, rather than "point of view" or hypotheses, at our primative level of knowledge development. However, it could be that over the past 20 years we have collected enough well-established facts that we are at the stage where we could attempt to formulate important theories that would take account of the most salient of these facts. Integrating these variables into a single theory will pose a most difficult challenge. In the meantime, I hope that those involved in such studies will take a broad eclectic approach to data collection while still getting the data necessary to test theory.

The Nature of Serious and Chronic Delinquency

Serious delinquency appears to be at the midpoint of a continuum. ranging from minor misbehaviors to serious persistent violent crime. No one single characteristic or quality that we are able to specify or measure distinguished serious offenders from others, but rather their extreme placement along a whole set of biological, psychological, sociological, and environmental variables. The more disadvantaged, the more retarded in school, the more negative the attitudes toward authority, the more criminal the family background, the looser the bonds to conventional society, the more frequent the associations with delinquent peers, the more lacking in social anxiety, and the more diverse and intense the involvement in minor antisocial acts, the higher are the probabilities for continued and chronic delinquency. Recent research on three samples of delinquents who had been institutionalized in California Youth Authority facilities indicate that most of the same variables that differentiate minor from more serious delinquents also distinguish the nonrecidivist and less serious

154   Carl F. Jesness

TABLE 6.1
Percentage of Fricot Juveniles Arrested
for a Violent Crime As An Adult

	Risk Level (Score)	N	% Arrested
	(9-17)	21	19
Low	(18-20)	24	29
	(21-22)	29	28
Medium	(23-25)	55	47
	(26-28)	35	69
	(29-31)	25	60
High	(32-41)	21	81
Total		210	

NOTE: The variables included and their weights are: age at first police contact ($\leqslant$ 9 = 6, 10 = 5, 11 = 4, 12 = 3, 13 = 2, 14 = 1, $\geqslant$ 15 = 0); number of prior police contacts (number). Diversity: Aggression and/or purse snatch (yes = 1), escape (yes = 1), breaking and entering (yes = 1), vehicle theft (yes = 1), petty theft (yes = 1), use of alcohol or glue (yes = 1); usually with 3 or more others during delinquency (yes = 1), family on welfare (yes = 1), father main support of family (no = 1), intact family (no = 1), number of siblings (3 = 1, 4 = 2, 5+ = 3), father has crime record (yes = 1), mother has crime record (yes = 1), low family supervision (yes = 1), mother rejects (yes = 1), father rejects (yes = 1), parents wanted youth committed (no = 1), verbal IQ ($\leqslant$ 69 = 4, 70-79 = 3, 80-89 = 2, 90-99 = 1, 100+ = 0); grade level (at grade level = 1; 1 year retarded = 2, 2 years = 3, 3 years = 4, 4+ years = 5); negative school attitude (0-3); school disciplinary problems (yes = 1). This formula has not been subject to cross validation.

adult recidivist from the most serious and violent chronic adult criminals (Haapanen & Jesness, 1982). Although there is not sufficient time here to discuss this project in any detail, let me illustrate the point by presenting just one table.

The youths involved in this cohort were very young institutionalized delinquents who were followed for approximately 16 years. The follow-up of these 11-year-old delinquents to about age 26 showed that violent adult criminality could be predicted with a fairly high degree of accuracy. Table 1 shows results using a simplified formula. Tests of linearity showed a progression from nonrecidivists to violent offenders on many of the variables. Few of the variables shown as predictive will surprise you after what you have heard at this conference.

However, conspicuous in their absence are indicators of more basic (i.e., genotypic) personality and character traits. Throughout this conference we have learned about the predictive power of various indirect indicators of delinquency. Behavioral, sociological, and demographic measures tell us something about the youth, but don't get very directly at the personal characteristics that may underly chronic delinquency. In our work, the closest we have come to this is in our finding that chronic violent delinquents scored lower on measures of social anxiety, super ego, and perceptual maturity than did those who were less persistent and violent. What I am suggesting is that underlying these indirect measures in many instances is a callous, hedonistic personality relatively lacking in emotional responsiveness and in the ability to anticipate punishment or learn from it. It will be a challenge in future research to see if better indices tapping these character traits can be devised and incorporated into predictive formulas.

Individual Differences

Although a number of potential delinquents tend to identify themselves very early in life by displaying repeated conspicuous and diverse antisocial behaviors, many others do not. One of the few references to individual differences among delinquents by the authors at this conference was made by the members of the Oregon Social Learning Center in articles not presented here, but which I would highly recommend for all to read (Loeber, 1982; Patterson, 1980). The distinction made between overt and covert offenders is an interesting and important one. In the I-level (Interpersonal Maturity Level) terminology, the careful manipulator, the conformist, and the introverted-anxious types of youths present a more difficult problem in early identification, for they do not show much overt aggressiveness. Although it would be desirable to base interventions on the presence of observable antisocial behaviors and avoid the whole problem of false-positives, such an approach ignores a large group of false-negatives, some of whom may later become the most active chronic offenders.

Labeling Theory and the
Problem of False-Positives

One of the most important constraints on the use of predictive measures has been in the concern over falsely labeling someone a potential delinquent. But what about the so-called "false-positives"—is it possible that many of them are in fact falsely labeled false-positives? There are scattered data available suggesting that this may be the case. West (1982) discovered, in following a group of youths who were at high risk for criminality but had no convictions, that they were not without problems. Some admitted to committing undetected offenses or had committed minor offenses; others were "social failures." West could offer no generalizations about those who appeared to defy the odds and were reasonably successful because they were too rare. Robbins (1966) found that virtually all youths referred for antisocial behavior were maladjusted as adults. Those few resilient children in the Kauai study who were at high risk for delinquency but did not later engage in delinquency were to some degree identifiable as actually being at lower risk in showing more positive personal characteristics as well as in having been raised in more supportive environments. Loeber and Dishion in their paper mentioned that the false-positive youths associated more often with troublesome peers. It would be reasonable to speculate that many of these youths were engaged in covert delinquent activities that would be revealed through self-reports. They also found that the false-negatives engaged in less serious crimes than the true-positives. Data from a CYA study in process involving the identification of youth in an 8th-grade cohort who were later involved in delinquency indicated that 74% of the male false-positives were in the top quartile in self-reported delinquency (Jesness, 1983).

Continued research in this area may provide considerable reassurance to the effect that the so-called false-positives are not very false at all. And the broader the domain of variables included in the predictions, the more likely is this to be the case. After all, who would not support the notion the children who are abused, neglected or rejected, who are falling behind in school, who may have congenital defects, who annoy and bully others, who are having problems with their parents, who feel little attachment to others, and so forth, are not all in need of attention? Somehow the term false-positive just doesn't seem to ring true as a very appropriate term as more of these risk factors are shown as present in a given individual.

Conclusion

It is my impression that while our predictions are not perfect, they are sufficiently accurate to be taken seriously and used in practice. The actuarily oriented caseworker who turned down the wealthy oilman's proposition was, unfortunately, probably correct in doing so. He or she, in going with the odds, likely saved himself or herself from having to pay back the $300,000. So what would have happened to the more optimistic treatment-oriented caseworker who took the case? Can we ask what the probabilities would be of his or her being successful? We can ask, but unfortunately, few answers will be forthcoming—we simply do not have the data available to provide the answer. I have seen no probability tables that present the odds for positive treatment outcomes given certain conditions. We do know that we can predict with a fairly high degree of certainty that this youth will continue his delinquency. Fortunately for the caseworker and the boy, the word is "fairly" certain not "very" certain.

Maybe it is better that way. I don't mean to say that we should not continue our efforts to improve the accuracy of our predictions; I am suggesting that we may hope that these efforts never prove to be extremely accurate unless dimensions of treatment/intervention are heavily weighted in the formulas. After all, the youths involved in these studies were not growing and developing in a vacuum. Changes were happening to them internally and externally. In all these studies modest efforts were being made with the youths to alter the course of their careers by members of their families, by probation staff, persons in private agencies, school teachers, and in some cases by the youths themselves. It would be a little frightening if the predictions had shown that antisocial behavior was even more stable and predictable and thus perhaps more immutable than it has already been shown to be.

References

Alfaro, J. D. (1981). Report on the relationship between child abuse and neglect and later socially deviant behavior. In R. J. Hunner & Y. E. Walker (Eds.), *Exploring the relationship between child abuse and delinquency* (pp. 175-219). Montclair, NJ: Allanheld, Osmun.

Carr, A. (1977). *Some preliminary findings on the association between child maltreatment and juvenile misconduct in eight New York counties.* A report to the Administration for Children, Youth, and Families: National Center on Child Abuse and Neglect.

Carr, A. (1978). *Refinements on the relationships between being reported as a maltreated child and later being reported as a juvenile offender.* Prepared as part of a final report: National Center on Child Abuse and Neglect.

Elliott, D. S., Dunford, F. W., & Huizinga, D. (1983, June). *The identification and prediction of career offenders utilizing self-reported and official data.* Paper pre-

158   Carl F. Jesness

sented at the Vermont Conference on the Primary Prevention of Psychopathology.

Glueck, S., & Glueck, E. (1950). *Unraveling juvenile delinquency.* Cambridge, MA: Harvard University Press.

Haapanen, R. A., & Jesness, C. F. (1982). *Early identification of the chronic offender.* Sacramento: California Department of the Youth Authority, 1982.

Herrenkahl, R. C., Herrenkahl, E. C., & Egolf, B. P. (1983). Circumstances surrounding the occurrence of child maltreatment. *Journal of Consulting and Clinical Psychology, 51,* 424-431.

Hindelang, M. J., Hirschi, T., & Weis, J. G. (1979). Correlates of delinquency: The illusion of discrepancy between self-report and official measures. *American Sociological Review, 44,* 995-1014.

Jesness, C. F. (1983). *Prediction of delinquency in an 8th grade cohort.* Unpublished raw data.

Jesness, C. F., & Wedge, R. F. (1983). *Classifying offenders: The Jesness inventory classification system.* Sacramento: California Youth Authority.

Lane, T. W., & Davis, G. E. (1983, June). *The relationship between child maltreatment and subsequent juvenile delinquency: Implications for the prevention of adolescent delinquent behavior.* Paper presented at the Vermont Conference on the Primary Prevention of Psychopathology.

Loeber, R. (1982). The stability of antisocial and delinquent child behavior: A review. *Child Development, 53,* 1431-1446.

Loeber, R., & Dishion, T. J. (in press). Early predictors of male delinquency: A review. *Psychological Bulletin.*

Loeber, R., & Dishion, T. J. (1983, June). *Antisocial and delinquent youths: Methods for their early identification.* Paper presented at the Vermont Conference on the Primary Prevention of Psychopathology.

McNemar, Q. (1969). *Psychological Statistics (4th ed.).* New York: John Wiley.

Patterson, G. T. (1980). Children who steal. In T. Hirschi & M. Gottfredson (Eds.), *Understanding crime.* Beverly Hills, CA: Sage.

Robins, L. N. (1966). *Deviant children grow up.* Baltimore: Williams and Wilkins.

Spivack, G., & Cianci, N. (1983 June). *High risk early behavior pattern and later delinquency.* Paper presented at the Vermont Conference on the Primary Prevention of Psychopathology.

Wedge, R. F. (1981, June). *Delinquency in a Sacramento birth cohort.* Sacramento: California Youth Authority.

Werner, E. E. (1983, June). *Vulnerability and resiliency in children at risk for delinquency: A longitudinal study from birth to young adulthood.* Paper presented at the Vermont Conference on the Primary Prevention of Psychopathology.

West, D. J. (1982). *Delinquency: its roots, careers and prospects.* Cambridge, MA: Harvard University Press.

Wolfgang, M. E., Figlio, R. M., & Sellin, T. (1972). *Delinquency in a birth cohort.* Chicago: University of Chicago Press.

PART III

Intervention Programs to Prevent Delinquent Behavior

7
Child Abuse Prevention
with At-Risk Parents
and Children

David A. Wolfe

Within the last decade it has become possible to define groups of children at risk of developing criminal and antisocial behavior. A Senate Committee of the Canadian parliament set about to discover the commonalities among these groups of children in the late seventies, and the findings of the Committee confirm what has long been suspected:

> Your committee was forcibly struck by the degree to which the theme of violence breeds violence permeated the testimony of the witnesses we heard and the literature we studied. The violence may be emotional or physical, direct or indirect, or all of these—the risk of later violent criminal behavior will increase with the amount experienced in childhood (Standing Senate Committee on Health, Welfare, & Science, 1980, p. 54).

Methods and directions for early intervention in the prevention of antisocial behavior have become a major priority in both the U.S. and Canada. A consensus appears to be forming in favor of targeting family factors associated with distress and violence at a point in time where help would be most beneficial. No single experience in a child's early years is sufficient, in itself, to cause violent behavior, yet

Author's Note: Preparation of this chapter was facilitated by a research grant from the Medical Research Council of Canada (MA-7807).

research has recognized that the interaction of multiple key factors, especially conflict and violence, has the most harmful effect upon the child (Emery, 1982; Rutter, 1979). We need now to concentrate heavily upon those factors that may be amenable to change, well in advance of the first signs of child deviance.

One specific action highlighted by researchers and committees investigating the prevention of criminal behavior has been to teach parents the skills necessary to avoid violence in the home. This recommendation is based not only on sound empirical evidence, but also on the knowledge that we have current means at our disposal that could be very effective in helping parents in their critical role. This chapter will report on four years of program development involving the implementation of parenting skills training with abusive parents. This population was chosen as the target of intervention primarily due to the strong correlational relationship between the major factors associated with physical abuse (e.g., negative family interactions; unrealistic expectations) and later child developmental and behavioral problems (Toro, 1982). Furthermore, we assumed from the start that parents could modify their child management strategies if provided with careful training and feedback, and therefore we chose to extend the available behavioral parent training procedures to this very crucial concern. In this manner, we are attempting to demonstrate that the availability of individualized parent education/ training for families in need will have a significant impact upon the later emergence of prosocial behavior in high-risk children. Three treatment outcome studies with child abusers are reviewed as background to our current early intervention program. This ongoing research program began by investigating parent training skills with child abusers, and has recently added a child competence component. The intention of the research, however, has been to investigate systematically the efficacy of each new treatment procedure and therefore we have not yet arrived at a comprehensive or unitary solution to child abuse prevention.

The Relationship Between Child Abuse and Delinquent Behavior

Links between severe punishment and later child behavior problems have been proposed by researchers in many different fields of human service (Maurer, 1974; Welsh, 1976), and child abuse in particular appears to be a highly relevant issue in the prevention of future deliquency (Hunner & Walker, 1981). Although longitudinal, prospective studies of abused children are very rare, confirmatory evidence for this abuse-delinquency relationship has appeared from a number of sources and methodologies, leading to strong concerns regarding shared causes.

In studies of abused children, aggressive behavior appears at an early and disproportionate level. In a study of 56 physically abused and 56 neglected first graders in foster homes, Timberlake (1981) investigated the relationship between overt expression of aggression and six predictor variables. As predicted, being a victim of physical abuse accounted for the highest proportion of variance (34%) in aggressive behavior among the children. Similarly, George and Main (1979) observed the interactions of abused and nonabused preschool children and their caregivers, and reported that abused children were more likely to assault or threaten their own caregivers than nonabused children. It appears that aggressive social interactions are more common, even at a young age, among children who have been victims of violence, which may be the precursors to later delinquent behavior (Emery, 1982).

Bentley (1981) reviewed the salient literature on juvenile delinquency, cross-cultural child rearing, and child abuse, and consolidated many of the prevalent features of abuse and delinquency. The variables most commonly associated with these two areas were combined under the labels "high aggression level" (e.g., severe parental discipline, abuse, marital discord) and "atypical family structure" (e.g., family disruption, younger parents, large families, single-parent households). Thus the author stresses that the major contributing and associated factors in both abuse and delinquency are highly related and, ipso facto, these similarities imply common etiological processes that warrant the attention of early intervention programs.

Until very recently, nearly all of the research on the consequences of child abuse had been limited to short-term effects, prohibiting a clear understanding of childhood trauma and its aftermath. To increase their knowledge base, The New York State Select Committee on Child Abuse (Alfaro, 1981) undertook an empirical study based on the official records of child protective agencies and courts during the period between 1950 to 1972 among eight counties in New York State.

One large sample (N = 5,136) of children was examined to determine which direction they went after their contact with the child protective services system, while a second sample (N = 1,963) was examined to see from which direction they had come before their contact with the juvenile justice system. The findings of the study confirmed an empirical relationship between child abuse and juvenile delinquency or ungovernability, and revealed the astounding significance of family violence in the perpetuation of antisocial behavior. For example, as many as 50% of the families reported for abuse or neglect (averaged over eight counties) had at least one child who was later taken to court as delinquent or ungovernable. Furthermore, delinquent children who were reported as abused or neglected tended to be more violent than other delinquents, according to the nature of their court offenses. This monumental effort, of which only a small part is summarized here, concluded that child maltreatment and juvenile misconduct are products of a common family environment, and strongly urged noninstitutional remedies, beyond supervision and child placement, to the recognized needs of these families far in advance of court and agency involvement.

This brief review of the relationship between abuse and delinquency highlights the critical importance of early intervention with families at risk. An integral part of prevention of antisocial behavior in youth should include efforts to reduce physical violence and abuse among family members. We can now turn to those factors associated with child abuse that may respond to our early intervention efforts.

Behavioral Intervention with Abusive Parents

In deciding on a practical and valuable intervention strategy with abusive parents, behavioral researchers have focused their efforts primarily on aspects of the parents' child-rearing and problem-solving abilities. Although child abuse is clearly a multiply determined event, common characteristics that may be amenable to treatment have been delineated. These include: knowledge of child development, child management skills, appropriate parental models and supports, and stress management (Friedman, Sandler, Hernandez, & Wolfe, 1981; Vasta, 1982). There is no consensus in deciding upon the highest priority for these families (Helfer, 1982), since these factors are clearly interactive and potentiate one another.

However, it is advantageous for intervention purposes to consider all methods that strengthen parental coping abilities (Wolfe, 1985). In light of these concerns, we have chosen to direct our research toward the dimensions of parenting to determine, first, will abusive parents learn and perform more acceptable child-rearing methods, and second, do these new methods lead to sustained improvements in the child's behavior and/or development? The goals and objectives of a prevention-oriented approach to child abuse, therefore, can be formulated on the theoretical assumption that abuse is a learned behavior and may be prevented if appropriate learning opportunities are available. These goals include (Wolfe, 1985): (1) the development of positive child-rearing habits through successful and nonaversive parent/child interactions at an early stage; (2) improvement in the parents' ability to cope with stress; and (3) the development of the child's adaptive behaviors that will contribute to their overall adjustment.

Changes in Parental Behaviors Following Training

The first three studies to be discussed were conducted to address the question of whether abusive parents would benefit from intensive individual training in behavioral parenting skills. The rationale for selecting a structured, hands-on training format that deals almost exclusively with managing/teaching children has been outlined elsewhere (Friedman et al., 1981; Wolfe, Kaufman, Aragona, & Sandler, 1981). In recognition of the contributing causes of abuse that may be only minimally related to the child (e.g., poverty, isolation, marital distress), the parents in these early studies were selected primarily on the basis of child management problems. However, these parents also suffered from multiple stress factors and disadvantage, and as such are viewed as representative of the large majority of abusive parents (e.g., Kempe & Helfer, 1972).

These studies employed both instructional and direct training components, in accordance with behavioral parent training developed by Forehai and McMahon (1981), Patterson, Reid, Jones, and Conger (1975), Wahler (1976), and others. Most training was conducted in the home, with weekly clinic meetings or rehearsals. Parent/child interactions were recorded in the home and clinic, and target behaviors were selected individually for each family. In all cases, parent behaviors were identified that were correlates and antecedents of abuse that could be observed and modified. Instruments to assess the parents' perceptions of their childrens' behavior problems were commonly employed, in addition to screening measures to determine the appropriateness and saliency of parent training intervention (e.g., Agency Referral Questionnaire, Wolfe et al., 1981).

Study One. The study by Wolfe and Sandler (1981) was designed to investigate the efficacy of parent training when combined with a delineated reward system to increase desirable parental behaviors. Subjects in this study were three family units, referred to treatment following investigation of child abuse. Observations in the home were conducted to establish the patterns of aversive parent/child interactions. Graphical data (Figure 1) indicated that Total Aversive Behavior (TAB) across the three families during baseline revealed three distinct interaction patterns: the child in F-1 was extemely aversive and his mother exhibited a moderate rate of aversive behavior. In F-2, both the parent and child exhibited high rates of aversive interactions during baseline, and in F-3, the parent was aversive and the child displayed very little deviant behavior. The components of intervention (parent training and contingency contracting) were introduced individually and then combined in accordance with a two-variable withdrawal design. As shown in Figure 1, rates of parental aversive behavior dropped significantly for all three families once intervention was begun. Although no functional relationship between treatment mode and TAB rate was demonstrated, positive changes were attributed to the combined effect of both treatment components. Changes in child aversive behavior also were evidenced during treatment, and three- eight- and twelve-month follow-up observations revealed that desired improvements in parent and child behaviors were maintained across time. We concluded from this exploratory treatment study that "parents seemed eager to try something different with their children. However, they approached each new technique with caution and skepticism, and needed constant reassurance and encouragement to continue rehearsing the method" (p. 332).

Study Two. In a study by Wolfe et al. (1982), an extremely abusive parent was taught to control her hostile physical and verbal responses to her two retarded 9-year-old boys and 2-year-old daughter. Through home and clinic observation, the investigators focused on parent/child interactions while engaged in compliance and cooperative tasks, and measured both hostile parental prompts and positive

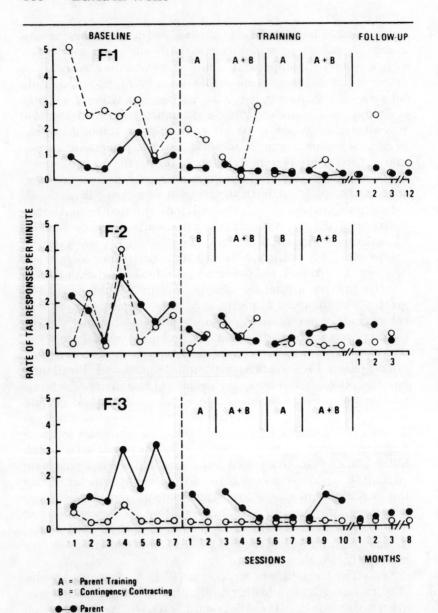

SOURCE: From D. A. Wolfe and J. Sandler, "Training abusive parents in effective child management," **Behavior Modification**, 5(3): 320-335, July 1981, © 1981 by Sage Publications, Inc. Reprinted by permission.

Figure 7.1 Rate Per Minute of Total Aversive Behavior for the Target Parent and Target Child

parental prompts. The study focused upon the evaluation of a direct parent training procedure (bug-in-the-ear) for modifying abuse-related behaviors and employed a multiple-baseline design across targeted parental behaviors. The results of this study are presented in Figure 2. As indicated, baseline interactions were characterized by high-frequency hostile physical and verbal behavior directed toward the children, whereas the parent seldom made positive verbal or physical gestures towards the children. When bug-in-the-ear parent training was initiated, there was an immediate reduction in both hostile physical and verbal behavior that was maintained throughout treatment and follow-up. Similarly, training in both positive verbal and physical behaviors produced increases in these categories. Desired changes in the mother's behavior were consistent across both the clinic and home settings and were maintained following withdrawal of the training procedure and at two month follow-up. This study offered further support for the use of structured parent training to reduce parent/child conflict that might escalate toward abuse by providing the parent with clear alternatives to corporal punishment. Although this single parent experienced a high level of stress due to economic disadvantage and extremely difficult child behavior, she was successful at modifying her physically abusive and overly critical methods of controlling her children. She expressed relief at being able to exercise more control over the children's negative behavior without becoming upset, and she began to spend a larger amount of time engaged in positive activities with them. Such individually based training involving simple instructions, modeling, rehearsal, and feedback was viewed, therefore, as an important component in the delivery of services to this family, in recognition of multiple stress factors that can interfere with or reduce parent effectiveness.

Study Three. In conjunction with these and similar small-N studies (Denicola & Sandler, 1980; Sandler, Van Dercar, & Milhoan, 1978), an effort was made to expand the evaluation of the program to a group design involving more parents, more evaluation criteria, and greater control of the effectiveness of intervention. In a study by Wolfe, Sandler, and Kaufman (1981), abusive parents were assigned to treatment and control conditions to compare the effects of parent training with a control group who received only the standard services provided by the child welfare agency. Sixteen abusive parents from a local child welfare agency participated in the study. We found that training in child management skills, delivered both in a group format

168   David A. Wolfe

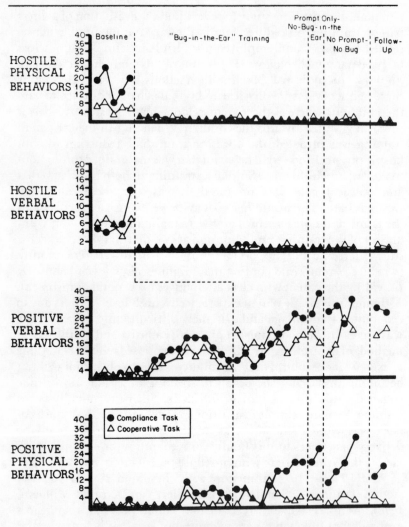

INTERACTION TRIALS

SOURCE: From D. A. Wolfe, J. St. Lawrence, K. Graves, K. Brehony, D. Bradlyn, and J. A. Kelly, "Intensive behavioral parent training for a child abusive mother," **Behavior Therapy.** 13: 438-451. © 1982 by the Association for Advancement of Behavior Therapy. Reprinted by permission.

NOTE: Frequencies per 10-minute sample of parent hostile physical and verbal behaviors (top 2 graphs) and parent positive verbal and physical behaviors (bottom 2 graphs) during compliance task and cooperative task are shown.

Figure 7.2 Clinic Observations of Parent Target Behaviors Across Experimental Conditions

and through competency-based training in the home, resulted in improvements in parent effectiveness. Group sessions focused primarily on general principles of child-rearing and common parental frustrations, while training in the home was more individualized and directed specifically toward current parent/child problems and concerns (e.g., parental criticism, inappropriate punishment, and child noncompliance, disruptive behavior, and so on). Parents were involved an average of 8.9 group hours and 16 individual training hours at home. Evaluation measures focused on three interrelated outcome criteria: observations of parenting skills in the home, parental report of child behavior problems, and caseworker ratings of family problems. The treatment and control group means for these measures at pre- and posttreatment assessments are shown in Table 1.

A two-factor multivariate analysis of covariance revealed a significant posttreatment increase in the use of child management skills by parents in the treatment group in comparison to controls. At one-year follow-up of agency records and caseworker report, no suspected or reported child abuse had occurred among the families who completed the treatment program. The authors pointed out in the discussion of this study that "a major benefit of an educational training approach with abusive families may lie in its ability to provide critical structure and direction for case planning, which may disburden social agencies and allow for increased flexibility in meeting the needs of these families" (Wolfe et al., 1981, p. 639). The results of this group study expanded previous reports of the utility of structured individual training with abusive parents, especially in comparison with current services from child protection agencies.

Conclusions from Child Abuse Intervention Studies. The findings from these studies suggested that parents who had previously used extrapunitive and harmful child management approaches could learn appropriate skills with relative ease. Moreover, parents reported fewer child behavior problems during posttreatment and follow-up, presumably due to their improved child-rearing ability. In general, these parents were initially quite resistent to efforts directed at their own behavior, and we found that the focus upon child behavior problems allowed for structure, direction, and readiness for the initiation of treatment. In this manner, modifying several aspects of parental behavior toward their child was viewed by the parents as a means to an end that they more readily accepted. Rather than complaining of "interfering in their affairs with their child," the

TABLE 7.1
Treatment and Control Group Means for Child Management
Skills (PCIF), ECBI Child Behavior Problems,
and Frequencies, and Caseworker Ratings

Variable	Treatment Group (N = 8)	Control Group (N = 8)
Child Management Skills (PCIF)[a]		
Pre	17.6	19.8
Post	91.1	14.8
Adjusted post[b]	84.8	21.1
Number of Child Behavior Problems (Problem Score)		
Pre	11.6	24.1
Post	1.8	22.4
Adjusted post[b]	7.2	17.0
Summed Frequency of Problem Occurrences (Intensity Score)		
Pre	130.0	184.0
Post	83.0	155.0
Adjusted post[b]	114.6	123.0
Caseworker Ratings of Family Treatment Needs[c]		
Pre	17.9	16.8
Post	7.0	17.0
Adjusted post[b]	7.5	16.4

SOURCE: Reprinted from D. Wolfe, J. Sandler, and K. Kaufman, A Competency Based Parent Training Program for Child Abusers. *Journal of Consulting and Clinical Psychology*, 1981, *49*, 633-641. Copyright 1981 by the American Psychological Association. Reprinted/Adapted by permission.
a. Percentage correct.
b. Regression of posttest on the pretest scores.
c. Range from 3 to 21; lower score indicates low treatment needs.

parents would respond to the new skills favorably once they realized the methods were not all that difficult or strange. We have cautioned, however, that these preliminary findings are far from conclusive since the generalizability of these gains (e.g., across time, families, behaviors, and so on) has not been thoroughly investigated.

A retrospective analysis of the referral characteristics and treatment outcome of 71 abusive families referred to our program over a three-year period was conducted to investigate the influence of demographic characteristics and court disposition upon parental participation and treatment benefit (Wolfe, Aragona, Kaufman, & Sandler, 1980). These analyses revealed that parents who were court-ordered to complete treatment as a requirement for full return of child custody were approximately five times more likely to complete treatment successfully than a family who was not required by the court to participate. Figure 3 indicates that 68% of the court-ordered referrals received a favorable disposition, whereas the majority of the nonordered families (59%) declined or withdrew from the program. Further analyses of 23 families who successfully completed the program revealed that the most salient factors related to success were age of the child (under age 5), court-ordered treatment, and two-parent families, although these conclusions are tentative and not predictive.

Based on these overall findings relating court-status to treatment outcome, we have suggested that a critical factor in the delivery of services to abusive families is the delineation of clear objectives that can be accomplished in a parent training program in order to avoid uncertain expectations and poor attendance. The use of family court or a contracting procedure to underscore to abusive parents the duration and nature of their expected involvement and behavioral changes was supported by these data. Furthermore, these studies supported the view that child abuse could be prevented by assisting parents in methods to handle difficult child behavior, rather than methods aimed at punishing the parent or dividing the family unnecessarily. Thus teaching abusive parents appropriate skills to deal with family problems provides a direction for intervention with this population that is concrete and problem-focused. Expansions of this approach into other areas affecting parenting may offer valuable assistance in limiting the short- and long-range consequences of family disturbance and violence.

Modifying Child Risk Factors Related to Abuse and Later Development

In a recent paper (Wolfe, 1985), I have outlined several of the major risk factors often associated with physical child abuse that may be amenable to early intervention. The abused child has been commonly described as abnormal on a number of significant behavioral-development dimensions (although I must caution that we do not know the direction of the effect, nor have researchers found consistent differences between abused and matched nonabused chil-

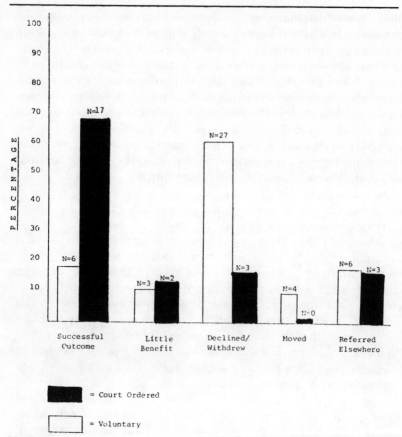

SOURCE: From D. Wolfe, J. Aragona, K. Kaufman, and J. Sandler, "The importance of adjudication in the treatment of child abusers: Some preliminary findings," **Child Abuse & Neglect**, 4: 127-135, 1980. © 1980 by Pergamon Press, Ltd. Reprinted by permission.

Figure 7.3 Dispositions of Court Ordered (n = 25) Versus Voluntary (n = 46) Child Abusers

dren—see Toro, 1982, for discussion). These include behavioral deficiencies such as poor speech and language abilities, slow cognitive development, and limited prosocial skills, and behavioral excesses such as aggression, unmanageability, hyperactivity, and poor self-control. These findings are not surprising, in view of the strong association reported between child behavior problems/developmental delay and marital conflict (Emery, 1982; Porter & O'Leary,

1980), parental maladjustment (Johnson & Lobitz, 1974), and limited extrafamilial resources and activities (Wahler, 1980). In order to arrest the pathological process that these family variables appear to have upon the child's development (and the reciprocal influence of developmental deviation upon family functioning), intervention with abusive parents must include strategies to enhance the developmental and adaptive abilities of the child, in addition to the adaptive skills of the parent.

Family Conflict and Child Deviance

In an attempt to formulate early interventions goals for abused and high-risk children, we have conducted two exploratory studies of the adaptive abilities and behavior problems of children from violent homes. These will be reviewed briefly prior to a description of the Parent/Child Early Intervention Program.

Behavioral Comparisons of Children from Abusive and Distressed Families. This study (Wolfe & Mosk, 1983) was designed to assess the abused child's behavioral and social impairments in relation to other child clinical and nonclinical populations in order to guide intervention and prevention efforts for abusive families. To control for family disturbance, both target samples were obtained from a child welfare department that was involved with the families due to extensive family instability and dysfunction. In this manner the study could more closely determine whether the behavior of abused children is distinguishable on any dimension from behaviors shown by children from nonabusive, distressed families. Thirty-five physically abused and 36 nonabused children from a child welfare agency and 35 nonabused children from the local community served as subjects. Specific criteria for inclusion in the study and group assignment of agency children were employed in order to obtain two samples of children from dysfunctional families who were distinguished primarily by degrees of physically aggressive child-rearing methods prevailing in the home.

Based on analyses of checklist symptoms and competencies completed by parents (Child Behavior Checklist; Achenbach & Edelbrock, 1982), we found that both the abused and nonabused children at the agency obtained significantly lower social competence scores than normals. Similarly, the two groups of children from the agency displayed higher rates of disruptive and deficient behavior than normals, but they did not differ from each other on any behavior problem dimension (see Table 2). These results were interpreted to indicate that abused children display a significantly greater number of behavior problems and fewer social competencies than normals. However, the comparison of the behavior patterns of abused children to children from distressed families revealed a strong similarity in the wide range of behavior problems displayed by the two groups. These conclusions support the hypothesis (e.g., Emery, 1982) that disturbances in the child's social and behavioral development may be more a function of family events and interaction patterns than isolated abusive episodes, and aversive elements besides physical aggression may be operative. The school-aged child, moreover, may be displaying behavior patterns that are adaptive when viewed in the context of family disturbance. Such patterns may pose difficulty for intervention programs unless the parents are assisted directly in their efforts to enforce rules and to encourage positive child behaviors, since the child may resist such efforts initially. Once the parent and child have grown accustomed to interacting in an aversive manner, efforts to alter such patterns will require considerable structure and supervision.

The Effects of Exposure to Family Violence upon Children (Wolfe, Jaffe, Wilson, & Zak, 1985). Our research team has been gathering data on the behavioral strengths and weaknesses of school-aged children who live amongst violent marital partners since these children could be considered "passive victims" of abuse, and they share many of the family distress factors seen in child abusive homes. In accordance with our findings of the behavioral development of children from abusive and distressed families, we anticipated that children exposed to violence in the home (not direct victims) would display adjustment problems similar to these other populations.

Current evidence highlights the harmful contribution of marital violence toward interpersonal adjustment problems among school-aged children (Porter & O'Leary, 1980; Rosenbaum & O'Leary, 1981). The male child, in particular, may be learning through repeated exposure to adult violence and threats of violence that physical aggression is an acceptable and successful method of conflict resolution. The child is often shielded from an awareness of the negative consequences of aggression, such as physical harm, family instability, arrest, and so forth, by well intentioned persons who find it difficult to explain the true nature of the family problems.

TABLE 7.2
Group Means and Standard Deviations of Measures of
Child Social Competence and Behavior Problems

	Group					
	Abused Children		Nonabused Agency Children		Nonabused Children in the Community	
Measures	M	SD	M	SD	M	SD
Social Competence						
Activities	47.89	11.76	45.72	11.74	52.83	9.93
Social	39.29	14.90	35.47	13.01	53.29	11.06
School	34.54	15.97	31.33	15.69	50.66	15.50
Total Competence	38.77	12.30	36.08	9.91	51.60	9.95
Behavior Problems						
Somatic Complaints	62.51	9.12	64.72	9.06	60.89	8.46
Anxious/Obsessive[a]	66.57	10.82	69.36	9.30	60.69	11.20
Depressed/Withdrawn[b]	70.00	10.34	71.06	9.65	60.34	13.16
Hyperactive	70.26	10.28	71.36	10.14	57.83	11.63
Delinquent	70.89	8.68	72.53	9.12	58.31	4.45
Aggressive	69.43	12.16	72.44	10.52	55.71	9.81
Total Internalizing	67.86	11.26	69.03	9.14	59.40	12.42
Total Externalizing	70.11	11.96	73.19	10.59	55.37	10.58

NOTE: T-scores from the Achenbach Child Behavior Profile.
a. This factor is termed "Obsessive-Compulsive" for profiles of younger and older boys, and is termed "Schizoid-Obsessive" for younger girls.
b. This factor is termed "Depressed" for profiles of younger girls and boys, and is termed "Hostile-Withdrawn" for older boys.
Reprinted from D. Wolfe, and M. Mosk, "Behavioral comparisons of children from abusive and distressed families." *Journal of Consulting and Clinical Psychology* 51(5): 702-708, 1983. Copyright 1983 by the American Psychological Association. Reprinted by permission.

Moreover, the absence of alternative, appropriate problem-solving approaches available to the child in a violent home contributes further to the likelihood of the child developing maladaptive interpersonal skills that become increasingly problematic. The development of intervention and prevention approaches for children from maritally violent homes depends heavily upon additional research to determine the extensive and far-reaching impact upon the child's development.

Social scientists have only recently begun to explore the effects of family violence upon children, and the available findings are preliminary. As stated above, the child's adjustment is likely to be a multivariate function of significant family events and patterns, which includes the child's role as a passive or active recipient of violence. Therefore, we have attempted to relate significant family variables, such as number of separations, number of male figures, amount of exposure to violence, and so on, to the child's overall adjustment at home and at school. We were interested particularly in the potentiating effects of multiple stress factors upon children's adjustment, in a manner similar to that described by Rutter (1979) and Sandler and Block (1979). This information would provide more direction for early detection and early intervention programming for many children from violent and distressed families.

To measure the relationship between selected family variables and child adjustment we developed a comprehensive interview format to elicit specific information from the child's mother, and had the parent and teacher complete the Achenbach Child Behavior Checklist and Teacher's Child Behavior Checklist. Unfamiliar observers were sent to each child's school to conduct six separate observations of classroom and peer interaction using a broad spectrum observation format (Achenbach, Direct Observation Form). The children included in this study had been exposed to physical violence between parents ranging from 4 to 20 times in the past year. They had also been repeated victims of threats of violence, but had not been physically abused (according to mothers' description and official records). Children and mothers were contacted through community shelters for battered wives, and they had been exposed to conflict within the last two weeks.

Similar to the findings of Porter and O'Leary (1980), we are finding that boys exposed to family violence have rates of externalizing behaviors (as reported by the parent) two standard deviations above the norm for their age. At school, however, these boys are reported as showing internalizing or externalizing behaviors that place them only 1 standard deviation above the norm, suggesting that to a certain extent their behavior problems are limited primarily to the home setting (since it is doubtful that a systematic reporting bias is operative across all families). This tentative conclusion is supported by the direct observation data at school, which found these boys to exhibit very few behavior problems during the day.

Children who are passive victims of family violence and its concomitants may be equally at risk for severe adjustment problems as the physically abused child and represent another critical target population for early intervention efforts. Staff members at emergency shelters for women have indicated to us that these children are subjected to a great deal of family disruption in addition to witnessing spouse abuse. A survey of staff opinions related to children's adjustment following exposure to family violence concurred with early research findings that indicated a strong relationship between family distress (especially violence) and child behavior problems (Wolfe et al., 1985). What has not been systematically studied, however, are the reports from staff and clinical studies indicating that some children from violent homes appear to be resilient to such stress factors. More information is needed to determine what health-promoting factors may influence a child's ability to withstand adverse family conditions, and to validate the assumption (Rutter, 1979) that cumulative effects of stress may be more harmful to the child than relatively isolated yet severe events in the family.

Implications for Early Intervention with Children from Abusive Families

The available evidence indicates that children from abusive families exhibit adjustment problems and developmental impairments that are related to major family variables. However, no distinctive pattern of adjustment, such as excessive aggression, depression, or similar behavioral dimension, accurately describes the majority of these children; they appear to exhibit problems of adjustment that, in the aggregate, exceed the majority of children from nonviolent homes. This suggests that certain pathogenic factors prevalent among dysfunctional families may be equally as powerful as physical abuse itself, and we should not limit our focus only to the prevention of physical abuse without equal concern being directed toward the less visible yet critical adaptive abilities of both the parent and child.

In order to develop a successful prevention strategy for at-risk families, we need to consider the critical events that form the foundation of the parent/child relationship. The observable short- and long-term psychological consequences of family violence upon the child do not likely result solely from abuse itself, but rather from the chronic absence of emotional and behavioral supports for the child (Garbarino, 1980). This assumption is similar to the conclusions brought forth in a recent review by Emery (1982) of the psychological effects of parental conflict and separation upon the child. He proposes that children who have established strong, positive relationships with one or both parents are more likely to adjust favorably to family changes, despite the adversity of family events. The prevention of child abuse and its long-term consequences, therefore, should be at a minimum a twofold process involving the strengthening of parental competence and pleasurable experiences with their young child, as well as the enhancement of the child's adaptive abilities (see Wolfe, 1985, for discussion). This conclusion has formed the basis for our current early intervention program with at-risk parents and children.

Promoting Competence in Parents and Children At Risk for Abuse

This longitudinal study is investigating the preventative benefits of early intervention with parents who have insufficient and inappropriate child-rearing abilities. We are applying many of the methods explored in previous studies with abusive and nonabusive parents to a younger population of parents who are at risk of abuse, and attempting to improve the overall quality of the parent/child relationship at a very early stage. This approach is certainly not unique in its purpose or conceptual basis, although very few controlled investigations of such an approach have been reported (Helfer, 1982). Although behavioral intervention for abusive parents has produced initial promising findings (reviewed above), modifying parent/child interaction patterns that have been in operation for several years is a difficult and costly task. In contrast, parents with very young children appear to be more willing to accept direction with their child-rearing methods, and involvement of the courts to protect the child becomes less necessary. Since these young parents have different needs and liabilities than most abusive parents, the current program has incorporated several new training methods into the program. These include greater emphasis on qualitative aspects of the parent-child relationship, developmentally appropriate activities and skill-rehearsal tasks, and enhancement of adaptive functioning in the child.

Developmental Process of the Parent/Child Relationship

Before discussing our program design and initial findings, a developmental, interactive research model will be presented. This model forms the foundation of our goals and procedures in working with high-risk families. The model is based upon empirical findings as well as theoretical assumptions derived from the disciplines of developmental and clinical psychology, pediatrics, and sociology, and has been arranged in a sequential, overlapping format.

Prenatal Factors

Although most of our early intervention methods are aimed at the young child, critical prenatal factors associated with abuse and related parent/child disorders are considered to be precursors to current parent-child problems. Thus, the developmental process of the parent/child relationship must first consider important correlational findings which are suggestive of early differences that may be predictive of healthy and at risk relationships.

Several major prenatal factors include:

a. Intrauterine Care. It is widely acknowledged that serious disturbances in fetal growth and development and later behavioral disturbances of the newborn child can be affected by maternal nutrition, age, and viral and bacterial infections (Erickson, 1982), which are especially problematic among teen parents. These health factors, in addition to genetic endowment, may have a significant impact on the mother's and child's later abilities to establish strong ties.

b. Maternal Adjustment and Functioning. Although less clear, maternal attitudes and feelings regarding pregnancy are believed to affect complications during pregnancy, labor, and delivery. This is a grave concern among mothers who experience extreme stress or depression. In addition, mother's (and perhaps father's) use of drugs, alcohol, and cigarettes have been linked to infant prematurity, low birth weight, slowed development, and the "difficult child pattern" (Erickson, 1982).

c. Parent's preparation and supports related to childrearing. Prospective studies (e.g., Egeland, Breitenbucher, & Rosenberg, 1980) have reported that high life stress and change during pregnancy are linked to abuse and related problems especially among mothers who were anxious, unknowledgeable about children, and ill-prepared.

The addition of natural caregivers, family members, and similar support opportunities seems to mitigate the effects of life stress and personal adaptation to a significant degree.

Postnatal Factors

During this developmental, interactive sequence we again see precursors to healthy versus high risk relationships. Infant caregiver attachment develops over time through interactional processes that may have a significant impact upon the quality of later patterns of care (Ainsworth, Blehar, Waters, and Wall, 1978). Children who were victims of abuse have been found to reveal more avoidant patterns than controls, which leads to further developmental decline. These patterns, in turn, have been linked to the quality of parenting rather than to the developmental status of the infant (e.g., prematurity, illness, etc.; Egeland and Sroufe, 1981), since parents who were poorly adjusted before the child's birth were more likely to have negative outcomes with their child somewhat unrelated to the child's birth status.

Conversely, the parent who is well-prepared for life changes associated with childrearing is less likely to succumb to the increasing stress factors that prevail. Skills, knowledge, experiences, and support that boost the individual's coping abilities will increase their resistance to forces which oppose their healthy adjustment. Some of these forces are inherent in the infants' early temperament and responsiveness, which may contribute in important ways to their own treatment.

Infancy and Early Childhood

Several of the critical factors related to prevention of child abuse at this stage include parental resources and responses to the child, and the child's opportunity and ability to develop adaptive behavior. Abusive parents have been found to be less involved and more passive with their infants than controls, especially in terms of intimacy, speech, and stimulation. Specific qualities of the parents' behavior which enhance the relationship include (Epstein, 1980): Verbal communication, freedom to explore, contingent and noncoercive responses to the infant's needs, and positive affect. Again, these are very similar to the factors reported by Werner (this volume) that discriminated delinquent from nondelinquent youth. It appears reasonable that deficiencies in these areas could be remediated through early intervention emphasizing skill-development and positive parent-child experiences.

Moreover, if these responses are age appropriate, peer supported, and otherwise successful for the parent at a very early point in the parental role, the risk of stress mediated aggression toward the child may be reduced. This is especially important for high risk parents who occasion aversive events on a daily basis (e.g., police, argument with family members, bill collectors) that interfere with their child-rearing abilities and impair the parent/child relationship (Wahler, 1980).

The child's own development at this stage becomes a significant preventative issue. Although we cannot determine whether atypical infant behavior patterns precipitate abuse or result from abuse, we are aware of the contributions of infant characteristics. The child's development of verbal and social abilities at a young age may foster continued favorable adult responses. For example, a child who does not express positive affect, moderate activity level, or age-appropriate language and social skills is more likely to receive diminished or negative attention from adults. Similarly, Patterson's (1982) research suggests that aggressive and disruptive children, even at a very young age, are at risk for increased punitive reactions from parents. Thus, infant cries, activity level, and responsiveness may significantly influence their care unless the parent is assisted in these efforts.

The culmination of this developmental process has been diagramed in Figure 4, where distinct health versus high risk outcomes are shown. This model implies not only the sequential, interactive nature of child abuse but underscores the major variables of significance to abuse prevention. Evidence of the initial effectiveness of this approach has recently emerged from the National Center for Child Abuse Prevention (Gray, 1983).

The Parent/Child Early Education Program Model

The translation of this developmental process into available intervention strategies is shown in Figure 5. These procedures stress the importance of intervention for the child as well as the parent, and the importance of supportive casework and community involvement. Although the actual training procedures employed are behaviorally based and empirically derived from other populations, it should be noted that several modifications have been made to adapt to the needs

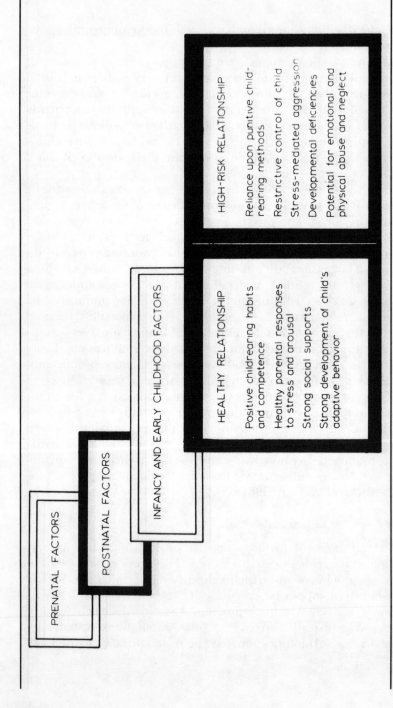

PRENATAL FACTORS

POSTNATAL FACTORS

INFANCY AND EARLY CHILDHOOD FACTORS

HEALTHY RELATIONSHIP

Positive childrearing habits
and competence

Healthy parental responses
to stress and arousal

Strong social supports

Strong development of child's
adaptive behavior

HIGH-RISK RELATIONSHIP

Reliance upon punitive child-
rearing methods

Restrictive control of child

Stress-mediated aggression

Developmental deficiencies

Potential for emotional and
physical abuse and neglect

Figure 7.4 The Developmental Process of the Parent-Child Relationship

PARENT/CHILD EARLY EDUCATION PROGRAM MODEL

Child Abuse Prevention With High-Risk Parents

EARLY INTERVENTION PROCEDURES
DURING INFANCY AND EARLY CHILDHOOD

PARENT

Behavioral Parent Training
Positive physical contact
Positive child experiences
Non-aversive control

Anger Control Training
Desensitization
Stress and anxiety management

CHILD

Parent-mediated Developmental
Stimulation
Language
Social interaction
Adaptive behaviors

Parent-mediated Training
of Prosocial Behaviors

Involvement in Nursery School
and Community Activities

ENVIRONMENT

Supportive Casework
Crisis relief
Family counseling

Peer Group Meetings

Figure 7.5   Early Intervention Procedures with High-Risk Families

183

of this population, such as a strong emphasis on positive physical contact and child experiences, the availability of self-control training involving child behaviors, and especially the importance of the parent's role in stimulating child development and prosocial behaviors, as opposed to alternative home care or professional treatment of the child.

The goal of the Parent/Child Early Education Program is to investigate the preventative benefits of early intervention procedures that emphasize qualitative and practical aspects of the parent-child relationship and the enhancement of child adaptive functioning. This program has been designed for young parents with less than five years of child-rearing experience who have been referred from the child protection agency following investigation of inadequate childcare. These parents can be generally described as single females in their late teens and early twenties who have completed one year of secondary education and exist on public support. Their children are infants or toddlers, who often show some decrement in their developmental progress (such as expressive or receptive language, social interaction, gross and fine motor abilities). Parents entering the program are assessed in terms of their current child management abilities through structured parent-child interactions, and measures of parental attitudes, personal adjustment, expectancies, and reported child-rearing problems are completed. The physical, cognitive, and behavioral development of each child is assessed by medical and psychological staff.

Parents receive training that involves positive reinforcement, ignoring, commands, and appropriate punishment in accordance with their needs and the developmental level of the child. In addition, therapists train parents to engage in daily activities with their child that serve to strengthen the child's areas of deficiency and to promote adaptive functioning. These activities include modeling and rehearsal of developmentally appropriate language abilities (e.g., eye contact, responding to simple sounds or phrases, producing sounds, and so on) and social interaction abilities (e.g., following directions, engaging in play with parent, expressing affection and needs). A criterion-based assessment and tracking system (Cone) provides the framework and guidance for training adaptive abilities with the parent and child. The purpose of training is to establish beneficial skills and positive experiences for both the parent and the young child, and therefore training continues until the parent has begun to employ the skills consistently and appropriately. Once these initial gains are apparent, therapist contact is reduced from twice a week to once every two weeks, and subsequently bimonthly follow-up sessions are begun for evaluative purposes.

The preliminary results of this early intervention program have been encouraging. The parents have been most receptive to a structured training approach that clearly demonstrates methods of eliciting desirable infant/toddler responses, and they spend more time engaging in positive, as opposed to disciplinary/restrictive, activities with their child. Following an average training period of two months, parents have shown improvements in critical child-rearing skills (e.g., direct commands, attention, praise) and report fewer child-rearing concerns and annoyances. Whereas the effectiveness of the program in developing adaptive abilities of the child must await longitudinal assessment, children appear to be responding to changes in their parent's behavior in terms of increased compliance and fewer undesirable behaviors following intervention (Wolfe, Edwards, Manion, & Koverola, 1986).

In sum, parents completing the program seem readily amenable to guidance and information concerning their parental role at this early point in time, and may be more capable of establishing positive experiences with their child than at any later date, despite multiple stress factors in their lives. Moreover, the young child's development can proceed with critical support and assistance from the parent, who is more attentive to the child's prosocial development and emotional needs.

Summary and Conclusions

Several studies focusing upon the treatment of abusive parents were presented that have led to considerable progress toward the prevention of child abuse. The available data suggest that a significant proportion of identified families can be assisted in altering abusive and coercive interaction patterns through the use of individualized skill-based training. These findings led to the development of early intervention procedures for high risk parents and children and the expansion of intervention techniques directed toward developmental competence in the child. We are optimistic that continued research efforts with this population will be successful in preventing disturbances in the developmental process of the parent/child relationship that have been linked to short- and long-term problems in the family.

In addition to favorable progress, however, these studies and experiences with abusive parents have uncovered very critical short-comings in service delivery and research directions that warrant continued investigation. Our efforts to modify patterns of coercive family interactions that have been in operation for several years were often rewarded with relatively small, yet important, gains in func-tioning, rather than major structural changes in family relations. Although a skill-based program was chosen as the most acceptable to parents, the most cost effective, and the most research supported with other populations, such an approach has limitations. Since child abuse is an extremely complex problem involving social as well as family factors, skill training with these families should be supple-mented by efforts to increase family social supports and life skills in areas beyond child management. The cumulation of minor life stresses, such as housing moves, transportation, health changes, and so forth, often contributed toward failure to complete training with some of our families, and we have launched new efforts directed at the understanding of these critical treatment interferences (Koverola, Elliot-Faust, and Wolfe, 1984). One of the few reliable discriminators of abusive and nonabusive families appears to be the presence of valuable social supports that may moderate the effects of environ-mental stress. Efforts to develop skill-based and supportive preven-tion programs will be required to assist parents in the acquisition and maintenance of social supports before a pattern of avoidance has been established (Kelly, 1983). Finally, the prevention of child abuse and the accompanying deterioration of family functioning will depend heavily upon increased involvement of fathers as well as mothers, greater community education efforts in addition to crisis intervention and alternative child care, and major national policy changes regarding family support and assistance in addition to child protec-tion laws and sanctions.

References

Achenbach, T. M., & Edelbrock, C. S. (1983). *Manual for the child behavior checklist and child behavior profile.* Burlington: University of Vermont.

Ainsworth, M.D.S., Blehar, M., Waters, E., & Wall, S. (1978). *Patterns of attachment: Observations in the strange situation at home.* Hillsdale, NJ: Lawrence.

Alfaro, J. D. (1981). Report on the relationship between child abuse and neglect and later socially deviant behavior. In R. J. Hunner & Y. E. Walker (Eds.), *Exploring the relationship between child abuse and delinquency.* Montclair, NJ: Allanheld, Osmun.

Bentley, R. J. (1981). Child abuse, cross-cultural childrearing practices and juvenile delinquency: A synthesis. In R. J. Hunner & Y. E. Walker (Eds.), *Exploring the relationship between child abuse and delinquency.* Montclair, NJ: Allanheld, Osmun.

Cone, J. (1984). *The pyramid scales: Criterion-referenced measures of adaptive behavior in handicapped persons.* Austin, TX: Pro-Ed.

Denicola, J., & Sandler, J. (1980). Training abusive parents in cognitive-behavioral techniques. *Behavior Therapy, 11,* 263-270.

Egeland, B., Breitenbucher, M., & Rosenberg, D. (1980). Prospective study of the significance of life stress in the etiology of child abuse. *Journal of Consulting and Clinical Psychology, 48,* 195-205.

Egeland, B., & Sroufe, L. A. (1981). Attachment and early maltreatment. *Child Development, 52,* 44-52.

Emery, R. E. (1982). Interparental conflict and the children of discord and divorce. *Psychological Bulletin, 82,* 310-330.

Epstein, A. S. (1980). *Assessing the child development information needed by adolescent parents with very young children* (Project report). Ypsilanti, MI: High/Scope Educational Research Foundation.

Erickson, M. T. (1982). *Child psychopathology* (2nd edition). Englewood Cliffs, NJ: Prentice-Hall.

Forehand, R. L., & McMahon, R. J. (1981). *Helping the noncompliant child: A clinician's guide to parent training.* New York: Guilford.

Friedman, R., Sandler, J., Hernandez, M., & Wolfe, D. (1981). Child abuse. In E. Mash & L. Terdal (Eds.), *Behavioral assessment of childhood disorders.* New York: Guilford.

Garbarino, J. (1980). Defining emotional maltreatment. The message is the meaning. *Journal of Pediatric Treatment and Evaluation, 2,* 105-110.

George, C., & Main, M. (1979). Social interactions of young abused children: Approach, avoidance, and aggression. *Child Development, 50,* 306-318.

Gray, E. (1983). What have we learned about preventing child abuse? Available from the author at the National Committee for Prevention of Child Abuse, 332 South Michigan Avenue, Chicago, Illinois 60604.

Helfer, R. E. (1982). A review of the literature on the prevention of child abuse and neglect. *Child Abuse and Neglect, 6,* 251-261.

Hunner, R. J., & Walker, Y. E. (Eds.). (1981). *Exploring the relationship between child abuse and delinquency.* Montclair, NJ: Allanheld, Osmun.

Johnson, S. M., & Lobitz, G. K.(1974). The personal and marital adjustment of parents as related to observed child deviance and parenting behaviors. *Journal of Abnormal Child Psychology, 2,* 193-207.

Kelly, J. A. (1983). *Treating child abusive families: Intervention based on skills training principles.* New York: Plenum Press.

Kempe, C. H., & Helfer, R. E. (1972). *Helping the battered child and his family.* Philadelphia: J. B. Lippincott.

Koverola, C., Elliot-Faust, D., & Wolfe, D. (1984). Clinical issues in the behavioral treatment of a child abusive mother experiencing multiple life stresses. *Journal of Clinical Child Psychology, 13,* 187-191.

Maurer, A. (1974). Corporal punishment. *American Psychologist, 29,* 614-426.

Patterson, G. R. (1982). *Coercive family process.* Eugene, OR: Castalia Publishing Company.

Patterson, G. R., Reid, J. B., Jones, R. R., & Conger, R. E. (1975). *A social learning approach to family intervention (Vol. 1).* Eugene, OR: Castalia.

Porter, B., & O'Leary, K. D. (1980). Marital discord and child behavior problems. *Journal of Abnormal Child Psychology, 8,* 287-295.

Rosenbaum, A., & O'Leary, K. D. (1981). Children: The unintended victims of marital violence. *American Journal of Orthopsychiatry, 51,* 692-699.

Rutter, M. (1979). Protective factors in children's responses to stress and disadvantage. In M. W. Kent & J. E. Rolf (Eds.), *Primary prevention of psychopathology. Volume III. Social competence in children.* Hanover, NH: University Press of New England.

Sandler, I., & Block, M. (1979). Life stress and maladaptation of children. *American Journal of Community Psychology, 7,* 425-450.

Sandler, J., Van Dercar, C., & Milhoan, M. (1978). Training child abusers in the use of positive reinforcement practices. *Behavior Research and Therapy, 16,* 169-175.

Standing Senate Committee on Health, Welfare and Science. (1980). *Child at risk.* Hull, Quebec: Minister of Supply & Services Canada.

Straus, M. A. (1979). Measuring intrafamily conflict and violence: The conflict tactics (CT) scales. *Journal of Marriage and the Family, 41,* 75-88.

Timberlake, E. M. (1981). Child abuse and externalized aggression: Preventing a delinquent life style. In R. J. Hunner & Y. B. Walker (Eds.), *Exploring the relationship between child abuse and delinquency.* Montclair, NJ: Allanheld, Osmun.

Toro, P. A. (1982). Developmental effects of child abuse: A review. *Child Abuse and Neglect, 6,* 423-431.

Vasta, R. (1982). Physical child abuse: A dual-component analysis. *Developmental Review, 2,* 125-149.

Wahler, R. (1976). Deviant child behavior within the family: Developmental speculations and behavior change strategies. In E. Mash, L. Hamerlynck, & L. Handy (Eds.), *Behavior modification and families.* New York: Brunner/Mazel.

Wahler, R. G. (1980). The insular mother: Her problems in parent-child treatment. *Journal of Applied Behavior Analysis, 13,* 207-219.

Welsh, R. S. (1976). Severe parental punishment and delinquency: A developmental theory. *Journal of Clinical Child Psychology, 5,* 17-21.

Wolfe, D. A. (1985). Parental competence and child abuse prevention. In R. J. McMahon & R. Peters (Eds.), *Childhood disorders: Behavioral-developmental approaches.* New York: Brunner/Mazel.

Wolfe, D. A., Aragona, J., Kaufman, K., & Sandler, J. (1980). The importance of adjudication in the treatment of child abusers: Some preliminary findings. *Child Abuse and Neglect, 4,* 127-135.

Wolfe, D. A., Edwards, B., Manion, I. G., & Koverola, C. (1976). *An evaluation of parent training and family support approaches to child abuse and neglect early intervention.* Manuscript submitted for publication.

Wolfe, D. A., Jaffe, P., Wilson, S., & Zak, L. (1985). Children of battered women: The relation of child behavior to family violence and maternal stress. *Journal of Consulting and Clinical Psychology, 53,* 657-665.

Wolfe, D. A., Kaufman, K., Aragona, J., & Sandler, J. (1981). *The child management program for abusive parents.* Winter Park, FL: Anna.

Wolfe, D. A., & Mosk, M. D. (1983). *Behavioral comparisons of children from abusive and distressed families.*

Wolfe, D. A., & Sandler, J. (1981). Training abusive parents in effective child management. *Behavior Modification, 5,* 320-335.

Wolfe, D. A., Sandler, J., & Kaufman, K. (1981). A competency-based parent training program for child abusers. *Journal of Consulting and Clinical Psychology, 49,* 633-640.

Wolfe, D. A., St. Lawrence, J., Graves, K., Brehony, K., Bradlyn, D., & Kelly, J. A. (1982). Intensive behavioral parent training for a child abusive mother. *Behavior Therapy, 13,* 438-451.

8

Stimulus Class Determinants of Mother-Child Coercive Interchanges in Multidistressed Families: Assessment and Intervention

Robert G. Wahler
Jean E. Dumas

It has become increasingly apparent that parent training will not always produce durable therapeutic changes in "high-risk" families marked by multiple social and material stressors. In particular, the use of this educational intervention with conduct problem children likely to become juvenile delinquents has been found wanting in families in which mothers suffer from social isolation, coercive entrapment with other adults, and socioeconomic disadvantage (see review by Griest & Forehand, 1982). Why this is so is unsettled (Dumas & Wahler, 1983a). Some investigators argue that multidistressed mothers may be deficient in those skills required to profit from any specific educational intervention (Salzinger, Kaplan, & Artemyeff, 1983). In essence, the skill deficiency argument implies a need for a much broader skill development than that typically seen in child management programs. Other investigators, focusing less on skills per se and more on the generalized use of these skills (Wahler & Graves, 1983), argue that multidistressed mothers live in environ-

Authors' Note: The data reported in this chapter were generated through research grant MH 18516 from the Crime and Delinquency Center of NIMH.

ments that prevent them from maintaining their child management skills and applying them across settings.

Upon close examination, the skill deficiency and skill generalization arguments can be seen to be two facets of the same position. If one assumes that a skill, such as direct statements of personal intent, is part of a mother's verbal repertoire, the validity of that assumption depends on maternal performance. However, one must also specify the environmental conditions under which that performance is to be observed. Few clinicians would be satisfied to see a despondent mother smile, make eye contact, and speak assertively within the confines of a clinic office. But, should these social skills become evident in the mother's home, at work, or in a recreation setting, the observing clinician is more apt to conclude: "I think she's got it." Thus meaningful judgments concerning the presence or absence of social skills always include a reference to the stimulus control of these skills (i.e., the environmental context in which the skills are expected to be performed).

Observational studies in parent training have documented the importance of stimulus control issues in the maternal skill deficiency problem. Green, Forehand, and McMahon (1979) compared the clinic playroom interactions of ten troubled mother-child pairs of dyads with ten nonproblem dyads. As suspected, the clinic-referred dyads produced a significantly greater number of aversive exchanges than did the control dyads. In the problem dyads the children were less compliant and their mothers were more demanding. But, when the clinicians then told the mothers to make their children "look" more obedient or more disobedient, both groups of dyads changed markedly. In making their children look good the mothers use more "question-like" commands as opposed to vague instructions, and used more reward-approval consequences for child compliance. Under these conditions, the two groups of mothers would have been considered equally skillful in child management. In a more pragmatic look at this issue, Wahler and Afton (1980) offered direct observational evidence that multidistressed mothers can learn the appropriate use of a time-out contingency, while reducing their child-directed aversive behaviors and maintaining their positive child interactions. This skill training package was associated with progressively shorter latencies between occurrences of child coercive behavior and mother use of time-out—a clearly desirable training outcome. As expected, the training results also showed reductions in the children's problem behaviors. However, in a follow-up phase these mothers, compared to another group of singularly distressed mothers, did not maintain their use of their newly acquired child management skills. In the same way, Griest, Forehand, Rogers, Breiner, Furey, and Williams (in press) demonstrated that mothers can acquire a set of parenting skills made up of the use of rewards, contingent attention to desirable child behavior, and clear instructions. Unfortunately, in follow-up these mothers reduced their use of the first two parenting skills, a reduction that was accompanied by a loss of therapeutic gains.

In referring to generalization as a crucial part of the skill deficiency question, the stimulus control issue merely describes that portion of the question. Put another way, we know from previously reviewed studies that an individual's performance of a particular social skill in one environmental context does not guarantee the transfer of that skill to other contexts. In order to explain this transfer problem, one might assume that multidistressed mothers do not generalize their child management skills because they have yet to attain the necessary learning experiences or because their natural environments are not conducive to skill generalization. While these two assumptions are not contradictory, they do point the interested clinician in somewhat different directions with respect to an expansion of parent training. If such training is to remediate an incomplete social-learning history (i.e., a deficit in learned social skills), the therapist would probably formulate a graded series of social skill experiences in a variety of different environments. On the other hand, if the remediation centers on interfering or competing stimulus factors in the mother's natural environment, the focus of training would be geared to attenuating such stimulus control. The key training consideration in these two remediation strategies concerns the behavioral skills the deficient mother is expected to acquire. In the former strategy, she would be expected to expand her repertoire of social skills, while in the latter she would be expected to develop her attentional tracking skills. In reference to the latter skills, one would be concerned about the mother's capability to specify those aspects of her environment that inhibit her desired performance.

While the social skill expansion strategy has received ample attention within the parent training literature (e.g., Kelley, Embry, & Baer, 1979; Martin & Twentyman, 1976; Mealiea, 1976), the systematic study of the attentional skills of multidistressed mothers has hardly begun. If these mothers fail to generalize their parent training benefits because their natural environments exert inhibitory stimulus control, it would obviously prove useful to pinpoint the sources of this control. Maternal attentional processes then become important indices of the stimulus patterns that reliably control a mother's day to day social behavior. Given that idiosyncratic stimulus patterns are identified, and their inhibitory functions demonstrated with respect to a mother's parenting behaviors, it might prove possible to attenuate the extent of that control without teaching the mother a broad array of new social skills. We turn to an examination of concepts and data that have some bearing on this possibility.

"Faulty" Stimulus Control: The Influence of Superstitious Reinforcement Contingencies

A troubled mother's attentional behavior is an important component of her social entrapment because recent findings suggest that the problem is not necessarily a *direct* function of reinforcement contingencies. From an operant viewpoint (the conceptual basis of parent training), a mother plays a role in a parent-child coercive interchange as long as her behavior remains under the reinforcement control of child, spouse, and other people who participate in this "pathological" social system. For example, a mother's aversive responses to her conduct problem child might be cued by her boyfriend's critical comments on her "wishy-washy" child management and her child's provocative nagging. In operant terms, it is assumed that this stimulus class (boyfriend criticism and child nagging) serves a discriminative function for her child-directed aversive responses (e.g., yell and hit). That is, when the mother responds by acting aversively, she is likely to receive a predictable stimulus consequence in the form of new child/boyfriend actions (e.g., the child might cry and the boyfriend praise her). The critical features of this 3-term sequential arrangement lie in its conditional probabilities. If the episode is understandable as an operant, then the probability of that stimulus consequence following mother aversive behavior will be different from that observed in other sequences (e.g., when the child nags but the boyfriend does not criticize). Thus if the mother acts aversively toward the child in the absence of this antecedent stimulus class, a different consequence (at least in terms of probability) ought to be evident.

Table 1 presents a hypothetical set of sequential arrangements as would be expected in a social system governed by operant principles of stimulus control. Sequence 1 should become a dependable facet of this coercive social system because the contingencies depicted are demonstrably different from the other sequential arrangement (sequence 2). While such system functioning does occur (see Patterson, 1976), it does not necessarily follow that it can be accounted for in strict operant terms. As stated above, recent findings suggest that a mother's coercive entrapment with her child may not necessarily be a *direct* function of observable reinforcement contingencies. For example, Wahler (1980) obtained correlational evidence pointing to the fact that aversive contact with extended family members and social service agents may accurately predict the level of aversive behaviors multidistressed mothers direct at their children. On days in which the mothers reported high proportions of social contacts with these adults, they were more likely to respond aversively to their conduct problem children. It is possible to consider that these predictors might serve a discriminative function since extended family members, helping agents, and child could have occasionally constituted a combined antecedent stimulus class for the mother. If so, the presence of this class might also predict some unique consequences for maternal aversive responses to the child. However, the fact that many of the mothers' contacts with these adults occurred outside the home setting and in the absence of the children leads us to wonder how a discriminative function could have been served in any consistent fashion.

Studies that have examined how accurately troubled mothers pay attention to the aversive behaviors of their conduct problem children are relevant to the discriminative stimulus issue just discussed. Griest, Wells, and Forehand (1979) considered the possibility that such mothers might be minimally responsive to their problem children as antecedent stimuli for their own behavior and maximally responsive to other stimulus sources of personal distress. In this study, maternal observational summary reports of child problem behavior were considered an index of maternal behavior directed at the child. The stimulus class used as a predictor of these summary reports was comprised of two variables: the child's behavior in the mother's presence (observed by professional observer) and a measure of maternal personal distress as obtained from the mother's self-report on a depression questionnaire. Results showed the maternal sum-

TABLE 8.1
Hypothetical Illustration of Discriminative Stimulus Control
of a Mother's Aversive Behavior Toward Her Child

	Antecedent Stimulus Class	Mother Response	Conditional Probability of Stimulus Consequence	
Sequence I:	Boyfriend criticizes and child nags	Aversive to child	Child cries	.50
			Boyfriend praises	.30
Sequence 2:	Child nags	Aversive to child	Child cries	.20
			Boyfriend praises	.00

mary reports were predicted by the distress component of this stimulus class *but not by the child behavior component*. In other words, the mothers' observations of their children appeared to be influenced by a class of stimuli broader than that produced by the children's immediate behaviors. These findings, along with those of Wahler (1980), pose an interesting question about the composition of such stimulus classes for troubled mothers. If extra-child stimuli are included in these classes, are they discriminative for these mothers' parenting style?

In asking this question we should consider a stimulus control process quite different from the reinforcement conception described in Table 1. Kantor (1959) has long argued that response-reinforcer relationships are often influenced by antecedent stimuli he called "setting events" (see Wahler & Dumas, in press). Although the operating principles of setting event control are not clearly understood, it is evident that such stimuli cannot be viewed simply as discriminative events. That is, the power of a setting event to influence behavior is not due to its prediction of reinforcement probabilities. For example, depriving an organism of food is a setting event that permits the prediction of food seeking reponses; the deprivation operation, however, does not predict the probability that such responses will be followed by food. Similarly, in reference to human behavior, there are documented examples of how stated rules and instructions can serve a setting event function. Fowler and Baer (1981) provided an especially clear demonstration of the process in a study of sharing behavior among preschoolers. First, the children's sharing with peers was brought under instructional control by making instructions to share discriminative for tangible reinforcement whenever sharing was observed to occur during an early free-play period. Next, the contingencies between instructions, sharing, and reinforcement were made ambiguous by delaying the reinforcement of sharing responses observed in this early period until the end of the school day. Following this step, the children showed marked increases in sharing during a late free-play period *even though these sharing responses were not contingently followed by reinforcers.* These latter sharing responses were under setting event control as opposed to discriminative stimulus control. The phenomenon proved to be durable across all experimental manipulation phases and provided a nice illustration of a puzzling process: Setting events can apparently induce functional connections between themselves and certain behavior-reinforcer relationships even though the observed connection between these events is random.

If we now return to the Wahler (1980) and Griest et al. (1979) studies of attentional processes in troubled mothers, it is tempting to consider that such maternal behaviors may be under setting event control. In other words, the extra-child or personal stimuli shown to predict a mother's aversive behavior toward her child and her observational reports about the child might bear only random (i.e., superstitious) relationships to the consequences of her behavior directed at the child. With multidistressed mothers this is tantamount to saying that their coercion problems with spouse, boyfriend, extended family members, and social service agents function as setting events within a stimulus class that also includes these mothers' problem children. The class can be considered "faulty" in the sense that their children represent the only discriminative components of the class as far as these mothers' parenting behavior is concerned. The other components influence their responses to their children, however, even though they are not contingently related to the consequences of these responses, this presumably through a stimulus control process best described as superstitious.

Attenuating Setting Event Control of
Mother-Child Coercion Traps

Based on the Griest et al. (1979) and Wahler (1980) studies, it seems likely that a multidistressed mother's adverse parenting behaviors are influenced by sources of distress beyond the child (e.g., her adult relationship problems). The first goal of the present investigation is to evaluate the nature of this influence process: Is it discriminative or superstitious? In other words, do the distress events bear some "rational" connection to the mother's child-rearing behaviors or is the connection adventitious and "irrational"? Given that superstitious stimulus control can be demonstrated, there would then be reason to suspect that such a mother's observational reports of her child's behavior play a key role in the control of her behavior. If a multidistressed mother *erroneously* reports her conduct problem child to be especially oppositional during a particular time period (Griest et al., 1979), she is also apt to act in ways that are consistent with this erroneous report (Wahler, 1980), that is, to provoke her child through coercive actions. Her child, who is behaving in a contingent fashion, ought to respond eventually in kind and, thus, provide her with superstitious reinforcers for her observational reports by increasing his or her level of aversiveness.

If the multidistressed mother's erroneous observational reports of child behavior are keystone factors in her coercive entrapment, improvements in her reporting accuracy ought to bolster her generalized use of skills acquired through parent training. But such improvements could not be achieved through simply teaching her to attend exclusively to her child's behavior. Wahler and Afton (1980) showed that, while such focused teaching was associated with the temporary use of parent training skills by all mothers, neither these skills nor the more accurate maternal observational reports generalized with multidistressed mothers. However, with singularly distressed mothers (mothers whose distress was restricted to their problem children) generalization was demonstrated for both reports and skills. Since the child directed actions of multidistressed mothers were presumably influenced by their adult relationship problems, the attentional tracking improvements produced by an intervention that focused exclusively on accurately reporting children's behaviors could not be expected to be maintained.

Another teaching strategy aimed at improving the accuracy of observational reports entails an expansion of the mother's report content to the point that *all* stimulus influences are reviewed. Suppose, for example, that a multidistressed mother's report about her child's "meanness" is erroneous because it is also influenced by her problems with a boyfriend. Instead of teaching the mother to focus her attention on her child's behavior only, this strategy would incorporate the boyfriend problem into her observational report of her child. Thus the report "child meanness" would come to summarize instances of boyfriend as well as child interchanges: "When I said that my child was mean today, I was also talking about my boyfriend being mean." Such a paradoxical report would be an accurate reflection of the stimulus class control of this mother's child-directed behavior. This teaching strategy, called "mand review" by Wahler and Dumas (in press), is intended to help a multidistressed mother review, that is, discriminate among, the many stimulus class determinants of her child observational report. Presumably, her ability to discriminate the full range of determining stimuli might lessen the influence of those stimuli that are only superstitiously related to her report. As an end product, the multidistressed mother might then demonstrate a generalized use of the child management skills she acquired in the course of parent training.

In summary, the present investigation addressed two research issues: First, it examines the stimulus class determinants of coercive interchanges between multidistressed mothers and their conduct problem children. Both child-produced stimuli and those emanating from these mothers' adult relationship problems constitute the stimulus class under scrutiny. It is expected that some of these stimuli will prove to be discriminative for the mothers' adverse parenting actions while others will better fit a superstitious or setting event function. Second, it provides pilot data about a new form of clinical intervention ("mand review") aimed at alleviating mother-child coercive entrapments. In a first phase, this intervention entails teaching multidistressed mothers traditional child management skills (i.e., parent training). In a second phase, the teaching efforts are aimed at an expansion of these mothers' observational summary reports about their children's problem behaviors. This expansion is governed by the stimulus class determinants obtained in the first phase of this intervention. It is expected that this expansion process will be associated with a reduction in the superstitious stimulus class control of these mothers' parenting actions.

Study I

Before attempting to address the issues raised above, we felt it necessary to further document the influence of mother-adult coercive interchanges on a mother's aversive behaviors directed at her child. While this influence process was described in Wahler (1980), all of the mothers studied in this sample were multidistressed. Thus a comparison group of singularly distressed mothers had not been evaluated. The data reported by Wahler and Afton (1980) would have permitted such a comparison between singularly and multiply distressed families. However, since the focus of that study was on parent training outcomes and on the quality of mother summary reports, such a comparison was not made.

Study 1 presents new analyses of the Wahler and Afton (1980) data. These data are composed of two sets of measures: home observations of mother-child interactions and maternal self-reports of adult community contacts in the 24-hour period immediately preceding each home observation (see Study II for a description of the instruments used to obtain these measures). On the basis of this second measure, the home observations were divided into two sets: those preceded by mother reports of a majority (80% or more) of aversive adult contacts, and those preceded by mother reports of a majority (80% or more) of positive adult contacts.

Table 2 presents the mean percentage occurrences (baserate probabilities) of aversive behaviors mothers directed at their children during the two sets of home observations. These probabilities are presented separately for multidistressed and singularly distressed mothers over the three study phases. Wahler and Afton had found that the mean levels of mother aversive behavior were significantly higher for the multidistressed mothers during the baseline and follow-up phases. An examination of these phases in Table 2 also shows that multidistressed mothers exhibited significantly higher levels of aversiveness on days in which they reported 80% of their adult contacts to have been aversive. The singularly distressed mothers, on the other hand, showed no significant tendency to respond differentially over the two sets of observations. As expected, these mothers reported fewer days marked by highly aversive adult contact and many more marked by highly positive adult contact.

The singularly distressed mothers in Wahler and Afton were middle-class, self-referred clients whose psychological concerns centered on their conduct problem children. Parent training not only appeared to help them improve their child relationship problems, Wahler and Afton also discovered that their summary reports about their children (expressed during clinic discussions between therapist and mother) changed during the parent training phase. The mothers used more specific examples of problem interchanges and became less

TABLE 8.2
Baserate Probability Measures of Mother Aversive Behavior
During Observations Preceded by Aversive or Positive
Maternal Community Contacts

Mothers	Mand Review Only	Parent Training and Mand Review	Mand Review Only
Observations preceded by aversive maternal community contacts			
Multidistressed	┌.079 (21)	┌.019 (18)	┌.082 (22
	*	*	*
Singularly distressed	.026 ┐ (8)	.009 ┐ (7)	.002 ┐ (9)
Observations preceded by positive maternal community contacts	N.S.	N.S.	N.S.
Multidistressed	└.041 (6)	└.009 (7)	└.046 (8)
Singularly distressed	.020 ┘ (30)	.006 ┘ (28)	.001 ┘ (26)

NOTE: The number of observations on which these measures are based are in parentheses. Mothers are classified as multidistressed (N = 8) and singular distressed (N = 7).
Their child directed aversive behavior is shown for each phase of a study reported by
Wahler and Afton (1980).
*p < .05; N.S. = No statistically significant difference.

likely to attribute blame to their children as training progressed. In
comparison, the multidistressed mothers were socioeconomically
disadvantaged clients who had been required by social agencies to
seek treatment for their conduct problem children. While these
mothers' psychological concerns did include their children, they also
voiced considerable distress about their relationships with spouses,
boyfriends, extended family members, and social service agents. In
these families, parent training produced only temporary changes in
the mothers' child relationship problems and *no* changes over study
phases in their summary reports expressed during the clinic discussions. In effect, when the mothers were encouraged by their therapists

to describe their child relationship problems, they continued to use global examples in which they generally attributed blame to the children.

It is important to point out a procedural aspect of the clinic discussion sessions reported by Wahler and Afton. These sessions marked the initial development of a means of helping multidistressed mothers improve the accuracy of their observational summary reports ("mand review"). At that stage of development, the change strategy used by a therapist was primarily reflective, in that the therapist simply restated a mother's descriptions or encouraged her to provide further descriptions of specific coercive incidents. The more active shaping of maternal reports into expanded summaries of coercion (described in the introduction) was not part of the initial procedure. The procedural point of interest concerns an apparent lack of impact of these early discussions on the levels of maternal aversive behavior depicted in Table 2. While the reflective, friendship style conversations occurred on a weekly basis in all phases of the study, there is no evidence that these experiences affected the mean levels of maternal aversiveness directed at the child or lessened the differential influence that adult contact exercised on this aversiveness. Parent training, however, did appear to have a positive, though temporary, impact on both facets of mother aversive behavior in these multidistressed families.

With Study I as a reference point for later comparison, we now turn to an examination of the issues raised in the introduction.

Study II

Method

Design

Six mother-child pairs of dyads took part in home-based assessments and clinical interventions over a period of 4 to 6 months. An ABAC experimental design specified that all mothers began the mand review intervention at the beginning of the study (A, 3 weeks), then started the parent training intervention while continuing mand review (B, 4 weeks), and third returned to mand review as the only intervention (A, 7 weeks). In this fashion, the impact of mand review as a maintenance supplement to parent training could be evaluated, bearing in mind the poor maintenance findings for multidistressed mothers reported in Table 2. Finally, a no intervention follow-up phase (C, approximately 4 months) was added to evaluate the natural environment maintenance of any intervention changes. The stimulus control issue was examined by comparing the probabilities that mothers would behave aversively toward their children given several different aversive or nonaversive antecedents. These probabilities were compared within two separate time frames: an "early" frame, comprised of the first 7 weeks of intervention, and a "late" frame comprised of the last 7 weeks of intervention. The logic of this design centered on the predicted impact of mand review on child and adult stimulus control of the mothers' child directed behaviors. This was done because we have found the summary report expansion required in mand review to be a fairly slow process with multidistressed mothers (Wahler and Dumas, in press) and, therefore, expected any impact of this expansion on such stimulus control not to appear until well into the review process.

Subjects

All six families were referred for clinical intervention because one child in each family had been designated as a conduct problem. In all six cases, the referral was "forced" by a social service agency following abuse/neglect charges brought against the parents. The mothers ranged in age from 24 to 42 years (mean age = 30). Only one mother had completed high school and two were married. Family incomes averaged $5,400 per year and number of siblings averaged two. The children ranged in age from 4 to 12 years (mean age = 7.75 years). Five of them were boys.

The children's referral problems included noncompliance with parental instructions (six children), physical assault (five children—severity ranged from fist fights and use of dangerous objects to sexual molestation and killing another person), property destruction (six children), stealing (six children), and drug use (two children).

All six of the mothers reported financial hardship and severe adult harassment. The latter included physical beatings by spouse or boyfriend (five mothers), and verbal threats and arguments several times weekly with extended family members, spouse or boyfriend, social service agents, and neighbors (six mothers). Four of the mothers had significant physical problems (Lupus, cancer, heart dysfunctions) and all six described themselves as experiencing frequent depression and anger.

Table 3 summarizes the mothers' self reported social contacts with adults outside their immediate family over the first 3 weeks of the study. Their pattern of social contacts is very similar to that of a much larger group of multidistressed mothers studied by Dumas and Wahler (1983b). These data were obtained with the help of the Community Interaction Checklist described below.

Measurement Procedures

Home observations. Following an initial interview, all mother-child dyads were observed twice weekly in their homes over the three clinical intervention phases and once weekly during the follow-up phase. Observation sessions were chosen by the mother as times of the day when interaction problems were most likely to occur in the home setting. All observations were conducted by trained observers, using the Standardized Observation Codes developed by Wahler, House, and Stambaugh (1976). This coding system provides a comprehensive (24 codes) picture of interactions between the target child and other family members. During each 30-minute observation session the observer is signaled through earphones to observe and record code occurrences on paper forms segmented into 15-second intervals. The observer is signaled for a total of 120 intervals. While a code can be scored only once per interval, there is no upper limit to the number of codes scorable in a single interval.

Of the 24 codes, 6 are relevant to the present study. These 6 codes can be grouped into two different behavior classes, one described as *mother aversive* (MA), and the other as *child aversive* (CA). MA represents all intervals in which either of 2 specific codes reflecting the mother's aversive behaviors directed at the child were scored: *Aversive instruction* was scored for any instance of discrete instruction accompanied by aggressive physical or verbal behavior; *aversive social attention* was scored for any instance of aggressive physical or verbal behavior. CA represents all intervals in which any of 4 specific codes reflecting the child's aversive behaviors directed at the mother were scored: *Opposition* was scored for any instance of noncompliance with a discrete instruction; *aversive opposition* was scored for any instance of noncompliance with a discrete instruction accompanied by physical aggression and/or verbal protest; *complaint* was scored for any instance of physical aggression and/or verbal protest; *rule violation* was scored for any instance of violation of an established household rule.

Referral problem index. Following each observation session, the observer asked the mother to provide a recall report on each of the

TABLE 8.3
Self Reported Patterns of Social Contacts of the Participants

	Average Daily Number Contacts	% Friend	% Kin	% Helper	% Neutral	% Aversive
Mother						
1	4.80	92.20	.00	5.00	33.20	18.40
2	6.00	56.20	33.60	.00	27.80	30.80
3	2.00	20.00	60.00	10.00	5.00	40.00
4	4.00	50.00	31.60	.00	15.00	12.00
5	2.60	15.60	71.40	12.80	.00	54.20
6	1.80	6.60	23.20	.00	16.60	26.60
Overall means	3.53	40.10	36.63	4.63	16.27	30.00

NOTE: These patterns were measured during the first 3 weeks of administration of the community interaction checklist. They include mean number of daily contacts, mean percentage of daily contacts with three categories of people, and mean percentage of daily contacts rated as neutral and aversive.

target child's referral problems. The list of these referral problems was derived from an initial structured interview with each mother and was comprised of those low-rate behaviors not likely to materialize during the observation sessions. Across all children, the lists included stealing, fighting, property destruction, running away, and tobacco and drug use. Mothers were simply asked to report whether or not each problem occurred within the 24-hour period that preceded the observation.

Community interaction checklist. Following each observation session, the observer also conducted a brief structured interview with the mother. The interview format, called the Community Interaction Checklist (Wahler, Leske, & Rogers, 1979), prompts maternal recall of all her adult social contacts in the preceding 24 hours. Each mother was asked to recall these contacts within the framework of several categories. Two categories are relevant to the purpose of the present study, namely, the identity of the contact person (e.g., friend, kinfolk, helping agency representative) and the valence of the contact for the mother (from +3 = very positive, through 0 = neutral to –3 = very aversive). The term "insularity" (from Wahler et al., 1979) refers to a mother's lack of friendship contacts and coerced status in her social network (see Table 3).

Mand review codes. Each mother met with her therapist once weekly for mand review sessions. The principal purpose of these sessions was to change the content of the mother's summary reports of personal coercion. As noted in the introduction, a multidistressed mother's description of a "bad" day with her conduct problem child presumably refers to her overlapping coercive experiences with adults as well. Thus whenever a mother offered a summary report of personal coercive problems with her child, the therapist systematically encouraged her to consider which other interpersonal problems might influence this report.

All mand review sessions were videotaped for later analyses with the Mand Oriented Review Codes (see Wahler and McEachern, 1983, for a detailed description of these codes). This coding system enables an observer to analyse a speaker's summary reports of personal coercion in the following manner: when a speaker (mother) describes one or more prior interchanges involving herself and other people the observer classifies that description as a *Tact Episode* or *Mand Episode*. The latter classification means that one or more aversive instructions or exchanges were involved in the episode. If none were involved, the episode description is classified as a tact. When a mand episode is scored, the observer listens until the topic changes or until the therapist offers a question or comment classified as a *Redirect*. This classification means that the therapist's question or comment is relevant to the episode but directs the speaker to new information. For example, if the episode concerns a mother's account of how her child made her feel "out of control," a therapist's redirect might be: "What kind of a mood were you when your child started to upset you?" When a redirect is scored or an episode topic changes, the prior maternal description is scored into several descriptive codes: the codes *Global* or *Specific* refer to the abstract versus concrete nature of the description; other codes designate the *Persons* involved in the descriptions by classifying the aversive instructions or exchanges in terms of their *Person Sources* and *Person Recipients* and note whether the speaker assigned *Blame* to someone through voice intonation or content. Each speaker description which is preceded by a redirect is called an *Interchange*. Each mand episode can include one or more interchanges, depending on the number of redirects which occurred during that episode.

Measurement Reliability

Home Observations. To assess the reliability of the Standardized Observation Codes, each mother-child dyad was observed once in each study phase by two observers (the standard observer and a reliability checker) simultaneously. Three reliability comparisons were collected across all phases of the study for each family.

TABLE 8.4

Measures of Session and Interval-By-Interval Reliability
of the Standardized Observation Codes

	Mand Review Only	Parent Training and Mand Review	Mand Review Only	All Phases
Mother Behavior				
Aversive instruction				
Sess.	.58	.97	.84	.77
Int.	.23	.46	.45	.39
Aversive social attention				
Sess.	.89	.97	.98	.95
Int.	.49	.37	.36	.41
Child Behavior				
Opposition				
Sess.	.92	.80	.53	.81
Int.	.56	.52	.28	.49
Aversive opposition				
Sess.	.99	.94	.90	.99
Int.	.63	.40	.99	.64
Complaint				
Sess.	.97	.99	.98	.97
Int.	.69	.45	.47	.56
Rule violation				
Sess.	.55	.75	.98	.82
Int.	.25	.75	.50	.34

NOTE: Reliability checks occurred once per family in each phase of the study, for a total of 18 checks over all study phases. Session measures are based on interclass correlation coefficients; interval measures are based on the statistic kappa.

Interclass correlation coefficients were computed to measure the session reliability of all behavioral codes. They are presented with their tests of significance in Table 4. All coefficients were found to be significantly different from zero. The use of this correlational technique to estimate the reliability of session level scores has been recommended by Hartman (1977); see Guilford and Fruchter (1978) or Winer (1971) for computational procedures. This measure of reliability was considered appropriate for all data analyses that compared total session scores across intervention phases (i.e., for all baseline probability comparisons).

Measures of interval-by-interval agreement for each observer pair were also obtained by tabulating (in 2×2 tables) the number of interval agreements and disagreements for occurrences and non-occurrence of each behavioral code. The totals of each corresponding table cell were then added and averaged to obtain one summary table for each behavioral code. A measure of agreement that controls for chance agreements was obtained by computing a statistic known as *kappa* (see Hartmann, 1977, or Hubert, 1977, for rationale and computational procedures) for each of the codes. As seen in Table 4, the measure was found to be significantly different from zero in all cases (see Hubert, 1977, for statistical test), indicating that interval-by-interval agreement among observers was systematically higher than would be expected by chance alone. This more stringent measure of reliability was necessary for all data analyses which compared within-sessions scores for each mother-child dyad (i.e., for all conditional probability comparisons).

Community interaction checklist. The reliability of the community intraction checklist was evaluated by computing a measure of internal consistency known as an intraclass correlation coefficient (Guilford & Fruchter, 1978; Winer, 1971). This measure was based on nine checklists for each mother (the first three, mid-three, and last three checklists she completed). Each checklist was scored as "insular" if it met at least one of two conditions: (a) the mother reported twice as many of her daily contacts with kinfolk and/or helping agency representatives as with friends, or (b) she reported at least a third of all her daily contacts as neutral or aversive (score of 0 to –3). Otherwise, it was scored as "noninsular." The resulting data matrix was subjected to a repeated measures analysis of variance. The reliability of the checklist was found to be equal to .94 ($F\,5,48 = 15.63$, $p < .001$). Since no direct intervention efforts were aimed at changing these maternal contact patterns, they were expected to remain stable throughout the study. The demonstration of this stability was a necessary precondition to an examination of changes in the stimulus influence of these contact patterns on mother-child interaction. Given that these contact patterns remained stable, meaningful statistics of association could then be computed between the patterns and the mothers' observed child-care behaviors.

Mand review codes. To assess the reliability of the mand-oriented review codes, one mand review videotape in each study phase was viewed independently by two observers. Measures of session reliability were then obtained for these 1-hour tapes by comparing observer code totals through a simple percentage agreement computation: (Observer 1 total/Observer 2 total) $\times$ 100. These agreement percentages were computed for each reliability check session on the following code totals: number of *Mand episodes*, number of *interchanges* comprising these episodes, number of *people* involved in these interchanges and *global* or *specific* quality of the interchange descriptions. All agreement percentages were fund to exceed .80 (range = .82 – .99).

Family Treatment

Parent training. Parent training was intitiated after a 3-week period of mand review intervention. As such, the latter intervention served as a baseline before the inititation of parent training, which was conducted as follows.

(1) Baseline data from the standardized observation codes were presented and discussed between mother and therapist. Emphasis was placed primarily on findings reflecting adverse child-parent interactions and deficits in the target child's behavioral repertoire. Mother's use of instructions was noted, particularly in reference to her follow-through efforts as evidenced by her use of positive and aversive attention directed to the child. The substance of this discussion was aimed at making a mother aware of how her child's aversive behavior was related to (and probably maintained by) her own behavior toward the child.

The baseline data were also used to pinpoint deficits in the child's prosocial behaviors, such as work, cooperative parent-child interactions, and/or independant play. Discussion of these topics functioned to show mothers how improvements in these behaviors might provide alternatives to the child's aversive behaviors.

(2) The baseline findings were then set within a social-learning explanation along the lines of Pattersons's (1974) coercion hypothesis. This teaching process was used to make the maintenance arguments from baseline more understandable to the mothers. As the logical conclusion of this explanation, the therapist emphasized the necessity of helping mother and child escape their "coercion trap."

(3) Specific means of escaping the coercion trap were next outlined for the mothers. These included a point reward system to facilitate the improvement of the child's behavior deficits and a time-out contingency as a means of not "giving in" to the child's aversive action. At this point, the target child was brought into the discussion for a summary of previous discussions, a setting of contractual arrangements for the reward system, and a detailed explanation, including modeling, of the time-out contingency. In all families, the deficit-improving part of the contract was to be carried out at least once per day. The child's participation in this contractual arrangement was

primarily related to the point reward system. If the child chose not to participate, consequences were limited to an absence of points. However, if the child protested the contract in an aversive manner, the time-out contingency was applicable as well.

(4) To insure that these treatment procedures were properly implemented, the therapist then made several home visits. In the course of these visits, the mothers were instructed to explain to the child and carry out an example of the point reward system. If necessary, modeling and rehearsal were used. If child aversive actions occurred during this demonstration, the therapist monitored and prompted (if necessary) the mothers' use of time-out. Home observations never occurred during these visits, or did they occur during parts of the day devoted to the target child's deficit-improving contract.

(5) Once the therapist was satisfied with a mother's understanding and use of the treatment procedures, the function of the home visits changed from prompting and instructing to a more reactive purpose, that is, the therapist was simply available to offer advice if the mothers asked for it. All such home consultations ended after 7 weeks of training.

Mand review. This intervention was initiated during the first week of the study and continued on a weekly basis over a 14-week period. Each mand review session occurred in a clinic setting for approximately 1 hour per week. This teaching process would probably be viewed by an untrained observer as serious, but friendly, conversations between mother and therapist. While this friendship orientation is considered an important part of mand review, the therapist follows a fairly structured teaching plan in reference to the mother's summary reports of personal coercion. This is done by encouraging mothers to focus their recall descriptions on their coercive interchanges with their target children and other people in their family and community settings. At first, most mothers offer these descriptions as global or abstract reports that summarize unknown specific encounters with a designated person (e.g., target child, Wahler & Afton, 1980). When a summary report of coercion is offered, the therapist encourages the mother to provide more information on: (1) the specifics of the encounter and (2) the global properties of her experience. While the former prompt is aimed at identifying the particular behaviors involved, the latter is aimed at obtaining the mother's global or summary labels for these behaviors, for examples: "When he kept climbing on the furniture after I had asked him not to" (a specific child behavior), "I felt like he was tearing out my heart" (a global maternal experience). In this initial part of mand review, therapist and mother learn to talk with one another in both specific and global terms. In addition, both parties establish the identities of all people who are typically involved in these coercive descriptions (e.g., target child, spouse, mother-in-law, and so on).

The next strategy in mand review is based on the assumption (see introduction) that a mother's global labels are inaccurate representations of her prior coercive interchanges. Thus when she offers a global label such as "I really bent over backwards with him" that designated a specific interchange with her target child, the therapist assumes that additional specific interchanges, some involving other people, are also summarized by this global label. In following this assumption, the therapist attempts to broaden the mother's coercive description, typically with "Is that like—?" questions. For example, the therapist might say, "When you felt he (target child) was tearing out your heart, was it like that time your boyfriend made you apologize?" In other words, a mother's labeled experience is matched with a previously labeled experience. The purpose is to encourage the mother to expand the specific people and behaviors she includes under her chosen global labels. If this is successful, a multidistressed mother will gradually be inclined to describe her global labels as multidetermined, rather than the product of some singular stress experience originating in her target child's aversive behavior.

Data Analyses

Treatment impact across all intervention phases. In order to evaluate the impact of parent training and mand review on child and mother behavior, the observation sessions were grouped into the four study phases: mand review only, parent training and mand review, mand review only, and follow-up. Baserate probabilities of aversive child and mother behaviors were computed within each phase. To do this, the number of observation intervals containing *child aversive* and *mother aversive* behavior were summed separately for each observation and divided by the total number of intervals per observation. Mean baserate probabilities were then obtained for each family, averaged across the six families, and compared across phases.

In the same manner, the *referral problem index* was computed for each child within each phase. This was done by calculating the number of maternal reports of occurrence of child referral problems for each observation and dividing it by the total number of referral problems. A mean percentage score (baserate probability) was then obtained for each child, averaged across the six children, and compared across phases.

"Early" and "late" treatment impact. Given a significant, overall treatment effect, the observation sessions of the first three intervention phases were grouped into two sequential sets, an "early" and a "late" set, which represented the first and last 7 weeks of clinical intervention, respectively. Three groups of measures were then obtained: (1) the baserate probability of child aversive behavior (CA); (2) the conditional probabilities of mother aversive behavior at Time 2 given child aversive behavior at Time 1 (MAt2/CAt1) and of mother aversive behavior at Time 2 given no child aversive behavior at Time 1 (MAt2/CAt1), where Time 1 and Time 2 are consecutive observation intervals; (3) the conditional probabilities of child aversive behavior at Time 3, given child aversive behavior at Time 1 and maternal aversive behavior at Time 2 (CAt3/CAt1 and MAt2), and of child aversive behavior at Time 3 given no child aversive behavior at Time 1 but maternal aversive behavior at Time 2 (CAt3/CAt1 and MAt1), where Time 1, 2, and 3 are consecutive observation intervals. Of these last two measures, the first one represents the probability that a child will continue to behave in an aversive manner despite a mother's disapproval or punishment of such behavior; the second one represents the probability that a mother will initiate an aversive interchange with her child in the absence of any immediate child provocation.

Within both the "early" and "late" sets, two subsets of observation sessions were also selected: one of them included only those observations preceded by maternal self-reports of a majority of aversive adult contacts in the previous 24-hour period, while the other included only those observations preceded by reports of a majority of positive adult contacts in the same period. Aversive and positive contacts were defined with the criteria used in Study 1. Three measures were then computed for these subsets: (1) the baserate probability of child aversive behavior (CA); (2) the baserate probability of mother aversive behavior (MA); and (3) the conditional probability of child aversive behavior at Time 2 given mother aversive behavior at Time 1 (CAt2/MAt1).

Expansion of maternal summary reports. Changes in maternal summary reports of personal coercion were studied in graphic form over the 14 weeks of mand review sessions. This was done by computing two indices of summary report expansion. The first one was obtained by dividing the number of different interchanges by the number of mand episodes for each session. This measure assumes that the higher the ratio of interchanges per episode, the broader the summary report nature of that episode. The second measure was obtained by adding the number of different people a mother related to her chosen summary report or metaphor in each session. This measure assumes that the more people a mother associated with her summary report, the broader the nature of that report. Both measures were obtained for each family separately and averaged across families.

Results

Table 5 presents and compares the mean levels of mother aversive behavior, child aversive behavior, and child referral problem index for the four phases of the study.

These comparisons are based on separate analyses of variance and paired comparisons for these three measures. The comparison of the first two phases on intervention indicate that significant reduction occurred in all three measures from mand review only (phase 1) to mand review and parent training (phase 2). The fact that the mean levels of all three measures were observed to remain stable over the six sessions (3 weeks) of phase 1 suggests that these reductions were a function of parent training. Of greater importance here, however, is the fact that these treatment gains were all maintained in the post-parent training phase (see comparisons of phases 1 and 3). While mand review cannot be assigned a specific causal function in these maintenance findings, the results suggest that such maintenance might be attributable to this period of intervention following parent training. This is tentatively suggested by the fact that maintenance was not obtained later under natural environmental conditions (phase 4). Note that the results of this last phase must be considered with considerable caution, as they are based on three mother-child dyads only. Three families dropped out of the program in the follow-up phase. Mothers gave the following reasons for dropping out: one was arrested for selling illegal drugs, while the other two reported threats of separation and bodily harm from spouse and boyfriend were they to continue.

Table 6 presents the stimulus control findings over the clinical intervention period of 14 weeks. All comparisons were based on t-tests

TABLE 8.5

Baserate Probability Measures of Mother Aversive and Child Aversive Behavior, and of Child Referral Problems, Over the Three Clinical Intervention Follow-up Phases

	Mand Review Only	Parent Training and Mand Review	Mand Review Only	Follow-up		
	Phase 1 (3 weeks) N = 6	Phase 2 (4 weeks) N = 6	Phase 3 (7 weeks) N = 6	Phase 4 (16 weeks) N = 3	$F(3, 17)$	Paired Comparisons*
Mother aversive	.054	.020	.014	.046	4.30*	P1 > P2 and P3; P4 > P3
Child aversive	.221	.100	.101	.200	4.83*	P1 > P2 and P3; P4 > P3
Child referral problems	.568	.350	.200	.204	10.25**	P1 > P2 and P3

*p < .05; **p < .001.

TABLE 8.6

Baserate and Conditional Probability Measures of
Mother Aversive (MA) and Child Aversive (CA) Behavior

	Early Intervention	Late Intervention
All Observations		
MA	.05	.02
CA	.14	.11
MAt2/CAt1	⌐.10	⌐.07
MAt2/CAt1	* ⌊.05	* ⌊.03
CAt3/CAt1 and MAt2	⌐.24	⌐.20
CAt3/CAt1 and MAt2	** ⌊.10	** ⌊.10
Observations Preceded by Aversive Maternal Community Contacts		
CA	.26	.11
MA	.09	.01
CAt2/MAt1	.09	.08
Observations Preceded by Positive Maternal Community Contacts		
CA	.13	.11
MA	.03	.02
CAt2/MAt1	.11	.09

NOTE: t1, t2, and t3 refer to consecutive observation intervals, for the "early" and "late" phases of clinical intervention. Some measures are based on all observations, others on only these observations preceded by aversive or positive maternal community contacts.
*p < .05; **p < .01.

for correlated means; only the significant differences are indicated. Considering first the "early" phase of intervention, the conditional probabilities based on all observations provide a correlational picture depicting child discriminative stimulus control of mother aversive behavior. That is, when the child behaves aversively, mother aversive behavior is more likely to follow and to lead in turn to further child aversive behavior than when the child does not provide an aversive antecedent stimulus. However, the baserate and conditional probabilities based on only those observations preceded by aversive or positive maternal community contact provide a different picture of stimulus control. Although aversive community contacts are followed by an increased likelihood of child and mother aversive behavior, the child is not more likely to respond to mother aversive behavior by being aversive in these observation sessions than he or she is when the sessions are preceded by positive maternal community contact. Thus while aversive contacts with adults clearly set the occasion for mother aversive behavior toward her child, their stimulus control function appears adventitious rather than discriminative. That is, the mothers behave *as if* their aversive encounters with adults were predictive of child aversive behavior when, in fact, their children demonstrate no differential response likelihood under these conditions. In our terminology, these encounters function as setting events rather than as discriminative stimuli.

As expected, the "late" phase of intervention provides no evidence of adventitious stimulus control of mother aversive behavior toward their children. The children still serve a discriminative function for their mothers' aversive responses, but the mothers' adult encounters no longer set the occasion for later coercive interchanges with their children. In effect, the mothers now act as if their adult interchanges were irrelevant to their child interchanges. As we suggested with respect to the treatment outcome results, mand review *may* have been responsible for this change.

Figure 1 documents the intended changes in maternal summary reports of personal coercion. The two measures depicted in this figure show a gradual expansion of the information summarized by these reports. They indicate that, over the mand review sessions, the mothers were apt to summarize a greater number of different coercive interchanges when describing an episode of coercion and to mention more people as related to their summary reports. As noted above, we suggest that these changes may have affected these mothers' attentional processes with regard to their coercive experiences within their family and community.

Discussion

In keeping with previous experimental analyses (e.g., Patterson & Fleischman, 1979; Wahler, 1980; Wahler & Afton, 1980), the results indicate that parent training was an effective treatment strategy associated with significant reductions in mother and child aversive behaviors, even in multidistressed families. Contrary to the same evidence, however, the results indicate that these treatment gains were maintained in a post-parent training phase during which mothers continued to take part in weekly mand review sessions. Although

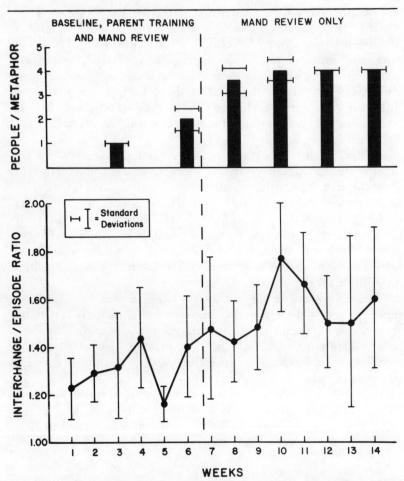

NOTE: The first graph depicts the mean number of interchanges per episode over the mand review sessions. The second graph depicts the mean number of people related to maternal summary reports over the same sessions.

Figure 8.1   The Gradual Expansion of Information Summarized by Maternal Reports of Personal Coercion

such maintenance cannot be directly attributed to mand review, this finding seems to warrant the further experimental study of mand review as a maintenance procedure. Specifically, its impact, if any, on long term treatment gains remains unclear.

The results also offer correlational support for the two assumptions outlined in the introduction. First, as did the results of Study 1, they indicate that the social interchanges of multidistressed mothers with adults influence the aversive behaviors they direct at their children. In the "early" stages of intervention, the base rate probabilities of maternal aversive responses to their children were significantly higher during those observation sessions that, according to the mothers, had been preceded by aversive interchanges between themselves and other adults. Furthermore, from an operant perspective, the results indicate that this stimulus influence was adventitious rather than discriminative. That is, the mother's aversive contacts with adults failed to predict the likelihood that their children would respond to them in kind, that is, by being more aversive toward them on days in which their mothers initiated more aversive interchanges. Second, the results of the "late" stages in intervention suggest that such adventitious stimulus influence might be attenuated through the systematic use of mand review. If this is correct, multidistressed mothers might be able to maintain their parent training gains, at least as long as they are able to maintain a change in their summary report definition of their parenting problems. Given that these mothers become able to describe their adult relationship problems as categorically related to their parenting problems, they might come to respond to the latter in a more discriminative manner. In other words, their behavior toward their children might come under the stimulus control of their children's behavior, instead of remaining under the wider setting event control of their aversive interchanges with adults.

We think that these correlational findings ought to strike a note of optimism for clinicians who are faced with the treatment of multidistressed mothers and their conduct problem children. We know that teaching such mothers to use demonstrably effective child-care methods does not ensure that they will continue to use them after the teaching process has ended. Our findings suggest that this lack of maintenance is associated, at least in part, with the existence of covarying relationships between these mothers' observational summary reports of their children's problem behaviors and their child-care methods. They also suggest that these summary reports might be "faulty," that is, under the control of a class of stimuli broader than that produced by the children's immediate behaviors. If this is correct, an expansion of maternal summary reports along the lines of our suggested strategy might alter this maladaptive form of setting event control, thus making the long-term maintenance of treatment gains more likely.

Our follow-up findings strike a note of pessimism equal to the optimism just voiced. Even if future experimental investigations support our correlational inferences, multidistressed mothers may still fail to maintain their therapeutic gains when clinical contacts are ended. This is at least what happened to the three families we followed-up in this study, who apparently all returned to pre-treatment levels of interpersonal problems. Such adverse outcome points the interested clinician in two compatible directions. Once multidistressed mothers become better able to discriminate their child and adult problems, they might also: (1) become better able to benefit from additional teaching experiences with regard to their adult problems, such as marital intervention; and (2) be more likely to engage themselves in more supportive relationships with friends, who could then be invited to join the mothers in therapy to learn to converse with them in the mand review style, thus helping them maintain their newly acquired discriminative skills. Some combination of both future directions might prove useful in helping these mothers maintain their treatment gains and thus prevent the development of their children's conduct problems into even more serious delinquent behaviors.

References

Dumas, J. E., & Wahler, R. G. (1983a). Predictors of treatment outcome in parent training: Mother insularity and socioeconomic disadvantage. *Behavioral Assessment, 5*: 301-313.

Dumas, J. E., & Wahler, R. G. (1983b). *Indiscriminate mothering as a contextual factor in aggressive-oppositional child behavior: "Damned if you do, damned if you don't."* Manuscript submitted for publication.

Fowler, S. A., & Baer, D. M. (1981). Do I have to be good all day? The timing of delayed reinforcement as a factor in generalization. *Journal of Applied Behavior Analysis, 14*, 13-24.

Green, K. D., Forehand, R., & McMahon, R. J. (1979). Parental manipulation of compliance and noncompliance in normal and deviant children. *Behavior Modification, 3*, 245-266.

Griest, D. L., & Forehand, R. (1982). How can I get any parent training done with all these other problems going on?: The role of family variables in child behavior therapy. *Child and Family Behavior Therapy, 4*, 73-80.

Griest, D. L., Forehand, R., Rogers, T., Breiner, J., Furey, W., & Williams, C. A. (in press). Effects of parent enhancement therapy on the treatment outcome and generalization of a parent training program. *Behavior Research and Therapy.*

Greist, D. L., Wells, K. C., & Forehand, R. (1979). An examination of predictors of maternal perceptions of maladjustment in clinic-referred children. *Journal of Abnormal Psychology, 88*, 277-281.

Guilford, J. P., & Fruchter, B. (1978). *Fundamental statistics in psychology and education (6th ed.)*. New York: McGraw-Hill.

Hartmann, D. P. (1977). Considerations in the choice of interobserver reliability estimates. *Journal of Applied Behavior Analysis, 10*, 103-116.

Hubert, L. (1977). Kappa revisited. *Psychological Bulletin, 84*, 289-297.

Kantor, J. R. (1959). *Interbehavioral psychology*. Granville, OH: Principia.

Kelley, M. L., Embry, L. H. & Baer, D. M. (1979). Skills for child management and family support: Training parents for maintenance. *Behavior Modification, 3*, 373-396.

Martin, B., & Twentyman, C. (1976). Teaching conflict resolution skills to parents and children. In E. J. Mash, L. A. Hamerlynck, & L. C. Handy (Eds.), *Behavior modification approaches to parenting*. New York: Brunner/Mazel.

Mealiea, W. L. (1976). Conjoint-behavior therapy: The modification of family constellations. In E. J. Mash, L. A. Hamerlynck & L. C. Handy, (Eds.), *Behavior modification approaches to parenting*. New York: Brunner/Mazel.

Patterson, G. R. (1974). Interventions for boys with conduct problems: Multiple settings, treatment and criteria. *Journal of Consulting and Clinical Psychology, 42*, 271-281.

Patterson, G. R. (1976). The aggressive child: Victim and architect of a coercive system. In E. J. Mash, L. A. Hamerlynck & L. C. Handy (Eds.), *Behavior mofification and families I. Theory and research*. New York: Brunner/Mazel.

Patterson, G. R., & Fleischman, M. J. (1979). Maintenance of treatment effects: Some considerations concerning family systems and follow-up data. *Behavior Therapy, 10*, 168-185.

Salzinger, S., Kaplan, S., & Artemyeff, C. (1983). Mothers' personal social networks and child maltreatment. *Journal of Abnormal Psychology, 92*, 68-76.

Wahler, R. G. (1980). The insular mother: Her problems in parent-child treatment. *Journal of Applied Behavior Analysis, 13*, 207-219.

Wahler, R. G., & Afton, A. D. (1980). Attentional processes in insular and noninsular mothers. *Child Behavior Therapy, 2*, 25-41.

Wahler, R. G., & Dumas, J. E. (in press). A chip off the old block: Some interpersonal characteristics of coercive children across generations. In P./Strain (Ed.), *Children's social behavior: Development, assessment, and modification*. New York: Academic Press.

Wahler, R. G., & Graves, M. G. (1983). Setting events in social networks: Ally or enemy in child behavior therapy? *Behavior Therapy, 14*, 19-36.

Wahler, R. G., House, A. E., & Stambaugh, E. E. (1976). *Ecological assessment of child problem behavior. A clinical package for home, school and institutional settings*. New York: Pergamon.

Wahler, R. G., Leske, G., & Rogers, E. S. (1979). The insular family: A deviance support system for oppositional children. In L. A. Hamerlynck (Ed.), *Behavioral systems for the developmentally disabled: I School and family environments*. New York: Brunner/Mazel.

Wahler, R. G., & McEachern, S. (1983). *Assessing parent verbal reports of personal coercion: A coding system*. Unpublished manuscript. Child Behavior Institute, The University of Tennessee.

Winer, B. J. (1971). *Statistical Principles in Experimental Design (2nd ed.)*. New York: McGraw-Hill.

9

The Effects of Early Educational Intervention on Crime and Delinquency in Adolescence and Early Adulthood

John R. Berrueta-Clement
Lawrence J. Schweinhart
William Steven Barnett
David P. Weikart

The Perry Preschool project began in 1962. Designed to prevent educational failure in a population judged to be at risk for high rates of early placement in special education and later school dropout, the study was based on a program of early intervention that included either one or two years of preschool education and weekly home visits. In order to evaluate the program's effects, study participants were divided into two groups of similar average characteristics at entry and assigned at random to experimental (treated) and control (untreated) conditions. Follow up of study participants has continued

Authors' Note: Financial support for data collection and analyses here reported has been received from the National Institute of Mental Health, the U.S. Office of Special Education and Rehabilitation Services, and Carnegie Corporation of New York. The opinions here expressed are, however, the responsibility of the authors and do not reflect official positions of these organizations. The support of other sources during the two decades of the study is also gratefully recognized: the public schools of Ypsilanti, Michigan; the U.S. Office of Education; the Spencer Foundation, and the U.S. Administration for Children, Youth, and Families. The collaboration of the Michigan State Police, the Michigan Department of Social Services and of various police departments and courts in providing information is also acknowledged. Our most important debt is to the study participants and their families, who have borne with and trusted us for twenty years.

to the present. The research has been reported regularly, principally through a monograph series; numerous summaries and articles have also appeared elsewhere (Berrueta-Clement, Schweinhart, & Weikart, 1983; Schweinhart and Weikart 1980; Weber, Foster, & Weikart, 1978; Weikart, Bond, & McNeil, 1978; Weikart, Rogers, Adcock, & McClelland, 1970).

This chapter summarizes results on delinquency and crime through early adulthood for the project, based on both self-report data and official records of juvenile and adult involvement with the legal system. Primary findings are based on the analysis of group differences; a preliminary examination of relational paths connecting characteristics at study entry with early intervention, intermediate variables and outcomes is also presented. In the final section we discuss implications of these findings for social policy and research.

Study Background

The study sample originated in one neighborhood in Ypsilanti, Michigan—an area whose inhabitants were (and still are) predominantly low-income black families. Children of preschool age were located for the study through a family census by the elementary school, through referral by neighborhood groups, and through door-to-door canvassing. Families were screened first for socioeconomic level (computed as the sum of scores, standardized within the surveyed population, for the average of parents' years of schooling, the father's or single mother's level of employment, and half of the ratio of rooms to persons in the household). Children from families below a certain socioeconomic level were given the Stanford-Binet Intelligence Test. Children with IQs between 60 and 88, and no evidence of organic handicap, were selected for the study.

Parents of sample members had a median value of 9.4 years of schooling at entry into the study, slightly less than the national value for blacks in 1970, but more than 2.5 years less than the overall national value across all ethnic groups. Table 1 displays the characteristics of the study sample at entry. Fewer than one in five of the parents had completed high school, compared to one in two nationally. About half of the sample families were headed by a single adult, compared to one in seven nationally. In two out of five families, no parent was employed. Among employed parents, jobs usually could be classified as unskilled labor. Half of the families

TABLE 9.1

Family Demographic Comparisons: Longitudinal Sample
at Entry and United States (1970 Census)

Category	Sample at Entry (1962-1965)	United States (1970) Blacks	All Races
Schooling of Parents			
Mothers/females 25 and over:			
Median years of school	9.7	10.0	12.1
Percentage elementary only	32	41	27
Percentage with some high school	47	26	20
Percentage completing high school	21	33	53
Fathers/males 25 and over:			
Median years of school	8.8	9.6	11.8
Percentage elementary only	46	45	27
Percentage with some high school	43	23	19
Percentage completing high school	11	32	54
Family Composition and Employment			
Husband-wife families:	53[a,b,c]	67	86
Percentage with both employed	7	29	29
Percentage with one employed	38	30	46
Percentage with none employed	7	9	11
Single-head families:[d]	47	33	14
Percentage with head employed	13	17	8
Percentage with none employed	34	16	6
All families:[e]			
Percentage employed adult male	50	60	74
Percentage employed adult female	20	47	38
Percentage none employed	42	25	17
Percentage receiving welfare	50	18	5
Employment level of working adult males:			
percentage professional	0	9	25
percentage skilled	5	25	39
percentage semiskilled	14	30	20
percentage unskilled	81	35	16
Household Density			
Median number of persons	6.7	3.1	2.7
Median number of rooms	4.8	4.7	4.8
Mean person/room ratio	1.2	.66	.56
Percentage ratio above 1.0	63	19	8

SOURCE: This table is reproduced with slight modifications from Schweinhart and Weikart, 1980: 18. Permission to reproduce is acknowledged.
a. The 123 children in the sample were in 100 families since siblings were included; since child conditions are being reported, n = 123 cases are used in calculations. The experimental group included six sibling pairs, one group of 3 and one group of 4. The control group had 12 sibling pairs.

TABLE 9.1   Continued

b. In 1973-1977, when youths were 15, the sample had 42% husband-wife families and 58% single-head families. Mothers' employment rate was 45%.
c. Labor force participation of unemployed persons was ignored in these categorizations.
d. Nationally 11% of families had a single female head, and 3% a single male head, in 1970.
e. Employment levels are given for 66 working fathers in the study sample. The employment level of mothers in the sample was either unskilled or not reported.

received welfare assistance, compared to only one in twenty families nationally. Residences were typical of local urban areas in size, but were crowded with more than twice the number of people in the typical household as indicated by the 1970 Census (6.7 versus 2.7).

The sample for the study consists of 123 youths in 5 waves, born each year between 1958 and 1962. The study began in 1962, with the selection of a group of 4-year-olds (Wave 0) and a group of 3-year-olds (Wave 1). The sample was completed over the next 3 years by the annual selection of additional groups of 3-year-olds: Wave 2 in 1963, Wave 3 in 1964, and Wave 4 in 1965. Wave 0 experimental-group children attended preschool for 1 year beginning in 1962; Waves 1 through 4 attended preschool for 2 years.

The scientific strength of the project is due to an experimental design in which study participants were randomly assigned to a group that went to preschool and another that did not. Each year participants were assigned to groups by a matching and randomization procedure. The children were ranked in order of increasing pretest IQ; these rankings were carried out separately by gender. Closest matching pairs of children were arbitrarily assigned to separate groups. Exchanges between groups were carried out to equate the ratio of boys to girls and the groups' average socioeconomic status. Finally, each year one of the groups was arbitrarily designated the experimental (preschool) group, and the other the control (no preschool) group. Siblings were assigned to the same group as their older siblings in order to maintain group independence. Five children were transferred from the preschool group to the no-preschool group; their mothers worked outside the home and there was no one who could take the children to the program or attend home visits. Once assigned to a group, none of the families withdrew from the program. It is clear that neither parents nor teachers participated in the decision about which children received the preschool intervention.

Group comparisons on entry-level and later socioeconomic characteristics show that there are no important differences between the two groups apart from treatment. The two groups showed no statistically significant differences (at p less than .10) on entry IQ, socioeconomic status, father's absence, father's education, boy-girl ratio, family size or birth order. As Table 2 shows, there was one statistically significant difference—on level of maternal employment. Multivariate testing of all background characteristics at entry showed that group differences did not attain the .10 level. The socioeconomic characteristics of the two groups were reexamined eleven years later through a new parent interview. This time, there were no significant differences between the two groups of families. Over the years, the effect of entry-level differences in maternal employment has been examined in outcome analyses; it has generally been found to be nonexistent (Schweinhart & Weikart, 1980; Weikart et al., 1978).

The preschool program to which the experimental group was assigned was an organized educational program directed at the intellectual and social development of young children. It was staffed by teaching teams that received extensive managerial support and inservice training. Children attended preschool for 2 school years at ages 3 and 4, except for Wave 0 children who attended for 1 school year at age 4. The school year began in October and ended in May. Classes were conducted for two and one-half hours in the morning, for 5 days a week; the staff-child ratio was approximately 1 adult for every 5 to 7 children enrolled. Teachers visited mothers and children in the home for one and one-half hours each week. The curriculum developed for this project is described in the book *The Cognitively Oriented Curriculum*, by Weikart et al., 1971; a more recent expression can be found in Hohmann, Banet, and Weikart, 1979.

The preschool education program (or the lack of it) was the entire extent of differential treatment of study participants by researchers. All study participants, regardless of treatment group, received the same schedule of measurements. Teachers in elementary or secondary school were not informed about the group membership of study participants; in fact, all information about treatment groups was kept from test administrators.

Theoretical Framework

We speculate that a principal link between preschool intervention and later misbehavior and delinquency is through school failure. In

TABLE 9.2

Demographic Comparisons: Experimental Versus Control Group

Category	Experimental Group	Control Group	p (var.)[a]
Number of Cases (Youths)[b]	58	65	
Gender–percentage female	43	40	ns
Age at entry, mean years: Wave 0	4.4	4.2	ns
Waves 1-4	3.3	3.3	ns
Mean number of older siblings	2.8	3.0	ns
Mean entry Stanford-Binet IQ	79.8	78.5	ns
Parents' Schooling			
Median years–mothers	10.0	9.5	ns
Median years–fathers	8.6	9.0	ns
Families[d,e]			
Socioeconomic status, mean score	8.0	7.9	ns
Percentage receiving welfare	55	45	ns
Percentage with no parents employed	51	34	ns
Two-parent families, percentage	54	51	ns
Mother works, percentage	5	9	ns
Father works, percentage	46	45	ns
Employment level: skilled	4	2	
semiskilled	10	3	ns
unskilled	32	40	
Female-headed families, percentage	46	49	
Mother works, percentage	4	22	.002 (13%)
Families 11 Years Later[c,f]			
No parent employed, percentage	46	40	ns
Two-parent families, percentage	39	42	ns
Mother works, percentage	10	6	ns
Father works, percentage	32	38	ns
Female-headed families, percentage	61	58	
Mother works, percentage	17	20	ns
Housing			
Mean person/room ratio	1.2[c]	1.3	ns
Family moves since child started school:			
percentage none	15	17	
percentage one	58	54	ns
percentage two or more	27	30	

SOURCE: This table is reproduced with slight modifications from Schweinhart and Weikart, 1980: 23. Permission to reproduce is acknowledged.

a. The two-tailed *p* value, based on a chi-squared test, is reported if less than .10, followed by the proportion of variance accounted for by group membership.

b. Data collected at project entry (1962-1965) unless otherwise noted.

c. Data collected 11 years after project entry (1973-1977).

d. The 123 children in the sample were in 100 families since siblings were included; since child conditions are being reported, n = 123 cases are used in calculations. The experimental group included six sibling pairs, one group of 3 and one group of 4. The control group had 12 sibling pairs.

TABLE 9.2 Continued

e. Socioeconomic status scores are standardized within the sample after summing the average of parents' schooling, the average of parents' levels of employment, and half of the ratio of rooms to persons in the household.
f. Labor force participation of unemployed persons was ignored in these calculations.

this view, children at risk of educational failure achieve enhanced success in early schooling through preschool; early school success is linked to later success and to higher educational attainment at the end of secondary education. School success, in turn, is linked to reduced rates of misbehavior and delinquency.

A number of longitudinal studies in educational research have begun to establish linkages between early education and school success in disadvantaged populations. Previous reports of the present study have documented a relation between preschool and increased academic achievement, reduced placement in special education, and improved ratings of academic performance and school motivation (Schweinhart & Weikart, 1980). Other studies corroborate these findings. The work of Gray and her colleagues (Gray, Ramsey, & Klaus, 1982) and that of Levenstein (1978) confirm a relation between early education and reductions in special education placement and dropout rates. Palmer's project (Palmer, Siegel, & Persons, 1979) has demonstrated a relation between early intervention, increased academic achievement, and reduced grade retention. The Consortium for Longitudinal Studies (1982) has assembled the findings from these and other efforts and has carried out corroborative secondary analyses. A number of other evaluative studies and long-term follow-ups can be cited to the same effect (e.g., Irvine, 1982; McDonald & Monroe, 1981).

A considerable body of literature in criminology substantiates links between school success and delinquency. Both the amounts of schooling received (Bachman, O'Malley, & Johnston, 1978; Conger & Miller, 1966; Elliott & Voss, 1974) and success during schooling (Hirschi, 1969; Silberberg & Silberberg, 1971) have been shown to be significantly related to early delinquency. A variety of theoretical explanations for this relation are offered. Hirschi's (1969) social bonding theory suggests that school failure weakens links of attachment to school and strengthens bonds of attachments to other elements, leading to delinquent behavior. Other connections are offered between school factors such as teachers' attitudes and behavior toward students (Gold, 1978; Simons, 1978) or curriculum track placement (Kelly & Pink, 1973; Schafer & Olexa, 1971; Wiatrowski, Hansell, Massey, & Wilson, 1982), and delinquency. Alternatively, personality and behavior problems evidenced in the school setting (Conger & Miller, 1966; Glueck & Glueck, 1950; Offord, Poushinsky, & Sullivan, 1978) or erosion of the self-image (Bachman et al., 1978; Gold & Mann, 1972; Jensen, 1972) are viewed as consequences of school failure and causes of delinquent behavior. A careful review of these theories, with special concentration on social bonding theory and its recent elaborations (Elliott, Ageton, & Canter, 1979; Wiatrowski et al., 1982) is available in a project report by Farnworth (1982). Farnworth's efforts provide the core of the present review.

When the linkage between school success and delinquency is examined empirically, it proves to be more complex than the connections suggested by theory. Hypothesis-testing efforts with this sample by Farnworth, using self-reports of delinquent behavior and misbehavior at age 15, suggest that there are distinct varieties of delinquent behavior and that predictive relations differ by both gender and behavior type (1982). Among the variables showing significant predictive power for some, though not all, delinquent outcomes are IQ, achievement, placement in special education, family and school attachment, educational expectations, family mobility in the school years, self-image—in short, every one of the elements mentioned by theorists.

The framework for the present chapter, in the presence of this congeries of relationships, is considerably more modest than what most theorists might expect. Preschool is linked to increased success in elementary school for low-income black youth, and through this link is associated with higher educational attainment by age 19. Higher educational attainment is linked to lower rates of delinquent involvement. The fact that educational attainment and delinquency are to some extent contemporaneous is recognized as a flaw in the model. This shortcoming of the present study will have to be remedied by future studies with larger sample sizes and a longer time frame. To some extent problems of variable specification for the present study may be remedied by the passage of time: current plans for data collection as study participants reach their mid-twenties may permit more exact specification of variable sequences over time.

Data Collection and Variables
for the Present Study

A broad variety of measures has been collected during the course of this study. Measurement was carried out at study entry and annually from ages 4 to 11, and at 14, 15, and 19 years of age. Measurement descriptions through age 15 are available in earlier reports (see Schweinhart & Weikart, 1980).

For the present chapter, variables of interest at the end of adolescence were collected from three sources. School records were collected for 112 individuals (91% of the study sample) and provide detailed educational progress data and information about special education placement. Interviews with study participants were conducted in 121 cases (98% of the sample); in all but 8 cases these interviews took place at age 19. Interview topics included self-reported delinquent behavior and misbehavior. Finally, juvenile and adult arrest and court records were searched for 121 study participants. Adult arrest and court records were searched through the services of the Michigan State Police, and are complete through mid-1982 (at which time the oldest study participants had almost turned 25 and the youngest were a few months shy of 20 years of age).

Variables presented in this chapter can be classified as entry level, intervening, or outcome. Dependent or outcome variables are measures of delinquency, including interview-based self-reports as well as variables obtained from the examination of official records. Intervening variables include measures of later educational attainment (based both on school records and on interview-derived information about postsecondary education and training) and measures of early school success (including special education placement, academic achievement, and teacher ratings). Entry-level characteristics of the family and the individual include family socioeconomic status and study participant IQs; the effects of preschool are assessed through IQ immediately prior to school entry. Finally, independent and fixed variables include preschool program participation and gender.

Analytic Methods

The principal method of analysis in the present chapter is the straightforward comparison of group differences. The study's experimental design and entry-level group comparability permit us to assume that, on the average, the behavior of control group members reflects the behavior that would have characterized experimental group members in the absence of treatment. This assumption is buttressed by a series of analyses of group differences over time presented in previous reports, which provide a consistent picture. Further corroboration is provided by analyses establishing causal relations between variables over time for the study sample, as well as by analyses reported elsewhere (e.g., Berrueta-Clement et al., 1983; Schweinhart & Weikart, 1980) controlling for initial differences between individuals.

Comparisons of group differences are carried out through the use of Student's t for the comparison of group means in continuous variables; for categorical variables, Fisher's exact test is used for 2×2 contingency tables (contrasting variables with two categories in the two treatment groups) and chi-squared is used for variables with more than two categories and for the comparison of event frequencies.

Analyses exploring relational sequences between variables over time are conducted by means of multiple regression techniques. All variables prior to a given dependent variable are entered into a multiple regression; nonsignificant variables are then eliminated and the regression is rerun. This process is repeated until only predictor variables significantly related to the dependent variable are left. Gender presents a complication in these analyses. Ideally, causal analyses would be performed separately for males and females, but study sample sizes make this impractical. As an interim strategy, gender is entered as a variable in all initial regressions, and retained where it makes a significant contribution.

In all analyses, a .100 two-tailed significance level is used to determine the region of null hypothesis rejection.

Results

Group Comparisons

Preschool led to a reduction in the number of persons involved with the legal system, and in the number of arrests of study participants. Data stemming from searches of juvenile and adult official records are presented in Table 3. These data cover the period from earliest offenses through mid-1982. At the end point of data

TABLE 9.3

Effects of Preschool on Crime and Delinquency:
Official Records Data

Category	Preschool (N = 58)	No Preschool (N = 63)	p
Percentage ever arrested or charged[a] (as juveniles or adults)	31	51	.022
Percentage ever detained as juveniles	16	25	ns
Percentage ever arrested as adults	25	40	.078
Total number of arrests	73	145	.0001
Percentage with no arrests	69	50	
Percentage with one or two arrests	19	25	.068
Percentage with three or more arrests	12	25	
Seriousness Scores[b]			
Percentage arrested for property or violent offenses	24	38	.078
Number of property/violence arrests	47	74	.005
Mean person total seriousness score	6.7	5.8	ns
Percentage with scores over 3	19	22	ns
Juvenile Records			
Total number of arrests	30	44	ns
Total petitions requested	11	25	.037
Percentage with petitions requested	7	13	ns
Total petitions adjudicated	2	5	ns
Percentage with adjudications	3	3	ns
Adult Records[c,d]			
Total minor arrests or charges	1	21	.0001
Percentage with minor arrests/charges	2	16	.007
Total nonminor arrests	42	80	.028
Total convictions	20	24	ns
Percentage convicted at least once	16	21	ns
Case dispositions:			
Percentage receiving probation	7	6	ns
Mean months probation received	12	33	.093
Percentage receiving fines	3	14	.037
Mean fine amounts	$168	$209	ns
Percentage confined	10	13	ns

NOTE: Statistical analyses in this table are Fisher's exact test to compare the proportion of persons (such as those ever arrested or charged); Student's t for comparison of means; and chi-squared for comparison of observed event frequencies (such as total number of arrests). Significance levels are presented for two-tailed p values below .100.

a. Juvenile arrest data without individual identification were obtained for 4 individuals in the preschool group (4 arrests total), and for 5 persons in the no preschool group (5 arrests total). These data are included in arrest counts, but are necessarily excluded from counts of persons ever arrested, since these individuals might already be counted in the data with individual identification.

TABLE 9.3   Continued

b. Seriousness scores were derived from ordinal rankings developed by Phillips and Votey (1981) on the basis of relative seriousness rankings in the work of Sellin and Wolfgang (1964) for crimes involving property or violence. Arrest charges were used; dismissed charges were ignored. In multiple-charge arrests, the most serious charge was scored. Where charges were changed, the final charge was used. For details of the scoring procedure, see text.
c. Minor adult offenses included traffic violations and breaches of the peace.
d. Confinement terms were not compared because sentences are quite variable (e.g., 2 to 20 years) and terms actually served were not available.

collection, study participants ranged between 19 and 24 years in age; thus the data presented cover longer time spans for some study participants than others.

Overall, preschool led to a reduction in the proportion of persons ever arrested or charged—from 51% to 31%. The total number of arrests per group was markedly different: 145 for the control and 73 for the experimental group. Fewer persons attending preschool were arrested for crimes involving property or violence: 24%, compared to 38% for those who had not attended preschool. The number of property or violence arrests was also markedly reduced (from 74 to 47). A further breakdown by number of arrests shows that, in the preschool group, both the number of persons with one or two arrests and the number of persons with three or more arrests are diminished.

Seriousness scores were assigned to juvenile and adult arrest charges. The scoring procedure was based on rankings developed by Phillips and Votey (1981) on the basis of work on the relative seriousness of offenses originally carried out by Sellin and Wolfgang (1964). The basic procedure was simple: offenses involving violence (rankings 1-11 in the Phillips and Votey scale) were assigned a score of 3; offenses generally involving losses of property exceeding $50.00 (rankings 12-27 in the Phillips and Votey scale) were assigned a score of 2; and other offenses (ranked 28-61 in the Phillips and Votey scale) were assigned a score of 1. Arrest charges were used for scoring; when multiple charges were made at the time of arrest, the most serious charge was scored. Dismissed charges were ignored. When charges were changed, the final charge was used. The mean seriousness score across all offenses for persons with assigned seriousness scores did not differ between groups.

Juvenile records showed similar trends to the overall data, although the only significant difference between groups appeared in the number of petitions requested of juvenile courts: 11 for the group that attended preschool and 25 for the group that did not.

Adult records showed notable effects favoring preschool. There was a remarkable reduction in the number of minor offenses recorded: 1 for the experimentals and 21 for the controls. The difference was also reflected in the number of persons with minor charges: respectively, 1 and 10. Minor offenses included traffic violations and breaches of public order. Other arrests for more serious offenses showed the same pattern: persons who had attended preschool had 42, while those who had not had 80. Although the number of persons sentenced did not differ by group, there were reductions in both the mean length of probation (from 33 to 12 months) and in the number of persons receiving fines. There were no differences in the number of persons jailed; lengths of confinement could not be compared, since sentences are extremely variable (2 to 20 years, for instance) and the figures for actual time served were usually not available.

Taken together, the data present a remarkable picture. Of the 121 study participants, 50 (41%) have been arrested at least once; half of the members of the control group have been arrested. Those sentenced at least once number 22, 18% of the total sample. The charges against study participants are varied; the most frequent are burglary and larceny. Assault charges are also common. Serious charges include one of murder, one of manslaughter and two of criminal sexual conduct. These rates can be compared to those found in other research. For example, Wolfgang, Figlio, and Sellin report an offense rate of 50% for nonwhite males in their Philadelphia birth cohort, considering only the period up to their 18th birthdays (1972: 66). Our overall rate through age 17, including both juvenile and adult offenses, is 31% in the study sample's control group.

Against this background, the effects of early intervention seem equally notable. Preschool reduced arrests by half, and the proportion of persons arrested from one-half to less than one-third. The effects of preschool extend to both minor and nonminor offenses. It should be noted that arrests carry no presumption of guilt, and that there is no difference between groups in the number of persons sentenced. And yet these data make a straightforward statement: this is a population at risk of involvement with the law, and early intervention reduces that risk.

Self-report data were also collected through interviews at age 19 for most study participants. The data obtained are summarized in Table

4. For a number of types of delinquent behavior or misbehavior, individuals were asked to note the number of instances: none, one, two, three, or four, and five or more. Each response was multiplied by the closest number of instances, thus recoding 1 as 1, 2 as 2, 3 or 4 as 3, and 5 or more as 5. The scoring procedure led to an undercount of the number of events of misbehavior reported. The total number of events was summed and compared across groups. A seriousness score was also derived by assigning Phillips and Votey seriousness scores of 3, 2, and 1 (as described earlier) to those varieties of misbehavior that could be categorized in this fashion. The original scale is similar to that used in the study to collect self-reported data at age 15 (see Schweinhart and Weikart, 1980).

Preschool led to lower numbers of self-reported offenses for four offense categories: *involvement in a serious fight; involvement in a group or gang fight; causing an injury requiring bandages or a doctor;* and *involvement with the police.* In all of these cases, the number of reported offenses was lower for the group that had attented preschool: 26 versus 52 events for involvement in a serious fight; 23 versus 58 events for involvement in a group or gang fight; 21 versus 43 events for causing someone an injury; and 29 versus 54 instances for involvement with the police. For other categories, there were no significant differences between groups. The consistency of differences for three of the four items dealing with violent behavior seems notable. The total number of events reported was summed across categories; there was no significant difference between groups on total self-reported delinquent events. In order to compare the proportion of individuals reporting relatively low offense levels, we collapsed together nonoffenders and one-time offenders. The proportion of such persons is higher in the group that attended preschool: 41%, as compared to 27% for the group that did not go to preschool (Fisher's exact test, p = .070). If the events are weighted by seriousness, there is no statistically significant difference between groups on means; but there is a significant difference by the median test, with the median seriousness-weighted number of offenses for the preschool group lower than the median value for the group that did not attend preschool.

Preschool led to a number of other important outcomes in late adolescence, complementing the picture portrayed by reductions in crime and delinquency. Study participants who attended preschool were more likely to graduate from high school and to undertake some

TABLE 9.4
Effects of Preschool on Misbehavior and Delinquent
Behavior: Self-Report Data at Age 19 Interview

| | Number of Self-Reported Offenses | | |
Behavior Category	Preschool (N = 58)	No Preschool (N = 63)	p
Hit an instructor or supervisor	12	16	ns
Involved in a serious fight	26 (n = 58)	52 (n = 62)	.009
Involved in a group or gang fight	23	58	.001
Caused someone an injury requiring bandage or a doctor	21	43	.016
Threatened someone with knife or gun	15	13	ns
Took something worth less than $50	62	56	ns
Took something worth more than $50	37	44	ns
Took something from a store	92	110	ns
Took a car without permission, other than from parent or relative	18	12	ns
Took part of a car	17 (n = 52)	12 (n = 57)	ns
Entered a place illegally	29 (n = 52)	23 (n = 57)	ns
Set a fire deliberately	7 (n = 52)	7 (n = 57)	ns
Vandalized school property	24 (n = 52)	24 (n = 57)	ns
Vandalized property at work	9 (n = 51)	5 (n = 56)	ns
Smoked marijuana	162 (n = 52)	196 (n = 57)	ns
Used other dangerous drugs	39 (n = 52)	29 (n = 57)	ns
Involved with police	29 (n = 52)	54 (n = 57)	.020
Mean number of self-reported offenses	6.76	7.54	ns
Mean self-reported offense score, weighted by seriousness	12.36	15.25	ns

NOTE: Statistical tests in this table are chi-squares with one degree of freedom. Significance levels are presented if two-tailed p is lower than .100. Seriousness weightings for offenses involving property or violence were assigned following the methods of Phillips and Votey (1981); for details see text.

form of postsecondary education or vocational training; they were more likely to be working at the time of their age 19 interview, and less likely to have received some forms of welfare assistance as cases in their own right. Women who attended preschool reported fewer pregnancies or live births through age 19. A more detailed examination of these findings will be found in a monograph currently under preparation.

Causal Analysis Over Time

A pertinent question at this point is "how"? Granted that the experimental design permits the claim that preschool led to the results obtained, by what mechanism did these results come about?

The theoretical framework outlined earlier claimed a central role for early school success. In essence, preschool is held to have produced some change in the study participants, a change to which the public school system responded by "rewarding" them with success through elementary school. In turn, this success leads to higher educational attainment, and educational attainment leads to reduced delinquent involvement with the law as well as to increases in other indicators of socioeconomic success and social responsibility.

We have already accepted that this modest relational attempt does not offer insight into underlying psychological or behavioral causative factors; it is not "educational attainment" in itself that leads to reduced delinquency, for example. Our goal in preparing a model for analysis is rather to point out the linkages that more sophisticated models will have to explain: we expect to learn as much from the linkages between variables as from the linkages that are absent.

A diagram of our preliminary relational model is presented as Figure 1. Variables for this analysis are defined as follows: *gender*—1 = male, 2 = female; *preschool education*—1 = no, 2 = yes; *IQ before study entry*—the test score obtained in the fall of the entering years; *IQ before school entry*—the test score obtained in the spring before entry into kindergarten; *teacher ratings of antisocial behavior*—combined ratings for kindergarten and grade 1, derived from factor analyses and including items relating to disobedience, disruption of classroom procedure, teasing or provoking other students, influencing others toward troublemaking, resistance, lying or cheating, resentment of criticism, and so on (see Farnworth et al., 1981—higher scores correspond to more acceptable behavior); *teacher ratings of affective skills*—combined ratings for kindergarten and grade 1, derived from factor analyses and including items relating to social relations with classmates, friendliness, trust of the environment, degree of introversion or extroversion, general happiness, isolation and communication (see Farnworth, Berrueta-Clement, & Rashid, 1981—higher scores correspond to more positive social behavior); *years in special education*—the number of years spent in integrated or self-contained special education programs, regardless of diagnostic category; *achievement test score average*—the average of at least four achievement tests across grade 1 to grade 5 and grade 8 (with missing data replaced by the sample overall mean score in 10 cases); *years of education attained*—the number of years of education successfully completed, with high school graduation = 12, and any college = 13;

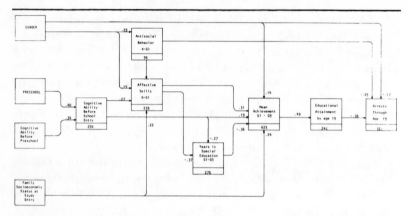

NOTES: The number of subjects for the analyses here reported is 112. Coefficients on arrows are beta weights from ordinary least squares regression equations; the arrows point to the dependent variable in each equation. Arrows connect variables only if the relationship is statistically significant with p = .10 or less. The proportion of variance in each dependent variable accounted for by significant independent variables appears at the bottom of the box for each dependent variable. For method and variable descriptions, see text.

Figure 9.1 A Relational Model for the Perry Preschool Study Over Time

and number of arrests through age 19 including both juvenile and adult arrests.

Two variables (other than gender) directly influence the number of arrests through age 19: educational attainment and early teacher ratings of antisocial behavior. Notably, neither IQ at school entry, years in special education, academic achievement or early teacher ratings of affective skills appear to affect the number of arrests— except through the intervention of educational attainment. Teacher ratings of affective skills, though not IQ or ratings of antisocial behavior, are related to family socioeconomic status. There may be an underlying variable causing both increases in educational attainment and reductions in the number of arrests; but if such a variable is related to academic achievement or special education placement, it works its effects through educational attainment. The other important finding is the significant and independent association over time between teacher ratings of antisocial behavior at ages 5 and 6 and number of arrests. This relation suggests that certain patterns of behavior already defined in the child extend with some constancy (or at least with strong relations to later behavior) from the earliest school years through late adolescence. Even more suggestive is the set of variables antecedent to these teacher ratings: the only significant relation between antecedent variables and teacher ratings of anitsocial behavior is for gender (with boys being rated as more likely to exhibit such behavior than girls). Neither the child's cognitive ability (at program entry or at school entry), nor treatment, nor the family's socioeconomic status are predictive of antisocial behavior at ages 5-6.

The relational analysis presented above offers at least one plausible path connecting preschool education with reduced delinquent behavior, going through school success. Preschool education and entry IQ together determine IQ just before entry into school, which is related to teacher ratings of affective skills, to years in special education, and to average academic achievement. These proxies for early- and middle-educational success are predictive of educational attainment through age 19, and this in turn causes reduced delinquent behavior as measured by official records data. The model also suggests that certain features of behavior that are significantly predictive of later delinquent activity can be identified by schoolteachers as early as kindergarden.

Conclusions and Implications for
Research and Policy

Preschool can reduce levels of delinquent behavior, and has other important lifetime outcomes, for individuals from low-income families viewed early in life as being at risk of educational failure. The outcomes extend to broadly varied aspects of the lives of individuals in late adolescence and early adulthood: school success, earnings and employment, teenage pregnancy, and both self-reported and official deliquent behavior and misbehavior. Economic analyses of these data (Barnett et al., in press) suggest that cost figures can be assigned to these outcome differences, and that under conservative assumptions early education more than pays for itself in terms of its returns to society and to the taxpayer.

Early education appears to act on long-term outcomes by helping to ensure successful early schooling experiences, which in turn lead to greater educational attainment. These findings occur in a sample of individuals judged to be at significant risk for educational failure prior to treatment. Thus it seems that this form of early interven-

238 Berrueta-Clement et al.

tion can have a preventive effect: it can help reduce the likelihood that individuals will engage in delinquent behavior or misbehavior. Because of its cost-effectiveness and the broad scope of the outcomes obtained, such a form of intervention appears to deserve serious consideration by policymakers. In both human and economic terms, the value of successful preventive efforts is much greater than that of remedial therapies, if the populations at risk can be accurately targeted.

The results obtained with experimental intervention appear to be complementary to those obtained by other methods, rather than to replicate them. Correlational approaches (for instance, in Coleman et al., 1966; Jencks et al., 1972; Jencks et al., 1979; Rehberg & Rosenthal, 1978) or approaches using subsample identification (e.g., Werner & Smith, 1982) provide no means for controlling for self-selection by individuals or their families. In situations in which long spans of time are covered, the opportunities for self-selection are repeated. If self-selection is not controlled by early and timely equation and random assignment, causal isolation remains problematic even after extensive statistical manipulation. It is for this reason, we feel, that correlational and descriptive studies have quite generally underestimated the relation between educational inputs and life outcomes. It should be noted that the pattern of relations found in correlational studies may be quite correct, in the sense of representing the typical relation found between variables in the absence of intervention; but it is not the best estimate of the sort of relational pattern that might be found if social policies were changed in some meaningful way.

The results of the Perry project argue powerfully for the broad extension of early educational interventions to low-income youngsters and to all persons at risk for educational failure.

References

Bachman, J. G., O'Malley, P. M., & Johnston, J. (1978). *Adolescence to adulthood: Change and stability in the lives of young men.* Ann Arbor, MI: University of Michigan Institute for Social Research.

Barnett, W. S., Berrueta-Clement, J. R., Schweinhart, L. J., & Weikart, D. P. (in press). *An extended economic analysis of the Perry Preschool program.*

Berrueta-Clement, J. R., Schweinhart, L. J., & Weikart, D. P. (1983). Lasting effects of preschool education on children from low-income families in the United States. In *Avoiding school failure: The relation between early education and primary school.* Ottawa, Canada: International Development Research Centre.

Coleman, J. S., Campbell, E. Q., Hobson, C. J., McPartland, J., Mood, A.M., Weinfeld, F. D., & York, R. L. (1966). *Equality of educational opportunity*. Washington, DC: Government Printing Office.

Conger, J. J., & Miller, W. C. (1966). *Personality, social class and delinquency*. New York: John Wiley.

Consortium for Longitudinal Studies. (1982). Lasting effects of early education. *Monographs of the Society for Research in Child Development, 47* (2-3, Serial No. 195).

Elliott, D. S., Ageton, S. S., & Canter, R. J. (1979). An integrated theoretical perspective on delinquent behavior. *Journal of Research in Crime and Delinquency, 15*(1), 2-27.

Elliott, D. S., & Voss, H. L. (1974). *Delinquency and dropout*. Lexington, MA: D.C. Heath.

Farnworth, M., Berrueta-Clement, J., & Rashid, H. (1981, December). *A longitudinal study of schooling and delinquency* (Preliminary technical report on NIMH grant RO1 MH33488). Ypsilanti, MI: High/Scope Foundation.

Farnworth, M. (1982). *Schooling and self-reported delinquency: A longitudinal study*. (Final report on NIMH grant RO1 MH 33488). Ypsilanti, MI: High/Scope Educational Research Foundation.

Glueck, S., & Glueck, E. (1950). *Unraveling juvenile delinquency*. Cambridge, MA: Harvard University Press.

Gold, M. (1978). Scholastic experiences, self-esteem and delinquent behavior: A theory for alternative schools. *Crime & Delinquency, 24*(3), 290-308.

Gold, M., & Mann, D. (1972). Delinquency as defense. *American Journal of Orthopsychiatry, 42*(3), 463-479.

Gray, S. W., Ramsey, B. K., & Klaus, R. A. (1982). *From 3 to 20: The early training project*. Baltimore, MD: University Park Press.

Hirschi, T. (1969). *Causes of delinquency*. Berkeley: University of California Press.

Hohmann, M., Banet, B., & Weikart, D. P. (1979). *Young children in action: A manual for preschool educators*. Ypsilanti, MI: The High/Scope Press.

Irvine, D. J. (1982, March). *Evaluation of the New York State Experimental Prekindergarten Program*. Paper presented at the annual meeting of the American Educational Research Association, New York.

Jencks, C., Bartlett, S., Corcoran, M., Crouse, J., Eaglesfield, D., Jackson, G., McClelland, K., Mueser, P., Olneck, M., Schwartz, J., Ward, S., & Williams, J. (1979). *Who gets ahead? The determinants of economic success in America*. New York: Basic Books.

Jencks, C., Smith, M. K., Acland, H., Bane, M. J., Cohen, D., Gintis, H., Heyns, B., & Michelson, S. (1972). *Inequality: A reassessment of the effect of family and schooling in America*. New York: Basic Books.

Jensen, G. F. (1972). Delinquency and adolescent self-conceptions: A study of the personal relevance of infraction. *Social Problems, 20*(1), 84-103.

Kelly, D. H., & Pink, W. T. (1973). School commitment, youth rebellion and delinquency. *Criminology 10*(4), 473-484.

Levenstein, P. (1978, April). Third grade effects of the mother-child home program (Final report of the Developmental Continuity Consortium Follow-up Study).

McDonald, M. S., & Monroe, E. (1981). A follow-up study of the 1966 Head Start program (mimeo). Rome, GA: Rome City Schools.

Offord, D. A., Poushinsky, M. F., & Sullivan, K. (1978). School performance, IQ and delinquency. *British Journal of Criminology, 18,* 110-127.

Palmer, F. H., Siegel, R. J., & Persons, W. A. (1979). *Harlem Study follow-up: Eighth grade reading achievement test scores and retained-in-grade data* (Final Report, Contract No. 26-79-15886). The Education Commission of the States to Early Intellective Development, Inc.

Phillips, L., & Votey, H. L. (1981). *The economics of crime control.* Beverly Hills, CA: Sage.

Rehberg, R. A., & Rosenthal, E. R. (1978). *Class and merit in the American high school.* New York: Longmans.

Schafer, W. E., & Olexa, C. (1971). *Tracking and opportunity: The locking-out process and beyond.* Scranton, PA: Chandler.

Schweinhart, L. J., & Weikart, D. P. (1980). Young children grow up: The effects of the Perry Preschool program on youths through age 15 (Monograph, No. 7). Ypsilanti, MI: High/Scope Educational Research Foundation.

Sellin, T., & Wolfgang, M. E. (1964). *The measurement of delinquency.* New York: John Wiley.

Silberberg, N. E., & Silberberg, M. C. (1971). School achievement and delinquency. *Review of Educational Research, 41*(1), 17-32.

Simons, R. L. (1978). The meaning of the IQ-delinquency relationship. *American Sociological Review, 43,* 268-280.

Weber, C. U., Foster, P. W., & Weikart, D. P. (1978). An economic analysis of the Ypsilanti Perry Preschool project. *Monographs of the High/Scope Educational Research Foundation* (No. 5).

Weikart, D. P., Bond, J. T., & McNeil, J. T. (1978). The Ypsilanti Perry Preschool project: Preschool years and longitudinal results through fourth grade. *Monographs of the High/Scope Educational Research Foundation* (No. 3).

Weikart, D. P., Deloria, D., Lawser, S., & Wiegerink, R. (1970). Longitudinal results of the Ypsilanti Perry Preschool project. *Monographs of the High/Scope Educational Research Foundation* (No. 1).

Weikart, D. P., Rogers, L., Adcock, C., & McClelland, D. (1971). *The cognitively oriented curriculum: A framework for preschool teachers.* Urbana, IL: National Association for the Education of Young Children.

Werner, E. E., & Smith, R. S. (1982). *Vulnerable but invincible.* New York: McGraw-Hill.

Wiatrowski, M. D., Hansell, S., Massey, C. R., & Wilson, D. L.. (1982). Curriculum tracking and delinquency. *American Sociological Review, 47,* 151-160.

Wolfgang, M. E., Figlio, R. M., & Sellin, T. (1972). *Delinquency in a birth cohort.* Chicago: The University of Chicago Press.

10

Teacher Practices, Social Development, and Delinquency

J. David Hawkins
Tony Lam

Background and Rationale

Delinquent behavior results from the interaction of a developing child and his or her social environment. The pathway to delinquency is influenced by experiences in the family, at school, and in the community. Apart from prior delinquent behavior, association with delinquent peers is the strongest predictor of adolescent delinquent behavior (Elliott, Huizinga, & Ageton, 1982; Elliott & Voss, 1974; Ginsberg & Greenley, 1978; Hirschi, 1969; Jensen, 1972; Jessor & Jessor, 1977; Johnson, 1979; Johnstone, 1981; Kandel & Adler, 1982; Meade & Marsden, 1981; Meier & Johnson, 1977; Weis et al., 1981; Winfree, Theis, & Griffiths, 1981). However, both family and school experiences also contribute to the process of "becoming delinquent."

There is disagreement about how and how much family and school experiences contribute. In their longitudinal study of the National Youth Panel, Elliott et al. (1982) found only indirect effects on delinquency of social bonds to family and school. However, other investigators have found evidence of more direct effects of family and/or school experiences on delinquency in both cross-sectional studies (Hirschi, 1969; Jensen, 1972; Johnson, 1979; Johnstone, 1981; Meade & Marsden, 1981) and perhaps, more important, longitudinal

Authors' Note: The authors wish to thank Denise Lishner for her assitance in preparing portions of this chapter. The research reported in this chapter was supported by Grant Number 80-JS-AX-0052 from the National Institute for Juvenile Justice and Delinquency Prevention, U.S. Department of Justice. Points of view or opinions on this document are those of the authors and do not necessarily represent official position or policies of the U.S. Department of Justice.

analyses (Elliott & Voss, 1974; Jessor & Jessor, 1977; Kandel, Kessler, & Margulies, 1978).

While debate continues regarding the ways in which family and school experiences affect delinquency, it appears reasonable to view the evolution of delinquency from a developmental perspective. Delinquent behavior is likely to be a response to or result of experiences from birth through adolescence. From a developmental perspective, it can be argued that early experiences in the family are likely to influence social bonding to the family (Hirschi, 1969), social and self-control (Reckless, 1961), and subsequent experiences in school, as well as the likelihood that social bonds of attachment to school and commitment to education will develop (Bahr, 1979). Similarly, school experiences themselves are likely to influence the extent to which a youth will develop social bonds of attachment and commitment to prosocial activities and prosocial others (Hirschi, 1969; Schafer & Polk, 1967). The social influence of peers becomes salient during adolescence itself. If the process of developing a social bond to prosocial others and prosocial activities has been interrupted by uncaring or inconsistent parents, by poor school performance, or by inconsistent teachers, youths are more likely to come under the influence of peers who are in the same situation and are also more likely to be influenced by such peers to engage in delinquent activities (Hawkin & Weis, 1985).

A developmental perspective on delinquency would suggest that prevention efforts that seek to address only the peer/delinquency linkage and that wait to intervene until adolescence may be misspecified. Intervention at this stage in the development of delinquent behavior may be too late to reverse a process that has been set in motion as the result of experiences in family and school.

This developmental view of delinquency has been integrated into a theory of delinquency and its prevention, the social development model (Hawkins & Weis, 1985; Weis & Hawkins, 1981). The theory integrates social control and social learning theories as has the work of others (Braukman, Kirigin, & Wolf, 1980; Conger, 1976, 1980; Elliott et al., 1982; Johnson, 1979; Johnstone, 1981; Linden & Hackler, 1973; Meade & Marsden, 1981). In contrast to others, our theoretical model seeks explicitly to serve as a basis for delinquency prevention. We have attempted to describe general stages of development and to identify intervention approaches that would appear appropriate at each stage.

Our social development theory identifies three general conditions that appear to be necessary in the formation of a social bond in each context of socialization. These conditions are opportunities for involvement, skills, and reinforcements. We posit that social bonds are developed in families, in school, or among peers when youths have the opportunity to be involved with others in activities and interactions in these settings, when they have the skills necessary to perform competently in the settings, and when they experience consistent rewards or reinforcement for their involvement. When youths experience opportunities for involvement in the family, when they develop the requisite social, cognitive, and behavioral skills to perform as expected in family activities and interactions and when they are rewarded consistently for adequate performance in the family, they will develop a bond of attachment, commitment, and belief in the family. When these three conditions are not present in the family, a bond to family is not likely to develop.

Bonding to school is conditioned by the extent to which social bonds to the family have developed by the time the child enters school as well as by the extent to which the child experiences opportunities for involvement, develops skills, and is rewarded for skillful performance at school. Similarly, social bonds to peers, whether prosocial or delinquent, will develop to the extent that youths have opportunities for involvement with those peers, the skills to perform as expected by those peers, and the rewards that are forthcoming from interaction with those peers. We do not suggest that strong bonds of attachment to family and school will preclude the development of strong bonds of attachment to peers so long as the norms of family members, school personnel, and peers regarding appropriate performance or behavior do not conflict. However, we suggest that the formation of social bonds to family and school will decrease the likelihood that youths will develop attachments to *delinquent* peers in adolescence, since the behaviors rewarded in family and school and those likely to be rewarded by delinquent youths are not compatible.

As a foundation for delinquency prevention, the social development model implies that families, schools, and peer groups are appropriate objects for intervention, depending on the developmental stage of the child. Interventions that seek to increase the likelihood of social bonding to the family are appropriate from early childhood through early adolescence. Interventions that seek to increase the likelihood of social bonding to school are appropriate throughout the years of school attendance. Interventions that seek to increase social bonding to prosocial peers are appropriate as youths approach and enter adolescence.

We are currently testing the combined effect of a set of developmentally sequenced interventions that are consistent with the social development model. We are seeking to identify the combined and, where possible, individual effects of the interventions to see (1) whether they create the conditions of increased opportunities, skills, and rewards; (2) the extent to which they generate increased social bonding to family, school, and prosocial peers; and (3) the extent to which they are successful in reducing delinquent behavior. The test is being conducted using an experimental and quasi-experimental longitudinal design. This chapter focuses on the portion of the project involving 1,166 seventh grade students in Seattle in 1981-1982.

If the process of becoming delinquent is a developmental one, then it can be expected that the process of developing social bonds that will inhibit delinquency also takes place over time. We do not expect the interventions that we are testing to be powerful enough to extinguish delinquent behavior over the course of a single academic year. We do hypothesize that the combined effects of a series of interventions consistent with the social development model should have cumulative effects on delinquency if the interventions are implemented with fidelity to the conditions outlined in the model.

It is reasonable to begin to assess results at the end of one academic year of the project to see whether the effort has, in fact, produced measurable changes in the contexts of socialization, in social bonding, and in behavior. This chapter reports the results of analyses focused on those questions. We discuss only one component of the project, the methods of instruction included in the school-focused interventions. We review the relationships between school experiences and delinquency to provide a foundation for suggesting that certain methods of classroom instruction in public schools should hold promise for preventing delinquency. The ways in which these instructional practices might address the correlates of juvenile delinquency are explored. Using the data from the first year of implementation with seventh-grade students in Seattle, we investigate:

(1) The extent to which teachers' instructional practices in experimental classrooms have been changed.

(2) The extent to which the teaching practices tested in this project are related to student classroom behaviors.
(3) The extent to which the teaching practices are related to academic achievement.
(4) The extent to which the teaching practices have produced greater student bonding to school.
(5) The extent to which the teaching practices tested in this project have produced changes in school related delinquent and antisocial behavior after 1 year of intervention.

It should be noted that the project we are discussing does not seek specifically to identify high-risk youths for intervention. Rather, the project intervenes with a general population sample in an urban school district. Although we are using various means to identify high-risk children within our samples and although some of our work focuses on these children, the project includes a sample of the general population of children at the participating grade levels.

Those familiar with the literature on delinquency and the growing body of knowledge in the area of prediction of antisocial behavior may question this focus on the general population. Only a small proportion of children engage in repeated serious delinquency (Elliott, Ageton, & Huizinga, 1978; Shannon, 1982; Wolfgang, Figlio, & Sellin, 1972).

Given this knowledge and a desire to be cost-effective in seeking to prevent delinquency, why do we intervene with a general population sample? There are several reasons for our choice. The first involves the problem of prediction. In our view, techniques for the prediction of delinquent behavior in individuals before they are apprehended are not sufficiently developed to justify intervention strategies that concentrate only on high-risk individuals (Weis & Sederstrom, 1981). It is possible to predict the delinquent behavior of individuals who have been apprehended previously for delinquent behavior with some confidence. However, waiting to intervene until a prediction of future delinquency can be made with some certainty requires waiting until much of the crime to be committed by a youth has already occurred. For example, Weis and Sederstrom (1981) estimate that *totally effective intervention* with the chronic recidivists in Wolfgang et al.'s cohort (1972) based on extrapolative prediction from prior patterns of delinquency could, at best, prevent only 21% of the entire cohort's total offenses. It is difficult to imagine that intervention with such recidivists would be totally effective since intervention using this type of predictive approach would not occur until the causal sequence of becoming alienated from family and school and enmeshed with delinquent peers had already occurred and would somehow have to be reversed.

An alternative approach is to predict delinquency on an individual basis from the known correlates of delinquency. A number of researchers have carried out longitudinal studies that have identified early predictors of adolescent delinquency. (See Loeber & Dishion, 1983, for a review.) The problem with the use of findings from large sample surveys as a basis for targeting high-risk individuals is that, even with the best prediction approaches currently available, the shift from the level of aggregate survey data to the individual level will result in a substantial number of false positives (prediction of delinquency which will not occur) and false negatives (prediction of no delinquency, but delinquency will occur) (Monahan, 1981). While recent advances at the Oregon Social Learning Center appear promising for reducing the likelihood of false-positive and false-negative predictions in identifying youths at risk for delinquency (Loeber, Dishion, & Patterson, 1983), this problem has not yet been overcome.

A second and equally important reason for our choice of a general population rather than individually targeted intervention approach is the assumption that the conditions that create social bonding and inhibit delinquency occur in social organizations such as school in the course of activities that are directed primarily toward other goals, such as socialization and education. The social development model suggests that when such organizations are successful in creating opportunities, skills, and rewards for youthful participants, social bonding is likely to occur and delinquency is likely to be inhibited. Thus it appears appropriate to seek changes in organizations to ensure that they provide opportunities, skills, and rewards to those youths who participate in them rather than to seek to change directly the behaviors of targeted high-risk individual youths. In this regard, it appears appropriate, in designing school-focused interventions, to seek to alter the general classroom and organizational environments of schools to increase the conditions for social bonding. Hence the focus here is on changing teacher practices rather than on removing high-risk students from classrooms for special attention.

These considerations led us to design our experiment as a test of primary or preclusive prevention approaches that seek to affect the practices of those in the family, school, and peer environments of developing children. Because rates of delinquency are higher in urban areas that have high proportions of people of lower socioeconomic status, minority populations, and unemployment (Weis & Sederstrom, 1981), this research is being conducted in an urban community with these characteristics.

SCHOOL EXPERIENCES AND DELINQUENCY

We turn now to the focus of this chapter, the evaluation of the promise of a set of classroom instructional methods for increasing social bonding and preventing delinquency, focusing first on the evidence regarding school experiences and delinquency (see Hawkins & Lishner, in press).

School Failure and Delinquency. There is considerable evidence that, whether measured by self-report or by official police data, male delinquency is related to academic performance at school (Elliott & Voss, 1974; Jensen, 1976; Johnson, 1979; Kelly & Balch, 1971; Linden, 1974; Noblit, 1976; Polk, 1969; Polk & Schafer, 1972; Schafer, 1969). While youths from low socioeconomic and minority background are more likely to experience academic failure than are while middle-class students, the experience of academic failure or success itself appears to be related to delinquency (Call, 1965; Jensen, 1972; Johnson, 1979; McPartland & McDill, 1977; Palmore & Hammond, 1964; Polk, 1969; Polk, Frease, & Richmond, 1974; Stinchcombe, 1964). Juvenile delinquents consistently perform more poorly in school than do nondelinquents (Kelly & Balch, 1971; Frease, 1973; Polk et al., 1974; Senna, Rathus, & Siegal, 1974; Slocum & Stone, 1963). Frease (1973) found that officially reported delinquency was highest among boys with low grades who did not like school and lowest among boys with high grades who liked school. Youths who experience success in school are less likely to become delinquent, while those who fail in school are more likely to engage in disruptive classroom behavior and delinquency (Frease, 1973; Kelly, 1975).

School failure, as measured in these studies, does not appear to be a surrogate for academic ability. While some research has shown an inverse relationship between IQ and delinquency (Farrington, 1973; Jerse & Fakouri, 1978), Hirschi (1969) found that this relationship disappeared when school performance and attachment were controlled, and Wolfgang et al. (1972) found the relationship between IQ and delinquency to be spurious. These results suggest that the process of succeeding or failing in school, the experience itself, may be related to delinquency.

A number of theorists have sought to explain this observed relationship between school failure and delinquency. Hirschi (1969) suggested that academic incompetence and poor school performance lead to dislike of school, which precipitates rejection of school authority and results in an increased likelihood of delinquent behavior. Elliott and Voss (1974) theorized that school failure leads to alienation from school and subsequently to drop out and delinquency. They viewed delinquency as an adaptation to school failure, arguing that those who fail in school become frustrated and are rejected and shunned by others, leading to negative attitudes to school and alternative standards of conduct. This is supported by Bachman's research (Bachman et al., 1978), which has shown that early school experiences are more relevant to predicting delinquency than late ones.

Gold (1978) viewed delinquency as a defense against feelings of low self-esteem derived from school failure. He suggested that youths who fail in school seek recognition by engaging in criminal behaviors with delinquent peers. Such students may provide each other with support, rewards, and reinforcements for delinquent behavior that they have not found in a conventional context (Cohen & Short, 1976). Research by Elliott and Voss (1974) indicated that when boys with police contacts dropped out of school, their rates of police contact systematically declined. A possible interpretation is that school experiences may reinforce delinquent behavior among some youths.

Commitment to Educational Goals and Delinquency. There is also evidence that a low degree of commitment to education is related to delinquency. Youths who are not successful academically may still be committed to school and educational attainment. However, it has been shown that students who are not committed to educational pursuits are more likely to engage in delinquent behavior (Elliott & Voss, 1974; Hirschi, 1969). Hirschi (1969) found an inverse relationship between an achievement orientation and delinquency, as well as a negative relationship between educational aspirations and self-reported delinquency. Epps (1967) and Pine (1965) found similar negative relationships between educational aspirations and self-reported delinquency. Factors such as how much students like school

(Kelly & Balch, 1971), time spent on homework, and perception of the relevance of coursework are also related to delinquency (Elliott & Voss, 1974). Glasser (1978) found that students who exhibit discipline problems generally have no stake in school and rarely participate in school activities. Johnstone's annual surveys of high school seniors (1981) have demonstrated that the use of hallucinogens, cocaine, heroin, stimulants, sedatives, or nonmedically prescribed tranquilizers is significantly lower among those students who expect to attend college than among those who do not plan to go on to college.

School Climate and Delinquency. Finally, there is evidence that school organization itself affects both academic achievement and student behavior. The Safe School Study (National Institute of Education, 1978) concluded that schools organized in certain ways experience lower levels of violence and vandalism than other schools. The authors concluded that schools are conducive to learning and to low rates of violence when they are organized so that the following conditions are present:

(1) Students perceive their courses to be relevant;
(2) Students perceive that they have some control over what happens to them at school;
(3) Students perceive school discipline policies as firm, fair, clear, and consistently enforced;
(4) Students see that there is a rational reward structure in the school that recognizes students for their achievements;
(5) There is a strong and effective school governance, with a consistent structure of order and strong principal leadership; and
(6) Ways are found to decrease the impersonality of the school and increase the amount of continuing contact between students and teachers.

The school-focused interventions tested in our project seek to improve instruction in public school classrooms, to promote successful school experiences for a larger proportion of students, and to enhance the development of social bonds to school that will decrease the likelihood of association with delinquent peers and delinquent behavior. The interventions include schools within a school, school-based management of change, reorientation of the curriculum, methods of instruction, student involvement and school/family programs. This chapter is limited to a discussion of the methods of classroom instruction tested in this project and their potential for preventing delinquency.

Classroom Instruction and
Delinquency Prevention

The three classroom-based instructional strategies being implemented to accomplish the project goals are proactive classroom management, interactive teaching, and cooperative learning. These are described briefly below. (See Cummings, 1983, for a more complete description.)

Proactive Classroom Management. Proactive classroom management is aimed at establishing an environment that is conducive to learning and that promotes appropriate student behavior, minimizing disruption of classroom activities. Such an environment increases opportunities for skill development for all students, and should therefore increase student commitment to learning. Teachers are taught to give clear and explicit instructions for student behavior and to recognize and reward attempts to cooperate. Classroom routines are to be established by the teacher at the beginning of the school year. These set up a consistent pattern of expectations between the teacher and students. Clear directions and consistent expectations should result in effective use of classroom time for skill development and should prevent discipline problems (Emmer & Evertson, 1980). Teachers are also taught methods for preventing minor classroom disruptions from interrupting instruction and decreasing opportunities for learning (Cummings, 1983). The teacher learns to take immediate and brief action to restore the learning environment while simultaneously downplaying the incident. Also integral to effective management of the classroom is the frequent, appropriate use of encouragement and praise. Praise should specify exactly what student behavior is being rewarded so that desired behaviors are reinforced (Martin, 1977). The contingent use of praise should increase social bonding of student to teacher and classroom. Together, these strategies should create a positive climate for learning and deter incidents of disruption, affording students a more productive classroom experience that should contribute to social bonding to school.

Interactive Teaching. Interactive teaching is a method based on the premise that virtually all students can and will develop the skills necessary to succeed in the classroom, under appropriate instructional conditions (Bloom, 1976). This approach has resulted in improved learning in a wide variety of classroom situations (Block, 1971, 1974; Peterson, 1972; Stallings, 1980). The components of interactive teaching used in this project are mental set, objectives, input, modeling, checking for understanding, remediation, and assessment. Interactive teaching requires that students master clearly specified learning objectives before proceeding to more advanced work. Grades are determined by demonstration of mastery and improvement over past performance, rather than in comparison with other students. Interactive teaching expands opportunities for students to attain success while reducing the risk of failure. This should enhance students' perceptions of their own competence as well as their commitment to educational pursuits. The use of clear and explicit objective standards in grading should promote students' belief in the fairness of the educational system.

Cooperative learning. Cooperative learning involves small, heterogeneous groups of students as learning partners. Students of differing abilities and backgrounds work together in teams to master curriculum material, and receive recognition as a team for their group's academic performance. Cooperative learning makes students dependent on one another for positive rewards (Slavin, 1980). Team scores are based on the individual student's academic improvement over past performance, allowing each student to contribute to the team's overall achievement. The cooperative learning techniques used in the project are Student Teams Achievement Divisions (STAD) (Slavin, 1980), Teams-Games-Tournaments (TGT) (DeVries & Slavin, 1978), and Jigsaw (Aronson, 1978).

Cooperative learning creates a classroom norm favoring learning and academic performance (Slavin, 1979). Mastery of learning tasks, motivation, positive student attitudes toward teachers and schools, and self-concept are greater in cooperative classrooms than in competitive or individualistic ones (Johnson & Johnson, 1980; Slavin, 1979). Research has shown that cooperative learning methods are more effective than traditional methods in increasing student achievement and in developing mutual concern among students across racial groups (Slavin, 1982). In combination with training in basic cooperative skills, this approach reinforces students in helping each other to succeed in classroom endeavors. Positive student interaction should reduce alienation in the classroom and promote attachment among students based on the pursuit of accepted academic goals (Slavin, 1980). This should, in turn, reduce the likelihood that students will form alternative attachments with delinquent peers that lead to delinquent behaviors (Hawkins, 1981).

Methods

Implementation of the Research

Prior to the 1981-1982 academic year, seventh-grade core subject (math, language arts, and social studies) teachers in three middle schools in Seattle were assigned to experimental or control classrooms. (One teacher assigned to an experimental classroom was not hired until late October). All core subject teachers in a fourth school were assigned to experimental classrooms and all core subject teachers in a fifth school were assigned to the control condition, resulting in a total of 15 experimental and 18 control teachers teaching a total of 54 experimental and 59 control classes, respectively. Experimental teachers received 5 days of initial training in the instructional methods described above. In addition, one teacher in each experimental school was assigned to perform the role of "clinical supervisor" or "coach." These teachers were trained to use a system of observation and routine feedback in order to encourage experimental teachers to use the methods of instruction that the project seeks to test. The "coaches" received one extra free period each day during which they were expected to observe and confer with experimental teachers regarding their use of the methods of instruction. Finally, the project provided three booster training sessions to experimental teachers during the academic year.

It should be noted that the experimental teachers were, for the most part, randomly assigned to participate in this project from existing staffs of participating schools. The teachers in the experimental conditions were not selected for their teaching expertise or for their reputations as innovators or "master teachers." The project is ambitious in this regard. The goal is to see whether existing schools and classrooms can be altered to create the conditions for social bonding to school and then to see if the creation of these conditions is related to reduced rates of delinquency.

With one exception, seventh-grade students in three Seattle middle schools were assigned to experimental and control classrooms on a stratified random basis to ensure racial balance in the groups. In one school, due to scheduling conflicts, those students requesting Spanish and German as an elective were scheduled into experimental classes while those requesting French as an elective were scheduled into control classes. All seventh-grade students in the fourth school were in experimental classes and all seventh graders in the fifth school were in control classes resulting in a total sample of 513 experimental and 653 control subjects in the Seattle project at the beginning of the 1981-1982 academic year.

The Sample

Experimental and control groups were compared for equivalence in the fall of 1981 using school record data. There were no significant differences between the two groups overall for proportion of males, age, ethnicity, with whom the subject lived, eligibility for free lunches (a measure of low socioeconomic status) or standardized achievement test scores in math, reading, language arts, and the total battery of the California Achievement Test. Of the sample, 53% were males, 54.4% were white, 24% were black, 4.4% were hispanic, 12.8% were Asian/Pacific islander, and 3.4% were native Americans. The mean age was 13.3 years. As indicated by free lunch eligibility, 36% were from low-income families.

There were, however, some significant differences within schools and between the school with all experimental classes and the school with all control classes. In one school, the experimental group's mean age was 1.76 months greater than the control group's and in another school, the experimental students had significantly lower average scores on the math, language arts, and total battery of the standardized achievement tests administered prior to the experimental intervention. A between-school comparison of the school with all experimental classes and the school with all control classes revealed two statistically significant differences between students. There was a higher proportion of Asians and Pacific islanders at the experimental school (26.5%) than at the control school (13.5%). Similarly, 23.0% of the experimental students in the school with all experimental classes were classified as nonnative English speakers versus 12.6% of the students in the all-control school. To the extent that these initial differences affect outcomes related to achievement and delinquency, they would appear to be slightly less favorable to the experimental group.

Measures

Teacher Instructional Practices. Teacher use of the instructional practices to be tested in this project was assessed through structured observations of experimental and control teachers using a closed observational recording system. Each experimental and control teacher was observed by trained researchers for one class period on three successive days in the fall, winter, and spring of the 1981-1982 academic year for a total of nine observations per teacher. Separate observations were made and recorded each 60 seconds for each class period observed. For each 60-second observation, the primary teacher activity was coded according to 11 predefined categories listed on the observation form. Additionally, the fidelity of the observed teacher behavior to the teaching practice as established in this project was coded using predetermined criteria. To provide a summary measure of the extent to which teachers were using the project methods of instruction, the minute-by-minute observational data for each class period observed were condensed into "valence scores" using a standardized procedure for assigning weights to each coded observation for each category of teaching practice (see Kerr et al., 1983). The valence scores for each 60-second observation were combined to create a valence score for the class period observed. Valence scores for each teacher were combined to provide a mean teacher valence score for each round of observations. Using another data set, the average interrater reliability (intraclass correlation) of the mean valence score generated from the observation instrument has been found to be 0.91 (Kerr et al., 1983). The valence scores also appear to be relatively stable indicators of teacher practices. The Pearson's correlation between teacher valence scores from winter and spring rounds of observation was $r = 0.78$ (n = 31 teachers). Therefore, winter and spring valence scores were combined to produce an overall valence score for each teacher. These valence scores are used in the analyses below as overall measures of the use of project teaching practices. The mean valence scores for observed teachers ranged from –36.33 for a teacher whose teaching practices violated many of the project's criteria for instruction to 16.67 for a teacher who consistently used a large number of the practices tested in the project.

Student Perceptions of Classroom Processes. The theoretical model to be assessed in this project postulates that youths must experience, in the classroom, the opportunities and rewards hypothesized as conditions for social bonding if they are to develop social bonds to schools that will inhibit delinquent behavior. One way of assessing the extent to which youths have such experiences is to assess the extent to which they perceive the events and processes taking place in the classroom as providing the hypothesized opportunities and rewards. Indicators of students' perceptions of the classroom were collected using a group-administered questionnaire given by project research staff to experimental and control students in October 1981 and again in May 1982.

A total of 1,012 (93.7% of 1,080 eligible students completed the student questionnaire in October, 1981. Of the 1,282 eligible students, 920 (71.8%) completed the survey in the spring of 1982. Completing both fall 1981 and spring 1982 surveys were 766 students (67.7% of the fall sample).

Six items that tap perceptions of opportunities and rewards provided through the classroom are included on the questionnaire (see appendix). Each item has a 5-point response scale (YES!, yes, ?, no, NO!). In addition, a 5-point index was constructed to tap student perceptions of classroom opportunities for positive peer interaction: "Opportunities for Positive Peer Interaction in Class" (Cronbach's alpha = 0.65) (see appendix). This index seeks to assess students' perceptions of the general opportunities provided in class for peer interaction.

Student Behaviors Linked to Achievement. Student achievement is inversely related to delinquent behavior. We hypothesize that the use of the project teaching practices will be accompanied by a corresponding level of student behavior that is likely to lead to student academic success. In other words, when teachers use the project teaching practices, students should be more likely to engage actively in the classroom learning activity presented and should be less likely to be "off task." Students' "engaged" and "off task" behavior in the classroom was measured as part of the classroom observation procedures described earlier. Behaviors of students while in each observed classroom were sampled and observed in the following manner. Five students were randomly chosen for observation during each class period. Each was rapidly observed in sequence during each minute of classroom coding and a determination was made as to whether each student was actively "engaged" in the lesson, "attending" to the lesson without visible indication of being actively involved, or "off task" with another student or alone. Mean interrater reliability (Kappa coefficient) of the student behavior ratings, calculated from another data set, was 0.40 (Kerr et al., 1983).

A second measure of student behavior linked to achievement is the proportion of free time spent on homework. Research has shown that the amount of time spent on homework, as measured by student self-report, contributes significantly in explaining high school student grades after controlling for race, family background, ability, and the student's program of study (Keith, 1982). This measure in the current study was constructed from items on the fall and spring student questionnaires. Students were asked to estimate the number of hours per week spent doing things with family, spent with friends outside of school, and spent doing homework. The total time reported for these three questions was calculated and the proportion of the total spent on homework was used as an indicator of student behavior linked to achievement.

Student Achievement. Test scores from the California Achievement Test (Forms 11C and D, 1977) on the math, reading, language, and total batteries are used as one measure of student achievement. The tests were administered by the school district in the spring of 1981 (before the project began) and again in the spring of 1982. A total of 1,034 (95.7%) students participated in the spring 1981 testing, and 1,058 (82.5%) participated in the spring 1982 testing.

A second measure of academic achievement is grades. Student grades for math, language arts, and social studies were obtained from district grade reports for the fall 1981 semester and for the spring 1982 semester. Fall grade reports were available for 847 (78.4%) students and spring grade reports were available for 1,092 (85.2%) students.

Student Bonding to School. It is hypothesized that teacher practices advocated in the project will lead both directly and through improved student achievement and perceptions of increased oportunities, skills, and rewards within the school setting to increased bonds of commitment and attachment to school. Social bonding to school is measured by 13 items on the student survey. Of these items, 3 have been combined into an attachment to school index (Cronbach's Alpha = 0.86) (see appendix).

Student Bonding to Peers. It is hypothesized that increased academic success and increased perceptions of opportunities, skills, and rewards from school resulting from teacher use of the project practices will lead to increased attachment to prosocial peers and decreased attachment to delinquent ones. Student bonding to prosocial peers and friends in trouble is measured by items from the student survey. (Classroom sociometric data were collected in the second year of the project, but are not available for this analysis.) The indicators of prosocial friends include "how good a student is your best friend," and the "number of close friends at school," reported by the respondent on the fall and spring surveys. Indicators of delinquency-prone friendships are the following: "My best friend gets into trouble a lot"; "If a friend asked to copy your exam in class would you let your friend copy it even if you knew you would get kicked out of class if you got caught?" and "What would you do if some friends asked you to cut school with them?"

Student Antisocial Behavior. In this longitudinal study, it is not expected that the project interventions will have measurable effects on either self-reported or official delinquent behavior within the first academic year. However, school-related misbehavior might be expected to change within this time period as a consequence of the use of the project teaching practices. Six school-related measures of antisocial behavior are included on the fall and spring student questionnaires. They are the reported frequency in the last year of staying away from school when parents thought the respondent was there, the number of times the respondent reports being sent out of the classroom in the past year, the number of times the respondent reports being suspended or expelled from school in the past year, the number of times the respondent reports taking things from a desk or locker at school in the past year, the number of times the respondent reports getting in trouble at school for drugs or alcohol in the past year, and the number of times the respondent reports being high on drugs at school in the past month. School record data also are available for school suspensions and expulsions.

Analysis

The theory to be assessed through this study is complex, and includes a large number of distinct concepts as well as both direct and indirect paths to delinquent behavior. The analysis reported here does not seek to test the theory, but rather to look for evidence of relationships between the teaching practices advocated in the project and the subsequent constructs in the theoretical model. To accomplish this goal, two types of analyses are conducted. Analysis of covariance (or analysis of variance where appropriate covariates are not available) is used to compare experimental and control teachers and students on variables of interest. Second, regression analyses in which teacher valence scores are entered as a predictor variable are conducted. The regression analyses were performed at the aggregated teacher level across classes, with teacher, rather than individual student, as the unit of analysis.[1]

Results

The results are arranged according to research questions addressed.

Did the Project Change Teaching Practices at the Classroom Level?

A fundamental question in any field experiment concerns the extent to which the intervention was actually implemented. This is especially important when the program relies on practitioners in existing institutions to change their behaviors. Previous prevention experiments have experienced difficulty in generating changes in teacher behaviors (Moskowitz et al., 1981a, 1981b).

Comparison of the teacher valence scores across experimental and control classrooms allows an assessment of the implementation of the project teaching methods in the experimental classrooms. The mean combined valence score for the 15 experimental teachers was 1.03 (s.d. = 12.99), while the mean valence score for the 17 observed control teachers was −13.11 (s.d. = 13.74). This difference was significant beyond the α = .05 level (t = 3.02, df = 31, p = .005), suggesting that, overall, experimental teachers were more likely to conform to the teaching practices advocated by the project than were control teachers. This difference in mean valence score was consistent within all three schools with a within building experimental design as well as between the two whole grade comparison schools. In contrast, analysis of variance of mean valence scores revealed no significant differences at the α = .05 level across experimental classrooms in the four experimental schools (F = 0.94, p = 0.46) or across control classrooms in four schools (F = .49, p = 0.69). It should be noted, however, that the valence score was constructed so that points are added for desired project practices while points are subtracted for undesired practices (Kerr et al., 1983). A mean score of 1.03 is nearly a neutral score. The observed difference between experimental and control teachers appears to reflect undesirable teaching practices of control teachers (as defined by the project) rather than exemplary implementation of the practices by experimental teachers. Nonetheless, there do appear to be differences between experimental and control teachers in the use of project practices during the first year of project implementation.

Did Students Perceive Differences in their Classrooms Associated with the Teaching Practices?

Six items and an index were used to assess possible differences between experimental and control classes as perceived by students. Using an analysis of covariance (ANCOVA) procedure in which student responses to these same items on the fall 1981 questionnaire were used as covariates, experimental and control students were compared within the three experimental schools and across the two schools with whole grade experimental and control conditions. This entailed 24 separate ANCOVAS, creating a problem of inflating Type I error rate from performing multiple tests of significance. If an α .05 significance level is chosen, it is likely that at least one of these ANCOVAS would produce significant results by chance alone. While this problem is recognized, individual building analyses were conducted in order to provide an indication of which of the teaching methods were implemented in each school as perceived by students.

Student team learning groups were the most consistently reported characteristics of experimental classrooms. In all comparisons, experimental students were more likely to report that they broke up into groups in their classes, and this difference in adjusted mean scores was significant in all comparisons at the $\alpha = .05$ level. At school 3, this finding was accompanied, as hypothesized, by greater involvement in classroom discussions and activities. However, no significant differences on this latter item were found at the $\alpha = .05$ level between experimental and control subjects in the other schools. Further, none of the comparisons revealed significant differences in perceptions of a classroom norm favoring achievement ("Other students in my classes want me to do my best work."), though while not significant, the differences in adjusted means for this item were in the expected direction in three schools. While students reported the use of student team learning groups in their classes, as implemented, these groups were not consistently accompanied by dramatic differences in student perceptions of classroom involvement or norms for achievement during the first project year. Further, the use of student learning groups was not accompanied by perceptions of generally greater opportunities for positive peer interaction in experimental classes as measured by the index of five items related to this construct.

The results regarding student perceptions of interactive teaching methods were scattered. Experimental students at school 4 reported greater opportunities for remediation (a second chance to learn the material) than did the corresponding control students in school 5. At school 2, experimental students reported that their teachers were more likely to seek to establish a mental set (showing the utility of the material). At school 3, experimental students perceived less use of competitive grading practices by their teachers. While all these findings are in the expected direction, the data do not reveal a consistent pattern of perceived differences in classrooms associated with the use of interactive teaching methods.

The valence score analyses revealed that in the first project year, experimental teachers were using some of the project teaching practices more than their control colleagues. They appear to have been most consistent in their use of student team learning groups. However, during the first year, none of the experimental faculties implemented the project teaching methods to the extent that a consistent pattern of predicted differences existed between experimental and control students' perceptions of the opportunities and rewards available in their classes.

Are the Project Teaching Practices Associated with Student Behaviors Linked to Achievement?

The previous analyses looked at how the project teaching methods were related to students' perceptions of their classrooms. These perceptions make up one set of variables that may relate to bonding and delinquent behavior. How are project teaching methods related to student classroom behaviors linked to academic success? Perhaps the best summary indication of the relationship between the teaching practices advocated by the project and student classroom behavior is shown in the correlations between the teacher summary implementation or valence scores and students' "engaged" and "off task" behavior in the classroom. The valence scores are positively related to engaged behavior by students ($r = 0.38$; $p < 0.001$) and negatively related to off-task behavior by students in the classroom ($r = -0.60$; $p < 0.001$). These relationships suggest that when teachers use the teaching methods advocated by the project, students engage in more behaviors likely to be associated with academic success and in fewer behaviors likely to be associated with academic failure and alienation from the classroom.

These data from the classroom are consistent with data regarding the proportion of time students spend on homework outside of school. Using teacher as the unit of analysis, the contribution of teacher valence scores to the proportion of time students reported they spent on homework during the 1981-1982 academic year was assessed in a regression analysis. After the contribution of proportion of time spent on homework during the previous year was removed, teacher valence scores explained 5.8% of the variance in time spent on homework (semipartial $r = 0.24$). Again, it appears that the project teaching practices are positively associated with student behaviors that are likely to be related to student academic success, though this relationship is relatively weak.

Are the Project Teaching Practices Related to Student Academic Achievements?

Academic success can be measured in at least two ways: student performance on standardized achievement tests and student grades as reported by teachers on report cards. Both measures are available in the project. Regression analyses controlling for spring 1981 scores on the California Achievement Test (CAT, 1977) were conducted at the teacher level to assess the relationship between teacher valence scores and CAT scores for the spring of 1982. The analyses were conducted by subject area. There was virtually no relationship between language arts teacher valence scores and CAT reading or CAT language arts scores. There was a relationship in the expected direction between math teacher valence scores and CAT math scores. Valence scores accounted for approximately 9% of the remaining variance in spring 1982 scores when the common variance between spring 1981 and spring 1982 math scores was removed (semipartial $r = 0.30$).

The relationship between grades and teacher valence scores was also assessed, though in this analysis, no control for previous grades was available. Again, the relationship was strongest, and in the predicted direction, for math teacher valence scores and math grades ($r = 0.46$). There was a weak relationship between social studies teacher valence scores and social studies grades, in the predicted direction ($r = 0.21$), and there was virtually no relationship between language arts teacher valence scores and language arts grades.

In sum, it appears that the relationship between the use of project teaching practices and student achievement is mixed. After one year of intervention, there is a consistent moderate relationship in the expected direction between the use of project teaching practices in math classes and math achievement scores as well as math grades. However, no relationship is found between the use of project teaching practices and student achievement measures for language arts.

It is possible that the practices advocated in the project are best suited for generating academic success in math and are not as well suited to teaching other subjects. Alternatively, it is possible that the outcome measures used to assess math achievement are more sensitive or more closely related to classroom activities allowing early documentation of relationships for math that may be observed over a longer period of time for other subject areas.

Are the Project Teaching Practices Associated with Student Bonding to School?

Perhaps the most direct indicator of a relationship between teacher use of the project practices and student attachment that might be related to those practices is the correlation between teacher valence scores and classroom mean scores on student reports of how much they like their classes. Consistent with previously reported findings, when analyzed at the teacher level, the correlation was strongest and in the expected direction for math classes. The correlation between the teacher valence score and liking math was $r = 0.54$. This relationship was paralleled by t-tests comparing experimental and control students' responses to the item "I like my math class this year" (1 = YES!, 5 = NO!). In schools 1, 2, and 3, experimental students responded more positively than did controls to this question on a 5-point response scale (for school 1, $t = -2.26$, df = 138, $p = .025$; for school 2, $t = -2.17$, df = 165, $p = .032$; for school 3, $t = -2.05$, df = 193, $p = .042$). No significant difference was found for this item between experimental students in school 4 and control students in school 5.

In contrast to the findings for math, the relationship between teacher valence scores and student reports of liking language arts classes was in the opposite direction from that hypothesized ($r = -0.30$). This relationship was not as strong as the positive relationship for math. Experimental and control group comparisons within schools suggest that individual teacher attributes other than project practices may have contributed to this result for language arts. Experimental subjects at school 1 were significantly more likely than controls to report *liking* their language arts class (t = -2.51, df = 125, p = 0.13) while a comparison between schools 4 and 5 showed that experimental students were significantly less likely than controls to report liking their language arts classes (t = 3.40, df = 473, p = .001). Experimental and control comparisons on this variable were not significant for schools 2 and 3.

Consistent with prior results, virtually no relationship was found at the teacher level between teacher valence scores and the mean degree to which students reported liking their social studies classes. Again, experimental and control comparisons revealed significant differences for two schools but not in the same direction. At school 1, experimental subjects liked their social studies classes less than did controls (t = 2.9, df = 124, p = .004) while at school 2, experimental subjects liked their social studies classes more than did controls (t = -3.30, df = 121, p = .001).

Undoubtedly, teacher and class characteristics other than the use of project practices influence the degree to which students report liking their classes. However, the consistency of results for math classes suggests that the project's teaching practices may have a relationship to favorable student attitudes toward math classes across teachers and buildings.

The project teaching practices also appear to be related to student educational aspirations and expectations. At the teacher level, teacher valence scores explain 9.5% of the variance in scores on a 7-point item indicating the amount of schooling expected when the common variance between spring 1982 and fall 1981 responses on this item is partialled out (semipartial r = 0.31). Similarly, teacher valence scores account for 14.4% of the variance in scores on a 7-point item indicating the amount of formal education desired by students when the common variance between spring 1982 and fall 1981 responses on this item is partialled out (semipartial r = .38). Both these relationships are in the expected direction; greater use of the project teaching practices is associated with greater educational aspirations and expectations on the part of students. These results are paralleled by analysis of covariance results comparing experimental and control students on these two items. In the fall of 1981, experimental students in three of four schools displayed lower mean educational aspirations than their control counterparts. By the spring of 1982, experimental students in all four schools had higher mean scores on the "amount of schooling wanted" survey item. Overall, the spring mean scores for experimental students adjusted for fall scores were significantly higher than the scores for controls using ANCOVA ($F = 14.42$; $p <$ .001). A similar difference between experimental and control students' adjusted spring educational expectation scores was also found ($F = 13.57$, $p < .001$). It appears that teacher use of project practices is associated with a significant improvement in students' interest in continuing their educations.

Looking at student bonding to school more globally, it is not clear whether the teaching practices or participation in the project as an experimental subject was associated with greater student attachment to school at the end of one year. Where this construct was measured by an index of three items ("I like my teachers," "I like my classes," and "I have good teachers"), it was unrelated to teacher use of the project practices (measured by the teacher valence scores). Similarly, no significant differences were found between experimental and control students' spring scores on this index adjusted for fall scores.

On the other hand, there was a weak relationship in the expected direction at the teacher level of analysis between teacher use of project practices (teacher valence scores) and student reports of liking school better this year than last year controlling for responses to a similar item on the fall, 1981, survey (semipartial $r = 0.23$). This weak association was not paralleled by a significant difference between experimental and control subjects on this item.

In summary, some relationship was found between teacher use of the project practices and student attitudes toward their math classes. Similarly, the use of the project practices was positively related to students' educational aspirations and expectations. However, it does not appear that the use of the practices, or participation as an experimental subject in the project more generally, was associated with desired changes in students' overall attachment to school and teachers after one year of intervention.

Are the Project Teaching Practices Related to Student Bonding to Peers?

No relationship was found between teacher valence scores and questions regarding subjects' best friends on the spring survey when shared variance in fall and spring survey items was partialled out. It does not appear that use of the teaching practices has led students to choose new best friends who are better students or in trouble less.

Further, the teaching practices were not related to the selection of more prosocial friends or to a commitment to more prosocial norms in peer interactions. No relationships were found between project teaching practices and students' reported willingness to let a friend copy an exam in class or students' willingness to cut school with friends.

Interestingly, it does appear that the use of the practices as measured by valence scores was accompanied by a greater total number of close friends reported by students (semipartial $r = .39$) as well as by a greater number of close friends at school reported by students (semipartial $r = .36$) when the common variance in spring data and fall data are partialled out. It is possible that the use of student team learning groups in classes increased the size of students' friendship networks.

Are the Project Teaching Practices Associated with Student Antisocial and Delinquent Behaviors?

The previous analyses do not suggest that the project teaching practices have had a sufficient impact on student bonding at the end of one year to affect antisocial behavior in major ways. Virtually no relationships were found between the use of the teaching practices as measured by teacher valence scores and student self-reports of truancy, theft from desks or lockers, or the frequency of getting in trouble at school for drugs or alcohol.

More promising results were found for suspensions and expulsions. We have seen that teacher use of the project practices appears to be associated with less off-task behavior in the classroom. Off-task behavior in the classroom may lead to a referral of the student to the vice principal for disciplinary action. Misbehavior is a prominent reason for suspension or expulsion. Of all officially reported disciplinary actions resulting in removal of cohort students from school, 89% were for misbehavior.

Interestingly, teacher valence scores were found to be related at the teacher level to both the mean number of official student disciplinary reports per student and the total number of days suspended from school (see Table 1). Greater use of the project teaching practices was associated with lower rates of official disciplinary action ($r = -0.41$)

TABLE 10.1

Correlations (r) Between Teacher Implementation (Valence)
Score and Frequency of Student Antisocial Behavior
for the 1981-1982 Academic Year (N = 33 teachers)

Antisocial Behavior	r	r^2
(1) From Student Disciplinary Report		
1.1 Total number of reports	−0.41**	0.16
1.2 Total number of days suspended	−0.44**	0.19
(2) From Student Survey		
2.1 Number of times high on drugs at school in the past year[1]	−0.28*	0.08
2.2 Number of times suspended or expelled from school in the past year[1]	−0.33*	0.11

1. Semipartial correlation between implementation score and student Spring 1982
survey response partialling out common variance between Spring 1982 and Fall 1981
survey response from Spring 1982 survey response.
*p < 0.05; **p < 0.01.

and fewer days of student suspension from school (r = −0.44). This
result was paralleled by results of an analysis of the relationship
between student self-reports of suspension or expulsion from school
in the past year and teacher valence scores. Again, a negative
relationship was found between teacher use of project teaching
practices and the number of suspensions reported by students during
the 1981-1982 school year on the spring 1982 survey, partialling out
the common variance between the spring 1982 and fall 1981 survey
responses on this item (semipartial r = −0.33). It is noteworthy that the
number of days suspended as determined from the official disciplinary
reports and the number of days suspended as reported by students on
the spring 1982 survey were highly correlated (r = 0.81), providing
some evidence of the validity of these self-report data.

It is impossible to determine from these results the extent to which
the desired effects on suspensions and expulsions reflect changes in
teacher behaviors versus changes in student behaviors, since suspension or expulsion is a response to a child's behavior by school
personnel. However, the results do suggest that the use of the project
teaching practices is associated with greater retention and participation in school. It appears that when teachers use the project
practices, they are better able to hold students in school without
having to resort to suspension or expulsion for misbehavior. Thus

the practices may assist in providing continuing opportunities for school participation and may reduce the likelihood of alienation from school as a consequence of being forcibly removed from school.

An additional finding of interest is the negative relationship between project teaching practices and student self-reports of getting high on drugs at school (semipartial $r = -0.28$). This early result suggests that the use of the teaching practices may be associated with less frequent drug use at school.

Discussion

In this chapter, we have reported the results of one component of a comprehensive longitudinal delinquency prevention project that seeks to test a set of interventions focused on institutional changes in the major units that affect child development. The chapter is a progress report on the feasibility and promise of one intervention that seeks to prevent antisocial behavior. Specifically, we have investigated the short-term results of an intervention seeking to change teachers' classroom practices in order to increase the opportunities, skills, and rewards available for students in the classroom. We have hypothesized that such changes should lead to greater academic success, greater student bonding to school and prosocial peers, and decreased antisocial behavior.

The first year results indicate that some of the desired changes have been made in experimental teachers' classrooms. Experimental teachers consistently scored higher than controls on measures of project implementation gathered from structured classroom observations. While implementation at the end of one year was not uniform across all teachers, experimental teachers as a whole used the desired teaching practices more than did control teachers. However, these differences in the use of the teaching practices captured by the classroom observations of researchers have not led to consistent differences in the perceptions of experimental and control students regarding the activities and norms of their classrooms. While experimental students reported more frequent use of student groups, they did not consistently report other classroom differences.

This finding raises the question of whether classroom changes of sufficient magnitude were made during the first project year to generate changes in student bonding to school that might inhibit delinquent behavior. In fact, it does not appear that experimental students generally were more strongly bonded to teachers and school at the end of the first year of intervention when compared with control subjects.

On the other hand, promising trends appeared in the first year data. There is evidence that the use of the project teaching practices was associated with improved use of student time in and out of the classroom. Students were more likely to engage in learning activities and less likely to be off task in the classroom when teachers used the project practices. Similarly, they spent more time on homework when their teachers used the practices. Additionally, students liked math classes better, and they developed greater educational aspirations and expectations for themselves when the practices were used. Finally, students were less likely to be suspended or expelled from school when their teachers used the project practices. These trends suggest that the experimental teaching practices may create an environment of greater opportunity for involvement and skill development in classrooms for a larger proportion of students. The data leave at least two important questions to be addressed before more definitive conclusions can be reached.

The first involves the amount of time required to make institutional change in schools at the classroom level. It may be unreasonable to expect major effects on student attitudes and behaviors related to delinquency to result during the first year that new teaching methods are being introduced to teachers. Change efforts may require a period of adjustment and adaptation on the part of both change agents and teachers before new practices are institutionalized and routinized in classrooms. It would have been desirable to pilot the teaching methods with teachers for a year prior to assessing their effect on students, though practical considerations of funding and teachers' annual transfers prevented this in the current project.

The larger question is whether the trends reported after the first year of the project will continue to develop during the second year. Will teacher use of the project practices increase during the second year of implementation? Preliminary analyses suggest increasing divergence between experimental and control teachers' valence scores in the desired direction over time. If greater differences occur, will they be accompanied by significant differences in student bonding and behavior during the second year of implementation? At this point, several outcomes appear plausible. It is possible that the project will not affect student antisocial behavior even though teacher behaviors change. It is possible that the project will affect student behaviors related to academic achievement and even school retention (suspensions and expulsions) without affecting bonding to school, peer associations, or antisocial behavior. On the other hand, it also appears possible that changes in classroom opportunity structures associated with the project's teaching practices may affect certain school-related delinquent behaviors such as drug use at school.

There are several findings in the first year data, including the results on math class attachment, educational aspirations and expectations, suspensions and explusions, and the use of drugs at school that suggest the plausibility of this latter outcome.

Note

1. Ideally, since the project sought to change teacher practices in the classroom, both experimental unit and the unit of analysis should be the class (Cronbach, 1976; Glass & Stanley, 1970; Poyner, 1979). However, the teacher was used as the unit of statistical analysis instead of the class because all teachers were observed in only one of the classes they taught. Teacher valence scores were applied to all classes taught by each teacher. Two shortcomings are recognized in this procedure of aggregating data to the teacher level: (1) unique classroom effects within teachers were ignored, and (2) for dependent variables not related to a specific subject area (e.g., antisocial behavior measures), student responses were included in the analysis multiple times because each student had more than one teacher in the project. (This problem would also be present using the class as the unit of analysis.) The alternative of analyzing at the individual student level was rejected because it ignores entirely the classroom effect (Cronbach, 1976; Packham et al., 1969), and assumes equal treatment for all students with the same teacher when the teacher's implementation score is assigned to each individual student taught by that teacher.

Appendix

Views of Classroom Practices

(1) In my classes, we break up into groups which compete with each other.

270 Hawkins and Lam

(2) In my classes, most students take part in class discussions or activities.
(3) In my classes, if you don't understand the material at first, you get another chance to learn it.
(4) In my classes, to get a good grade you have to do better than other students.
(5) In my classes, teachers show us how what we are studying is useful.
(6) Other students in my classes want me to do my best work.

**Opportunities for Positive
Peer Interaction in Class**

(1) In my classes I learn to get along with other people.
(2) Other students in my classes want me to do my best work.
(3) Students in my classes help each other with school work.
(4) In my classes most students take part in class discussions or activities.
(5) When my classmates and I disagree we usually talk things out.

Attachment to School

(1) I like my teachers.
(2) I like my classes this year.
(3) I have good teachers this year.

References

Aronson, E. (1978). *The jigsaw classroom.* Beverly Hills, CA: Sage.
Bachman, J. G., O'Malley, P. M., & Johnston, J. (1978). Adolescence to adulthood; change and stability in the lives of young men. In *Youth in transition.* Ann Arbor, MI: Institute for Social Research.
Bahr, S. J. (1979). Family determinants and effects of deviance. In W. R. Burr, R. F. Hill, I. Nye, I. L. Reiss (Eds.), *Contemporary theories about the family. Vol. 1.* New York: Free Press.
Block, J. H. (1971). *Mastery learning: Theory and Practice.* New York: Holt, Rinehart, & Winston.
Block, J. H. (1974). *Schools, society, and mastery learning.* New York: Holt, Rinehart, & Winston.
Bloom, B. S. (1976). *Human characteristics and school learning.* New York: McGraw-Hill.
Braukman, C. J., Kirigin, K. A., & Wolf, M. M. (1980). Group home treatment research: Social learning and social control perspectives. In T. Hirschi & M. Gottlieb (Eds.), *Understanding crime* (pp. 117-130). Beverly Hills, CA: Sage.
California Achievement Tests (1977). CTB/McGraw-Hill, Monterey, CA.
Call, D. J. (1965). *Delinquency, frustration and non-commitment.* Unpublished doctoral dissertation. University of Oregon, Eugene, OR.

Cohen, A. K., & Short, J. F. Jr. (1976). Crime and juvenile delinquency. In R. K. Merton & R. Nisbet (Eds.), *Contemporary social problems* (pp. 45-102). New York: Harcourt.

Cohen, E. G. (1982). *Expectation states theory and classroom learning.* Paper presented at the American Education Research Association meeting, New York.

Conger, R. D. (1976). Social control and social learning models of delinquent behavior: A synthesis. *Criminology, 14,* 17-40.

Conger, R. D. (1980). Juvenile delinquency: Behavior restraint or behavior facilitation. In T. Hirschi & M. Gottfredson (Eds.), *Understanding Crime,* pp. 131-142. Beverly Hills, CA: Sage.

Cronbach, L. J. (1976). *Research on classroom and schools: Formulation of questions, design and analysis.* Occasional Paper of the Stanford Evaluation Consortium, Stanford University.

Cronbach, L. J., & Snow, R. E. (1977). *Aptitude and instructional methods: Handbook for research on interactions.* New York: Irvington.

Cummings, C. (1983). *Managing to teach.* Snohomish, WA: Snohomish.

DeVries, D. L., & Slavin, R. E. (1978). Teams-Games-Tournament: A research review. *Journal of Research and Development in Education, 12,* 28-38.

Elliott, D. S., & Voss, H. L. (1974). *Delinquency and dropout.* Lexington, MA: D. C. Heath.

Elliott, D. S., Ageton, S. S., & Huizinga, D. (1978). *Self-reported delinquency estimates by sex, race, class, and age.* Boulder, CO: Behavioral Research Institute.

Elliott, D. S., Huizinga, D., & Ageton, S. S. (1982). *Explaining delinquency and drug use.* Boulder, CO: Behavioral Research Institute.

Emmer, E. T., & Evertson, C. M. (1980). *Effective management at the beginning of the school year in junior high classes.* Austin, TX: Research and Development Center for Teacher Education, University of Texas at Austin.

Epps, E. G. (1967). Socioeconomic status, race, level of aspiration, and juvenile delinquency: A limited empirical test of Merton's conception of deviation. *Phylon, 28,* 16-27.

Frease, D. E. (1972). The schools, self-concept, and juvenile delinquency. *British Journal of Criminology, 12,* 133-146.

Frease, D. E. (1973). Schools and delinquency: Some intervening processes. *Pacific Sociological Review, 16,* 426-448.

Farrington, D. P. (1973). Self-reports of deviant behavior: Predictive and stable? *Journal of Criminal Law and Criminology, 64,* 99-110.

Ginsberg, I. J., & Greeney, J. R. (1978). Competing theories of marijuana use: A longitudinal study. *Journal of Health and Social Behavior, 19,* 22-34.

Glass, G. V., & Stanley, J. C. (1970). *Statistical methods in education and psychology.* Englewood Cliffs, NJ: Prentice-Hall.

Glasser, W. (1978). Disorders in our schools: Causes and remedies. *Phi Delta Kappan, 59,* 331-333.

Gold, M. (1978). Scholastic experiences, self-esteem, and delinquent behavior: A theory for alternative schools. *Crime & Delinquency, 24(3),* 290-308.

Hawkins, J. D. (1981). Student team learning: Preventing the flocking and feathering of delinquents. *Journal of Primary Prevention, 2(1),* 50-55.

Hawkins, J. D., & Lishner, D. L. (in press). "Schooling and Delinquency." In E. H. Johnson (Ed.), *Handbook on Crime and Delinquency Prevention.* Westport, CT: Greenwood Press.

Hawkins, J. D., & Wall, J. S. (1980). *Alternative education: Exploring the delinquency prevention potential*. Washington, DC: National Institute for Juvenile Justice and Delinquency Prevention, Office of Juvenile Justice and Delinquency Prevention, Law Enforcement Assistance Administration, U.S. Department of Justice.

Hawkins, J. D., & Weis, J. G. (1985). The social development model: An integrated approach to delinquency prevention. *Journal of Primary Prevention, 6*(2), 73-97.

Hirschi, T. (1969). *Causes of Delinquency*. Berkeley, CA: University of California Press.

Jensen, G. F. (1972). Race, achievement, and delinquency: A further look at delinquency association perspective. *American Journal of Sociology, 78*, 562-575.

Jerse, F. W., & Fakouri, M. E. (1978). Juvenile delinquency and academic deficiency. *Contemporary Education, 49*, 106-109.

Jessor, R., & Jessor, S. L. (1977). *Problem behavior and psychosocial development: A longitudinal study of youth*. New York: Academic Press.

Johnson, R. E. (1979). *Juvenile delinquency and its origins: An integrated theoretical approach*. New York: Cambridge University Press.

Johnson, D. W., & Johnson, R. W. (1980). Cooperative learning: The power of positive goal interdependence. In M. Lyons (Ed.), *Structuring cooperative experiences in the classroom: The 1980 handbook*. Minneapolis, MN: Cooperation Network.

Johnston, L. D. (1973). *Drugs and American youth*. Ann Arbor, MI: Institute for Social Research.

Johnston, L. D., Bachman, J. G., & O'Malley, P. M. (1981). *Student drug use in America 1975-1981*. Rockville, MD: National Institute on Drug Abuse.

Johnston, L. D., O'Malley, P. M., & Eveland, L. K. (1978). Drugs and delinquency: A search for causal connections. In D. B. Kandel (Ed.), *Longitudinal research on drug use* (pp. 137-156). Washington, DC: Hemisphere-Wiley.

Johnstone, J. W. C. (1981). The family and delinquency: A reappraisal. In A. C. Meade (Ed.), *Youth and society: Studies of adolescent deviance* (pp. 25-63). Chicago: Institute for Juvenile Research.

Kandel, D. B., & Adler, I. (1982). Socialization into marijuana use among French adolescents: A cross-cultural comparison with the United States. *Journal of Health and Social Behavior, 23*(Dec.), 295-309.

Kandel, D. B., Kessler, R. C., & Margulies, R. F. (1978). Antecedents of adolescent initiation into stages of drug use: A developmental analysis. In D. B. Kandel (Ed.), *Longitudinal research on drug use* (pp. 73-99). Washington, DC: Hemisphere-Wiley.

Keith, T. Z. (1982). Time spent on homework and high school grades: A large sample path analysis. *Journal of Educational Psychology 74*(2), 248-253.

Kellam, S. G., Stevenson, D. L., & Rubin, B. R. (1982). How specific are the early predictors of teenage drug use? In L. S. Harris (Ed.), *Problems of drug dependence, 1982*. Rockville, MD: National Institute on Drug Abuse.

Kelly, D. H. (1975). Status origins, track position and delinquent involvement: A self-report analysis. *Sociological Quarterly, 16*, 264-271.

Kelly, D. H., & Balch, R. W. (1971). Social origins and school failure: A re-examination of Cohen's theory of working class delinquency. *Pacific Sociological Review, 14*, 413-430.

Kerr, D. M., Kent, L., & Lam, T. (1983, March). *Measuring program implementation through classroom observation.* Paper presented at the annual meeting of the American Educational Research Association, Montreal.

Linden, E. W. (1974). *Interpersonal ties and delinquent behavior.* Doctoral dissertation. University of Washington, Department of Sociology, Seattle.

Linden, E., & Hackler, J. C. (1973). Affective ties and delinquency. *Pacific Sociological Review, 16*(1), 27-46.

Loeber, R., & Dishion, T. (1983). Early predictors of male delinquency: A review. *Psychological Bulletin, 94*(1), 68-99.

Loeber, R., Dishion, T. J., & Patterson, G. R. (1983). Multiple gating: A multistage assessment procedure for identifying youths at risk for delinquency. Eugene, OR: Oregon Social Learning Center.

McPartland, J. M., & McDill, E. L. (Eds.). (1977). *Violence in schools: Perspectives, programs, and positions.* Lexington, MA: D. C. Heath.

Martin, D. L. (1977). Your praise can smother learning. *Learning, 5*(6), 42-51.

Meade, A. C., & Marsden, M. E. (1981). An integration of classic theories of delinquency. In A. C. Meade (Ed.), *Youth and society: Studies of adolescent deviance.* Chicago: Institute for Juvenile Research.

Meier, R. F., & Johnson, W. J. (1977). Deterrence as social control: The legal and extra legal production of conformity. *American Sociological Review, 42*(2), 292-304.

Monahan, J. (1981). *The clinical prediction of violent behavior.* Washington, DC: Government Printing Office.

Moskowitz, J. M., Malvin, J. H., Schaeffer, G. A., Schaps, E., & Condon, J. W. (1981a). *The effects of a classroom management teacher training primary prevention program on fifth-grade students.* Napa, CA: Pacific Institute for Research and Evaluation.

Moskowitz, J. M., Malvin, J. H., Schaeffer, G. A., Schaps, E., & Condon, J. W. (1981b). *A process and outcome evaluation of a peer teaching primary prevention program.* Napa, CA: Pacific Institute for Research and Evaluation.

National Institute of Education. (1978). *Violent schools—safe schools: The safe school study report, vol. 1.* Washington, DC: Goverment Printing Office.

Noblit, G. W. (1976). The adolescent experience and delinquency: School versus subcultural effects. *Youth and Society, 8,* 27-44.

Palmore, E. B., & Hammond, P. E. (1964). Interacting factors in juvenile delinquency. *American Sociological Review* 29:848-854.

Packham, P. D., Glass, G. V., & Hopkins, K. D. (1969). The experimental unit in statistical analyses. *Journal of Special Education, 3,* 337-349.

Peterson, P. (1972). *A review of research on mastery learning strategies.* Unpublished manuscript. Stockholm: International Association for the Evaluation of Educational Achievement.

Pine, G. J. (1965). Social class, social mobility, and delinquent behavior. *Personnel and Guidance Journal, 43,* 770-774.

Polk, K. (1967). Urban social areas and delinquency. *Social Problems,*14(Winter), 320-325.

Polk, K. (1969). Class, strain, and rebellion among adolescents. *Social Problems, 17,* 214-224.

Polk, K., & Schafer, W. E. (1972) *School and delinquency.* Englewood Cliffs, NJ: Prentice-Hall.

Polk, K., Frease, D., & Richmond, F. L. (1974). Social class, school experience and delinquency. *Criminology, 12*, 84-96.

Poyner, H. (1979). Selecting units of analysis. In G. Borich (Ed.), *Evaluating educational programs and products*. Englewood Cliffs, NJ: Educational Technology.

Reckless, W. (1969). *The crime problem*. New York: Appleton-Century-Crofts.

Schafer, W. E. (1969). Participation in interscholastic athletics and delinquency: A preliminary study. *Social Problems, 17*, 40-47.

Schafer, W. E., & Polk, K. (1967). Delinquency and the schools. In *President's commission on law enforcement and administration of justice, juvenile delinquency and youth crime* (pp. 222-277). Washington, DC: Government Printing Office.

Senna, J., Rathus, S. A., & Siegel, L. (1974). Delinquent behavior and academic investment among suburban youth. *Adolescence, 9*, 481-494.

Slavin, R. E. (1979). *Using student team learning*. Baltimore, MD: Center for Social Organization of Schools, Johns Hopkins University.

Slavin, R. E. (1980). Cooperative learning. *Review of Educational Research, 50*, 315-342.

Slavin, R. E. (1982). *Cooperative learning groups: What the research says to the teacher*. Washington, DC: National Education Association.

Slocum, W. L., & Stone, C. L. (1963). Family culture patterns and delinquent-type behavior. *Marriage and Family Living, 25*, 202-208.

Shannon, L. (1982). *Assessing the relationship of adult criminal careers to juvenile careers*. Washington, DC: National Institute for Juvenile Justice and Delinquency Prevention.

Stallings, J. (1980). Allocated academic learning time revisited, or beyond time on task. *Educational Researcher, 9*(11), 11-16.

Stinchcombe, A. C. (1964). *Rebellion in a high school* Chicago: Quadrangle.

Van de Ven, A. H., & Ferry, D. L. (1981). *Measuring and assessing organizations*. New York: John Wiley.

Weis, J. G., Hall, J. B., Henney, J. S., Sederstrom, J., Worsley, K., & Zeiss, C. (1981). *Peer influence and delinquency: An evaluation of theory and practice, part I and part II*. Washington, DC: Government Printing Office.

Weis, J. G., & Hawkins, J. D. (1981). *Preventing delinquency*. Washington, DC: National Institute for Juvenile Justice and Delinquency Prevention, Government Printing Office.

Weis, J. G., & Sederstrom, J. (1981). *The prevention of serious delinquency: What to do?* Washington, DC: Government Printing Office.

West, D. J., & Farrington, D. P. (1973). *Who becomes delinquent?* London: Heinemann.

Winfree, L. T., Theis, H. E., & Griffiths, C. T. (1981). Drug use in rural America: A cross cultural examination of complementary social deviance theories. *Youth and Society, 12*(4), 465-489.

Wolfgang, M. E., Figlio, R. M., & Sellin, T. (1972). *Delinquency in a birth cohort*. Chicago: University of Chicago Press.

11

Cognitive-Behavioral Strategies in the Prevention and Treatment of Antisocial Disorders in Children and Adolescents

Larry Michelson

Antisocial Behavior

Antisocial behavior among youth is a complex and multidimensional phenomenon that presents a significant challenge to mental health, legal, and social systems in comtemporary society. Children and adolescents who engage in antisocial and acting-out behaviors and related illegal acts are typically labeled as conduct disordered and delinquent. While there are wide variations in the continuum from normative to pathological behaviors, these youth present significant patterns of dysfunction, including physical and verbal aggression, stealing, lying, fire-setting, destruction of property, noncompliance, school truancy and/or academic failure, and marked interpersonal deficits. The level of dysfunction varies, of course, depending upon factors including the nature, intensity, density, duration, and combination of antisocial acts.

Despite the varied nature of diagnostic and nosological studies, utilizing diverse symptoms, criteria, and heterogeneous populations, there is a general consensus regarding the factors that make up antisocial behavior. Indeed, there is significant concordance between clinical and multivariate strategies for delineating the syndrome, which includes aggression, covert or overt illicit behaviors, defiance,

Author's Note: Appreciation is expressed to the Pittsburgh Child Guidance Clinic Foundation, Alan Kazdin, Ph.D., University of Pittsburgh, and James Breiling, Ph.D., National Institute of Mental Health, for conceptual and methodological ideas and refinements, which were so generously offered. This paper was supported in part by NIMH (MH39642).

and oppositionalism (Achenbach & Edlebrock, 1978; American Psychiatric Association [APA], 1980; Kazdin, 1984; Quay, 1980; Rutter, Shaffer, & Shepherd, 1975). The DSM-III manual of psychiatric disorders defines conduct disorder as a repetitive and persistent pattern, of at least six months' duration, in which either the rights of others are violated or major age-appropriate societal norms are ignored. Moreover, DSM-III provides four subtypes of conduct disorder that consider whether there are aggressive components (aggressive versus nonaggressive) and social behavior (social versus undersocialized). Aggressive subtypes engage in physical violence, stealing, assaults, robbery, and so on, while the nonaggressive counterparts exhibit behaviors such as chronic stealing, lying, truancy, or running away. Socialized subtypes are described as being capable of exhibiting genuine concern for others and experiencing guilt and remorse, while the undersocialized subtypes do not.

Antisocial youth typically fail to demonstrate the requisite social skills necessary to perform effectively and appropriately in interpersonal domains. Socially aggressive and antisocial children tend to behave in a manner that is both unpleasant to others and, in the long term, self-defeating. A number of researchers, including Quay (1980) and Patterson, Reid, Jones, and Conger (1975), have highlighted many of the commonalities that describe aggressive youth. These include verbal and physical assaultiveness, teasing, provoking, quarreling, and fighting as a means of resolving conflicts, and violating or ignoring the rights of others. They may use tactics that are personally effective on a short-term basis but rarely appropriate from a social or moral perspective and that result in myriad negative long-term effects. Aggressive youth may directly violate the legal or human rights of others by the use of physical, psychological, or emotional force. Not surprisingly, this type of social behavior generates numerous deleterious side effects. As described by Patterson et al. (1975, p. 4):

> The socialization process appears to be severely impeded for many aggressive children. Their behavioral adjustments are often immature, and they do not seem to have learned the key social skills necessary for initiating and maintaining positive social relationships with others. Peer groups often reject, avoid and/or punish aggressive children, thereby excluding them from positive learning experiences with others, Socially negative/aggressive children often have academic difficulties and they achieve at lower levels than their classmates.

Aggressive and antisocial youth not only acquire academic skills at greatly diminished rates compared to their nonaggressive peer cohorts, but their antisocial interpersonal interactions tend to elicit counteraggression from their peers and social rejection from significant others, including parents, siblings, teachers, and other adults in their environment. On a long-term basis, the loss of friends, reduced interpersonal contact, frustration, guilt and decreased opportunities for academic enrichment as a result of alienating both peers and adults far outweigh the possible short-term benefits of their aggressive behavior. Moreover, left untreated, aggressive children appear to make significantly unsatisfactory adjustments as adults (Robins, 1974, 1978). Antisocial youth manifest decreased popularity with their peers (Winder & Rau, 1962) and experience a greater incidence of academic failure (Schindler, 1941), substance abuse, legal violations, and psychiatric disturbances as adults (cf. Michelson & Wood, 1980b; Morris, Escoll & Wexler, 1956).

Antisocial behavior and conduct disorders among youth represents a serious social, legal and clinical problem. While exact epidemiological estimates are not available due to divergent criteria used to classify children as antisocial, varying definitions, and geographic locales employed (Kazdin, 1984), extrapolations indicate that among childhood disorders the presence of antisocial behavior is high (Kazdin, 1984). Elliott, Dunford, and Huizinga (this volume) found that while the proportion of youth classified as "serious career offenders" was small (2.5%), this highly delinquent group accounted for 25% of all reported violent, index, and total offenses committed. Moreover, Elliott et al.'s (this volume) research clearly suggests that the vast majority (86%) of self-reported "career offenders" are unknown to the police and, in fact, had no arrests. Hence generalizations of the prevalence of antisocial behavior, from a purely legal (arrest data) perspective, are likely to greatly underestimate the extent of the problem. As noted by Achenbach (1982, p. 480):

> Children officially judged (adjudicated) delinquent represent a small tip of a large iceberg. Even the tip of the iceberg is obscured by inconsistent reporting practices and inconsistent reasons for adjudication, such as the seriousness of the crime versus the need for court supervision because of parental neglect. According to the U.S. Department of Justice (1979), juveniles under 18 are arrested for 28% of the major offenses comprising the FBI's Crime Index (the major crimes are

murder. manslaughter, forceable rape, robbery, aggravated assault, burglary, larceny and auto theft). Offenses cleared by arrests of juveniles range from about 5% of murders to about 34% of burglaries. . . . [Hence] for all offenses, over two million juveniles are arrested per year.

In addition to these estimates of juvenile delinquency, derived from actual court cases, aggressiveness, conduct disorder, and antisocial behavior in children and adolescents represent the most frequent referral problems for outpatient clinics (i.e., from one-third to two-thirds of all referrals) Gersten, Langner, Eisenberg, Simcha-Fagen, & McCarthy, 1976; Herbert, 1978; Patterson, 1982; Robins, 1981). Moreover, the actual number of cases identified for psychological screening or treatment is, in all likelihood, an underestimate of the exact extent of the dysfunction (Robins, 1974, 1978; Kazdin, 1984). In school these youth may be identified as underachievers or learning disabled because of their related academic and social difficulties. Others come directly into contact with the police and the juvenile court system rather than with treatment facilities.

The vast majority of the symptoms that characterize conduct disorders and antisocial behavior among youth typically evolve from an extended history of serious rule violation. Antisocial behavior in adulthood has been found to be preceded almost invariably by a youthful history of serious antisocial behavior (Robins, 1978). Even within childhood, the level of severity and density of antisocial behaviors are powerfully associated with and typically precede the emergence of more serious behaviors associated with delinquency (Block, 1977; Kazdin, 1984; Livson & Peskin, 1967; Loeber & Dishion, 1983; Patterson, 1982).

The clinical and social impact of antisocial disorders is noted by both its high prevalence and its chronicity. Indeed, unlike a variety of childhood disorders, antisocial patterns appear to crystallize and become relatively stable over time (Graham & Rutter, 1973; Olweus, 1979; Robins, 1974, 1978, 1981). As noted by Kazdin (1984), the temporal stability of conduct problems departs from several other childhood disorders that are more age specific, such as phobias. Likewise, antisocial behavior patterns among youth portend significant problems of adulthood, including alcoholism, substance abuse, psychoses, psychiatric disturbance, and criminal behavior (see Robins & Hill, 1976; Wolfgang, Figlio, & Sellin, 1972). Legal and psychiatric complications aside, antisocial youth manifest significant interpersonal dysfunctions including difficulties and life dissatisfaction in adulthood. As discussed by Kazdin (1984, p. 5):

> The long-term effects of severe antisocial behavior has untoward consequences not only for the persons themselves but also for their children (Robins, 1981). Males with conduct problems father as many children as other men (despite their higher rates of marital disruption), and their children have increased risks for childhood deviance and antisocial behavior. Finally, and perhaps obviously, many of the problems encompassed by conduct disorder can have serious untoward consequences for innocent victims. Serious aggressive behavior and antisocial acts against persons and/or property (e.g., fire setting) can result directly in injury and fatality to others.

Transient and mild antisocial behaviors are evident in many children, only some of whom eventually develop conduct disorders. Although precise epidemiological estimates are not available due to the varying definitions and characteristics of the samples employed, it appears that among school-aged children the prevalence of behavioral problems is approximately 25% with a range from 1.5% to 30% or greater depending upon the source (Cowen, Trost, Lorion, Door, Izzo, & Isaacson, 1975; Glidewell & Swallow, 1969). Thus despite the varying criteria for delineating antisocial behaviors among school children, there appears to be a relatively high rate of prevalence. Furthermore, it is probable that such behaviors may portend some form of subsequent social maladjustment, possibly even delinquency and conduct disorders. Longitudinal studies suggest there is reasonable temporal stability over the years throughout elementary school with regard to teacher ratings of antisocial behavior and interpersonal problems with children (Herbert, 1978; Eron, 1980; Patterson, 1982; Quay, 1972).

In recognition of the prevalence, severity, chronicity, and prognosis of antisocial behavior among youth, it is critical that effective intervention strategies be devised. From both economic and social perspectives, the development of effective prevention and/or treatment strategies is important because these disorders are among the most costly to society (Robins, 1981). Indeed, a significant proportion of markedly aggressive youth eventually enter into either adult mental health or criminal justice systems. Hence the requisite monetary expenditures involved in managing these persons as adults are quite high (Kazdin, 1984).

Contemporary estimates of the costs associated with this social problem may actually represent underestimates of the total cost of antisocial behavior among youth given the substantial expenditures in mental health services used by this population. Psychiatric research inpatient units, which specialize in evaluation and treatment of antisocial behavior and conduct disorders in children and adolescents, can cost between $36,000 and $63,000 for a 3-month program (Kazdin, 1984, personal communication). Furthermore, these efforts are typically of a secondary prevention nature and directed more toward stabilizing the youth and reducing florid symptomatology rather than eliminating pervasive antisocial behavioral patterns.

Recognizing the prevalence of antisocial behavior among youth, the need for clinical research is clear. However, there are relatively few prevention or treatment studies that have demonstrated unequivocal efficacy with antisocial youth. Clinically, there is a consensus that antisocial children are difficult to work with. Numerous interventions have been proposed and applied, including both individual and group therapy, psychotherapy, family therapy, transactional analysis, behavior therapy, pharmacotherapy, and residential treatment (see Campbell, Cohen, & Small, 1982; Kazdin & Frame, 1983; Morrison, 1978). Unfortunately, no treatment has been shown empirically to remediate completely the disorder once it has solidified or to reduce reliably its tertiary negative consequences. In light of these considerations, several interventions have recently been proposed as potentially viable modalities for the prevention and/or treatment of antisocial disorders among youth; these interventions will now be reviewed.

Intervention Strategies

Research on the community prevention or outpatient treatment of antisocial disorders in children and adolescents is relatively sparse. As noted earlier, no psychosocial or biological form of treatment has been unequivocally demonstrated in outcome studies to prevent or reduce the risk or severity of conduct disorder, or to remediate the disorder once it has become diagnosed. However, three promising psychosocial treatments have emerged from social-learning theory, cognitive-developmental theories, and behavior therapy strategies. These include Parent Management Training (PMT), Cognitive Therapy, as applied in the form of Interpersonal Cognitive Problem-

Solving Skills Training (ICPS), and Behavioral Social Skills Training (BSST). Although ICPS and BSST serve as the major prevention and treatment strategies of focus in the present review, PMT warrants comment and will be briefly critiqued.

Parent Management Training (PMT)

Parent management strategies typically entail training parents to interact more effectively with their children and to use various behavioral principles (e.g., reinforcement, extinction, and punishment) to increase prosocial behavior. PMT has been applied to parents of diverse clinical populations, including aggressive, acting-out, autistic, and mentally retarded children. Numerous studies have applied PMT to children with marked antisocial and oppositional behavior (for reviews, see Kazdin, 1984; Kazdin & Frame, 1983; Patterson, 1982; Wahler, 1976). The most programmatic work has been completed by Patterson and his colleagues, who have developed a model relating how antisocial behavior develops. The model emphasizes the role of coercive interactions between and among family members that serves to exacerbate aggressive behavior (see Patterson, 1982). PMT focuses on directly altering these negative interaction patterns, reducing coercive interchanges between parent and child, and enhancing prosocial behavior through systematic reinforcement (Kazdin, 1984). A number of outcome investigations have been reported over the past fifteen years that clearly demonstrate the efficacy of Patterson's program with systematic replication within the program itself and extensions by other clinical researchers (e.g., Fleischman, & Szykula, 1981; Patterson & Fleischman, 1979).

Although PMT is a promising treatment technique, it is not without limitations. First, PMT is not, of course, invariably effective. The efficacy of PMT appears to depend upon the types of families that participate, the intensity of the treatment (e.g., duration, supervision in the home), and several parent and family factors (e.g., parental discord and psychopathology) (see Kazdin, 1984). In dysfunctional families, the treatment may produce little or no change or gains may not be maintained once they are achieved (Wahler, Berland, & Coe, 1979). A related concern with PMT is the breadth of its applicability. For clinically severe children, it is not always a viable strategy. Limitations may not exclusively rest with the children per se, but rather with the families and associated familial conditions in which they are embedded. For example, in one local project to investigate inpatient treatments for children with serious conduct disorder, approximately 75% of the families of the children were not suitable for PMT. Parent psychiatric dysfunction, apathy, or disinterest in contributing further attention to their children were limiting conditions for the effective use of PMT. For this reason, the clinical services' intensive treatment efforts have been focused on the child rather than the child and parent combined.

At the other end of the spectrum, PMT might appear to be applicable for large-scale preventive efforts. Based on existing evidence, there may be some benefit to large-scale dissemination of PMT. However, such an extensive application of PMT currently exceeds the present status of the evidence. PMT can be highly effective when administered intensively to an individual family or small groups of families. With regard to large-scale preventive efforts, the administration of this form of treatment raises multiple problems including feasibility. Wide-scale application of PMT may sacrifice the intensity of treatment and the integrity of its execution. Large groups of parents would need to be seen and individual consultations during and between sessions along with monitoring the contingencies of reinforcement and punishment used in the homes would be required.

PMT, without careful execution and monitoring of treatment and that departs from the superb model developed by Patterson and his colleagues, is likely to have commensurately reduced efficacy. Also, the conceptual model developed by Patterson and his associates using aggressive children does not necessarily imply that child-parent interaction is the only point of effective intervention for children who have yet to achieve clinically severe levels of dysfunction. It is not clear, at this point in time, that children at risk for subsequent conduct disorder eventually become identified cases specifically because of their family interaction. Problems with family interaction have been shown to be related to child deviance. However, for possible preventive purposes, the interactions of parents and their children may not be the only place of intervening effectively to reduce the risk, severity, and subsequent appearance of conduct disorder. Other factors may contribute to or correlate with child deviance (e.g., cognitive processes) and may serve as the focus of effective interventions for treatment and preventive purposes. A focus on cognitive processes is not incompatible with the model of PMT developed by Patterson (1982). The emergence of maladaptive cognitive processes that underlie interpersonal problems and behavioral adjustment have also been attributed to parent-child interactions (Spivack & Shure, 1974, 1982). However, for preventive and treatment purposes, focusing on the child, rather than the parents, represents a conceptually attractive and empirically based approach that has an added advantage of feasibility.

PMT places numerous demands on parents, including mastering educational materials, conducting home observations, successfully implementing treatment techniques, and attending weekly treatment sessions over a period of several months. These demands may, of course, affect the attrition rate that is reported between 17% and 32% (Eyberg & Johnson, 1974; McMahon, Forehand, Griest, & Wells, 1981; Patterson & Fleishman, 1979). Moreover, other factors may mediate dropout including low socioeconomic status, depression, social insularity, and parental psychopathology (Kazdin, 1984; McMahon et al., 1981). While many parents undertake and successfully complete parent management training, others may refuse even to participate or only become minimally involved in implementing the comprehensive therapeutic regimen.

Overall, the PMT literature reveals treatment gains in adaptive child behavior both at home and at school. Follow-up studies ranging from 1 (Fleishman & Szykula, 1981) to 4½ years (Baum & Forehand, 1981) support the efficacy of PMT with regard to decreasing aggressive, noncompliant, and antisocial behavior in children from ages 3 through 12 years (Patterson, 1982). Eyberg and Johnson (1974), Patterson (1974), and Wells et al. (1980), have also reported that PMT is effective in reducing antisocial and deviant behavior in children to within normative levels of functioning as compared to adjusted peer cohorts.

While PMT has been shown to yield positive effects, it cannot, at present, be regarded as a panacea for antisocial behavior in children. First, several studies have reported only minimal therapeutic impact of the strategy. In addition, a number of critical mediating factors such as typology of antisocial behavior, family characteristics, socioeconomic status, psychiatric conditions in the family, and so on, may greatly influence the outcome of the intervention. Hence risk variables that have typically not been fully integrated within PMT, such as marital dysfunction, social insularity, family disharmony, and parental psychopathology, may need to be clinically addressed, either initially or concurrently, if maximum gains are to be achieved

284   Larry Michelson

for these high-risk families (Griest et al., 1982; Kazdin, 1984; Wahler & Afton, 1980).

Clearly, further research is needed to identify and mollify those factors that mediate both short- and long-term outcome. In addition, specific adjunctive interventions may be necessary to remediate concomitantly the presence of parental and/or family factors that have a deleterious implication for the successful implementation of PMT. Furthermore, strategies to encourage those families who are at high risk and who, coincidentally, may be less likely to undertake training, will be needed. Hence while PMT is regarded as one of the more effective and currently practiced behaviorally based treatment strategies for antisocial youth, it cannot be professed as the primary or sole therapy of choice. Indeed, the previously cited problems with PMT strategies have, in part, served as an impetus for the search for alternative therapeutic approaches. In light of the critical importance of developing and implementing diverse treatment strategies, particularly those directed specifically to antisocial children and adolescents, two therapeutic strategies have become the subject of increased clinical-research attention. These include cognitive therapy, principally interpersonal cognitive problem-solving interventions, and behavioral social competency training, both of which will now be reviewed, with discussion of their advances, limitations, and issues for further investigation.

Interpersonal Cognitive Problem-Solving (ICPS)

Interpersonal cognitive problem-solving skills training emphasizes the importance of cognitive processes in understanding, mediating, and resolving interpersonal conflicts. Cognitive (problem-solving) treatments focus on modifying dysfunctional thinking processes that are presumed to result in antisocial behavior. The specific cognitive processes that are targeted for change differ according to the varying characteristics of the child or adolescent. However, a number of cognitive operations are commonly focused upon in treatment, including remediating negative perceptions, attributions, self-statements, and expectations, and enhancing effective problem-solving strategies. As discussed by Kazdin (1984, p. 14):

> The assumption of cognitive therapy is that children with deviant behavior suffer a deficiency in particular processes, or an inability to use their applied cognitive skills. At present, it is premature to provide

a complete account to cognitive processes that emerge as part of normal development and their aberrations that result in deviant behavior. However, research has progressed by showing that maladjusted children vary in diverse processes including perceptions of social situations, thought processes and problem-solving skills.

Five major cognitive skills have been identified as underlying interpersonal behavior and social adjustment by Spivack, Platt, & Shure (1976) and include: (1) alternative solution thinking; (2) means-ends thinking; (3) consequential thinking; (4) causal thinking; and (5) sensitivity to interpersonal problems.

The importance of these and related cognitive processes in social adjustment and aggression has received increasing attention in the scientific literature. Several investigations have found that the ability to engage in the above problem-solving skills is related to behavioral adjustment (Spivack et al., 1976). In general, maladjusted youth generate fewer constructive alternative solutions to interpersonal problems, tend to focus on ends or goals rather than the intermediate steps required to achieve them, to recognize fewer consequences associated with their dysfunctional behaviors, to fail to understand the causes of other peoples' behavior, and to be less sensitive to interpersonal conflict (Spivack et al., 1976). Moreover, a number of studies have reported that deficits in problem-solving skills and their association with adaptive functioning cannot be accounted for by variables such as the child's socioeconomic class, intelligence, or gender (Kazdin, 1984).

Beyond these specific skills, cognitive processes have been frequently accorded a major role in aggressive behavior (Berkowitz, 1977; Novaco, 1978). Aggression is not simply activated by external environmental events, but rather by the way these events are idiosyncratically perceived and cognitively processed. The processing refers to the youth's appraisal of the situation, anticipated reactions of others, and self-statements in response to particular environmental cues (Kazdin, 1984). Child psychiatric inpatients and aggressive school children both exhibit a predisposition to attribute hostile intent to others, particularly in social interactions where the cues of actual intent are ambiguous (Dodge, 1980; Nasby, Hayden, & DePaulo, 1980). In addition, when situations are initially perceived as threatening or hostile, antisocial youth are even more likely to respond aggressively (Deluty, 1981).

General cognitive deficits in perceiving the actions and intent of others have been identified as well. The relationship of empathy and role-taking (also called perspective-taking [PT] ability to aggression has also been investigated. *PT* has been defined as "the ability to view a situation from another person's point of view and to anticipate his or her reactions to future events" (Kennedy, 1982). It appears that empathy and PT involve complex and multiphasic components, including affective inferences about other persons' internal emotional responses and perceptual inferences about another person's perspective of a given situation.

Despite the fact that it is by no means a unitary construct, findings have emerged indicating that the hypothesis suggesting a relationship between PT and antisocial behavior and aggression may be empirically supported. For example, young delinquents evidence greater egocentrism than nondelinquents on test of cognitive PT (Chandler, 1973) and affective PT (Rotenberg, 1974). Perspective taking among children appears to be inversely related to the expression of aggression (Feshbach, 1975). Aggressive delinquents exhibit less empathy than nonaggressive delinquents (Aleksic, 1976; Ellis, 1982). However, the relationship is not as clear with aggressive adolescents (Ellis, 1982). Thus the development of aggressive behavior appears to be associated, although not necessarily causally, with deficits in PT.

Chandler (1973) found significant differences in PT ability between delinquent versus nondelinquent youth. Recognizing the importance of PT skills in the socialization process, he randomly assigned delinquent subjects to one of three treatment conditions (role-taking, placebo attention control, no-treatment control groups). In an innovative role-taking condition, subjects were informed they were participating in a video film workshop and were providing remedial training in PT skills. Statistically significant differences in favor of the active role-taking treatment were obtained on PT ability. Positive and significant reductions in subsequent delinquent acts were also found at the 18-month follow-up. Moreover, the training substantially reduced their social egocentrism. Furthermore, the development of these social-cognitive skills was associated with observable reductions in delinquent behavior. The study provides empirical support for the conceptualization of delinquents as deficient in role- and perspective-taking skills, lagging behind their peer cohorts on these critical social-moral developmental capacities. These results highlight the importance of preventing and/or remediating developmental deficits in social reasoning and fostering social cognition in youth, particularly those identified as "at-risk" for antisocial and conduct disorders.

In a subsequent study Chandler, Greenspan, and Barenboim (1974) further explored the relationship between role-taking, referential communication, and social deviancy. The authors found that institutionalized, emotionally disturbed children were significantly delayed in their developmental capacity to utilize role-taking or referential communications skills. Following a ten-week program that met for two hours per week, subjects who received role-taking training and referential communications training evinced statistically significant improvements as a result of the intervention. In addition, follow-up analyses revealed significant correlations ($r = .40 - .49$) between behavioral ratings of improvement and improved social cognition. These results reaffirmed the presence of developmental delays in emotionally disturbed children and the viability of cognitive-social skills interventions to remediate such deficits. The data also provide added support for the hypothesis that improvement in these interpersonal skills may be associated with observable and clinically salient behavioral improvements.

In regard to problem-solving skills in conduct-disordered youth, Little and Kendall (1979) state, "In each case, when a non-normal group was compared with a matched group of normals, those adolescents who were having adjustment problems were found to be deficient in three ICPS skills: (1) means-end thinking; (2) alternative thinking; and, (3) perspective taking" (p. 84). Furthermore, the authors concluded that adolescents who exhibited interpersonal problem-solving deficits were much more likely to be classified as emotionally disturbed or delinquent. Overall, the research indicates that youth who exhibit behavioral problems appear to suffer deficits in social problem-solving skills. While such deficits may not necessarily be causally related to maladaptive behavior, Spivack et al. (1976) have found that training youth to engage in problem-solving skills improved classroom performance and increased popularity and concern for and helping behavior toward other children.

The efficacy of problem-solving interventions has been examined in several treatment studies (Abikoff, 1979; Kennedy, 1982; Urban & Kendall, 1980). Most of these studies involved impulsive or "emotionally disturbed" children, who were seen either individually or in small groups, and trained in problem-solving skills on related analogue tasks. Reviews of this literature indicate that treatment has generally been effective in significantly altering cognitive processes to which the procedures are directed. However, objective behavioral improvement has not been as systematically monitored and results appear more equivocal.

Several ICPS programs have been administered in the schools using teachers as trainers and have encompassed aggressive, hyperactive, mentally retarded, and normal elementary school children ranging from preschoolers to high school students (e.g., Camp & Bash, 1975; Elardo & Caldwell, in press; Gesten et al., 1979; Healey 1977; Kirschenbaum et al., 1981). For example, Camp and Bash (1981) developed an 8-week program entitled "Think Aloud" for use by individual small groups of children ages 6 to 8, who manifested aggressive and/or hyperactive behaviors and deficient self-control. The program combined techniques from Spivack, Platt, and Shure (1976) with self-instructional techniques from Meichenbaum and Goodman (1971). Thus children developed inner dialogues, in addition to problem-solving strategies. Program goals included both impersonal and interpersonal skills, incorporating both alternative solution and consequential thinking properties, As reported by the authors, relative to control subjects, the treated group evinced significant gains and observed classroom prosocial behaviors and increased academic achievement/cognitive skills. There were also reported increases in independent, teacher-rated prosocial behaviors and decreases in hostility and hyperactivity among children.

Elardo and Caldwell (in press) described a program for social development entitled "Project AWARE." AWARE was targeted for fourth and fifth graders and sought to enhance social competency through small-group discussions by (1) facilitating understanding of the thoughts and feelings of others; (2) increasing the children's ability to be more understanding and accepting of individual differences; (3) facilitating the generation of alternative solutions and consequential thinking skills; and (4) increasing self-respect and concern for others. The 72-lesson program was divided into 4 units that met twice weekly for 30 minutes over a 6-month period. According to the authors, the program was successful for both mixed racial and social classes among fourth and fifth graders, compared to untreated controls on numerous variables including alternative solution skills and behavioral adjustment, but not on perspective-taking ability. Children who had received the full curriculum evidenced significantly greater improvement than controls on measures of willingness to share experiences with the group, impulsivity, inappropriately blaming others, improved self-control, and creativity.

Recently, Natov (1981), in a study of 45 selected AWARE lessons using lower-class emotionally disturbed fifth graders, found increases in solution skills but not in means-end thinking, which was not part of the AWARE curriculum. Interestingly, Spivack and Shure (1974) reported that solutions and means-ends are uncorrelated, that is, an improvement in one skill area does not necessarily generalize to the untrained area and that these skills must be trained specifically. Natov reported that these children improved more than the controls with respect to achievement and learning, attending to class discussions, performing assigned work with increased care, and greater comprehension of class lessons.

Several studies also suggest promise of the ICPS approach as a means of preventing social maladjustment (Shure & Spivack, 1979b, 1982). For example, Shure and Spivack (1982) trained inner-city, black 4 to 5-year-olds in problem-solving skills. Children who were having problems of adjustment improved with treatment compared to nontreated individuals. Those who were considered to be adjusted already were less likely, over the course of a one-year follow-up, to show deviant behavior. Recently, Shure and Spivack (1983) adapted their program for young children to fourth- and fifth-grade school children in a developmentally adjusted package consisting of 55 lessons, administered in a classroom setting. As with the program for younger children, processes to develop problem-solving skills to be learned included alternative, consequential, and means-end thinking. Over a four-month program, administered in 40-minute sessions, three to four times a week, children received the ICPS training. The program was not specifically tested, using a comparative methodology (i.e., control versus treated subjects) with regard to the efficacy of the intervention. Instead, a priori, theoretical questions were addressed (e.g., did the children who manifested increases in ICPS skills also evidence concurrent improvements in classroom behaviors?). The results indicated that significant gains were made in the extent to which children decreased impulsive and inhibitive behaviors after the program, and correlates with ICPS and behavioral-change scores emerged most consistently with positive prosocial behaviors such as social ability, concern for others, and popularity. Another interesting effect reported by the authors was that ICPS training may have led to significant enhancement in academic achievement, including mathematics and reading grade levels, as well as general comprehension of task-oriented classroom activities. Thus ICPS improvement appears to have some functional relationship as a positive mediator of academic achievement, in that although the children manifested a wide range of IQs, they were still able to acquire, consolidate, and apply these newly learned skills in the academic setting. Unfortunately, due to the noncomparative nature of this research, the long-term efficacy vis-à-vis untreated controls remains unknown.

Overall, the above studies suggest several important features of the ICPS approach. First, laboratory evidence reveals a strong association between social-cognitive processes among school-age children and problem behavior at home and in school. Second, treatment studies with maladjusted, antisocial children have shown, although not as consistently, that school behavior, classroom performance, and peer relations (popularity and likeability) can be significantly improved using these strategies. Third, preliminary preventive approaches suggest that behavioral problems among adjusted children are less likely to emerge subsequent to ICPS training (see Spivack & Shure, 1982).

Thus the ICPS literature, on both a conceptual and clinical level, supports the utility of enhancing social problem solving of antisocial youth. The diversity of its application to a wide variety of populations, for varying lengths of time, conducted by a range of trainers lends support to its short-term effectiveness. However, the long-term efficacy (i.e., maintenance and generalization) of ICPS vis-à-vis prevention/treatment of antisocial behavior in youth has not been systematically investigated and is an area requiring further study.

While ICPS training programs have generated encouraging results, there are a number of significant issues that need to be addressed in future research. First, clinical outcome studies examining the effectiveness of ICPS strategies should include behavioral measures of adjustment. While teaching children problem-solving skills is both theoretically and intuitively appealing, it is important to demonstrate that these skills are functionally related to adaptive behavior. Thus ICPS programs should routinely include not just measures of problem-solving ability, but also use behavioral assessment to establish empirically that these skills do in fact mediate observable gains in adaptive functioning.

A significant and ubiquitous problem with regard to ICPS training programs in the past has been their failure routinely to include attention-placebo control groups as a means of controlling for nonspecific therapist factors such as trainer attention and social reinforcement. It also is unknown whether teaching ICPS skills significantly enhances long-term adaptation of maladjusted anti-social children. The equivocal findings are, in large part, the result of the relative absence of long-term follow-up studies with regard to the application of the strategy, occasional successes, and some failures. As reviewed by Kazdin (1984, p. 18):

> Relatively few studies have evaluated cognitive therapy with clinical child populations. In some cases where clinical populations are used, the focus is on impulsivity rather than on the problems that precipitated treatment or hospitalization. . . . When clinical populations are studied, measures of cognitive function often reflect change but measures of overt behavior (e.g., the classroom) yield equivocal results. Thus, the clinical efficacy of treatment has not been clearly demonstrated (p. 18).

A number of other critical issues await more programmatic research with regard to ascertaining the efficacy of ICPS strategies for antisocial youth. These include: (1) what is the optimal duration, intensity, and sequence of training; (2) which factors may mediate short- and long-term effectiveness; (3) are there interaction effects between problem-type, cognitive level of maturation, and treatment strategy; and (4) what are the cognitive correlates of the antisocial typologies? Resolving these questions would allow for more careful prescriptive treatments where specific antisocial disorder subtypes could be assigned to their optimal interventions, based upon identified deficits.

Recently, Michelson and Mannarino (1984) have proposed that ICPS training may need to be combined with other intensive therapeutic experiences such as PMT or behavioral social competency training to significantly affect antisocial youth who manifest severe behavioral deficits. Finally, the issue of treatment generalization has received scant attention in the ICPS literature. Unless ICPS training programs can actually demonstrate that the children use these skills across multiple settings and individuals, the training efforts will certainly have fallen short of their ultimate aims. Hence generalization assessment and programming procedures should be more systematically undertaken with ICPS programs.

Behavioral Social Skills Training (BSST)

Another strategy that holds much promise for the prevention and/or treatment of antisocial disorders in children and adolescents is BSST. This modality is directed at developing specific and complex interpersonal behaviors that encompass a wide variety of social situations to promote prosocial interactions. BSST is based on the view that children with antisocial, aggressive, noncompliant, and acting-out behaviors have not sufficiently developed the requisite skills to function optimally, both inter- and intrapersonally. BSST focuses on developing complex and adaptive behavioral repertoires to enhance personal competencies.

The conceptual basis of BSST and research on the underpinnings of childhood dysfunction are more diffuse than work on the ICPS. BSST stems from the view that maladjustment is defined in terms of both intra- and interpersonal behavior. Further, it is assumed that appropriate social behaviors develop or fail to thrive in part as a function of learning experiences. Evidence, culled from a variety of sources, suggests the potential importance of learning experiences in promoting maladjustment. For example, as previously discussed, research has suggested that aggressive behavior in the home of conduct-disoriented children is maintained by direct and consistent (albeit unwitting) reinforcement of that behavior by the parents (see Patterson, 1982). Moreover, prosocial behavior is usually not reinforced by parents of deviant children and, indeed, is likely to be ignored. Other learning influences may play a role in the development of aggressive behavior. Aggressive youth are more likely to come from homes where there is child or spouse abuse, and from parents who use harsh (corporal) punishment practices (e.g., Glueck & Glueck, 1952; McCord, McCord, & Zola, 1959). Sources of violence and punitiveness might provide modeling experiences to children, training them how to interact with others. Indeed, evidence has suggested that children interact with their peers in the ways that their parents interact with them. Thus aggressive and deviant parent-child or parent-parent interactions may provide a training regimen for deviant behavior in the youth. Modeling opportunities to learn aggressiveness might also come from other sources such as violence on television. Children who view aggressive television in early childhood tend to be much more aggressive and this influence is still evident into late adolescence (Eron, 1980). The above evidence documents some of the learning influences on acting-out behaviors. While no theory can lay compete claim to understanding and proving the etiological basis for aggressive behavior, there is a strong conceptual basis for providing BSST to high-risk and antisocial youth.

BSST emphasizes development of those interpersonal skills that are identified via social validation, developmental, and child clinical psychology literatures as being critical to the social, psychological, and cognitive adjustment in children. Hence training focuses on multiple skills, including (but not limited to): Empathy, role taking, giving and receiving compliments, expressing appreciation, entering, participating in conversations, asking questions, dealing with interruptions, nonverbal behavior, giving and receiving complaints, apologies, and criticism, making requests, asking why, learning to say no, how to accept others saying no, standing up for one's and other's rights, recognizing the rights of others, dealing with anger, behavioral self-management, and self-control strategies for anger, stress, and impulse control, dealing with aggressive feelings and behavior, conflict resolution training, dealing with teasing, accusations, rejection, disappointment, and group pressure, decision making, honesty, interacting with adults, accepting responsibility, cooperation, paying attention, dealing with authority figures, increasing frustration tolerance, and increasing delay for immediate gratification.

The primary objective of the BSST program is to train children and adolescents in specific adaptive behaviors related to critical areas of interpersonal functioning. The specific skills trained vary as a function of the characteristics of the youth, their specific problems, age, and social situations. Over the past eight years, I have been actively involved in assessing and promoting social competence in youth. As a result of these programmatic studies, it became progressively apparent that one of the most efficient and effective strategies for teaching and disseminating social skills programs would be through the systematic development of empirically derived modules, each covering specific content areas deemed of clinical and social importance by children, parents, and teachers. Through a series of social validation procedures, including normative surveys, questionnaires, behavioral observation, panel reviews, and as a result of several large-scale investigations, a series of sixty modules were developed (see Michelson, Sugai, Wood, & Kazdin, 1983), The BSST modules have yielded significant treatment effects across normal, at-risk, maladjusted, outpatient, and inpatient populations. Specifically, social skills content areas that were identified as being important to the overall social competency of children were developed into separate instructional units. The modules were designed in sequence in a progressively more complex manner with earlier modules focusing on more simple social skills and later modules describing more complex skills that are built upon the fundamental ones.

One of the primary goals of the BSST program is to reduce aggressive, acting-out, and antisocial behavior. To accomplish this aim, participants are instructed in a variety of content areas, all directed toward achieving positive and mutually satisfying solutions that enhance both short- and long-term goals and relationships. The youth are encouraged to express themselves, but in ways that do not violate other peoples' rights or feelings and to engage in self-control procedures as a means of deflecting and redirecting anger, hostility, and aggressive behavior. They are also encouraged to behave in an honest, positive, nonpunitive, fair, considerate, direct, nondefensive, sensitive, and constructive manner. The use of aggressive and antisocial behavior that ignores or restricts the feelings, opinions, needs, or rights of others, or uses manipulative, impulsive, punishing, or socially inappropriate strategies to achieve their goals is eschewed. Likewise, the use of aggressive responses that are bossy, demanding, self-centered, insensitive, callous, or that depict disregard for others' feelings are replaced with adaptive social repertoires. Thus, from a behavioral perspective, the use of the term *social skills* refers to repertoires of social interaction and social knowledge that, when used interpersonally, tend to evoke positive reinforcement on both a short- *and* long-term basis, resulting in positive outcomes for *both* parties. Acquisition of effective and appropriate social skills prepares the youth for competent and rewarding participation in diverse aspects of human interaction.

While social skills training is, in essence, a program to teach and enhance communication in interpersonal skills (both implicit and explicit), the preventive approach used in BSST prepares the youth for the intricacies of social interaction by formalizing the development of successful inter- and intrapersonal repertoires. These socially skilled youth are then better prepared to develop and thrive in their complex social environments. Parents or teachers may admonish these youth to behave with greater self-control, empathy, and decreased aggressiveness. Unfortunately, mere insistence that they behave in such a manner does little to remediate their social deficits and excesses. However, through the use of clinically salient programmed modules, the youth are exposed to, reinforced, instructed, modeled, and given feedback (with treatment generalization designed into the program) to facilitate development of these more effective and appropriate skills. The strength of BSST derives from evidence that behaviors that relate to maladjustment can, in fact, be altered. BSST has been applied to a variety of inpatient, outpatient, and normal populations including children and adolescents who are socially aggressive, withdrawn, mentally retarded, learning disabled, delinquent, and others (see Michelson & Wood, 1980a & b; Michelson et al., 1983; Rinn & Markle, 1979; Van Hasselt, Hersen, Bellack & Whitehall, 1979).

Various components of BSST are designed to promote social behavior in different ways. *Instructions, coaching,* and *modeling* refer to antecedent components that help prompt the desired target behaviors. With instructions, the trainer details the situation and the behaviors that are to be performed for effective social functioning. The behavior may then be modeled by the trainer or peers who actually engage in the requisite behaviors. Through observation, the youth learns the behaviors that are required and how they are performed. When the youth then engages in trying the behavior himself or herself, coaching is provided to help prompt individual behaviors to make the responses more refined and effective. Other components, such as rehearsal and practice, provide additional opportunities to perform the response. Verbal and nonverbal behaviors are also enacted to provide proprioceptive cues not readily available from observation. Through repeated practice, the appropriate behaviors become stable in the youth's repertoire. Feedback and social reinforcement, as components of training, provide consequences designed to increase the frequency of correctly responding so that appropriate social behavior becomes firmly established in the youth's repertoire. In recent years, the individual procedures (instructions, coaching, modeling, rehearsal and practice, feedback and social reinforcement) typically have been combined into a "treatment package" to maximize development and generalization of behavior in a variety of interpersonal situations (Michelson et al., 1983).

Thus while a number of programs have used the individual

techniques just described to promote prosocial behavior, a number of innovative programs have appeared that offer multifaceted treatments or packages in which the above procedures are combined (Filipczak, Archer, & Friedman, 1980; Michelson et al., 1982; Michelson & Wood, 1980b; Michelson, Mannarino, Marchione, Stern, Figueroa, & Beck, 1983). It is assumed that combining alternative strategies maximizes the *impact, durability,* and *generality* of the treatment effects. Also, as increasingly more severe clinical populations have been studied, the need for these more intensive interventions has increased.

Recently, Michelson et al. (1983) compared ICPS, BSST, and Rogerian (control) treatments for child psychiatric outpatients referred for problems of marked antisocial behavior and conduct disorders ($n = 61$). The children ranged in age from 8 to 12 years old and included 62% black and 38% white children. All children manifested severe social adjustment problems with referral complaints of marked aggression, dysfunctional peer relations, deficient anger control, social skill deficits, and social rejection. The majority of subjects experienced related problems, including academic failure, acting-out, noncompliance, and related behavioral adjustment problems. Treatment consisted of 12 weekly one-hour sessions with follow-up conducted at 6 and 12 months. The assessment battery used to evaluate outcome included direct behavioral observations, parent-, teacher-, peer-, self-report, and academic performance measures.

The BSST and ICPS treatments made significant within-group improvements on several measures whereas control group children did not. Major between-group analyses indicated that, at posttreatment, there were no group differences. However, at one-year follow-up, children in BSST and ICPS groups were significantly better than the nondirective group on several measures of adjustment and behavioral problems at home and at school. Significantly greater gains were evident for the BSST condition than for the ICPS condition on a few measures. However, on an overall basis these were both significantly and equally effective on long-term outcome. These findings are significant because of the paucity of evidence on the efficacy of psychosocial treatments for conduct disordered children. Of additional interest was the fact that children in the BSST and ICPS training continued to improve over the course of follow-up in academic, social, and emotional areas of functioning while children in the control condition did not.

While these results were encouraging with regard to the short-term efficacy of these interventions, a number of clinical issues arose with regard to the project. First, it became readily apparent that although significant gains were achieved, not all of these children would, by social-normative standards, be considered well adjusted. Furthermore, while significant treatment effects were observed on a short-term basis, the absence of continued improvements on direct behavioral observation measures suggested that in order to effect the ongoing behavioral components of the antisocial disorder, the use of more intensive and prolonged interventions may be necessary. Thus one of the major recommendations of the study was to apply these effective treatment modalities on a preventive basis. Specific suggestions were offered advocating early screening and identification of "at-risk" children, who could then receive the interventions on a more intensive and extended basis (e.g., covering one to two school years). This would help obviate the need for prolonged and costly treatment of crystalized, and perhaps intractable, antisocial disorders seen in older youths. In light of these findings, a study was undertaken (Marchione, Michelson, & Mannarino, 1984) to examine the efficacy of BSST, ICPS, and a combined BSST *plus* ICPS modality, for possible synergistic effects, which will be described subsequently.

Combined Cognitive-Behavioral Treatments

BSST and ICPS both represent highly promising procedures for the prevention and treatment of antisocial behavior in youth. The techniques can draw upon underlying conceptual approaches about the basis of deviant behavior and have been subjected to considerable controlled outcome research. Although the treatments are quite different, they are not incompatible at either the conceptual or practical levels. Indeed, the focus on cognitive processes and behaviors (i.e., combining features of the modalities) might optimize treatment effects in the long run. Although ICPS and BSST have not been systematically evaluated as preventive techniques for conduct disorder per se, they have been applied widely to children with diverse interpersonal and adjustment problems.

The current empirical status of ICPS and BSST indicates considerable promise as behavior change techniques. There are several important reasons for examining combined cognitive-behavioral strategies as viable preventive/treatment modalities. First, the approaches are derived from different (but not incompatible) conceptual positions about the basis of social maladjustment and conduct problems and how they should be ameliorated. BSST is based on the view that maladjustment can be translated into objective, identifiable, and treatable deficits in socially adaptive interpersonal behaviors. These deficits can be altered by training that actively develops new ways of responding in interpersonal situations. BSST develops the behavior through repeated practice, feedback, reinforcement, and modeling experiences across a large number of critical interpersonal situations. ICPS is based on the view that social maladjustment results from deficits in several cognitive processes and verbal mediation skills and the control that these processes and skills exert over behavior. Therefore, training is directed toward the development of internalized verbal repertoires that control overt social behavior.

Second, research underlying both approaches suggests that the focus on specific overt behaviors and cognitive process is important to ameliorate maladjustment. Children who are identified as acting-out problems in schools, as well as those whose dysfunctions are sufficiently severe as to be identified and diagnosed clinically as conduct disorders, have been shown to differ from children functioning well in their overt behavior and in their cognitive processes related to social situations. A treatment approach that targets both overt behavior and underlying cognitive processes maximizes the likelihood of controverting antisocial behavior and reducing the likelihood of subsequent clinical solidification and dysfunction. Because of their different but complementary treatment foci, the combination of ICPS and BSST may maximize therapeutic change. Hence both the cognitive processes that underlie behavior and specific response repertoires can be directly altered with a combined treatment.

A number of studies support the use of ICPS, BSST, and combined ICPS/BSST treatments. Kendall and Zubin (1981) investigated a cognitive-behavioral intervention to facilitate self-control in impulsive/aggressive acting-out children. The authors compared individual and group treatment with a control condition with 30 teacher-referred children in grades 3 to 5 who participated in 12 sessions with practice on psychoeducational tasks, interpersonal play situations, and personal problem areas. Individual and group cognitive-behavioral treatment conditions evidenced statistically significant improvement, utilizing blind teacher ratings of self-control, posttreatment, and perspective taking at follow-up. Both the group and individual cognitive-behavioral treatments evidence generalization as seen on the teachers' blind rating of self-control. Moreover, the improvement in self-control and hyperactivity ratings for the cognitive-behavioral intervention placed the treatment children within one standard deviation of the normative mean. Finally, the maintenance of role-taking improvements appeared to be directly attributable to their individual or group treatment. These findings suggest the potential of cognitive-behavioral strategies in enhancing children's self-control and the efficiency of employing group treatment.

Recently, Kendall and Braswell (1982) compared a cognitive-behavioral treatment, a behavioral treatment, and an attention-placebo control condition with 27 non-self-controlled problem children ranging in age from 8 to 12 years. Subjects were randomly assigned to one of the treatment conditions, which entailed 12 sessions of individual therapist contact focusing on psychoeducational play, interpersonal tasks, and situations with the cognitive-behavioral treatment including self-instructional training via modeling and behavioral contingencies in the behavioral treatment involving modeling in contingencies. The cognitive-behavioral intervention improved teathers' blind ratings of self-control and both the cognitive-behavioral and the behavioral interventions manifested significantly greater improvement on teacher blind ratings of hyperactivity. Parent ratings did not evince treatment improvements, possibly as a result of the brief intervention. While several performance measures, including cognitive style, academic achievement, and so forth, reflected improvements for the cognitive-behavioral and behavioral conditions, only the cognitive-behavioral (combined intervention) yielded improved children's self-concept. While naturalistic observations in the classroom were highly variable, several observational codes revealed positive treatment effects. Likewise, normative comparisons conducted at the ten-week follow-up period provided additional evidence for the effectiveness of the combined intervention. These models are useful for illustrative purposes and reveal initial intervention effects. Moreover, treatment potency would probably be significantly enhanced by increasing its duration and specifically programming generalization procedures into the interventions, as successfully reported by Michelson et al. (1983).

Kettlewell and Kausch (1983) conducted a cognitive-behavioral treatment program for aggressive children, ages 7-12 years, attending a summer daycamp. Twenty children participated in 4 weeks of biweekly 90-minute sessions during which they received an integrated cognitive behavioral treatment. A no-treatment control group was also employed. The treatment group evidenced statistically significant and clinically superior performance on coping skills, self-report of anger, problem-solving ability and need for the use of time-out as a disciplinary action. While no follow-up data were collected, these results suggest that aggressive behavior can be positively affected by the combined treatment, at least on a short-term basis.

Marchione et al. (1984) recently compared BSST, ICPS, and a combined BSST plus ICPS program for high-risk youth in a large-scale comparative outcome study. The primary objective of this investigation was to examine issues regarding the effectiveness, generalizability, and feasibility of the three interventions as prevention programs for antisocial fourth and fifth grade elementary school children and to establish the relative and combined efficacy of Cognitive and Behavioral social competency strategies. Two-hundred forty children from fourth and fifth grade elementary school classes were screened using the AML scale (Cowen et al., 1973) to identify those youth "at risk" in regard to marked antisocial behavior. The upper one-third, or 80 children, were selected for random assignment to one of the four conditions (behavioral, cognitive, combined, control groups).

The four experimental conditions were compared at posttreatment using ANCOVAS that yielded statistically significant differences $(p < .05)$ on the major dependent measures, including the children's assertive behavior scale-aggressive factor, passive factor, and total score. The interventions were also significantly different on the parent's and teacher's measures of children's social skills problem-solving effectiveness and on peer sociometric ratings. Post-hoc anlyses indicated that in all cases, the active treatments demonstrated statistically superior functioning compared to the control group. To ascertain the long-term impact of the active interventions, ANCOVAS were performed on the six-month follow-up assessment measures. The analyses and post-hoc test revealed significant between-group differences on the CABS-total (Combined, BSST > ICPS), problem-solving goals (Combined > ICPS, BSST), and solutions (Combined > BSST, ICPS). These results suggest that the Combined ICPS *plus* BSST treatment was most effective and led to improvement across a wider dimension of functioning on both a short- and long-term basis.

These results provide empirical support for the relative and combined effectiveness of the BSST and ICPS treatment modalities with high-risk youth. Each of the three prevention strategies yielded statistically significant effects across the critical domains of social functioning. These findings suggest that the modalities are promising and potentially efficacious strategies for reducing antisocial behavior among high-risk children. Moreover, given a comprehensive intervention of extended duration, considerably magnified short- and long-term effects would probably be generated.

Recommendations for Enhancing the Effectiveness of Cognitive and Behavioral Strategies

Based upon my clinical-research experience in cognitive-behavioral strategies for antisocial youth, and in light of findings from the scientific literature, there appear to be several refinements which, if pursued, would enhance the effectiveness of these interventions. First, in the vast majority of studies where treatment effects were either not obtained or of negligible significance, the duration of treatment was relatively brief. In almost all cases where generalization and maintenance effects were not observed at follow-up assessments there were typically no booster sessions provided. Indeed, both the ICPS and BSST literatures reveal a paucity of extended, sequential, or booster interventions. Benefits from extending these modalities for longer periods of time might include: (1) facilitating maintenance and generalization across settings, individuals, and time; (2) increased opportunities to acquire, practice, and refine these newly acquired skills; (3) improved consolidation of treatment effects due to longer exposure of at-risk children to these strategies; and (4) increased probability of success with slow learners, learning disabled, or at-risk children with attention deficits, due to their having increased opportunities to attend to, process, and acquire these skills.

Recognizing the chronicity and intensity of antisocial behavior in children and adolescents, it is important initially to identify effective strategies in the reduction and/or elimination of the at-risk behavior. Once the actual efficacy of these strategies is demonstrated, subsequent studies to improve efficiency (i.e., dissection investigations) can then be undertaken to delineate more cost-efficient variations and employ prescriptive treatments where children are matched to alternative interventions based upon empirically derived "best fit" subject-treatment response profiles. Currently, much of the research literature is limited to brief treatments, yielding mixed treatment effects. Particularly problematic are studies obtaining short-term effects that often dissipate following termination of the brief interventions and are less often observed during long-term follow-up. Thus conclusions regarding the long-term effects of many of these approaches cannot be fully determined due to the clinical confound of attenuated treatments. Present conceptualization of the current status of the prevention/treatment field, in particular with regard to child psychopathology, reveals that numerous child-oriented short-term studies have demonstrated the clinical use of BSST, ICPS, and combined cognitive-behavioral strategies. Recognizing that these modalities represent highly promising interventions at present, it is important that they be subjected to more programmatic research.

Treatment integrity is an often ignored, though potentially important aspect of enhancing the effectiveness of any therapeutic intervention. (Sechrest, et al., 1979). *Treatment integrity* refers to the process that the intervention is carried out specifically as intended. Merely labeling an intervention as "cognitive" or "behavioral" says relatively little of its particular content. Indeed, clinicians using the same modality may differ widely in their application, style, content, scope, duration, and sequence of treatment. Therefore, it is important that treatment integrity be considered as an integral component of any intervention. To ensure that they are carried out as intended, it is critical that treatment integrity be systematically undertaken (Yeaton & Sechrest, 1981). This can be accomplished by developing a quantifiable scoring procedure that employs a fidelity index derived from verbatim ratings of the treatment sessions that are then coded on a sentence-by-sentence basis for the presence of a particular type of modality. The coding procedure could directly utilize the actual treatment manuals as specific training guides as to what defines treatment fidelity. Furthermore, the ratings should be conducted in a random and nonsequential manner by independent assessors to reduce potential rater biases and related methodological artifacts.

To clinically use the treatment fidelity index, trainers should strive to maintain high levels of procedural integrity to ensure the modality is faithfully reproduced and carried out as specified. Moreover, the utility of treatment integrity is further enhanced by its potential application to training new therapists, cross-center comparisions, and retrospectively identifying salient process aspects of the intervention that are associated with therapeutic outcome.

Multiple Gate Screening. As discussed earlier in this volume (see Loeber & Dishion) the use of multiple gate screening provides an effective strategy for identifying high-risk children, using increasingly stringent inclusion criteria with mass screening being performed initially and progressively more in-depth and restrictive assessments being undertaken subsequently. Recently, Loeber and Dishion (1983) examined the reliability and validity of this multistage assessment procedure for identifying youths at risk for antisocial behavior and delinquency. The authors correctly classified 86% of recidivist youths based upon the sophisticated multiple gating procedure, wherein teachers, parents, and home contact/assessments were performed. Furthermore, the multiple gating procedure was 58% less expensive than the unitary stage screening procedures typically employed.

The success of the multiple gating procedure lies, in part, in its recognition that factors related to increased risk status can be directly associated with increased *density, multiple settings, variety,* and *early onset* of antisocial behaviors. Specifically, this refers to the increased frequency of these antisocial behaviors compared to normal cohorts, the multiple settings in which they occur such as the home and school, the variety of acts such as truancy, stealing, lying, bullying, and so on, and their early onset as a portent of subsequent maladjustment. Thus using multiple gating procedures it appears that the youth's own behavior is a relatively reliable and powerful index of antisocial patterns when it is frequently reported across multiple settings by various informants who observe varied violations. Hence the use of multiple gate screening procedures should receive serious consideration as a means of identifying at-risk youth who might then benefit from cognitive, behavioral, combined, or alternative interventions.

Generalization programming. A critical issue underlying any therapeutic endeavor for antisocial youth is generalization programming. If these vital but fragile skills are to be applied in appropriate situations outside the original setting in which they were trained, procedures must be undertaken to ensure that therapeutic benefits generalize across time, multiple settings, and individuals. There has been increasing evidence that generalization does not naturally occur for most educational or treatment programs (Baer, Wolf, & Risley, 1968; Kazdin, 1980). Research indicates that socially deficient children also do not automatically acquire the necessary social skills through mere contact with regular (adjusted) students (Cooke & Appoloni, 1977). Behaviorally disordered and antisocial youth are often ignored or rejected by peers rather than becoming involved in actions that facilitate the development of more appropriate social behaviors (Strain & Timm, 1974). Therefore, generalization cannot be regarded as a passive function where a skill once taught magically appears and continues to operate thereafter. On the contrary, generalization requires an active stance by the trainer and must be specifically designed and programmed into interventions, if they are to result in meaningful and lasting benefit.

Although the most common approach to generalization is to "train and hope," this strategy is not likely to yield optimal results. A number of techniques for promoting generalization beyond the training setting, including maintenance over time and transfer across settings, have been elaborated by Stokes and Baer (1977), Michelson and Mannarino (1984), and Michelson et al. (1983). Procedures to promote generalization include:

(1) teaching behaviors that will be supported by the natural environment;
(2) teaching a variety of responses;
(3) training loosely under varied conditions;
(4) training across multiple persons and settings common to the natural environment;
(5) fading training consequences to approximate natural contingencies;
(6) reinforcing accurate self-reports of performance;
(7) training the ability to generalize by reinforcing new, appropriate applications; and
(8) utilize peers in training.

Therefore, generalization programming should be an essential feature of ICPS, BSST, and combined cognitive-behavioral interventions for antisocial youth. Without generalization programming these newly acquired inter- and intrapersonal skills may be limited with regard to their transfer to other settings, individuals, or across time. It is important that generalization be incorporated directly into the training process rather than assuming it will occur. This will provide a more systematic approach to fostering maximum therapeutic maintenance.

Conceptual and Methodological Issues

Currently, a number of critical issues remain with regard to cognitive and behavioral strategies for antisocial youth. First, it remains problematic that the vast majority of studies do not employ objective diagnostic criteria such as DSM-III for subject inclusion. Similarly, until target populations are clearly specified, conclusions regarding both appropriateness and efficacy of the interventions remain tentative. Research is also needed to identify which specific cognitive and behavioral deficits reliably differentiate adjusted versus antisocial youth. Moreover, well-adjusted peers should be used as comparative cohorts to provide an estimate of the social and clinical impact of the intervention in restoring at-risk youth to "non-risk" status. The use of multitrait-multimethod assessments should also be considered to provide a more refined and meaningful triangulation of the effects of a given treatment strategy.

In summary, behavioral, cognitive, and combined modalities can produce beneficial changes in antisocial youth with mild to moderate adjustment problems. Remediation of more severe and/or chronic antisocial behavior in youth is clearly more difficult and requires further investigation. Combined cognitive-behavioral strategies, however, offer much encouragement, based upon current research. Moreover, issues of attenuated treatment, absence of generalization programming, treatment integrity, booster sessions, and heterogeneous subject selection need to be more fully addressed, if more specific prescriptive prevention/treatment recommendations are to be offered.

References

Abikoff, H. (1979). Cognitive training interventions in children: Review of a new approach. *Journal of Learning Disabilities, 12*, 65-77.

Achenbach, T. M. (1982). *Developmental psychopathology* (2nd ed.). New York: John Wiley.

Achenbach, T. M., & Edelbrock, C. S. (1978). The classification of child psychopathology: A review and analysis of empirical efforts. *Psychological Bulletin, 85*, 1275-1301.

Adler, F. (1977). The interaction between women's emancipation and female criminality: a cross-cultural perspective. *International Journal of Criminology and Penology, 5*, 101-112.

Aleksic, P. (1976). A study of empathic inhibition of aggression in juvenile delinquents (Doctoral dissertation, Miami University, 1975). *Dissertation Abstracts International, 36*, 4675-4676B.

American Psychiatric Association. (1980). *Diagnostic and statistical manual of psychiatric disorders* (3rd ed.). Washington, DC: Author.

Baer, D. M., Wolf, M. M., & Risley, T. R. (1968). Some current dimensions of applied behavior analysis. *Journal of Applied Behavior Analysis, 1*, 91-97.

Baum, C. G., & Forehand, R. (1981). Long-term follow-up assessment of parent training by use of multiple outcome measures. *Behavior Therapy, 12*, 643-652.

Berkowitz, L. (1977). Situational and personal conditions governing reactions to aggressive cues. In D. Magnusson & N. S. Ender (Eds.), *Personality at the crossroads: Current issues in interactional psychology*. Hillsdale, NJ: Erlbaum.

Block, J. (1977). *Lives through time*. Berkeley: Bancroft.

Camp, B. W. (n.d). Verbal mediation in young aggressive boys. *Journal of Abnormal Psychology, 86*, 145-153.

Camp, B. W., & Bash, M. (1975). *Think aloud program group manual.* Boulder: University of Colorado Medical Center.

Camp, B. W., & Bash, M. (1981). *Think aloud: Increasing social and cognitive skills—A problem-solving program for children.* Champaign, IL: Research Press.

Campbell, M., Cohen, I. L., & Small, A. M. (1982). Drugs in aggressive behavior. *Journal of the American Academy of Child Psychiatry, 21,* 107-117.

Chandler, M. (1973). Egocentrism and antisocial behavior: The assessment and training of social perspective-taking skills. *Developmental Psychology, 9,* 326-332.

Chandler, M., Greenspan, S., & Barenboim, C. (1974). Assessment and training of role-taking and referential communication skills in institutionalized emotionally disturbed children. *Developmental Psychology, 10,* 546-553.

Cooke, T. P., & Appolloni, T. (1976). Developing positive social-emotional behaviors: A study of training and generalization effects. *Journal of Applied Behavior Analysis, 9,* 65-78.

Cowen, E. L., Trost, M. A., Lorion, R. P., Door, D., Izzo, L. D., & Isaacson, R. V. (1975). *New ways in school mental health.* New York: Human Sciences Press.

Deluty, R. H. (1981). Alternative-thinking ability of aggressive, assertive, and submissive children. *Cognitive Therapy and Research, 5,* 309-312.

Dodge, K. A. (1980). Social cognition and children's aggressive behavior. *Child Development, 51,* 162-170.

Elardo, P. T., & Caldwell, B. M. (in press). The effects of an experimental social development program on children in the middle childhood period. *Psychology in the schools.*

Ellis, P. L. (1982). Empathy: A factor in antisocial behavior. *Journal of Abnormal Child Psychology, 10,* 123-134.

Eron, C. D. (1980). Prescription for reduction of aggression. *American Psychologist, 35,* 244-252.

Eyberg, S. M., & Johnson, S. M. (1974). Multiple assessment of behavior modification with families: Effects of contingency contracting and order of treated problems. *Journal of Consulting and Clinical Psychology, 42,* 594-606.

Feshbach, N. D. (1975). Empathy in children: Some theoretical and empirical considerations. *The Counseling Psychologist, 5,* 25-30.

Filipczak, J., Archer, M., & Friedman, R. M. (1980). Inschool social skills training: Use with disruptive adolescents. *Behavior Modification, 4,* 243-263.

Fleischman, M. J., & Szykula, S. A. (1981). A community setting replication of social learning treatment for aggressive children. *Behavior Therapy, 12,* 115-122.

Gersten, J. C., Langner, T. S., Eisenberg, J. B., Simcha-Fagen, O., & McCarthy, E. D. (1976). Stability and change in types of behavioral disturbance of children and adolescents. *Journal of Abnormal Child Psychology, 4,* 111-127.

Gesten, E., Flores de Apodaca, R., Rains, M., Weissberg, R., & Cowen, E. (1979). In M. W. Kent & J. E. Rolf (Eds.). *Social competence in children.* Hanover, NH: University Press of New England.

Glidewell, J. C., & Swallow, C. S. (1969). *The prevalence of maladjustment in elementary schools: A report prepared for the Joint Commission on The Mental Health of Children.* Chicago: University of Chicago Press.

Glueck, S., & Glueck, E. T. (1952). *Delinquents in the making: Paths to prevention.* New York: Harper.

Graham, P., & Rutter, M. (1973). Psychiatric disorder in the young adolescent: A follow-up study. *Proceedings of the Royal Society of Medicine, 66,* 1226-1229.

Griest, D. L., Forehand, R., Rogers, T., Breiner, J., Furey, W., & Williams, C. A. (1982). Effects of parent enhancement therapy on the treatment outcome and generalization of a parent training program. *Behavior Research and Therapy, 20,* 429-436.

Healey, K. (1977). *An investigation of the relationship between certain social cognitive abilities and social behavior, and the efficacy of training in social cognitive skills for elementary retarded-educable children.* Unpublished doctoral dissertation, Bryn Mawr College.

Herbert, M. (1978). *Conduct disorders of childhood and adolescence: A behavioral approach to assessment and treatment.* Chichester, England: John Wiley.

Kazdin, A. E. (1980). *Research design in clinical psychology.* New York: Harper & Row.

Kazdin, A. E. (1984). Treatment of conduct disorders. In J.B.W. Williams & R. L. Spitzer (Eds.), *Psychotherapy research: Where are we and where should we go?* (pp. 3-27). New York: Guilford.

Kazdin, A. E., & Frame, C. (1983). Treatment of aggressive behavior and conduct disorder. In R. J. Morris & T. R. Kratochwill (Eds.), *The practice of child therapy.* New York: Pergamon.

Kendall, P. & Braswell, L. (1982). Cognitive behavioral treatment of inpulsivity: concrete versus conceptual training. *Journal of Consulting and Clinical Psychology, 50,* 672-689.

Kendall, P. C., & Zubin, B. A. (1981). Individual versus group application of cognitive-behavioral self-control procedures with children. *Behavior Therapy, 12,* 344-359.

Kennedy, R. E. (1982). Cognitive-behavioral approaches to the modification of aggressive behavior in children. *School Psychology Review, 11,* 47-55.

Little, V. L., & Kendall, P. C. (1979). Cognitive-behavioral interventions with delinquents: Problem-solving, role-taking, and self-control. In P. C. Kendall & S. D. Hollon (Eds.), *Cognitive behavioral interventions: Theory, research and procedures.* New York: Academic Press.

Livson, N., & Peskin, H. (1967). Prediction of adult psychological health in a longitudinal study. *Journal of Abnormal Psychology, 72,* 509-518.

Loeber, R., & Dishion, T. J. (1983). Early predictors of male delinquency: A review. *Psychological Bulletin, 94,* 68-99.

Marchione, K., Michelson, L., & Mannarino, A. (1984). Cognitive behavioral treatment of antisocial behavior. University of Pittsburgh. (unpublished)

McCord, W., McCord, J., & Zola, I. K. (1959). *Origins of crime.* New York: Columbia University Press.

McMahon, R. J., Forehand, R., Griest, D. L., & Wells, K. C. (1981). Who drops out of treatment during parent behavioral training? *Behavioral Counseling Quarterly, 1,* 79-85.

Meichenbaum, D., & Goodman, J. (1971). Training impulsive children to talk to themselves: A means of developing self-control. *Journal of Abnormal Psychology, 77,* 115-126.

Michelson, L. (1981). Behavioral approaches to prevention. In L. Michelson, M. Hersen, & S. M. Turner (Eds.), *Future perspectives in behavior therapy.* New York: Plenum.

Michelson, L., Foster, S., & Richey, W. (1981). Behavioral assessment of children's social skills. In B. B. Lahey & A. E. Kazdin (Eds.), *Advances in clinical child psychology* (Vol. 3). New York: Plenum.

Michelson, L., Hersen, M., & Turner, S. M. (Eds.). (1981). *Future perspectives in therapy.* New York: Plenum.

Michelson, L., & Mannarino, A. (1984). Social skills training with children: Research and clinical application. In P. S. Strain, J. M. Guralnick, & H. Walker (Eds.), *Children's social behavior: Development, assessment, and modification.* New York: Academic Press.

Michelson, L., Mannarino, T., Marchione, K., Stern, M., Figueroa, J., & Beck, S. (1983). A comparative outcome study of behavioral social skills training, cognitive problem solving, and Rogerian treatments for child psychiatric outpatients: Process, outcome, and generalization effects. *Behaviour Research and Therapy, 21,* 545-556.

Michelson, L., & Wood, R. (1980a). A group assertive training program for elementary school children. *Child Behavior Therapy, 2,* 1-9.

Michelson, L., & Wood, R. (1980b). Behavioral assessment and training of children's social skills. In M. Hersen, P. Miller, & R. Eisler (Eds.), *Progress in behavior modification* (Vol. 9). New York: Academic Press.

Michelson, L., & Wood, R. (1982). Development and psychometric properties of the Children's Assertive Behavior Scale. *Journal of Behavioral Assessment, 4,* 3-13.

Michelson, L., Sugai, D., Wood, R., & Kazdin, A. E. (1983). *Social skills assessment and training with children: An empirically-based handbook.* New York: Plenum.

Morris, H. H., Escoll, P. S., & Wexler, R. (1956). Aggressive behavior disorders of childhood: A follow-up study. *American Journal of Psychiatry, 112,* 991-997.

Morrison, H. L. (1978). The asocial child: A destiny of sociopathy? In W. H. Reid (Ed.), *The psychopath: A comprehensive study of antisocial disorders and behaviors.* New York: Brunner/Mazel.

Nasby, W., Hayden, B., & DePaulo, B. M. (1980). Attributional bias among aggressive boys to interpret unambiguous social stimuli as displays of hostility. *Journal of Abnormal Psychology, 89,* 459-468.

Natov, I. (1981). *An intervention to facilitate interpersonal cognitive problem-solving skills and behavioral adjustment among emotionally handicapped children.* Unpublished doctoral dissertation, Fordham University.

Novaco, R. W. (1978). Anger and coping with stress. In J. Foreyt & D. Rathjen (Eds.), *Cognitive behavior therapy: Therapy, research and practice.* New York: Plenum.

Olweus, D. (1979). Stability of aggressive reaction patterns in males: A review. *Psychological Bulletin, 86,* 852-875.

Patterson, G. R. (1974). Interventions for boys with conduct problems: Multiple settings, treatments, criteria. *Journal of Consulting and Clinical Psychology, 42,* 471-481.

Patterson, G. R. (1982). *A social learning approach, Vol. 3: Coercive family process.* Eugene OR: Castalia.

Patterson, G. R., & Fleishman, M. J. (1979). Maintenance of treatment effects? Some considerations concerning family systems and follow-up data. *Behavior Therapy, 1,* 168-185.

Patterson, G. R., Reid, J. B., Jones, R. R., & Conger, R. E. (1975). *A social learning approach to family intervention. Families with aggressive children* (Vol. 1). Eugene, OR: Castalia.

Quay, H. (1972). Patterns of aggression, withdrawal and immaturity. In H. Quay & J. Weng (Eds.), *Psychopathological disorder of childhood.* New York: Wiley.

Quay, H. C. (1979). Classification. In H. C. Quay & J. S. Werry (Eds.) *Psychopathological disorders of childhood* (2nd ed.). New York: John Wiley.

Rinn, R. C., & Markle, A. (1979). Modification of social skills deficits in children. In A. S. Bellack & M. Hersen (Eds.), *Research and practice in social skills training*. New York: Plenum.

Robins, L. N. (1974). *Deviant children grown up*. Baltimore: Williams and Wilkins.

Robins, L. N. (1978). Study of childhood predictors of adult antisocial behavior: Replication from longitudinal studies. *Psychological Medicine, 8*, 611-622.

Robins, L. N. (1981). Epidemiological approaches to natural history research: Antisocial disorders in children. *Journal of the American Academy of Child Psychiatry, 20*, 566-580.

Robins, L. N., & Hill, S. Y. (1976). Assessing the contributions of family structure, class, and peer groups to juvenile delinquency. *Journal of Criminal Law, Criminology and Police Science, 57*, 325-334.

Rotenberg, M. (1974). Conceptual and methodological notes on affective and cognitive role-taking (sympathy and empathy): An illustrative experiment with delinquent and non-delinquent boys. *Journal of Genetic Psychology, 124* (2), 177-185.

Rutter, M., Shaffer, D., & Shepherd, M. (1975). *A multi-axial classification of child psychiatric disorders*. Geneva: World Health Organization.

Schindler, P. (1941). The psychogenesis of alcoholism. *Quarterly Journal of the Study of Alcoholism*. 2: 277-292.

Sechrest, L., West, S. G., Phillips, M. A., Redner, R., & Yeaton, W. (1979). Some neglected problems in evaluation research: Strength and integrity of treatments. In L. Sechrest, S. G. West, M. A. Phillips, R. Redner, & W. Yeaton (Eds.), *Evaluation studies: Review annual* (Vol. 4), Beverly Hils, CA: Sage.

Shure, M. B., & Spivack, G. (1978). *Problem-solving techniques in childrearing*. San Francisco: Jossey-Bass.

Shure, M. B., & Spivack, G. (1982). Interpersonal problem-solving in young children: A cognitive approach to prevention. *American Journal of Community Psychology, 10*, 341-356.

Shure, M. B., & Spivack, G. (1983) *Manual for interpersonal cognitive problem solving for fourth and fifth grade elementary school students*. Philadelphia, PA: Hahnemann Hospital.

Shure, M. B., & Spivack, G. (1979a). Interpersonal cognitive problem solving and primary prevention: Programming for preschool and kindergarten children. *Journal of Clinical Child Psychology, 2*, 89-94.

Shure, M. B., & Spivack, G. (1979b). Interpersonal problem-solving thinking and adjustment in the mother-child dyad. In M. Kent & J. Rolf (Eds.), *Primary prevention of psychopathology, Vol. 3. Social competence in children*. Hanover, NH: University Press of New England.

Spivack, G., Platt, J. J., & Shure, M. B. (1976). *The problem-solving approach to adjustment*. San Francisco: Jossey-Bass.

Spivack, G., & Shure, M. B. (1982). *Social adjustment of young children: A cognitive approach to solving real-life problems*. San Francisco: Jossey-Bass.

Spivack, G., & Shure, M. B. (1979). The cognition of social adjustment: Interpersonal cognitive problem-solving thinking. In B. B. Lahey and A. E. Kazdin (Eds.), *Advances in clinical child psychology* (Vol. 5). New York: Plenum.

Stokes, T. F., & Baer, D. M. (1977). An implicit technology of generalization. *Journal of Applied Behavior Analysis, 10*, 349-367.

Strain, P. S., & Timm, M. A. (1974). An experimental analysis of social interaction between a behaviorally disordered preschool child and her classmate peer. *Journal of Applied Behavior Analysis, 7*, 583-592.

Urbain, E. S., & Kendall, P. C. (1980). Review of social-cognitive problem-solving interventions with children. *Psychological Bulletin, 88*, 109-143.

Van Hasselt, V. B., Hersen, M., Bellack, A. S., & Whitehall, M. B. (1979). Social skill assessment and training for children: An evaluative review. *Behavior Research and Therapy, 17*, 413-438.

Vedder, C. B. (1979). *Juvenile offenders (Revised, 6th printing)*. Springfield, IL: Thomas.

Wahler, R. G. (1976). Deviant child behavior within the family: Developmental speculations and behavior change strategies. In H. Leitenberg (Ed.), *Handbook of behavior modification and behavior therapy*. Englewood Cliffs, NJ: Prentice-Hall.

Wahler, R. G., & Afton, A. D. (1980). Attentional processes in insular and noninsular mothers: Some differences in their summary reports about child problem behavior. *Child Behavior Therapy, 2*, 25-42.

Wahler, R. G., Berland, R. M., & Coe, T. D. (1979). Generalization processes in child behavior change. In B. B. Lahey & A. E. Kazdin (Eds.), *Advances in clinical and child psychology* (Vol. 2) New York: Plenum.

Wells, K. C., Griest, D. L., & Forehand, R. (1980). The use of self-control package to enhance temporal generality of a partner training program. *Behavior Research and Therapy, 18*, 347-354.

Winder, C., & Rau L. (1962). Parental attitudes associated with social deviance in pre-adolescent boys. *Journal of Abnormal and Social Psychology, 69*, 418-424.

Wolfgang, M. E., Figlio. R. M., & Sellin, T. (1972). *Delinquency in a birth cohort*. Chicago: University of Chicago Press.

Yeaton, W. H., & Sechrest, L. (1981). Critical dimensions in the choice and maintenance of successful treatments: Strength, integrity and effectiveness. *Journal of Consulting and Clinical Psychology, 49*, 156-167.

PART IV

Discussion

**Intervention Programs to Prevent
Delinquent Behavior**

12

Primary Prevention of Delinquency

Harold Leitenberg

I thought it would be most useful to first provide a general overview or critique of the topic "primary prevention of delinquency" and then to go on to discuss the primary prevention implications of each of the intervention papers presented.

Reviews of the delinquency prevention literature tend to be depressing. Not much success has been demonstrated and there is not much prospect of sweeping solutions in the near future. In 1967 the President's Commission on Law Enforcement and Administration of Justice concluded "that there is little in the way of research or evaluation to back claims of success for any programs designed to prevent delinquency." The intervening decade has not changed this picture. In 1981, Wall, Hawkins, Lishner, and Fraser wrote: "While a broad range of programs with potential to prevent juvenile crime have been initiated, few of these programs have been adequately evaluated for prevention effects, and even fewer have demonstrated effectiveness when evaluated" (p. 1). My own reading of the situation suggests that what is most likely to be done in the name of delinquency prevention is least likely to be effective, and what is most likely to be effective is least likely to be done. Before expanding on this theme, let's take a look at what we are trying to prevent, and what is meant by *primary prevention*.

Extent of the Problem

Juvenile delinquency refers to crimes committed by youth in a particular age range, usually under age 18 and over age 12, though

312

this depends to some extent on the type of crime and varies somewhat from state to state. The types of crimes usually considered include breaking and entering, robbery, arson, motor vehicle theft, homicide, rape, larceny, aggravated assault, vandalism, and so on. These crimes need to be distinguished from so-called *status offenses* such as truancy, running away from home, and unmanageability, which would not be considered an offense if the individual were not a minor. No matter what the source of statistics, police contacts, arrests, court records, convictions, reports of victims, self-reported delinquency, it is clear we are trying to prevent a very high-frequency problem. This is no small outbreak of legionnaires disease. The following point in time arrest statistics give some idea of the extent of the problem.

- In 1975, males between ages 13 through 17 accounted for nearly 50% of all arrests for robbery and nearly 30% of all arrests for violent offenses (Zimring, 1979).
- In New York City in 1979, there were approximately 12,000 arrests for robbery. Children *under* 16 accounted for approximately half of these (New York Times, March, 1982).
- Uniform crime records in 1979 indicated that juveniles account for 40% of the total arrests for all index crimes (Weis & Sederstrom, 1981).
- A majority of the arrests for arson (53%) and auto theft (52%) are committed by juveniles (Weis & Sederstrom, 1981).

Males account for the bulk of these arrests. Zimring (1979) calculated the sex distribution for all arrests for homicide, robbery, and aggravated assault in 1975 by persons under age 18. A total of 90% of the homicide arrests, 93% of robbery arrests, and 84% of aggravated assaults (excluding rape) involved males. Black youth are also way overrepresented in these arrest figures. An often cited estimate is that approximately half of all juvenile arrests involve blacks (Calvin, 1981). Perhaps this is not surprising given that crime rates are so much higher in slum neighborhoods where, unfortunately, so many black children live.

Lifetime prevalence arrest statistics are even more grim. Several longitudinal studies suggest that a substantial minority of male youth will be arrested prior to age 18. In a study conducted in Philadelphia, Wolfgang, Figlio, and Sellin (1972) found that 35% of males born in 1948 who lived in Philadelphia when they were between 10 and 18 years of age were arrested before age 18. In another

Philadelphia study, Savitz (1970) found that 59% of boys living in Philadelphia for the full period between age 7 and 18 had juvenile court records. More rural areas of the country report lower figures. For example, in a Kentucky study, 20% of boys and 5% of girls had juvenile court records (Ball, Ross, & Simpson, 1964).

It is always interesting to compare U.S. statistics with those obtained in other countries. A study conducted in a working class area in London, England found that 20% of males by age 17 were convicted for a criminal offense (West & Farrington, 1977), while a study in Stockholm, Sweden found that only 9% of boys had an official delinquency record by age 16 (Janson, 1977, as cited in Farrington, 1979).

All of the above statistics reflect official arrest records and as several researchers have shown only about 5% of delinquent acts are known to the police and fewer still result in an official arrest (Elliott & Voss, 1974; Haney & Gould, 1973).

What Is Primary Prevention

This meeting is part of a series of conferences held at the University of Vermont under the overall title of Primary Prevention of Psychopathology. No matter what the area of concern, health, mental health, crime and delinquency, everybody I know is in favor of the *idea* of primary prevention. Obviously it is far more preferable to prevent problems from arising in the first place, than to try and relieve them after they occur. All we need to do, advocates argue, is to follow the example of public health. It is standard public health doctrine that major diseases are seldom brought under control or eliminated by attempting to treat individuals who are already sick (Albee, 1982). Instead, the most impact is achieved through prevention programs directed at large groups or entire populations. In the public health field, *primary prevention* refers to programs designed to reduce the incidence of *new* cases of a particular disease within a specified time. In other words, a primary prevention program tries to prevent the onset of a disorder; it is a proactive rather than a reactive approach.

It should be noted that early diagnosis and early treatment to reduce the duration, severity, negative sequelae, or chances of repetition of a disease is called *secondary prevention* rather than primary prevention. This distinction between primary prevention and secondary prevention can get terribly confused in the delinquency prevention area. For example, many family intervention programs involve referred children who are already exhibiting visible problems assumed to be linked to later delinquency, for example, aggression, stealing, and noncompliance. Since parent training or family therapy is introduced *after* the child has begun to demonstrate problem behavior, this would normally be considered an example of secondary prevention. However, if the explicit goal of the parent training program is to prevent subsequent delinquency when it has not yet occurred, then it could be considered primary prevention. Nevertheless, it should be understood that programs put into place *after* a delinquent act has been committed, for example diversion programs, are not considered primary prevention because delinquency has already occurred.

The three major strategies of primary prevention in public health involve: (a) finding the noxious agent and *eliminating* or neutralizing it; (b) *blocking* the *transmission* of the noxious agent to the host; and (c) *strengthening* the host's *resistance* to the noxious agent. That these prevention strategies have been successful in the health field is without question. In economically developed countries, cholera, typhoid fever, smallpox, scarlet fever, measles, polio, diphtheria, and whooping cough have been largely brought under control through the application of public health methods of prevention. Removing the sources of infectious disease through treatment of sewage and water purification and increasing resistance to disease through mass immunization programs have done wonders.

A skeptic may point out that this is all very well for infectious diseases that are linked to specific manageable causes, but what does all this have to do with delinquency. The medical model of treatment via drugs and surgery will not cure delinquency. Why should one think that the public health model of prevention is any more apt. To some extent I agree. The public health model may offer a false promise. This is because the causes of delinquency are inseparable from the causes of other problems; they are multiple rather than single; they are also often entangled in complex political and economic and organizational concerns, not microbes or air conditioning cooling towers. In the words of the musical "West Side Story," delinquency is a social disease not a physical disease.

The Causes of Delinquency

Prevention programs are usually predicated on some knowledge of the causal links to a disorder. Accordingly, critics sometimes argue that primary prevention efforts in areas such as delinquency and mental health are premature because we do not yet know the specific causes of delinquency. Please note this is *not* my position. I think we know many of the causes only too well, but we have not been too successful in eliminating them, or preventing them from reaching children, or increasing children's resistance to them.

When I suggest we know the causes, what I mean is that we have long known a number of factors that are associated with the increased likelihood of committing delinquent acts. The list of associated factors is no deep mystery. At the least it includes the following:

(1) Being male rather than female, especially in a society that glorifies violence, power, winning, and makes cultural heroes out of the "cool and lawless."

(2) Living in a slum neighborhood.

(3) Experiencing harsh, rejecting, and inconsistent parental discipline coupled with inadequate supervision.

(4) Growing up in a home with marital discord and lack of family affection and cohesion.

(5) Being rejected or abandoned by parents, and for males perhaps particularly by fathers.

(6) Having a "difficult temperament" and exhibiting hyperactive, aggressive, and other "externalizing" problem behaviors as a child.

(7) Experiencing repeated failure in school.

(8) Being black and unemployed with little stake in mainstream society.

(9) Having parents or siblings who engage in criminal activity.

(10) Having a negative self-concept.

(11) Associating with deinquent peers.

Some might argue that these factors are not true causes of delinquency. For instance, it is obvious that not all males growing up in a multidistressed family in an urban slum neighborhood become delinquent. However, it is also true that not all people who smoke develop lung cancer. Yet we are willing to say that smoking cigarettes causes cancer even though the evidence is statistical and correlational rather than experimental. Also, as Rutter (1979) showed, it is the combination of these risk factors that makes the difference. Experiencing only one item on the above list may be no different than experiencing none. But having two together, or three, or four increases the chance of a negative effect geometrically.

Why the Promise
of Delinquency Prevention
Has Not Been Realized

Unfortunately, having a decent understanding of many of the factors that contribute to delinquency has not led to any large-scale breakthroughs in efforts to prevent delinquency. The reasons for this failure are many. First, most of the work of the juvenile justice system is directed at police control and at interventions after delinquency has taken place. In the related field of mental health only between 1% to 2% of the total expenditures of federal, state, and local governments is devoted to prevention (Albee, 1982). Though I do not have the exact figures for delinquency prevention, I doubt that the situation is substantially different.

Second, programs that are advertised as delinquency prevention often fail to target delinquency or the causes of delinquency directly. Good examples are after-school recreation programs. These are well intentioned, and I certainly support providing swimming pools, basketball courts, hockey rinks, and arts and crafts for our children. These can be fun activities, physically healthy, and easily defended in the name of youth development. But they should not masquerade as delinquency prevention. Despite the anecdotal reports of athletes who believe they were saved from a "life of crime" by programs sponsored by organizations such as the Police Athletic League or Boys Clubs, there is no statistical or experimental evidence that I know of that suggests that lack of organized recreation opportunities causes deinquency. There is also no statistical evidence that I know of to support the belief that the provision of such opportunities reduces the incidence of delinquency (Wright & Dixon, 1977). Yet this is almost always the first program introduced in a community in the name of delinquency prevention. The second is a drop-in center. We have to stop kidding ourselves that relatively easily implemented programs prevent delinquency when the evidence indicates they do not.

In their 1975 review of primary prevention of psychopathology my colleagues Marc Kessler and George Albee wrote:

> During the past year we found ourselves constantly writing references on scraps of paper and emptying our pockets each day of notes on the

primary prevention relevance of children's group homes, titanium paint, parent effectiveness-training, consciousness raising, Zoom, Sesame Street, the guaranteed annual wage, legalized abortion, school integration, limits on international cartels, unpolished rice, free prenatal clinics, antipollution laws, a yoghurt and vegetable diet, free V.D. clinics, and a host of other topics. Nearly everything, it appears, has implications for primary prevention [p. 560].

The danger of including everything under the sun is that often the paths of least resistance will be chosen in mounting programs of primary prevention, even though they will lead us nowhere. Meanwhile the important causes will remain untouched.

A third reason for the lack of progress in delinquency prevention is that adequate evaluation of primary prevention efforts to determine what works and what does not work is seldom carried out. In preparing a review of delinquency prevention, Wright and Dixon (1977) noted they initially went through 6,600 abstracts. After excluding those school, job, and drug programs that failed to mention explicitly delinquency prevention in the abstract, and after excluding programs that involved removing children from their home, they were left with 350 references. Of these only 96 contained any empirical data. Of these 96, the majority (66%) were treatment studies and only 9 contained the elements of a methodologically appropriate study, that is, random assignment of subjects to programs, direct measures of delinquency, statistical analyses, and at least a 6-month follow-up. (It might be noted that of these 9 only 3 reported marginally successful outcomes.)

In a 1979 report of the preliminary findings of a national evaluation of delinquency prevention programs funded by the Office of Juvenile Justice and Delinquency Prevention, Krisberg concluded that "measuring the results of these OJJDP funded projects has proved highly problematic. After 2 years of research we will probably possess insufficient data to judge if agencies prevented youth crime to any appreciable extent. Only one of the 16 agencies provide sufficient cooperation to try and evaluate their effects. And in any case, few of these projects actually attempted to prevent delinquency" (cited in Weis & Sederstrom, 1981, p. 3).

Wall, Hawkins, Lishner, and Fraser put out a report in 1981 for the National Center for the Assessment of Delinquent Behavior and its Prevention entitled *Juvenile Delinquency Prevention: A Com-*

pendium of *36 Program Models.* A questionnaire was sent to 898 different public and private agencies in 261 cities in 50 states and Puerto Rico. Respondents were asked to nominate three programs they thought were most promising or effective for preventing delinquency. There were 512 responses and the authors reported they used three criteria in selecting the 36 programs from the 512 (program should address at least one empirically supported cause of delinquency; those showing the most promising evaluation results were included; a range of programs focusing on the major institutions affecting the lives of youth were selected). What is so sad about this is that only 2 of these 36 had any semblance of an adequate evaluation, and even these two are questionable in terms of primary prevention. One was the Alexander and Parsons' family training project in Utah that involved youth who had already committed delinquent acts. The other was a community crime prevention program in Seattle, Washington where neighborhoods were selected and provided better locks, equipment for engraving property, and organized so that neighbors watched each others' houses. The results were that burglary rates went down relative to matched control neighborhoods, but there is no way to determine how much of this reduction was due to youth or to adult crime.

It could be argued that the most massive and longest existing delinquency prevention program in this country involves removal of abused, neglected, and unmanageable children from their homes. In 1978, when my colleagues and I conducted some research in this area, we were not able to find a single experimental study that attempted to evaluate whether children who were removed from their home did better than children who were not removed. We could not find a single comparison of the relative long-term effectiveness of different types of placements, for example, foster homes versus group homes (Leitenberg, Burchard, Healy, & Fuller, 1981).

Much more effort obviously needs to be placed on evaluating what prevention programs work best with what populations if we are to make progress in this area. It would also help if we paid some attention to the results of evaluations that have been conducted, rather than repeating programs that have already been demonstrated to be ineffectual. This is very difficult because we are all very skilled at explaining away negative results so that we can keep on doing what we want to do. For example, although individual therapy and group therapy of children identified as predelinquent have been shown to be worthless time after time, one can simply argue the therapy was not done right, the wrong type of therapy was tried, the studies were poorly designed, and so on. It is discouraging but if often seems that intuitive appeal, ease of administration, opportunities for financial reimbursement, and political interests determine what is and is not done, rather than results of evaluation studies.

It should be noted that according to reviews conducted by Romig (1978) and Wright and Dixon (1977) almost nothing has so far been demonstrated in controlled studies to work. Excepting behaviorally oriented and communication-skills-oriented parent training, which have shown some promise, the failures they cite include almost everything that is popular: individual and group counseling, recreation, social casework, street work with gangs, vocational programs that contain no chance of advancement, scared-straight programs, diversion programs, remedial education, outward bound wilderness programs, residential programs, tougher law enforcement, and community involvement programs. Also, as Elliott, Dunford, and Huizinga suggest in the paper in this volume, there is reason to be skeptical about the eventual effectiveness of the newest fad, selective "incapacitation" of "career offenders." Although some juvenile offenders clearly commit a disproportinately large number of serious and nonserious juvenile crimes, locking these individuals up is not going to be that easy since these investigators found that 86% of chronic juvenile offenders are never apprehended while they are still juveniles.

The fourth and greatest impediment to successful delinquency prevention is the failure to address adequately the ultimate causes of delinquency. Because these causal conditions are so complex and so enmeshed in our political and economic system, they are hard to change. As a result, I do not think it is too much of an exaggeration to characterize much of what we are doing as akin to putting Band-Aids designed for pimples on gaping wounds. It really should be no surprise that this seldom helps, and sometimes hurts. In 1967 when the President's Commission on Law Enforcement and Administration of Justice issued their report they made a number of recommendations. They said something had to be done about slum neighborhoods, that massing multiproblem families together in one community is destructive. They said that our public schools are failing to meet the needs of large segments of our population, and made a number of recommendations as to the changes that needed to be made. They said that high rates of youth unemployment, particularly evident in the black population in urban centers, was destructive. They also recommended that Youth Service Bureaus be established to coordinate services. Unfortunately only the last recommendation was acted upon, even though the services these bureaus were supposed to coordinate were largely ones that had never been demonstrated to be effective in preventing delinquency. Meanwhile, the more root causes were left relatively untouched. Schools are still exclusionary and punitive with huge dropout populations. The rate of black unemployed youth is still about 50% in our cities.

Not only have we been unable to implement successfully many mass prevention programs to eradicate some of the more important conditions responsible for delinquency, it sometimes seems as if we have actually gone out of our way to create those very same conditions we are supposedly trying to eliminate. Consider the example of low-cost housing projects. All the evidence we have suggests that living in a poor neighborhood is more destructive than actually being poor. Therefore, when all the costs are taken into account, would not an effective voucher system (with enough money behind it so that the people involved could move into middle-class neighborhoods) be an alternative worth trying rather than creating new enclaves of poverty stricken multiproblem families? Obviously I am talking about giant political issues, but I do not see how they can be avoided if the topic of primary prevention of delinquency is to be taken seriously.

When large scale social, political, and economic issues are raised, they often evoke a sense of futility and exasperation in social scientists—as well they might. Most of us are not politicians, and the interventions that we are interested in and can manage ourselves are indeed elsewhere. As a result some of the leaders in the field of primary prevention have argued that those professionals interested in primary prevention should get away from "vague, ponderous, infeasible giant steps" and concentrate instead on "concrete, achievable, baby steps" (Cowen, 1977). It sounds good, but I'm skeptical. Baby steps often produce baby effects. Consider the following analogy in the dental health area. Imagine that instead of advocating putting fluoride in the water supply system to prevent cavities, one instead promoted parent training programs to get children to use dental floss three times a day. Good luck! Of course limited effects are better than no effects but I do not think we can just give up on trying to persuade those in political leadership positions to push for those programs that are most likely to have the most impact. Radical steps may be doomed because they are not achievable but smaller, supposedly practical, steps may be equally doomed because they are far too limited in scope and too divorced from the ultimate causes of delinquency. Which is more ephemeral, baby steps or giant steps, or are they both hopeless?

Discussion of Intervention Papers

This brings me back to the four prevention papers presented at this conference. My purpose here is not to provide a detailed summary and critique of each of these papers. Instead, I want to restrict my comments to a few major implications I saw in each of these papers for primary prevention of delinquency.

Two of the papers were concerned with family intervention in homes with young children. After reviewing some of the literature demonstrating a relationship between physical child abuse and delinquency, Wolfe described a series of studies he and his colleagues have conducted to determine whether abusive parents and their children can benefit if behavioral parenting skills are taught. At one level the results were quite positive in that parents who completed the training showed significant gains in their behavior and their children's behavior as compared to control parents who did not receive such training. There are certain cautions, however. First, these studies clearly do not target delinquency directly and thus their ultimate relevance to delinquency prevention is, of course, questionable. Second, it is important to note that in the absence of court referral, the majority of parents (59%) declined or withdrew from the training program. Third, there is insufficient follow-up data to know if a large number of the parents who received training will sustain their use of the parenting or child-rearing skills they were taught, and, if so, whether this will have any lasting impact on their children.

What struck me most, however, were two other related issues. As Wolfe indicates, child abuse is a multidetermined event. Lack of knowledge about child-rearing skills is obviously only one part of the problem. Other important contributing factors include marital conflict, lack of appropriate parental models, lack of education, and a variety of stressors associated with povery and being a single parent. I doubt that in the long run these issues can be ignored and that parent training in isolation will suffice. Moreover, as Wolfe points out, incidents of physical abuse of children, awful and dangerous as they are in their own right, may not be separable in their effects on delinquency from other concommitant pathological family characteristics. When the behavior of abused children was compared with the behavior of children from other distressed families who had not been physically abused (but who were referred by the same welfare agency), the two welfare agency groups of children were equally disturbed compared to a group of children from nondysfunctional control families. In other words, chronic family conflict and instability and lack of emotional support rather than abuse itself may be the more critical concern. In terms of primary prevention, I do not know if we can be sanguine that the provision of parent training alone will be sufficient to overcome the negative impact of these disturbed families.

In fact, although not stressing physical abuse of children per se, the second family intervention paper presented at this volume by Wahler and Dumas strongly suggests that parent training in multiproblem families is often insufficient. Wahler and Dumas note that prior research has demonstrated that parent training often fails to have lasting beneficial effects in chaotic families whose problems include severe marital conflict, socioeconomic disadvantage, social isolation, alcoholism, and depression. Although these parents can learn appropriate behavior management and other child-rearing skills, they fail to generalize or maintain these skills for very long, presumably because the multiple other stressors in their lives interfere in various ways. In the paper presented, Wahler and Dumas apparently assumed, and probably realistically so, that amelioration of these additional stressors was beyond their reach. They therefore tried a novel approach. After demonstrating that negative and coercive interactions with children had less to do with the child's behavior and more to do with stressful interactions mothers had with other adults, they tried to teach mothers to distinguish between the two. To simplify, the essence of their study was to teach mothers that "when you are angry at someone else, or even yourself, recognize this and don't blame it on your kids' behavior and take it out on them." If mothers could learn this discrimination, it was hoped they would maintain the use of effective parenting behaviors they were being taught. Before evaluting the results of this study, I think it would be useful to repeat the authors' description of the families they were working with. The parent sample consisted of 6 mothers ranging in age from 21 to 42, two were married, only one completed high school, and the average annual family income was $5,400. Four out of the six mothers had serious physical problems (Lupus, cancer, and heart dysfunctions), five out of six had been physically abused by their spouse or boyfriends, and all 6 reported arguments several times weekly with other adults they had contact with. Five out of the six target children were male, the mean age of all the children was 7.75 and the children's referral problems included noncompliance (all six), property destruction (all six), stealing (all six), drug use (two children), and physical assault in 5 out of 6 ranging from fist fights, use of dangerous objects, sexual molestation, and killing another person. In all six families the referral was forced by a social service agency following abuse and/or neglect charges.

As I read it, the nub of the results of this study was that yes, these parents can learn behavior management skills, and yes, these parents can learn that their aversive interactions with their children are often governed not by their child's behavior, but instead by aversive interactions they are having with other adults, and yes, this helps maintain the parenting skills for a little longer than usual, but in the end it is not nearly enough. There was no maintenance in the use of these parenting skills during the follow-up period. In fact, three mothers discontinued the program "prematurely," one because she was arrested for drug dealing, and two because their spouse or boyfriend threatened to leave them or beat them up if they continued. Obviously, parent training in multidistressed families such as these is often futile in and of itself. Perhaps, if combined with attempts to relieve some of the other stressors as well, the results might be different, though I am skeptical. In situations like this, foster home placement of children, although no panecea, is often a better alternative (Leitenberg et al., 1981).

I would like to expand the discussion of parent training to another dimension. When considered in the context of primary prevention, I think it is time to advocate proactive programs for the entire population. Research in the past two decades has taught us a good deal about what goes into effective parenting. I think it is about time that every high school in this country *require* a two semester course in parenting or child rearing. In conjunction with such a course, every high school should have as its laboratory a free day-care center for younger children and a free preschool for 3- and 4-year-olds. I would even go so far as to advocate that as a condition for obtaining a marriage license, people must pass such a course. Granted this will not ensure perfect parents just as passing a driver's test and passing a driver's education course does not ensure perfect drivers. Also, a minority of people obviously will continue to have children whether married or not. Nevertheless, the mass impact of such a proposal, if ever implemented, is likely to be greater than piecemeal programs for families having problems with their children. In terms of the importance of the subject matter, it certainly seems as important as foreign languages, social studies, and algebra. I saw a note the other day in the New York Times Sunday Book Review that over 100 books on parenting have been published each year since 1979. Perhaps we are ready for this. Obviously I can't prove that parenting and child behavior would improve if such courses were required, but based on the fact that such training has already been documented to be effective over and over again in *non*-multiproblem families who enter such programs *after* they have already experienced serious difficulties with their children, I think there is sufficient reason to be optimistic. Also, I would point out that we do not know for sure that passing the requirements for a driver's license reduces accident rates, yet we continue to enforce this requirement in the absence of any evidence of benefit. Is not delinquency prevention and healthy adjustment of children as important as accident prevention and safe driving?

As Hawkins and Lam argue in the introduction of their paper, if social bonds to family and school are strong, children are less likely to associate with delinquent peers and are less likely to be influenced to commit delinquent acts. Although from a developmental perspective, family bonding may be the initial foundation stone upon which much else depends, presumably school failure and dropout or school success and retention are to some extent under the independent influence of the school. From this perspective programs that increase the likelihood of school success and school retention might have a delinquency prevention effect. Two of the prevention papers presented in this volume describe programs with this purpose in mind, one dealing with preschool education and the other with a junior high school sample.

The project described by Berrueta-Clement, Schweinhart, Barnett, and Weikart is a model of its kind. A high-risk, low-IQ, socioeconomically disadvantaged, predominantly black male population of preschool children were identified. They were then randomly assigned to preschool and no preschool conditions, relevant measures were obtained on a regular basis over a 20-year period, and appropriate statistical analyses were carried out. Even the results were somewhat impressive, though unfortunately less so than the design and execution of the study itself. There were a total of 123 children age 3 to 4 in the initial sample and 58 were randomly assigned to receive preschool services and 65 served as control subjects (no preschool). In all other regards they were the same. Children in the experimental group attended the preschool 5 mornings a week, typically for 2 years. In addition, teachers visited the homes of these children for 1½ hours every week during the school year. The hypothesis was that the preschool experience might reduce later school failure that in turn would lead to increased school retention, increased self-esteem, increased expectancy of educational and occupational success, decreased behavior problems while in school, decreased rejection by teachers, and decreased alienation from mainstream social values— and thus ultimately result in decreased rates of later delinquency. At follow-up, during early adulthood, when the preschool and no preschool groups' lifetime arrest records were compared, 31% of the experimental group versus 51% of the control group had been arrested as either a juvenile or as an adult. Thus, although the arrest rates were high for both groups (41% of the combined sample), they were significantly higher for the group that had not had the early preschool experience. However, if only juvenile arrest records are considered, there was no significant difference between the experimental and control groups, though the trend was toward fewer arrests in the preschool group; also, the number of juvenile court petitions was significantly less in the preschool group. There was no statistically significant difference, however, between the groups in number of convictions as distinguished from arrests; or in the number of persons in each group involved in serious offenses, or in total self-reported delinquency. The exciting outcome, however, was that there was a difference in arrests even though the intervention was limited to two preschool years some 15 or so years earlier in time. Any positive results in controlled evaluations of delinquency prevention studies are hard to come by and should be savored.

How did the preschool intervention manage to produce this effect? According to the investigators, the most likely explanation had to do with the different rates of intervening school success between the two groups of children. A high percentage of the preschool group compared to the controls completed high school (67% versus 49%). The preschool group also received fewer years of special education services (1.8 years versus 3.8 years). It's also noteworthy that a higher percentage of the preschool group had some postsecondary educational and/or vocational training (38% versus 21%) and a higher percentage of the preschool group were employed at the time of the latest interview (50% versus 32%). It should be observed that a potentially important component of the preschool program may have included training in parenting and child-rearing skills. I am referring to the weekly home visit contained in this program. Perhaps without such parental involvement, cognitive and social enrichment in the preschool setting itself would not have produced the same results. Another implication of this study, of course, is that a preschool program may *reduce* subsequent delinquency, but it certainly does not come close to reducing it to acceptable levels. It should be remembered that after all is said and done, 31% of the preschool group were arrested for criminal acts during adolescence and young adulthood. Nevertheless, this represents a substantial reduction relative to the control group, and thus lends further support to the often heard recommendation that preschool programs should be made universally available. Unfortunately, this is easier said than done. For example, in a city very close to where the conference on which this book is based was held, the voters have yet to approve free kindergarten, no less free preschool.

The final intervention paper presented at the conference described one component of a school program. The specific purpose of this particular study was to provide a preliminary evaluation of a teacher training program in three specific instructional methods, namely, proactive classroom management, interactive teaching, and co-operative learning. (These instructional methods are described in detail in the Hawkins and Lam paper.) The study was conducted at the Junior High School level (seventh grade) in Seattle, Washington, and involved 15 experimental and 18 control teachers, resulting in 54 experimental and 59 control classes and a total of 1,166 children (513 experimental and 653 control). Teachers were for the most part randomly selected to be in experimental or control conditions. Prior to the school year, those teachers in the experimental condition received 5 days of training. During the school year they received 3 more days of booster training. In addition, one teacher in each school served as a consultant to the other experimental teachers.

The study is in its early stages so it is too soon to determine long-term impact, but some short-term results are noteworthy. Although the teachers in the experimental group did improve their instructional practices in the desired direction, they still had a long way to go. In addition, there was little sign of an effect on children's interest in school, delinquent behavior, or peer associations. Students taught by trained teachers for the most part did not like school any more than when they were taught by control teachers (the exception was math classes). There was also no relationship between teacher practices and self-reported truancy, theft, or getting into trouble because of drug or alcohol use, though suspensions and expulsions were less in the experimental group. Perhaps most discouraging in light of the original assumptions of this study, there was no association between changes in teacher practices and choice of friends. Hawkins and Lam remain somewhat hopeful that experimental and control teachers' instructional methods will diverge even further in subsequent years, yielding a greater effect on school bonding, peer associatons, and antisocial behavior than could be observed after only only year. Of course, only time will tell if their optimism is warranted.

From the larger perspective of primary prevention I would like to discuss two issues raised by this study. The first is that intervention was directed at a general population of junior high school students rather than a selected group of children assumed to be at risk for delinquency. The authors cogently argue that delinquency prediction for individuals is not accurate enough (too many false positives and false negatives). Hawkins, and Lam also go on to say:

> A second reason for our choice of a general population rather than an individually targeted intervention approach is the assumption that the conditions that create social bonding and inhibit delinquency occur in social organizations and aggregations (families, schools, peer groups) in the course of activities that are directed primarily toward other goals such as socialization, education, and interaction. The social development model suggests that when these oganizations and aggregations are successful in creating opportunities, skills and rewards for youthful participants, social bonding is likely to occur and delinquency is likely to be inhibited. Thus it appears appropriate to seek changes in organizations to ensure that they provide opportunities, skills, and rewards to those youths who participate in them rather than to seek directly to change the individual behaviors of targeted high-risk individual youths (Hawkins & Lam, p. 246).

This brings me to the second issue. Once this is said, that is, put the emphasis on organizations rather than individuals, it is hard not to be somewhat cynical about a delinquency prevention project that is concerned with improving teaching. Of course this is a desirable goal and I hope every College of Education in the country incorporates instruction in the pedagogic methods described in this study. But once again, if we are to take primary prevention seriously, we cannot ignore the larger social, political, and economic issues that affect the quality of teachers and educational programs in our public schools.

The sad fact is that our society pays only lip service to the value of teachers and teaching. For example, where I live, starting teachers are paid $12,700. I do not know if these figures are completely accurate, but I am told that starting postal workers are paid around $20.000 a year and sanitation workers in New York City are paid $35,000 a year. National statistics indicate that about 40% of teachers leave the profession within 7 years, and clearly many more who would be interested and talented teachers never start in the first place because the pay is so abysmally low. Given the meager appreciation they receive, is it any wonder that teachers usually prefer to work with motivated children and breathe a sigh of relief when uninterested, disruptive children are expelled or drop out of school?

In summary, my thoughts about primary prevention programs in delinquency tend to be pessimistic. Unless the larger political, organizational, economic, and social issues are addressed, I think we will make small headway, at best, in preventing delinquency. As I said in the introduction to this chapter, past efforts in this area indicate that what is most likely to be done in the name of delinquency prevention is least likely to be effective, and what is most likely to be effective is least likely to be done. This is not the fault of people working in this field. They do the best they can, given the organizational inertia and the political and economic restraints they have to face. Although this may sound like a cop-out, I think the most productive area for delinquency prevention is not within the realm of psychology, sociology, psychiatry, social work, or criminology—it is within the area of politics.

References

Albee, G. W. (1982). Preventing psychopathology and promoting human potential. *Psychologist, 37,* 1043-1050.

Ball, J. C., Ross, A., & Simpson, A. (1964). Incidence and estimated prevalence of recorded delinquency in a metropolitan area. *American Sociological Review, 29,* 90-93.

Calvin, A. D. (1981). Unemployment among black youths, demographics, and crime. *Crime & Delinquency, 27,* 234-244.

Cowen, E. L. (1977). Baby-steps toward primary prevention. *American Journal of Community Psychology, 5,* 1-22.

Elliott, D. S., & Voss, H. L. (1974). *Delinquency and Dropout.* Lexington, MA: Lexington Books.

Farrington, D. P. (1979). Longitudinal research on crime and delinquency. In N. Morris & M. Tonry (Eds.), *Crime and justice: An annual review of research, Vol. 1.* Chicago: University of Chicago Press.

Haney, B., & Gould, M. (1973). The juvenile delinquent nobody knows. *Psychology Today, Sept.,* 49-55.

Janson, C. G. (1977). *Project metropolitan, research report No. 7.* Stockholm: Stockholm University, Department of Sociology.

Kessler, M., & Albee, G. W. (1975). Primary Prevention. *Annual Review of Psychology, 26,* 557-591.

Leitenberg, H., Burchard, J. D., Healy, D., & Fuller, E. J. (1981). Nondelinquent children in state custody: Does type of placement matter? *American Journal of Community Psychology, 9,* 347-359.

Romig, D. A. (1978). *Justice for our children.* Lexington, MA: Lexington Books.

Rutter, M. (1979). Protective factors in children's response to stress and disadvantage. In M. Kent & J. Rolf (Eds.), *Primary prevention of psychopathology; Social competence in children.* Hanover, NH: University Press of New England.

Savitz, L. (1970). Delinquency and migration. In M. E. Wolfgang, L. Savitz, & N. Johnson (Eds.), *The sociology of crime and delinquency* (2nd Ed.). New York: John Wiley.

Wall, J. S., Hawkins, J. D., Lishner, D., & Fraser, M. (1981). *Juvenile delinquency prevention: A compendium of 36 program models.* Washington, DC: Government Printing Office.

Weis, J. G., & Sederstrom, J. (1981). *The prevention of serious delinquency: What to do?* Washington, DC: Government Printing Office.

West, D. J., & Farrington, D. P. (1973). *Who becomes delinquent?* London: Heinemann.

Wolfgang, M. R., Figlio, R. M., & Sellin, T. (1972). *Delinquency in a birth cohort.* Chicago: University of Chicago Press.

Wright, W. E., & Dixon, M. C. (1977). Community prevention and treatment of juvenile delinquency: A review of evaluation studies. *Journal of Research in Crime and Delinquency, 14,* 35-67.

Zimring, F. E. (1979). American youth violence: Issues and trends. In N. Morris & M. Torey (Eds.), *Crime and justice: An annual review of research, Vol. 1.* Chicago: University of Chicago Press.

PART V

Social Policy and the Prevention of Antisocial and Delinquent Behavior

13

Social Policy and the Prevention of Delinquency

Jay G. Lindgren

This consideration of the policy and program implications of the foregoing research reflects the perspective, or perhaps more accurately the bias, of a practitioner in the field of juvenile and adult corrections. Corrections is the "deep end" of society's response to the detected behavior of young adults and older adolescents, which has become in part at least what those attempting prevention desire to prevent. This experience has led to a rather cautious optimism. This optimism is reserved primarily for the people with whom we would intervene and the caution is primarily for what intervention might actually accomplish. Hopefully, what follows is advanced, however, without "disparaging potential for interventions (which) could be supporting, guiding, or nuturing" (Currie, July, 1982, p. 17).

This chapter will first summarize the major findings that have emerged during the past 20 years of correctional practice and reform that have relevance to delinquency prevention. The second section will highlight the findings and conclusions in the preceding contributions that have the most important policy implications. Finally, three fundamental principles for delinquency prevention will be advanced. The first and superordinate principle is that, delinquency prevention should be primary prevention focusing on the social and environmental correlates of delinquency. Second, prevention efforts that are direct services to families, children, youth, and communities should be structured such that major authority for definition of need and acceptance of service rests with "the client." Finally, a major role of policymakers, researchers, and practitioners ought to be finding "arrangements to join, not sever, personal troubles and political

issues in long-term efforts to reduce human misconduct and misery"
(Rosenheim, 1976, p. 56).

A "Deep End" Perspective

A Minnesota friend and colleague has been critical of corrections
for not doing more about prevention. This friend's favorite analogy
portrays people in corrections as lifeguards standing on a riverbank
watching more kids than they can respond to flounder down the
rapids. Occasionally one is reached in time; many, however, elude
the "lifeguard's" grasp. He laments that no one goes upstream and
identifies what is causing these kids to fall in so that this can be
prevented. Such a preventive perspective, he argues, would be more
effective and less costly than corrections high effort, low yield
"lifesaving" efforts. My response to such a challenge has been
resistance. The mission of juvenile corrections is to administer
control proportional to the harm done and to provide appropriate
services during the period of control to those youth who have been
justly and accurately identified as offenders. It is further argued that
this mission must be clearly separated from prevention services and
programs, which should by their very nature be voluntary, and
should not be targeted on identified individuals (Lindgren, 1982).
Finally, this friendly critic is reminded that scant evidence, if any,
exists to document the effectiveness of past preventive efforts in
reducing future delinquency (Weis & Hawkins, 1982).

After first reading the nine research papers contained in this
collection, it appeared that this friend's analogy should be turned
even further against him. The research provided the author an
opportunity to vicariously go to the source of the small stream where
corrections has been stationed. The source, it turns out, is a huge lake
with miles and miles of shoreline and beach where a multitude of
children frolic, many quietly playing on the beach or in safe water.
Those "at risk" are spread far and wide, and most of them do not
reach the dangerous river. There is, of course, danger in conclusions
from first readings and even greater danger in the over simplifications
of argument by analogy. Nevertheless, the identification studies in
this volume lend further support that the antecedents of delinquency
like most human problems are protean. Effective prevention efforts, it
follows, will have to be exceedingly diverse.

Major attempts have been made during the past 20 years to measure the effectiveness of a variety of corrections programs. Much of this effort has been summed up by the conclusion that "nothing works" (Martinson, 1974). That conclusion, together with increasing empirical evidence and growing public awareness that juveniles are disproportionately represented among the total group of *known* offenders, has resulted in decreasing tolerance for juvenile offenders and a growing movement toward a more punitive response (Boy 15, who killed two, 1978). In many states this has taken the form of moving juvenile corrrections toward a retribution model similar to adult corrections (State of Washington, 1977), and in other states, an effort to transfer more offenders who formally were treated as juveniles into the adult correctional system (Feld, 1978). This is ironic in that the evidence on the effectiveness of adult corrections is, if anything, less encouraging than the results of juvenile corrections. Moreover, the conclusions that "nothing works" and that juveniles constitute a major threat oversimplify a complex set of data that must be fully considered before policy and programs can be improved.

Three additional lines of inquiry seem to be particularly relevant to preventive efforts: (1) How many individual youth offend and how persistent is individual offending? (2) How accurately have correctional and diversion programs targeted on specifically identified groups or individuals? (3) What has been the immediate quality of the correctional response to "identified youth?" These are important empirical questions, and the past 20 years experience has provided partial but helpful answers to each of these questions.

Most juvenile offending is endemic and transient. Self-report research, with all of its inherent methodological problems, gives direct support to the first half of this contention. For example, Gold (1970) reported that 80% of the randomly selected youth in his Flint Michigan Study, engaged in delinquent behavior sometime during their adolescence. Elliot et al. (this volume), using stricter criteria over a shorter reporting period of two years, indicates that 60% of their cohort offended. Most adolescent offending is nonviolent, and a great deal is relatively trivial. Just as important, of those juveniles who have even experienced one or two arrests, most do not become adult criminals. (Greenwood, Lipson, Abrahamse, & Zimring, 1983). It is logical to conclude that even if "nothing works", that is, formal interventions, this transient quality of most juvenile offending must have to do with maturation and natural support.

The endemic and transient quality of juvenile offending has been known for some time. This knowledge informed the agenda of the 1967 President's Commission on Law Enforcement and the Administration of Justice, particularly the emphasis on deinstitutionalization, decriminalization of status offenses, and diversion of youth from formal court proceedings into public and private treatment programs (Empey, 1973). Evaluations of many of these reforms, however, have shown that a major unintended consequence has been a "net-widening" that includes less serious offenders than those originally targeted. Alternative programs have not accurately or consistently targeted on specific individuals or groups, even when relatively specific behavior criteria are available, for example, charged or adjudicated offenses. Programs set up as substitutes for existing methods of intervention have ended up as supplements. For example, pretrial diversion programs admitted individuals who formally would have been dismissed (Zimring, 1974). Community residences designed as alternatives to incarceration accepted individuals who formally would have been placed on probation (Minnesota Department of Corrections, 1977). Indeed, the deinstitutionalization movement has often served to move youth into different institutions rather than into more open community setting (Lerman, 1982).

Finally, what of the juvenile justice programs themselves? It appears that many programs designed to respond to juvenile offenders have not only been ineffective in producing lasting positive changes in individual behavior, but have often failed to meet basic standards of human decency and fairness (Wooden, 1976). The "failure of rehabilitation" may be excusable in that our assumptions about our ability to affect others positively were naively optimistic. The failure to meet basic standards, however, is inexcusable in that program quality is a variable that can be immediately known (Moos, 1975; Patton, 1978) and substantially influenced by those who administer such programs. Despite the "failure of rehabilitation" to effect long term changes in offender behavior, there is empirical evidence that movement from custodial goals to rehabilitative goals does improve the immediate social climate of correctional institutions (Feld, 1978; Geis, 1984; Street, Vinter & Perrow, 1966). Moreover, youth correctional programs, which are more closely identified with rehabilitative goals than adult correctional programs, are usually more compatible with democratic standards of decency than adult programs (Greenwood et al., 1983). The dilemma may be that it is in part the improved climate that drives the "net widening" (Miller, 1980; Morris, 1974; Rothman, 1980).

What Should Follow Early Identification?

The disappointing results and the net widening of past delinquency intervention efforts should cast an air of caution over attempts at early identification. Identification for what purpose? We have known since before the invention of the juvenile court that family functioning and neighborhood organization correlate with official delinquency. Massive government interventions into both areas have been made. Children and youth have been removed from their natural homes and have been placed into "more suitable homes." Neighborhoods have been eliminated and "neighborhoods" have been created through urban renewal. Have these interventions improved the circumstances of those affected? Leitenberg (this volume) reminds us that "we do not know if children placed out of home do better than children who have stayed at home." Indeed, the thrust of recent social policy has been to counteract the frequent phenomenon of children placed out of home who have not found the permanency essential for an experience to be properly called home (Public Law, 1980). Similarly, urban renewal "projects," particularly those that are "high rise" where the occupants must "face from five to seven hundred people without knowing for certain why they are there" (Suttles, 1968, p. 138), cannot be described as a neighborhood that will foster and support law-abiding behavior.

Intervention: Providing Help
and Coercing Services

The state of the art, of course, has advanced. The identification research in this volume provides much more sophisticated measurement and yields more specific antecedent factors than gross factors such as "family functioning" and "neighborhood organization." Even with a deeper understanding of some of the predictive factors, however, important value choices confront policymakers and practitioners. For example, in his overview of the identification research in this volume, Jesness has listed 23 factors identified with 11-year-old delinquents that strongly correlate with arrest for a violent crime by age 26. Most of these factors parallel those identified in the identification research in this volume. What should be done about these factors? Should 11-year-olds who have a significant number of these factors be placed under intensive control measures until their 26th birthday? Can social programs be instituted to eliminate or ameliorate some or all of these factors?

Jesness's 23 factors can be roughly placed in four categories. The most heavily weighted predictive factor, age at first police contact, is the most complex. It is well demonstrated that the earlier the onset of delinquent behavior, the more persistent the behavior. Yet present social policy allows for and should continue to allow for "diminished responsibility" for younger offenders (Zimring, 1975, pp. 80-81). A few of Jesness's factors, for example, number of police contacts, type of offense, and school disciplinary problems, are largely measures of the child's behavior and therefore should be considered to be under the power of the child to change or influence. Many of the factors are clearly not under the child's influence; for example, family on welfare, broken family, father not main support, number of siblings, father has crime record, mother has crime record, low family supervision, and low verbal IQ. Other factors appear more complex and result from interactions between child and peers, child and parent, or child and school, for example, mother rejects, father rejects, parents wants youth committed, grade level, and negative school attitude.

Early identification of delinquent prone children should only under very rare and specific circumstances result in the exercise of the coercive power of the state (Underwood, 1979). The factors identified by Jesness serve to underscore the importance of this principle. Social policy has to do with the allocation of money, services, opportunity, and coercion. It is essential to be clear about which of these resources is to be allocated or reallocated in an attempt to address the factors related to later delinquency. The net widening of formal coercive control following reform efforts in juvenile corrections should raise serious caution in the use of early identification factors. Prediction, it seems, becomes easily linked to control, especially when the intent is benevolent (Gaylin, Glasser, Marcus, & Rothman, 1978).

Several of the identification studies detect significant factors that are difficult to obtain without the cooperation of the youth or their family. The most obvious example is the self-report study by Elliott et al. (this volume). Likewise, Loeber and Dishion (this volume) develop a gating technique which progressively screens at three stages by first using teacher ratings, then conducting five daily telephone interviews with parents regarding the child's recent "antisocial" behavior, and finally an assessment of the mother's "child rearing methods" is completed.

Ethical as well as practical considerations argue that coercive interventions should not follow such identification techniques. As some families and most youth become aware of how such information is to be used, less information will be provided and what information is provided will become less reliable. Moreover, if coercive responses can follow, those who are honest and cooperative are more likely to be coerced.

Jesness (this volume) in his overview of the identification papers, concludes that "while our predictions are not perfect, they are sufficiently accurate to be taken seriously and used in practice." The policymaker and practitioner, of course, must weigh the costs and benefits of their use (Monahan, 1982). What are the possible responses to the findings of Elliott et al. (this volume) that chronic recidivists, who are identified by five or more arrests, only account for 14% of the career offenders identified by their self-reported delinquency? The career offenders, thus identified, represent 15.5% of their cohort. If 6% of the youth population that are chronic recidivists is too large a population "for a general application of intensive control measures" (Zimring, 1979, p. 95), obviously 15.5% becomes even more unwieldy. Generally, interventions that might be described as opportunities and services are much less costly than intensive control measures. Educating a youth and keeping a child at home, even in a public supported household, is less costly than incarceration or an out of home placement (Hubert H. Humphrey Institute, 1983; National Resource Center on Family Based Services, 1982).

The four intervention efforts researched in this volume focus on two major social institutions: the family and the school. The identification research in this volume on delinquency prone children underscores the importance of the developing child's interaction with these two institutions. All four efforts, then, proceed in promising directions.[1]

Intervening with Families

The family intervention experiments reported by Wolfe (this volume) and by Wahlen and Dumas (this volume) have been summarized and critiqued by Leitenberg (this volume). He questions the relevance of Wolfe's research in that delinquency is not targeted directly and that insufficient follow-up data are available. His conclusion on the Wahler and Dumas research is that, "parent training in multi-distressed families such as these is often futile *in and of itself . . .* foster placement of children, although no panacea is often a better alternative" (Leitenberg, this volume, emphasis added).

He then recommends that every high school require a two semester course in child rearing and that such a course be a condition of obtaining a marriage license. The progression from conclusions to recommendations is difficult to follow. As discussed earlier, Leitenberg's own review of the research concluded that there is no evidence that children placed out of home "do better." A compulsory child-rearing education approach would not be without financial cost at a time that a great deal of retrenchment is occurring in education. This approach may even be less likely to reach the "target population" than the agency referrals to parent training reported by Wolfe. Obviously, not every parent will get married or complete high school.

Leitenberg's proposal may have benefits even if it does not reach parents of delinquency-prone children. However, a critical social policy question, from a cautious perspective, is whether it might become mandatory to pass such a course before one is able to keep a child, a variation of "net widening." This would raise serious empirical, value, and legal questions. What is the relationship between passing a course and practicing good child rearing? Indeed what is "good child rearing"? When should parental rights be terminated? The answer to Leitenberg's question, "Isn't delinquency prevention and a healthy adjustment of children as important as accident prevention and safe driving?" (this volume), is of course, yes! The most difficult part of this issue is, however, that social policy and the law wisely recognizes a much deeper, more sacred bond between parents and children than between drivers and their licenses. Clearly, improved child rearing is an extremely important focus for future research and intervention. Despite the tentative and inconclusive results of the two family intervention experiments, such difficult work should be encouraged. If we are to progress, we must understand what is harmful and what works best in supporting and guiding the critical relationship between parent and child.

Intervening in Schools

Hawlins and Lam (this volume) present a social development theory that stresses that school and peer bonds as well as family bonds have important effects on delinquency behavior. This theory provides a rich set of hypotheses that can be tested in the real world of children and youth. They report on their experiment at the junior high level which varies the teacher instructional methods. The teachers in the experimental group, however, continue to have teaching practices that fall significantly below standards prescribed by the the researchers. The net effect of the teacher training appeared to be the unlearning of former poor practices rather than the learning and practice of improved methods. The authors offer a compelling argument for seeking changes in the way that schools are organized and teachers are trained to interact with children. Like the family, these mainstream institutions are essential to social success and well being. Schools should and can be more responsive to "high risk" youth. As Leitenberg (this volume) emphasizes, lasting improvement requires a greater fiscal commitment to educating our young (Hacker, 1984). Second, there often must be fundamental reorganization within the school system that supports changes in teacher practices (Janowitz, 1969). Third, the practice level must also be researched and modified. Despite the limited and negligible preliminary effects of the Hawkins and Lam experiments, more research of this type must be done. Finally, we should seek ways to enlist the support of the child's family for their education.

The project described by Berrueta-Clement et al. (this volume) is most encouraging in this regard. Utilizing an experimental design, the Perry Project provided preschool education and encouraged parental participation and support. The results of the research show improved school and employment performance by the experimental subjects. The effect on delinquent behavior 15 years later is limited but positive.

**What If an Intervention Is Helpful
but Does Not Prevent Crime?**

None of the four intervention projects yield the clear positive results hoped for. Yet some of the results, particularly those of the Perry Project, are encouraging. What is to be concluded about a project that has limited positive effects on later delinquent and criminal behavior but demonstrably improves education and employment performance? What of a project that attempts to improve the social climate in the classroom and provides greater opportunity for involvement and skill development in the important social arena of the classroom for a larger proportion of students but may have negligible long-term effects on delinquent behavior? What of a program that offers support and guidance to multidistressed mothers and enables them to begin to better discriminate between their child's misbehavior and pressures from other actors in their life but does not produce permanent changes in their child-rearing techniques?

Perhaps delinquency prevention should not be the *major* purpose for these types of interventions. There are other even more basic arguments for the provision of opportunities and services. This is the position eloquently argued by Graham Hughes (1983, p. 37).

> The case for expending resources on improving opportunities for poor children ought to turn on general moral principles of fairness in social arrangements, and not on hopes about the impact on the crime rate. The claim for equality is too important to rest on a promise that will not bear its weight. Similarly the case for making vigorous efforts to rehabilitate criminals derives from the moral duty to give them every chance to acquire skills and insights that may lead to different choices; the case does not depend on demonstrating that such programs will limit recidivism.

Lane and Davis's review of the research on the relationship between child abuse and neglect and later delinquency (this volume) raises surprising and serious questions about the existence let alone strength of such a relationship (Jesness, this volume). Does this mean there should be no interventions? Of course not! There must be intervention out of concern for the *immediate* safety and well being of the child.

When Are Interventions Most Helpful?

Considered together, the five research papers on identification and the four intervention experiments illustrate the complex interactive nature of child and youth development. Jesness (this volume) implies that the concern with incorrect labeling of potential delinquents has been overemphasized in past delinquency policy. Perhaps this perspective has weakened necessary support for juvenile justice agencies in doing their job with older youth who have been justly adjudicated for serious criminal level acts. However, the labeling-social reaction approach (Lemert, 1967) has been and continues to be an extremely important perspective for policymakers and practitioners, particularly those in youth and family service agencies. Such a perspective recognizes that we have a considerable amount of influence over how a social problem is defined. Furthermore, the labeling perspective emphasizes that ultimately we can and should exercise much greater control over our public responses to social problems than the problems themselves. On the micro interpersonal level, this is clearly recognized by Spivack and Cianci (this volume) where they emphasize the importance of teacher and school administrators' *responses* to early grade school misbehavior.

Werner (this volume) speculates from her cohort data that significant kith and extended kin relationships increase a child's ability to resist many physical and early emotional traumas that might otherwise contribute to later delinquency. We need more research on healthy development, particularly from "unhealthy" circumstances. It is not possible to conclude from her study whether these resilient children had these supportive relationships because of their ability to solicit those relationships or whether these significant others were unusual in their willingness to support troubled children. The most likely explanation is that such natural emotional support is two sided. It would seem that the essential characteristics of these relationships is that they are natural, informal, relatively continuous, and mutually formed. What might best be referred to as "loved ones." Social policy and programs should enhance such relationships and must avoid erecting obstacles to their continuance.

Formal helping agencies, whether public or private, all too often exclude this kind of help for troubled children and youth in developing their treatment plans and intervention strategies. Yet these agencies can rarely, if ever, hope to provide directly what can be provided by "love ones." Again, Werner (this volume) emphasizes that formal helping agencies provide services to only 30% of the high-risk children in her cohort and only successfully intervened with half of those youth. Jesness (this volume) concludes that the fact that half were helped is to be celebrated. Maybe so, but the critical policy and program implication is that natural informal relationships, even distant ones, should be actively involved with formal agencies in plans to assist children suffering from early trauma or neglect to overcome those experiences (Whitaker & Garbarino, 1983).

A major goal for formal helping agencies ought to be to provide services in a social climate that clearly evidences a sensitivity to and respect for the individuals being "served." This implication gains additional support in that one of the significant stresses on child abusing mothers identified by Wahler and Dumas (this volume) was contact with welfare agency workers. The mothers had to be taught to discriminate between agency created stress and the stress created by their children's behavior so that their children were not wrongly disciplined or abused following the agency induced stress.

As with the social climate of correctional programs discussed in the previous section, policymakers and practitioners have a great deal of influence over the immediate experience of children and families interacting with helping agencies. Policymakers and practitioners must ask, "when are we part of the cure and when are we part of the disease?" We should take full responsibility for the unintended as well as the intended consequences of our actions. Competent research will illuminate both types of consequences (Lerman, 1975; Newberger, 1983) and engage practitioners in the evaluation process so that the results are utilized (Patton, 1978).

Future research and intervention should not concentrate solely on the micro interactions between child and parent; child, parent, and teacher; child, kith, and kin; counselor and family; and social agency and family. There also must be research and reform at the macro societal level. Emphasis on family, friendships, and school is correct; however, this cannot be detached from the larger social and economic context. Repeatedly, the family intervention experiments in this volume demonstrate the environmental stresses present in these families' lives. As Elliott Currie has advocated, we need comprehensive "family oriented policies which include family allowances, improved child care, more flexible and humane working conditions" (Currie, May 1982, pp. 31-32). These policies would change "the terms and conditions of women's work and begin to control the forces that so want only to separate families from kin and friendship networks" (Currie, July 1982, p. 22). Currie has suggested several specific programs:

> There are no serious *technical* problems that prevent us now from providing adequate income support for family heads who are unable to work, or from developing on a large scale, the already tested supported work strategy for welfare mothers (as distinguished from Reagan-style "work fare"). . . . Another promising avenue is the development of comprehensive multiservice programs for high risk families. One notable example is the HEW-sponsored Child and Family Resource Programs . . . combined services include crisis intervention, education against child abuse, family counseling, Head Start and tutoring programs, meals for children and pre- and post-natal health counseling. . . . The General Accounting Office concluded . . . that the programs significantly improved the quality of life in poor families and could substantially reduce expenditures for later health care, welfare assistance, and youth and adult corrections—all at a cost of about $3,000 per family in 1977 dollars [Currie, July, 1982, pp. 22-23, emphasis in original].

344   Jay G. Lindgren

It should be noted that these multiservice programs encouraged "substantial parent involvement in policy making," an important principle that will be returned to in the final section.

Policy Implications

In summary, there are several social policy and program implications that emerge from the foregoing identification and intervention research:

- Delinquency prevention will be most effective if interventions are comprehensive and multileveled. Individual behavior changes are unlikely to continue without complementary supporting changes within the basic economic and social structure as well as at the institutional and interpersonal level.
- Preventive interventions focused on the individual should be voluntary. Coercive interventions should only occur following due process safeguards and be based on adjudicated past behavior, not prediction of future behavior. The latter intervention, by definition, is not prevention.
- Natural informal relationships may be more helpful to "delinquent prone" children than expert practitioners. Formal policies and programs should be developed so that the former relationships are strengthened through inclusion and assistance rather than weakened through exclusion and attempts at replacement.
- Interventions that address antecedent correlates of delinquency should rarely have as their *raison d'être* promised decreases in future delinquency. Prevention of delinquency may be *a* goal for intervention but should not be *the* goal. Most of these efforts can and should be justified on grounds of fundamental fairness.
- Social agency administrators should be held accountable for the context of their services. Evaluation research should be refined so that client (consumer) satisfaction with the fairness and respect with which services are provided, as well as the effectiveness of the service, is systematically measured. Such accountability may not decrease delinquency; however, it will serve to move public agency practice closer to the ideals of a pluralistic democracy.
- Extensive social research and intervention experiments should be encouraged and financially supported by the federal government. State, local, and federal financial support for helping agencies should be contingent on the agency administrator's participation in and utilization of such research and evaluation. Research and evaluation should measure unintended as well as intended consequences of social policies and programs and actively engage practitioners in the

evaluation process. The results of these efforts should be clearly and systematically abstracted by a federally supported national reference service. These abstracts should be widely distributed to policymakers and practitioners.

None of these implications results from optimistic conclusions about our ability to decrease delinquency in the foreseeable future. Most of them are exceedingly difficult to respond to at a time when the "tax payers' revolt" and the public's fear of crime pushes elected officials to offer quick, cheap "solutions." However, to avoid these implications is intellectually dishonest and denies many of the fundamental values we espouse as a society. We must move forward! The final section proposes and develops organizing principles that are responsive to these implications.

Preventing Delinquency Through Social Policy and Social Action

Once you bring life into the world, you must protect it. We must protect it by changing the world [Elie Wiesel, Interview].

Future social policy and program development for the prevention of juvenile delinquency should be primary prevention. Furthermore, this primary prevention should be from a situational model rather than a personal model. A situational model would emphasize the context of developing children, youth, and their families rather than identifying and intervening with individuals. The model would enhance the development of each individual's competence rather than diagnosing and treating individual defects (Albee, 1980). The physical well-being of the child would be stressed and the highest quality of social psychological support possible would be provided, preferably within the family. Resources would be targeted to schools, neighborhoods, and other normal mainstream agencies. These agencies would be supported to improve their safety, operational fairness, and respect for individual differences and autonomy so that, the mutual obligations between each developing child, their family, and their community are reinforced.

Primary prevention focusing on social and environmental correlates of delinquency has at least two major advantages. First, primary prevention avoids the problems inherent in prediction of future delinquent behavior. As Hawkins and Lam have stated, "Interventions at the individual level based on such predictions are likely to miss a number of youths who will become delinquent and also risk identifying and treating some individuals as 'predelinquent' even though they will never engage in serious delinquent behavior" (this volume). Second, allocating resources to improve or support everyday institutions and groupings such as families, employers, schools, and peer groups benefits all disadvantaged people, not only those who are identified "predelinquent." Fundamental fairness demands such an allocation when real opportunities, services, and resources are at stake.

This does not mean that services should not be directed at individuals and families or that such services cannot contribute to delinquency prevention. A frequently stated maxim frequently lost in the provision of service to disadvantaged people, is that people do not resist change; they resist being changed. The practitioners' continual faith in our ability to predict and change delinquent behavior, particularly at the "predelinquent" point in human development, contributes an even more corrupting motive for intervention than the benevolent motive seeking the "best interests of the child" (Gaylin et al., 1978). It would seem that we are even more likely to do harm when we intervene to avoid future wrong doing than when we intervene to cause future good.

Direct services to children, youth, families, and to whole communities should be structured such that major authority for definition of need and acceptance of services rests with the "client." Such an approach might be enhanced through a variety of provisions:

- Provision of money or vouchers to families, youth, and communities, that allow them to select a specific agency, service, or practitioner.
- Penetration of the policy and administrative core of public and private helping agencies by those served. This might be done through meaningful representation on advisory and administrative boards.
- Penetration at the day-to-day activity level of helping agencies by the "loved ones" and peers of those served. This would require full and active participation in intervention strategy meetings and the intervention process itself by these "interested parties."
- Utilization-based and consumer-based program evaluation. The formal evaluation process should include practitioners and clients such that the clients' evaluation of their experiences is measured as well as the effectiveness of the intervention in meeting formal agency goals. Program evaluation should be "utilization based" (Patton, 1978) such that results do in fact influence agency practice.

It would seem that social agencies and programs that embrace these provisions would have a number of hallmark virtues. They would demonstrate a respect for and friendliness toward those served. The services would respond to authentic and practical client "wants" as well as agency identified "needs." They would provide services that are accessible and timely. A few such agencies and programs exist; however, most of our public and many quasipublic (nonprofit) agencies serving disadvantaged people do not begin to approach these ideals.

The action necessary for the primary prevention of delinquency must be faced directly. The psychiatrist Seymour Halleck has been quoted as saying, "Any treatment that removes symptoms without simultaneously increasing the patient's awareness of his (sic) environment is potentially repressive" (quoted in Albee, 1981, p. 22). Authentic service, particularly to disadvantaged people, will encourage "consciousness raising" and organization for social action as well as individual behavior change. Following this argument to conclusion will require that agency administrators and practitioners not only structure services for open and meaningful client participation, there are two additional avenues that must be pursued: voluntary associations and professionals advocating for social action as informed experts.

Voluntary associations have been and continue to be an essential force undergirding self-determination in the United States (Trotter, 1981, pp. 263-274). These associations provide "mediating structures" between the individual and the agencies of the state (Currie, July, 1982, p. 24). By definition, professionals will rarely lead these indigenous organizations. However, professionals should support their struggles and offer technical expertise when requested.

Social researchers, agency executives, and practitioners often avoid the commitments and risks necessary for political change. Effective political action requires clearly articulated values, recommendations for specific actions, and public confrontation. Lloyd Ohlin, one of the more thoughtful and humane observers of juvenile justice in America, has recently commented:

> I would like to call attention to a persistent nagging problem—the emphasis on job security of professionals in the field as a major obstacle to the change in the years ahead. We must meet this problem head-on, be honest about it to begin with, and then see what has gone

wrong. What are the positive as well as negative effects of professional treatment of youth problems? How do we combine the strength and motivation of community leadership and participation with the trained sensibilities, experience, and counsel of professionals? This issue intersects and confronts all others [1984, p. 471].

Professionals have critical knowledge and the responsibility to use that knowledge to inform executive, legislative, and judicial decisions (Konopka, 1981). James Jacobs, in his thorough study of the sociological and historical changes in an Illinois prison between 1925 and 1975, concluded that "the federal court's abandonment of the 'hands off' doctrine was the most important development in the prison environment" (1977, p. 9). Some correctional professionals undoubtely were obstacles to such changes. Others provided critical testimony as expert witnesses for court decisions and even more important have stepped forward to carry out the actual implementation of court orders (Brodsky & Miller, 1981).

Less dramatic, but no less difficult, opportunities are open to practitioners every day. Again, to quote from Halleck, "There is no way a psychiatrist can deal with behavior that is partly generated by a social system without either strengthening or altering that system. Every encounter with a psychiatrist, therefore, has political implications" (quoted in Albee, 1981, pp. 21-22). Leitenberg (this volume) is correct: many significant issues in the prevention of delinquency are political; however, he falls short when he seems to conclude that improvement is therefore in the hands of politicians. Researchers, academics, and practitioners, in concert with those who suffer most from current social arrangements, can provide the clearest articulation of the real issues and most helpful responses. Necessary political action is unlikely without these coalitions taking their experience into public forums. Most politicians are not experts and need to have the relevant facts and value choices clearly formulated. Federal and state tax allocations and reallocations are necessary for many of the changes (Currie, July, 1982; Silberman, 1978; Trotter, 1981). Blueprints exist (Childrens Defense Fund, 1983).

The future will be ours to the degree we participate in the present. To paraphrase Camus, if those of us who base our hopes on human nature are fools, those who give up under current circumstances are cowards. With courage and a great deal of patience, we must move forward.

Note

1. There are at least three other promising areas where more research and intervention experiments should be encouraged: employment, peer support, and community development. Employment programs for youth and single parent households have been developed that have met with limited but promising results (Auletta, 1982; Currie, July 1982). Peer support projects, particularly those that have intermixed and guided "pro social" and "high risk" youth interactions have demonstrated positive effects (Weis et al., 1981; Smith, Farrant, & Marchant, 1972). Community development, although a somewhat amorphous concept, is an important context for social research and intervention experiments and, again, models exist (Silberman 1978, pp. 424-446; Currie July, 1982, pp. 24-25; Schlossman and Sedlack 1983; Trotter 1981).

References

Albee, G. W. (1980). A competency model must replace the defect model. In. L. A. Bond & J. C. Rosen (Eds.), *Competency and coping during adulthood* (pp. 75-104). Hanover, NH: University of New England Press.

Albee, G. W. (1981). Politics, power, prevention and social change. In J. M. Joffe & G. W. Albee (Eds.), *Prevention through political action and social change* (pp. 5-25). Hanover, NH: University of New England Press.

Auletta, K. (1982). *The underclass.* New York: Random House.

Boy 15, who killed two and tried to kill a third is given five years. (1978, June 29). *New York Times.* p. 1.

Brodsky, S. L., & Miller, K. S. (1981). Coercing change in prisons and mental hospitals: The social scientist and the class action suit. In J. M. Joffe & G. W. Albee (Eds.), *Prevention through social action and social change* (pp. 208-227). Hanover, NH: University of New England Press.

Children's Defense Fund. (1983). *A children's defense budget: An analysis of the president's FY 1984 budget and children.* Washington, DC: Author.

Currie, E. (1982, May-June). Crime and ideology. *Working Papers, 9*(3), 26-35.

Currie, E. (1982, July-August). Fighting crime. *Working Papers, 9*(4), 16-25.

Empey, L. T. (1973). Juvenile justice reform: Diversion, due process and deinstitutionalization. In L. E. Ohlin (Ed.), *Prisoners in America* pp. 13-48). Englewood Cliffs, NJ: Prentice-Hall.

Farrington, D. P., & West, D. J. (1982). The Cambridge Study in delinquency development, 1980. (Cited by J. Monahan, Childhood predictors of adult criminal behavior) In F. N. Dutile, C. H. Foust, & D. R. Webster (Eds.), *Early childhood intervention and juvenile delinquency* (pp. 11-21). Lexington, MA: D. C. Heath.

Feld, B. (1978a), *Neutralizing inmate violence: Juvenile offenders in institutions.* Cambridge, MA: Ballinger.

Feld, B. (1978b). Reference of juvenile offenders for adult prosecution: The legislative alternative to asking unanswerable questions. *Minnesota Law Review, 62,* 515.

Gaylin, W., Glasser, I., Marcus, S., & Rothman, D. (1978). *Doing good: The limits of benevolence.* New York: Pantheon.

Geis, G. (1984. Book review of Cullen, F. T. & Gilbert, K. E., Reaffirming rehabilitation. *Crime & Delinquency, 30*(1), 159-160.

Gold, M. (1970). *Delinquent behavior in an American city.* Belmont, CA: Brooks/Cole.

Greenwood, P., Lipson, A., Abrahamse, A., & Zimring, F. (1983). *Youth crime and juvenile justice in California: A report to the legislature.* Santa Monica, CA: Rand.

Hacker, A. (1984). The schools flunk out. *The New York Review of Books, 31*(6), 35-40.

Hubert H. Humphrey Institute of Public Affairs. (1983). The cost of locking-up juveniles. In *Rethinking juvenile justice.* Minneapolis, MN: University of Minnesota.

Hughes, G. (1983, November) How bad are the courts? *New York Review of Books, 30*,(17), 28-39.

Jacobs, J. B. (1977). *Stateville: The penitentiary in mass society.* Chicago: University of Chicago Press.

Janowitz, M. (1969). *Institution building in urban education.* Chicago: Chicago University Press.

Konopka, G. (1981). Social change, social action as prevention: The role of the professional. In J. M. Joffe & G. W. Albee (Eds.), *Prevention through social action and social change* (pp. 228-239). Hanover, NH: University of New England Press.

Lemert, E. M. (1967). *Human deviance, social problems, and social control.* New York: Prentice-Hall.

Lerman, P. (1975). *Community treatment and social control.* Chicago: University of Chicago Press.

Lerman, P. (1982). *Deinstitutionalization and the welfare state.* New Brunswick, NJ: Rutgers University Press.

Lindgren, J. G. (1982). Commentary on Monahan, J. Childhood predictors of adult criminal behavior. In F. Dutile, C. Foust, & D. R. Webster (Eds.), *Early childhood intervention and juvenile delinquency* (pp. 23-29). Lexington, MA: D. C. Heath.

Martinson, R. (1974). What Works? Questions and answers about prison reform. *The Public Interest, 35*(Spring).

Miller, D. (1980). *Alternatives to incarceration: From total institutions to total systems.* Ph.D. dissertation, University of California, Berkeley.

Minnesota Department of Corrections Research Information Systems. (1977). *The effect of the availability of community alternatives to state incarceration on sentencing practices: The social control issue.* St. Paul, MN: Author.

Monahan, J. (1982). Childhood predictors of adult criminal behavior. In F. N. Dutile, C. H. Foust, & D. R. Webster (Eds.), *Early childhood intervention and juvenile delinquency* (pp. 11-21). Lexington, MA: D. C. Heath.

Moos, R. H. (1975) *Evaluating corrections and community settings.* New York: John Wiley.

Morris, N. (1974) *The future of imprisonment.* Chicago: University of Chicago Press.

National Resource Center on Family Based Services. (1982, Summer). *Prevention at what cost?* (Prevention Report). University of Iowa.

Newberger, E. (1983, April 11). *The helping hand strikes again: Unintended consequences of child abuse reporting.* Testimony given before the Subcommittee on Family and Human Service, Committee on Labor and Human Resources, U.S. Senate.

Ohlin, L. E. (1983). The future of juvenile justice policy and research. *Crime & Delinquency, 29*(3), 463-472.

Patton, M. Q. (1978). *Utilization-focused evaluation.* Beverly Hills, CA: Sage.

Public Law (1980). *The adoption assistance and child welfare act.* 96-272.

Rosenheim, M. (1976). Notes on helping juvenile nuisances. In M. Rosenheim (ed.), *Pursuing justice for the child* (pp. 43-66). Chicago: University of Chicago Press.

Rothman, D. J. (1980). *Conscience and convenience.* Boston: Little Brown.

Schlossman, S., & Sedlack, M. (1983). The Chicago Area Project revisited. *Crime & Delinquency, 29*(3), 398-462.

Silberman, C. E. (1978). *Criminal violence: criminal justice.* New York: Random House.

Smith, C., Farrant, M., & Marchant, M. (1972). *The Wincraft Youth Project: A social work program in a slum area.* London: Tavistock.

State of Washington. (1977). *Juvenile Justice Code* (House Bill 371).

Street, D., Vinter, R. D., & Perrow, C. (1966). *Organization for treatment.* New York: Free Press.

Suttles, G. (1968). *The social order of the slum.* Chicago: University of Chicago Press.

Trotter, S. (1981). Neighborhood, politics, and mental health. In J. Joffe & G. W. Albee (Eds.), *Prevention through political action and social change* (pp. 263-274). Hanover, NH: University Press of New England.

Underwood, B. (1979). Law and the crystal ball: Predicting behavior with statistical inference and individualized judgement. *Yale Law Journal, 88,* 1408-1448.

Weis, J. G., Hall, J., Henney, J., Seldstrom, J., Worsley, J., & Zeiss, C. (1981). *Peer influence and delinquency: An evaluation of theory and practice, part I and II.* Washington, DC: Government Printing Office.

Weis, J. G., & Hawkins, J. D. (1982). *Preventing delinquency.* Washington, DC: Government Printing Office.

Whittaker, J. K., & Garbarino, J. (1983). *Social support networks: Informal helping in the human services.* New York: Aldine.

Wolfgang, M. E., Figlio, R. M., & Sellin, T. (1972). *Delinquency in a birth cohort.* Chicago: University of Chicago Press.

Wooden, K. (1976) *Weeping in the playtime of others.* New York: McGraw-Hill.

Zimring, F. E. (1974). Measuring the impact of pretrail diversion from the criminal justice system. *University of Chicago Law Review, 41,* 224-241.

Zimring, F. E. (1975). *Confronting youth crime: Report of the twentieth century fund task force on sentencing policy toward young offenders.* New York: Holme and Meier.

Zimring, F. E. (1979). American youth violence: Issues and trends. In N. Morris & M. Torey (Eds.), *Crime and justice: An annual review of literature* (pp. 67-107). Chicago: University of Chicago Press.

14

Contributors

William Steven Barnett, Ph.D., is Research Associate at the Early Intervention Research Institute, Utah State University at Logan. He is interested in policy analysis, in the economics of early education, and in research into mental retardation and early childhood programs.

John R. Berrueta-Clement, Ph.D., is an anthropologist by training. His professional interests deal with the integration of scientific research and information for policy purposes, with research methods and with the impact of information technologies on society. He is currently Director of Governmental Activities with the American Federation of Information Processing Societies (AFIPS), located in Washington, D. C.

John D. Burchard is Professor of Clinical Psychology at the University of Vermont where he teaches courses in social policy and children, child behavior therapy, and juvenile delinquency. From 1980 to 1985 he served as the Commissioner of the Vermont Department of Social and Rehabilitation Services, the State Agency mandated to provide services to delinquent, abused/neglected, and unmanageable children and their families. John Burchard has written many articles and book chapters in the general areas of behavior modification, juvenile delinquency, child abuse and neglect, and social policy and children. His most recent writing, "Social and Political Challenges to Behavioral Programs with Delinquents and Criminals," will appear in *Behavioral Approaches to Crime and Delinquency: Applications, Research, and Theory*, edited by E. Morris and C. Braukman.

Sara N. Burchard, Ph.D. is Assistant Professor of Psychology at the University of Vermont where she teaches graduate and undergraduate courses in developmental psychology, disabilities of learning and development, and supervises student research in these areas. She is a licensed psychologist and staff member of the Behavior Therapy, Psychotherapy Center of the University where she supervises student delivery of clinical and developmental services to children, adolescents, and developmentally disabled adults. She received her degree in developmental psychology from the University of Vermont where she engaged in research and therapeutic interventions with children and adolescents with adjustment problems or who were engaging in delinquent behavior. She has served as a research assistant at a treatment center for juvenile delinquents in Washington state and coordinated a statewide program of consultation, staff training, and applied research for community mental health centers in Vermont.

Norma Cianci is the Director of Mathematics Laboratory/Teacher of Mathematics, at the Baldwin School, Bryn Mawr, Pennsylvania. In addition, she is completing her doctoral studies in special education at Temple University where she previously obtained a Masters in Special Education and a Bachelor of Arts in mathematics. From 1979 to 1983 she was Director of the Longitudinal Study on Delinquency at Hahemann University. She has had 25 years of experience in teaching, administration, and research in the fields of regular and special education.

Glen E. Davis, Ph.D., is a clinical psychologist at the Kennebec Valley Mental Health Center in Waterville, Maine where he engages in therapy primarily with children, adolescents, and families, and group treatment of adolescent and adult sex offenders. His most recent research has focused on teenage stress that is culminated in a number of articles on the measurment of life events in adolescence. He is currently working on a manuscript that reviews the empirical literature on sexual offenses committed by adolescents.

Thomas J. Dishion is a researcher and therapist at the Oregon Social Learning Center and a doctoral candidate in clinical psychology at the University of Oregon. His primary research interest involves the interactional study of child socialization and the design and evaluation of theory-driven preventive interventions. Most recently he has been involved in the design of a family-based early intervention strategy for preadolescents involved in drug use. The design of such an intervention is to follow closely the findings from a passive longitudinal study currently under way. Clinically he is interested in child and family therapy and community level interventions.

Jean E. Dumas is an Assistant Professor of Psychology at the University of Western Ontario in London. His research work is focused on naturalistic observations of parent-child interactions in home settings. In particular, he is concerned with understanding the development of pathological family relationships and how these are maintained over time. He is currently assessing the role of parental control and predictability in this maladaptive process.

Franklyn W. Dunford is the Associate Director of the Behavioral Research Institute, Boulder, Colorado and a Research Associate at the Institute of Behavioral Science, University of Colorado. He is currently conducting research in criminal careers, police response to domestic assault and transient crime.

Delbert S. Elliott is the Director, Behavioral Research Institute and Professor of Sociology at the University of Colorado. His research concerns adolescent problem behavior (delinquency, drug use, runaway, mental health problems), domestic violence and the evaluation of delinquency prevention and treatment programs. He is coauthor of *Delinquency and Dropout* (1974), *The Social Psychology of Runaways* (1978), and *Explaining Delinquency and Drug Use* (1985). He served as Chairman of the Crime and Violent Behavior Review Committee for NIMH from 1984-1986. He is a member of The American Society of Criminology and The American Sociological Association. He received a BA degree from Pomona College and an MA and Ph.D. from the University of Washington.

J. David Hawkins, Ph.D., is the director of the Center for Social Welfare Research and Associate Professor in the School for Social Work at the University of Washington in Seattle. He is engaged in research on prevention and treatment of antisocial behavior in youth and adults based on the Social Development Model, an empirically derived theory of human behavior.

David Huizinga is a Senior Research Associate at the Behavioral Research Institute, Boulder, Colorado and Research Associate at the Institute of Behavioral Science, University of Colorado. He is co-author of *Explaining Delinquency and Drug Use* (1985) and *The Social Psychology of Runaways* (1978). His current research involvement includes a national longitudinal study of delinquency and crime and a study of police response to domestic violence.

Carl F. Jesness, Ph.D., received his degree from the University of Minnesota. A Clinical Psychologist, he soon became disenchanted with the progress shown by chronic schizophrenics and turned hopefully to the treatment of juvenile delinquents, where equal disenchantment soon turned his interest to research. After 26 years of such research with the California Youth Authority, Jesness retired and is now working as a consultant. Among his several publications are the *Jesness Inventory, Jesness Behavior Checklist,* and the *Jesness Inventory Classification System.*

Tony Lam, Ph.D., is the Senior Research Scientist at SRA Technologies, Inc. in Mountain View, California. He is engaged in educational research.

Theodore W. Lane, Ph.D., received his doctoral degree in 1982 from the University of Vermont, where he subsequently was an Assistant Professor of Psychology. During that time he consulted with several state agencies regarding the development of treatment and education services for children and adolescents. He currently directs the Children & Youth Program at Cumberland County Mental Health Center in Fayetteville, North Carolina, which includes a continuum of intensive treatment services for emotionally disturbed and violent/assaultive adolescents. His research interests and publications are primarily in the areas of child abuse and neglect, delinquency, and adolescence. His most recent research focused on early in-home intervention with parents of abused and neglected preschool children.

Harold Leitenberg, Ph.D., is Professor of Psychology, Clinical Professor of Psychiatry, and Director of the Behavior Therapy and Psychotherapy Center at the University of Vermont. He is a past Director of the Ph.D. Program in Clinical Psychology at the University of Vermont (1969-74; 1980-84), past President of the Vermont Psychological Association, and in 1982-83 he was named University Scholar in Social Sciences and Humanities. He is the author and coauthor of over 60 professional articles and chapters, and is currently a Fellow of two divisions of the American Psychological Association, and Consulting Editor of the *Journal of Consulting and Clinical Psychology.* He is editor of *Handbook of Behavior Modification and Behavior Therapy* (1976 main selection of the Behavioral Science Book Service), coeditor with G. W. Albee and S. Gordon of *Promoting Sexual Responsibility and Preventing Sexual Problems*

(1983) and coauthor with J. Geer and J. Heiman of *Human Sexuality* (1984).

Jay G. Lindgren is executive officer of juvenile release, Minnesota Department of Corrections. Mr. Lindgren was project director, Serious Juvenile Offender Program, Minnesota Department of Corrections, 1978 to 1981; and executive director, PORT of Olmsted County, Rochester, MN, 1972 to 1977. He has worked in varying capacities in juvenile and adult corrections programs in institutions and the community since 1966. Mr. Lindgren received an M.S.W. from the University of Minnesota in 1967 and was a visiting fellow at the Center For Studies in Criminal Justice at the University of Chicago in 1976.

Rolf Loeber, Ph.D., was trained as a clinical psychologist in Holland and in Canada. He received his Ph.D. from Queen's University in Kingston, Ontario. After working as a clinician in a psychiatric hospital, he embarked on a research career, working for approximately five years at the Oregon Social Learning Center in Eugene, Oregon where he studied family aspects of juvenile conduct problems and delinquency. While there, he developed an interest in the continuity of these problems over time, and this led to several studies on the prediction of delinquency. Currently, he is a member of a panel on criminal careers, sponsored by the National Academy of Sciences. He is an Assistant Professor of Psychiatry in the University of Pittsburgh School of Medicine where, with his wife, Magda Stouthamer-Loeber, Ph.D., he is codirector of the Child Conduct Problems Program at Western Psychiatric Institute and Clinic.

Larry Michelson, Ph.D., is an Assistant Professor of Psychiatry and Psychology at the University of Pittsburgh, Western Psychiatric Institute and Clinic, School of Medicine, Department of Psychiatry. Dr. Michelson has authored over sixty publications and books addressing cognitive-behavioral theory, assessment, prevention, and treatment strategies with children and adults. Some of Dr. Michelson's volumes include *Social Skills Assessment and Training With Children: An Empirical-Based Handbook; Handbook of Prevention* and *Issues in Psychotherapy Research*. He is currently conducting a large-scale NIMH prevention and longitudinal investigation with children using cognitive-behavioral modalities.

Lawrence J. Schweinhart, Ph.D., is a project director at the High/ Scope Educational Research Foundation in Ypsilanti, Michigan. His interests are in the effects of early childhood programs and their national status.

George Spivack, Ph.D., is professor of Psychology in the Department of Mental Health Sciences, Coordinator of Postdoctoral Training in Clinical Psychology, and Director of the Preventive Intervention Research Center at Hahnemann University, in Philadelphia. He has published extensively in the areas of clinical research, school psychology, and most recently interpersonal cognitive problem solving skills as an area of research and intervention aimed at preventing maladjustment in children and youth. He is currently engaged in an 18-year longitudinal study of urban school children, begun when they were in kindergarten. His research work in the area of prevention has been recognized through receipt of the Lela Rowland Prevention Award from the National Association for Mental Health in 1982, and the Award for Distinguished Contribution to Community Psychology and Community Mental Health from Division 27 of the American Psychological Association in 1984.

Robert G. Wahler is a Professor of Psychology at the University of Tennessee in Knoxville, Tennessee. His research work is focused on therapeutic interventions with conduct disordered children and their families. He is primarily interested in those chronic child-parent relationship problems that maintain conduct disorders. His current work is geared to evaluating a new intervention strategy with such chronic problems.

David P. Weikart, Ph.D., is President of the High/Scope Educational Research Foundation in Ypsilanti, Michigan. His current interests are in international research on young children and in dissemination of a child-development based curriculum model.

Emmy E. Werner is Professor of Human Development and research Child Psychologist at the University of California at Davis. She was formerly a Research Associate at the University of Minnesota's Institute of Child Development, a Visiting Scientist at the National Institutes of Health and Associate Research Child Psychologist at the University of California, Berkeley's School of Public Health. She is author of *Cross-Cultural Child Development: A View from the Planet Earth* and *Child Care: Kith, Kin and Hired Hands* as well as senior author of *The Children of Kauai; Kauai's Children Come of Age* and *Vulnerable but Invincible: A Longitudinal Study of Resilient Children and Youth.* She has written numerous articles on her cross-cultural and longitudinal research with high risk children and families. She is currently engaged in a follow-up at age 30 of a group of multiracial adults who successfully coped with perinatal stress, poverty, and parental psychopathology in infancy and childhood.

David A. Wolfe (Ph.D. University of South Florida) is Associate Professor of Psychology at the University of Western Ontario in Canada, where he teaches in both child and community subspecialties of clinical psychology and is Codirector of Clinical Training. He studies the prevention of child abuse, psychological disorders among physically and sexually abused children, and anger and arousal problems among abusive parents. His editorial board memberships include *Child Abuse & Neglect, Journal of Consulting and Clinical Psychology, Journal of Family Violence,* and the *Journal of Clinical Child Psychology.* He is coauthor of *The Child Management Program for Abusive Parents,* with K. Kaufman, J. Aragona, & J. Sandler.

NAME INDEX

Abikoff, H., 287, 305
Abrahamse, A., 35, 50
Achenbach, T. M., 173, 176, 186, 276, 277, 297
Acland, H., 240
Adcock, C., 221, 240
Adler, I., 241, 272
Afton, A. D., 197, 199, 201, 209, 215, 219, 284, 310
Ageton, S. S., 8, 14, 50, 71, 94, 95, 118, 227, 239, 241, 245, 271
Ainsworth, M. D. S., 180, 187
Albee, G. W., 315, 318, 330, 331, 346, 348, 349, 350, 351, 352
Aleksic, P., 286, 305
Alexander, J. F., 135, 136
Alfaro, J. D., 129, 130, 131, 132, 133, 136, 145, 157, 162, 187
American Psychiatric Association (APA), 276, 305
Anderegg, T. R., 124, 138
Andrew, J. M., 122, 136
Anthony, E. J., 43
Antonovsky, A., 42
Appoloni, T., 236, 305
Aragona, J., 164, 170, 172, 188, 189
Archer, M., 296, 306
Aronson, E., 120, 244, 251, 270
Artemyeff, C., 219
Auletta, K., 349, 350
Austin, J., 8, 14, 108, 119

Babigian, H., 46, 71
Bachman, J. G., 226, 227, 238, 248, 270
Baer, D. M., 218, 219, 303, 305, 309
Bahr, S. J., 242, 270
Baker, J. W., 46, 71
Balch, R. W., 247, 249, 272
Ball, J. C., 315, 331
Bane, M. J., 239
Banet, B., 224, 239
Barahal, R. M., 122, 136
Barenboim, C., 287, 305
Barnett, W., 13
Barnett, W. S., 237, 238, 236, 353
Bartlett, S., 239

Bash, M., 281, 305
Bates, J. E., 68, 71
Baum, C. G., 283, 305
Beck, S., 305, 307
Becker, H. S., 92, 117
Beezley, P., 123, 124, 137
Bell, R. Q., 82, 89
Bellack, A. S., 295, 308, 309
Benning, J. J., 16, 42, 47, 72, 89
Bentley, R. J., 162, 187
Berkowitz, L., 285, 305
Berland, R. M., 281, 310
Bermann, E., 45, 74
Berreuta-Clement, J. R., 13, 221, 229, 238, 239, 326, 341, 373
Bierman, J. M., 16, 43
Billis, D., 85, 89
Birch, H. G., 67, 71
Black, D. J., 92, 117
Blehar, M., 180, 187
Block, J., 22, 42, 278, 305
Block, J. H., 240, 270
Block, M., 176, 188
Bloom, B. S., 250, 270
Blumstein, A., 91, 117
Bogaslav, B., 49, 55, 74
Bolton, F. G., 125, 136
Bond, J. T., 221, 240
Bond, L. A., 350
Borich, G., 274
Bradlyn, D., 168, 189
Braithwaite, J., 104, 117
Brandon, S., 134, 137
Braswell, L., 299, 307
Braukman, C., 353
Braukman, C. J., 242, 270
Brehony, K., 168, 189
Breiner, J., 192, 218, 306
Breitenbucher, M., 177, 187
Briar, S., 92, 119
Brill, H., 119
Brodsky, S. L., 348, 350
Bronson, W. C., 70, 71
Burchard, J. D., 14, 320, 331
Burchard, S. N., 14, 354
Burgess, R. I., 135, 136
Burruss, G., 48, 73

359

SUBJECT INDEX

NOTES

NOTES